Life beyond the Holocaust

To Chaoph and Dinah
with best wishes —

Nina Kimelman

12/4/05

Life beyond the Holocaust

MEMORIES AND REALITIES

MIRA RYCZKE KIMMELMAN

EDITED AND WITH AN INTRODUCTION BY GILYA GERDA SCHMIDT
FOREWORD BY BEVERLY A. ASBURY

THE UNIVERSITY OF TENNESSEE PRESS / KNOXVILLE

Copyright © 2005 by The University of Tennessee Press / Knoxville.
All Rights Reserved. Manufactured in the United States of America.
First Edition.

Frontispiece: Mira Ryczke Kimmelman, 2004. Peter Holz, Photography Inc.

This book is printed on acid-free paper.

Library of Congress Cataloging-in-Publication Data

Kimmelman, Mira Ryczke, 1923–
    Life beyond the Holocaust : memories and realities / Mira Ryczke Kimmelman ;
edited and with an introduction by Gilya Gerda Schmidt ; foreword by Beverly A.
Asbury.— 1st ed.
        p. cm.
        Includes bibliographical references and index.
        ISBN 1-57233-435-5 (hardcover : alk. paper)
        ISBN 1-57233-436-3 (pbk. : alk. paper)
    1. Kimmelman, Mira Ryczke, 1923– 2. Holocaust survivors—United States—Biography.
I. Schmidt, Gilya Gerda. II. Title.
E184.37.K54 2005   2005003896

This book is written with love
for my children and grandchildren—
Benno, Gene, Joy, Caroline, and Melanie,
Michael, Max, and Ellie

Contents

Part 2

Part 3

Illustrations

FIGURES

Maps

Family Trees

Foreword

Mira Ryczke Kimmelman spoke at a Holocaust conference sponsored by the Tennessee Holocaust Commission. Addressing both teachers and their students from area schools, she related her experiences as a survivor. That was about fifteen years ago. It was my first exposure to her. She was so articulate, so warm and expressive, so open and patient in answering questions. Some of the questions were poorly stated by students raised in a state still largely marked by religious singularity. She may well have been the first Jew they had ever seen, and, no doubt, the first survivor of the Holocaust they had heard.

Mira Kimmelman provided a moment that audience is likely never to forget, as she did for so many others. Those who hear her may forget her name, but not her, not her presence, not her story. Such moments form memories that constitute and shape our being human. Those moments in life are relatively rare. Moments of birth and death. Moments of crisis. Moments of transcendental clarity. They form touchstones by which we find our place, our being in the world. From those moments we unconsciously form the symbols and stories by which we live. Mira's story surely became such a moment for those in attendance.

That moment may be "lost," repressed, sublimated for a while. But I don't believe that the story will ever be beyond recall for those who hear it or read it. Another moment will bring it back. A film. A concert. A war photograph. An AIDS statistic. And then we remember, and we discern who we are or want to be and what it was that touched us so deeply.

Mira created such moments for us because there are so many moments for her that her love and courage have led her to confront and relate. In her own words:

Through the years I overcame the fear of death. . . . There is still the hoarding of food and the fear of cold when winter comes.

We wanted our children to be born in a country free of hatred and discrimination.

I had nightmares and constant fears about our [American] children being taken from us.

[People ask], "How and when did you tell your children about the Holocaust?" . . . I have no easy answer. [We] never hid the fact that we were in . . . concentration camps. Our sons saw the tattoo on my left arm. . . . I told them what it meant.

Mira traveled back to places her families came from, where her brother and mother and grandparents perished—to the very places where she had suffered the most. She tells of revisiting the death camps at Birkenau/Auschwitz on July 29, 1990: "It was August 1, 1944, a steaming hot day when our cattle cars were opened. . . . Today was to be my return to this hell on earth."

Mira makes what Robert Jay Lifton has termed "the painful wisdom of the survivor" available to us, and with it the capacity to incorporate into our own lives her rededication to enhancing human life and opposing human destructiveness. That is the remarkable achievement of a remarkable woman; indeed, her gift to us.

Her tracing of moments of her history and of her people's history allows us and invites us to be touched by them and to make them moments of our own lives. Her "memories and realities" lure us toward wanting to leave our own trace of human goodness, justice, hope, and love alongside hers.

THE REVEREND BEVERLY A. ASBURY
VANDERBILT UNIVERSITY CHAPLAIN EMERITUS
CHAIR, THE TENNESSEE HOLOCAUST COMMISSION, 1986–98

Acknowledgments

The Holocaust did not end with liberation. The painful memories, the feelings of loss and guilt are still with me. The need to tell how we lived and survived as survivors prompted me to write this book. This subject came up time and again when I shared my Holocaust experiences with students. I could not have done it without the staunch support and encouragement from my children and friends.

First and foremost, I am greatly indebted to my friend and editor, Professor Gilya Gerda Schmidt, head of the Department of Religious Studies at the University of Tennessee and chair of the Fern and Manfred Steinfeld Program in Judaic Studies, who graciously accepted the task of editing what I had written. Her expertise and knowledge were invaluable, and I owe her my deepest gratitude. I am especially grateful to Rev. Beverly Asbury, chaplain emeritus at Vanderbilt University, Nashville, Tennessee, and past chairman of the Tennessee Holocaust Commission, for his willingness to write the foreword to this book. Many sincere thanks to the readers of my manuscript, whose ideas as well as counsel were greatly appreciated: Wendy Lowe Besmann, author of *A Separate Circle;* Leonard Dinnerstein, professor of history and director of Judaic Studies, University of Arizona; David Patterson, chair of Judaic Studies, University of Memphis.

I wish to thank the friends who helped with suggestions and opinions: John Bohstedt, professor of history, University of Tennessee; Alice Feldman Good and Jocelyn Bursten; Peter Höyng, associate professor of Germanic languages and literatures, University of Tennessee, for finding my brother's records at Vienna; special thanks to Hanna Shapira for her help with the maps, as well as to Carol Minarick; to Nicki Russler, Ruth Gove, and Professor

Herbert Lazarow for helping me in searching for ancestral records; Avigail Rashkovsky and Luda and Victor Olman for translating the Russian registry records into English; to Rachel Carlson, my appreciation and deepest thanks for the family trees, and to Frank Meisler, for permission to use the map from his book *On the Vistula Facing East.* I owe special thanks to the Department of Religious Studies at the University of Tennessee and specifically to Daniel Headrick, Stephen Holcombe, Erika Magnuson, and Joan Riedl for their help and assistance with the word processing and proofreading of my manuscript. Rick Robinson, Ph.D. student in history at the University of Tennessee, employed his considerable expertise in Photoshop and all the complicated software applications to digitize all of the photos and documents. He also prepared the final version of the manuscript for publication. My deepest gratitude. I greatly appreciate all the moral support from Joyce Harrison, former acquisitions editor of the University of Tennessee Press, and her successor, Scot Danforth. Without the help of the above-mentioned friends, I could not have written this book.

Last but not least my profound thanks go to my children. Their love, tireless encouragement, and understanding gave me the physical and emotional boost necessary for this task. This book has been conceived and written for my dear children and grandchildren.

Introduction

In order to orient the reader of Mira Ryczke Kimmelman's personal memoir to the situation of Holocaust survivors immediately following the end of World War II, it may be helpful to take a look at post–World War II events. How does one survive survival? Where does one go if going home is not an option? How did soldiers know how to deal with survivors of concentration and death camps? Who qualified as a displaced person? What assistance was available to these unfortunate stateless individuals?

The military defeat of the German army in World War II and the end of the Nazi regime, as well as the end of the Holocaust, did not come about suddenly but over the period of more than a year. Action in the Pacific theater did not end until August 15, 1945, but the invasion of Normandy took place as early as June 6, 1944. On July 23, 1944, the Soviet army stumbled upon the death camp of Majdanek, where 360,000 Jews had been murdered. By the end of 1944 the Soviet military had not only pushed the German army out of the Soviet Union, the Baltic States, and Poland, but also entered German territory. The Western Allies likewise entered German territory after the dramatic and successful Battle of the Bulge. It is a common misperception that the end of the war on May 8, 1945, and therefore the end of the Holocaust, also meant the end of suffering for the survivors. Nothing could be further from the truth. The end of the Holocaust for those persecuted by Hitler's regime spelled new challenges for those who lived through the hell of the Nazis—Jewish as well as non-Jewish individuals.

While many of us who are fortunate to only study the Holocaust marvel at the determination, perseverance, willpower, and courage of the victims of the Nazi atrocities, we probably have little understanding of and appreciation for the personal wasteland Holocaust survivors faced upon liberation.

Initially there were no more than 50,000 to 100,000 Jewish survivors—the figures vary—out of approximately 500,000 survivors. More Jewish survivors returned from the Soviet Union later in 1945. We know that tens of thousands of survivors died in the days and weeks following their release. In Bergen-Belsen alone 13,944 prisoners died immediately after liberation because they simply could not hold on anymore, let alone recover.[1] Many survivors would whisper with their last breath, "too late." And then there were those who joyously ate rich foods given to them by their liberators, only to die almost immediately upon consumption from the inability to digest. Those who already knew with certainty that loved ones, and sometimes all of their loved ones, had been murdered suffered from survivors' guilt and sometimes ended their own lives in order to end the torment of being left behind. And then there were those who hung on in the hope of finding relatives still alive. Some survivors, like Max Kimmelman and "Uncle" Nathan Laznowski, simply walked away from the liberated camps immediately after the Allied troops had arrived.[2] They, like many others, were assigned housing with German families or placed in the homes of Germans who were evicted for that purpose, where they lived either by themselves or in small groups until their future was decided. Max's and Uncle Nathan's postwar experiences illustrate the positive as well as the negative reception survivors received from their former tormentors. Some, like Mira's father, undertook dangerous journeys through a devastated Europe to try and learn more about their loved ones.[3]

There were no ready-made solutions to any of the tremendous problems that existed, each of which posed mind-boggling challenges. Nor were there sufficient organizations or adequate staff to deal with the approximately seven million uprooted civilians who crowded into the areas occupied by the Western Allies.[4] These displaced masses included "forced laborers . . . prisoners of war, former concentration camp inmates, and Eastern Europeans who had either voluntarily sought work in Germany at the beginning of the war or had fled from their homelands to escape the advancing Soviet Army in 1944."[5]

One thing is for sure, "immediate experiences differed from camp to camp and from person to person," so it is very difficult to generalize about survivor experiences.[6] In 2000 Eva Fogelman, herself a survivor, told a gathering of survivors in Washington, D.C., "To explain how individuals cope with massive psychic trauma, one cannot reduce the process to a few common characteristics. Not all the displaced persons were the same. Emotional states are multidimensionally determined, and are dependent on internal and external factors. There was no stability around Shoah survivors." Survivors also differed in "age and duration of persecution, the mode of survival, and the extent of loss."[7]

While providing emergency medical care certainly was the most urgent and immediate task that confronted the Allied soldiers, "the need to care for the survivors of the concentration camps was only one of many problems confronting the victorious Allied armies."[8] Many people simply wanted to go home. However, the very issue of repatriation set in stark relief the difference between the refugees. Now their original nationalities became important. Some could be repatriated and some—approximately one million—could not. In spite of these difficulties, within months most individuals from UN-affiliated countries were repatriated—almost six million by September 1945.[9] While organizations such as the United Nations Relief and Rehabilitation Agency (UNRRA), established in 1943,[10] and its successor, the International Refugee Organization (IRO), established on December 15, 1946,[11] were able to help those who wanted to go home,[12] much more was needed to care for Holocaust survivors, and Jewish Holocaust survivors in particular who, for the most part, couldn't go home. Königseder and Wetzel write that the soldiers who had been trained for combat "were not equipped to deal with the survivors of Nazi terror . . . with physically and psychologically abused human beings who were in need of urgent care. . . . The ordinary soldier . . . was often at a loss for how to deal with the Jews. He did not have the necessary background knowledge or psychological training to understand their unique situation."[13] In fact, immediate and total "immersion relief" would have been the only action that would have come close to a solution. Yet international organizations either "did not attempt major relief efforts" or were "understaffed and inexperienced" when it came to caring for survivors.[14] One of the biggest obstacles facing voluntary relief agencies was the military's refusal to allow these private agencies to operate independently in the occupied areas. The military wanted total control in the occupied areas.[15] Jewish agencies were only supposed to "assist military and civil authorities in an advisory and consultative capacity."[16] Only UNRRA and the military could carry out "functional relief activities."[17] The "Joint," or American Jewish Joint Distribution Committee (AJJDC)—which had been founded on November 27, 1914, by merging three separate Jewish assistance initiatives[18]—would have been ready to help even before the war was over but "met resistance all along the line to the idea that a civilian voluntary agency should be granted this opportunity."[19] AJJDC representatives were not admitted to the camps until late summer of 1945.[20] The Hebrew Immigrant Aid Society (HIAS) is another Jewish agency that has helped Jewish immigrants to adjust to their new life in the United States since the end of the nineteenth century. Yet representatives of HIAS were only able to establish offices in Germany and Austria toward the end of 1945.

Beyond that, those individuals who did not want to or could not go home, both Jews and non-Jews, among them those persecuted for racial reasons and those now under Communist rule, posed a special problem. For these refugees, the Allied liberators as well as the international agencies played an important role in transforming them into official displaced persons. The Allied liberators "provided official recognition" that the survivors "had been the victims of Nazi persecution,"[21] while the international agencies "decided which groups of people could receive the status of displaced persons."[22] Among the stateless, the Jewish survivors who called themselves *Sherit HaPletah*, the "saved remnant,"[23] were the largest in number and could not be repatriated; they could at best be "resettled."[24]

The most important issue for Jewish displaced persons was the status of Jewish survivors vis-à-vis all other survivors. At first, "the Allies . . . refused to recognize Jews as a separate ethnic group, arguing that acceptance of a classification based on religion would perpetuate Nazi policies."[25] Thus, initially no special provisions were made for them in any way by the victorious Allied forces. They were treated exactly like all other displaced persons. Because of the shortage of housing and staff, they often continued to live in concentration camps or the Nazi quarters in the camp. The locales often retained the electrified barbed wire fences of the oppression period, and the guards in these camps were often Germans and sometimes even former Nazis.[26] Specially established displaced persons camps were not much better, with flimsy and crude housing and few if any services, let alone "perks." "Supplies and amenities were almost non-existent. DPs lacked shoes, underwear, handkerchiefs, toilet paper, and toothbrushes."[27] Königseder and Wetzel explain that "there was no efficient way to supply the DP camps with everything they needed."[28] Because it was easier to control the large numbers of people in a confined area, the liberating forces preferred to keep survivors inside the liberated camps or in newly established assembly centers. While they were free, survivors nevertheless still found themselves inside a camp, "penned in behind barbed wires," and guarded by soldiers. They were in fact treated "as merely another battalion," having to live like soldiers, with rules and regulations. They were even "required to obtain passes before leaving the premises."[29] One can imagine the mental anguish this caused Holocaust survivors. Their only desire was to leave the location of their suffering as quickly as possible, yet this was a complicated wish and a drawn-out process at best.

In July of 1945 the four victorious powers held a conference at Potsdam, Germany. As a result, Germany was divided into four occupation zones—French, British, American, and Russian. Although the Allies established an Allied Control Council to oversee postwar activities from Berlin, when discussions about the nonrepatriable displaced persons arose, each group dealt with them according to their own interpretation. "Attitudes . . . toward the survivors differed from zone to zone."[30]

The Soviets flat out refused to acknowledge a displaced persons problem,[31] so they were not even part of this conversation. They "saw no reason to set up DP camps in their zone or to provide for thousands of displaced persons. . . . Holocaust survivors were given the choice of being repatriated or forgoing any public assistance."[32] Jewish survivors from the Soviet zone oftentimes gravitated toward the Western-occupied zones for help.[33]

Only small numbers of Jewish survivors—one thousand—lived in the French zone.[34] There was no need for any camps; they could be housed in private homes. Survivors in the French zone "did not establish a Central Committee" to look after their interests "until December 1945."[35]

A number of displaced persons camps were established in the British zone. The largest was the camp at Belsen, roughly on the terrain of the former concentration camp. The concentration camp had consisted of four camps. The barracks of the actual camp were burned down immediately after liberation to eradicate the many diseases running rampant there. The displaced persons assembly center was established in "nearby German army barracks that had previously housed a *Panzer* training school."[36]

Already after a few weeks, Jewish displaced persons "gradually began to organize administrative, occupational, cultural and religious facilities."[37] In April 1945, survivors first established a temporary committee under the leadership of survivor Josef Rosensaft, "whose charisma made him a natural leader."[38] In spite of British noncooperation, the survivors in Belsen by their sheer number managed to transform the camp "into a common liberated community,"[39] a shining example of Jewish creativity and determination.[40] On September 7, 1945, this temporary committee at Belsen published the first book in the British zone, which contained "the list of Jewish survivors in the camp."[41] At the same time, the Central Committee of the Liberated Jews in the British Zone also emerged.

Officially, the British resisted the suggestion to establish separate Jewish displaced persons camps, partly as a result of Britain's troubled relationship with worldwide Jewry over Palestine.[42] Great Britain, charged by the League of Nations in 1920 with administering the Mandate in Palestine, in 1939 laid down its latest policy concerning Palestine in a white paper that limited Jewish immigration into Palestine to an all-time total of seventy-five thousand, or fifteen thousand per year over a five-year period unless the Arabs agreed to additional immigration. This came exactly at a time when the Jews of Europe desperately needed a refuge. Now, the survivors who streamed into the British zone were seen as "part of a well-organized Zionist scheme, financed by American Jewry, to force Britain to open the gates of Palestine to the survivors."[43]

The largest number of displaced persons who were Jewish Holocaust survivors were in the American zone—140,000, according to Königseder and Wetzel.[44] Here, too, the Americans at first based their refusal to grant Jewish survivors separate status "on a tradition that granted international recognition only to nations and not to ethnic groups."[45] However, things took a positive turn in the U.S. zone when Jews were recognized "as a special category who were to be treated differently from the multitude of other victims of the war."[46]

Initially it was also difficult to get information to and from the survivors, because they had to depend on the support of Jewish soldiers in the military to communicate, since the postal service was not working and the Armed Forces did not allow civilians to send or receive mail until November 1945. In addition to Jewish soldiers, contact between survivors and relatives was also facilitated by "Jewish military chaplains" in the U.S. Army as well as "voluntary agency personnel."[47] Even within the American zone, treatment of Holocaust survivors by the military varied tremendously in different areas. Not all U.S. commanders treated Jewish displaced persons the same way. The Seventh Army, under the command of Gen. Alexander Patch in Württemberg and Hessen,[48] "attempted to deal with DPs in a humane fashion. . . . Residents of the assembly centers could come and go at will, disturbances were few, and morale seemed relatively good."[49] Gen. George S. Patton's Third Army, which controlled Bavaria,[50] on the other hand, "insisted that every camp be surrounded by barbed wire and manned by armed guards to watch over the detainees as if they were prisoners."[51] General Patton was blatantly anti-Semitic, describing the Jewish camp survivors in debasing and derogatory terms, calling Jewish displaced persons "lower than animals."[52]

Organizing survivors in the American zone was much more complicated than in the British zone because of the far larger number of Jewish survivors and the existence of many different camps and centers—forty-one, according to Königseder and Wetzel.[53] The first committee with wide influence was formed in Bavaria by Zalman Grinberg, a Jewish survivor from Kovno who worked closely with Rabbi Abraham J. Klausner, an American military chaplain from Memphis, Tennessee,[54] who was seen as "unequipped for this encounter with Holocaust survivors."[55] Klausner, however, was the first one to publish a survivor list in the American zone in book form on June 1, 1945.[56] He also established a tracing service that was "crucial . . . to restoring the mental health of former concentration camp inmates" desperately trying to find out if their relatives were still alive.[57] In July 1945, the first all-Jewish displaced persons camp was established in Feldafing, Bavaria. On July 1, 1945, representatives from all displaced persons camps in Bavaria met "to set up a permanent committee."[58] "Only in January 1946 did this committee expand into one that included the entire American zone. It was known as the Central Committee of the Liberated Jews in the U.S. Zone."[59]

The outcry against the military's sometimes insensitive and inadequate treatment of Jewish displaced persons was eventually heard back in the United States.[60] As a result, on June 22, 1945, President Harry S. Truman allowed a Commission of Inquiry to be convened. Luckily, its chair, Earl G. Harrison, dean of the University of Pennsylvania Law School, took his assignment seriously, and the subsequent report, submitted August 24, 1945, received much attention. The fortunate result was the establishment of separate displaced persons camps for Jewish survivors, on the model of Feldafing. These camps were no longer enclosed with barbed wire, nor were they guarded. Previously, only international relief agencies had been allowed to provide emergency assistance to the displaced persons. Now American Jewish social welfare agencies were allowed to enter and assist the victims in myriad ways. Most important, "after satisfying the requirement of survival— medical services, food, clothing, and housing—the Jewish committees and the Jewish relief agencies moved to provide Jewish substance for the lives of the survivors."[61] This substance was crucial for the survivors' mental well-being. Thus they enterprisingly organized camp schools, religious schools, even *yeshivot* (religious colleges), theater groups, a sports club, and a library. They also published newspapers and magazines, organized religious services, ran kosher kitchens and *mikvaot* (ritual baths), and managed a radio station and cinema. Many assembly centers were run as *kibbutzim,* a communal way of living at its zenith in Israel during the prestate period.

Although the world had considerable knowledge about the atrocities perpetrated by the Nazis primarily, though not exclusively, against the Jews, the attitude of allied countries and its citizens toward the surviving Jews had not progressed much beyond 1938. In July of that year representatives of thirty-two nations had met at Evian on Lake Geneva to discuss the Jewish refugee question in Europe. With the exception of one country, the

Dominican Republic, which was willing to take 100,000 Jewish refugees, all other countries refused to take in a sizable number of European Jews. Now, again, the problem of where to go loomed large and weighed heavily on survivors' minds. Nothing had changed. The United States, concerned about the employment situation for returning GIs, did not rush to admit large numbers of refugees or survivors. Anti-Semitism and antiforeigner sentiments were also strong among Americans, as was the fear of admitting former Nazis or current Communists.[62] It took a directive from President Truman, effective December 22, 1945, to allow several thousand survivors into the country. Although the result was merely "a small trickle" of 2,477, this directive contained a very important change in immigration requirements.[63] Ordinarily relatives, friends, and employers provided affidavits that vouched for immigrants once they were in the United States, to ensure that they would not become a burden to the government. The Truman directive included a very important provision for these stateless individuals. Through "corporate affidavits"[64] welfare agencies were, for the first time, permitted to guarantee "that immigrants would not become public charges."[65] Mira, her father, and Max were sponsored by friends of the family, but "Uncle" Nathan, who did not have family in the United States, benefited from this clause, which was retained in the 1948 Displaced Persons Act. By "June 30, 1947, 22,950 visas had been issued to DPs in Germany," 15,478 of them to Jews.[66] Many more Jewish refugees needed to find a new home.

Great Britain likewise did not let up on their immigration embargo to Palestine. In spite of President Truman's personal intervention with British Prime Minister Clement Attlee on August 31, 1945, pleading for "100,000 immigration certificates for Palestine,"[67] nothing changed officially.[68] In November of 1945 President Truman and Prime Minister Attlee together set up the Anglo-American Committee of Inquiry.[69] The Committee consisted of twelve members, six British representatives and six Americans, who were charged with investigating the situation in the displaced persons camps and the feasibility of allowing 100,000 displaced persons to enter Palestine. Upon the conclusion of their work in the spring of 1946, one of the committee members, Bartley C. Crum, wrote down his thoughts on the experience in a book, *Behind the Silken Curtain*. His sobering conclusion was that British fear of the loss of Arab goodwill (and oil) weighed heavier than the survival of starving, frail individuals who had been through hell. American policy did not fare too well in his assessment either, but Crum looked to our government to change course and step in with deeds.

Another effort to help the survivors, *Aliyah Bet,* or illegal immigration into Palestine, began with the moment of liberation and continued until the declaration of the State of Israel on May 14, 1948. When the British were not able to stem the flow of illegal immigrants in 1946, they established nine detention camps on Cyprus.[70] The tragedy of the *Exodus* (July 1947) provided another dramatic example of British heartlessness and Jewish survivors' determination to reach Palestine. Some survivors spent another year or two in those camps until the State of Israel was created. Many survivors simply had no choice but to stay in Europe, even if they hoped it would be only temporary.

During this time, surviving German Jews, who were small in numbers (no more than twenty-five thousand), began to organize communities again. They "reestablished community offices, opened temporary synagogues, and attempted to provide a variety of social services."[71] Eastern European Jews joined them and together they created a support network for all Jews in a given town. Mira's uncle Heniek Hammer joined such a community in Plattling, Bavaria, and was elected president of the Jewish Committee of Survivors in Plattling.[72]

Some Jewish survivors even tried to return to their hometowns in Eastern Europe. Unfortunately, "traditional Polish antisemitism had not declined."[73] They were attacked and abused or even worse. Yaffa Eliach's bloodcurdling experience of October 20, 1944, after liberation of her hometown of Eishyshok from the Nazis, serves as just one example. After having survived in hiding in underground pits on farms in the countryside for three years, about twenty survivors returned and reclaimed some of the homes they had owned before the Holocaust. In a brutal attack on their little group by neighbors, Yaffa's mother and baby brother were murdered in cold blood while she, her older brother, and her father looked on.[74] Like many others, they thus had no choice but to flee again, eventually making their way to the displaced persons camps in Germany, and await their fate.

During this time a clandestine Jewish organization, *Brichah* ("escape"), assisted by soldiers of the Jewish Brigade, who served in the British army, helped individuals to escape from Eastern Europe to the West and then to Palestine via the Jewish "underground railroad."[75] There were many postwar anti-Jewish pogroms in Poland. The "age-old blood libel that was part of the classic pattern of anti-Jewish violence" resurfaced quickly and strongly.[76] According to Dinnerstein, "between September and December 1945, 26 minor pogroms" took place against Jews in Poland, and "between May 1945 and January 1946, 300 Jews were murdered in Poland."[77] Königseder and Wetzel put the figure at 351 between November 1944 and October 1945.[78] The best known and most shocking incident was the attack on July 4, 1946, on 150 survivors who had returned to Kielce, their hometown, "114 miles southeast of Warsaw," only to be attacked by a mob of Poles, with 42 killed.[79] This horrible occurrence unleashed a major exodus of thousands of terrified Jewish survivors from Poland to the West.[80]

In 1946 President Truman decided to ask Congress to approve the admission of more displaced persons to the United States.[81] As Dinnerstein's book painstakingly documents, the journey from the Truman directive of 1945 to the Displaced Persons Act of 1948 was, however, fraught with attempts at sabotaging any further efforts on behalf of refugees, because of the American public's antiforeigner sentiments, anti-Semitism, and "fear that the Jews and other Eastern Europeans . . . would bring Russian ideology [read Communism] to these shores."[82] Thus, "the U.S. did not widely open the gates for immigrants until the congressional enactment of the Displaced Persons Act of [April 1,] 1948, revised in 1950, admitted large numbers of non-Jewish and also [some] Jewish displaced persons and ended the European refugee crisis."[83] This latest legislation had one major drawback, however, it "repealed the Truman Directive."[84] That is to say, it wiped out all of the preapprovals for visas (23,000) that had been granted under the Truman directive and had not been used by July 1, 1948.[85] Fortunately, the Displaced Persons Commission (DPC), which went into effect on August 27, 1948, knew how to deal with the rules and regulations of the new legislation to the advantage of the refugees. According to Dinnerstein, when the DPC was disbanded at the end of 1952, "more than

400,000 Europeans had arrived in the United States as a result of American efforts at resettlement. . . . the government had invested $250 million in the DP program, including $11,897,000 for the DPC. A spokesman for the DPC calculated that placing all of the DPs who reached the U.S. cost $100,601,000 or $1.93 per taxpayer."[86]

The question no one had a ready answer for was: how does one survive survival? What is "the psychology of the prisoner after his [or her] liberation"?[87] Dr. Viktor Frankl, himself a survivor of Nazi death camps, wrote in his acclaimed book, *Man's Search for Meaning,* that "it would be an error to think that a liberated prisoner was not in need of spiritual care any more."[88] Dr. Frankl gives the example of his own liberation. "'Freedom'—we repeated to ourselves, and yet we could not grasp it. . . . Its reality did not penetrate into our consciousness; we could not grasp the fact that freedom was ours. We came to meadows full of flowers. We saw and realized that they were there, but we had no feelings about them. . . . We had literally lost the ability to be pleased and had to relearn it slowly."[89] Fogelman explains that "one common denominator . . . existed for all DPs . . . emotional numbness or shallowness," also known as "'affective anesthesia.' The condition developed as a defense against daily dangers and anxieties that they suffered during the war."[90] Frankl calls this condition "depersonalization."[91]

While there was tremendous hope for the survivors in some ways, these hopes were often cruelly dashed when they learned what they had feared all along, yet did not dare to believe—that their loved ones were in fact dead. "How does one restore oneself when the sustaining fantasy does not come true?" asks Eva Fogelman.[92] How not to become bitter and disillusioned as the bad news about the loss of family and home sank in?[93] Frankl explains that "those who know how close the connection is between the state of mind of a [person] . . . and the state of immunity of his body will understand that the sudden loss of hope and courage can have a deadly effect."[94] Many lost the "why" of living,[95] experiencing "emotional voids"[96] that needed to be filled as quickly as possible for emotional stability.

Few Holocaust survivors received crisis counseling the way we know it today. Survivors often times had only each other. In Mira's story, this is expressed very clearly in Uncle Nathan's strong attachment to Max.[97] Thus, after initial basic needs were taken care of, it was crucial for survivors to give their life meaning, to fill the emotional voids, often without any help from any professionals. How does one return to one's pre-Holocaust self? How does one make the connection between what was and what is? Fogelman explains that "the DPs had to reconnect themselves to their pre-Holocaust selves and reintegrate this with their most recent horrific past and thereby ready themselves to rejoin the human race."[98]

Dr. Frankl notes that there are three ways in which "we can discover . . . meaning in life: 1) by creating a work or doing a deed; 2) by experiencing something or encountering someone; and 3) by the attitude we take toward unavoidable suffering."[99] In this way, survivors were able to empower themselves to resume living. Königseder and Wetzel state it this way: "Immeasurably more difficult was restoring the survivors' self-respect. In this regard, self-government allowed them to take control of their lives and demonstrate that Hitler's thugs had not banished them forever from the ranks of civilized humanity."[100]

Mira kept busy after liberation, until she collapsed, and then again after she recovered. Menachem Rosensaft, who was born to two survivors at Belsen, told the 2000 gathering of Holocaust survivors in Washington, D.C., about his mother's part in saving survivors, which no doubt also helped her. She was recruited by the deputy director of medical services of the British Army "to organize and head a group of doctors and nurses among the survivors to help care for the camp's thousands of critically ill inmates. For weeks on end, my mother and her team of 28 doctors and 620 other female and male volunteers, only a few of whom were trained nurses, worked round the clock with the military doctors to try to save as many of the survivors as possible."[101]

Mira also again experienced a human community that rose literally like a phoenix from the ashes. Sam Bloch remembers that "post-1945 Bergen-Belsen . . . proved that the flames that had consumed Jewish flesh and bones were powerless to kill the sources of our dreams for life and regeneration."[102]

As early as June 1945, communal activities began with a Jewish elementary school that taught "Hebrew, reading, arithmetic, Jewish and world history, the history of Eretz Yisrael, biology, drawing."[103] As in the American zone, this camp excelled at organizing educational and leisure activities for the Jewish survivors. A kindergarten and nursery school were "the most visible sign" of a renewed Jewish life in Belsen.[104]

Perhaps the most difficult to comprehend is Dr. Frankl's third goal, to find meaning even "when facing a fate that cannot be changed."[105] This one can perhaps attain by transforming "a personal tragedy into a triumph."[106] In Mira's case the triumph was that she lived, that she lived to tell her story and that of her loved ones, that she was reunited with her father, and, most important, that she was able to start a family of her own. Dr. Frankl also points out that it was important to talk not only of the future but also of the past—"all its joys, and how its light shone even in the present darkness."[107] Bloch understands this when he reminds us that we must remember not only death "but also life—the flourishing Jewish communities of Eastern and Central Europe. . . . We must remember not only *whom* we lost, but *what* we lost."[108] Therapists like Eva Fogelman recognize the importance for survivors "to include the histories of their prewar families and lives" when they write their memoirs. She explains that it is often "these family histories that inspired the survivors and drove them to choose life."[109] Telling the story serves the purpose of healing for the author.

Telling the story serves another purpose as well. Mira's first book, *Echoes from the Holocaust: A Memoir,* was for the record; it provided testimony of the atrocities committed by the Nazis against innocent human beings. This memoir has an additional function—it provides a legacy for future generations. Judaism has an honored tradition, that of bequeathing an ethical will to one's children and grandchildren, so that they can integrate the values of their parents, grandparents, and other relatives they might not have known personally into their own value system. The tradition of an ethical will goes back to Genesis 49, where Jacob blesses his children and grandchildren, extolling their unique qualities and instructing them how to live their lives. An ethical will is first and foremost communication, to an individual's family and friends. In a literate world, these communications often take the form of letters to loved ones, of stories that share a writer's personal values and experiences, such as the ones in Mira's book. Although an ethical will is a private communication, several have made it into collections of documents so that they can be enjoyed by everyone. The most precious collection is Jacob Rader Marcus's *This I Believe,* which includes Art Buchwald's touching reverse ethical will to his beloved and now deceased Pop.[110] The best-known examples of a "classical" ethical will come from Marcus's collection, *The Jew in the Medieval World,* which contains two antithetical examples by Judah Ibn Tibbon of twelfth-century Spain and Eleazar of Mainz from fourteenth-century Germany.[111]

Jewish ethical wills continue to be written to this day, both within Judaism and beyond. There are even workshops and instructional "how-to" books. In choosing to write much of this book as letters to her children and grandchildren, Mira's legacy becomes part of the future generations' ethical inheritance. Through this literary form, she also stresses the importance of establishing links between the generations—links such as a name. A good name, like a good wife, is priced above all else in Judaism. In speaking of the importance of names, Rabbi Nachman of Bratzlav, an important eighteenth-century Hasidic teacher in Eastern Europe, noted that "a name . . . contain[s] the secret of a person's existence"[112] as well as his or her "essence."[113] Professor David Patterson of the University of Memphis points out that "the name contains the essence and the mission of the soul." One is also reminded that the Nazis violated the sacrality of names in Judaism by forcing all Jews to adopt the name of Israel or Sarah as a badge of shame and, in the camps, by robbing inmates of their essence and in fact their soul by branding individuals with numbers and obliterating their names. By once again bringing to life her grandparents, parents, and other relatives, Mira connects them and their values as well as her own to the recipients of the letters. "The names," in Patterson's words, "bear not only a memory but also a responsibility." The lives that are bound up in these names are Mira's teachings and admonitions to her family and friends.

In conclusion, a few words about the amazing woman who is the author of this memoir are in order. In the chapter on Oak Ridge, Mira herself mentions some of the organizations she joined and was active in over the past forty years.[114] Yet she is too modest to state what those people she has been associated with know beyond any doubt—that Mira has been a valuable addition to the communal life of the Oak Ridge Jewish community, to East Tennessee, and, in fact, to the South. In her history of Jewish life in Knoxville, which includes Oak Ridge, Wendy Besmann wrote, "Mira Kimmelman herself had received a thorough European Jewish education. This made her especially precious to the growing Oak Ridge congregation."[115] Not only was she connected with school activities that benefited her sons, such as serving on the Oak Ridge High School PTA Board and teaching in the religious school of the Jewish Congregation of Oak Ridge for almost forty years, as well as serving as education chair and directing the religious school three different times (1968–70, 1993–94, and 1997–99), but Mira is such a caring and giving person that her services and advice have been sought in all areas of Jewish life and education. She has taught and prepared Bar and Bat Mitzvah students (1980–present), served on the *Chevrah Kadisha* (Burial Society) (1972–present), and presided as president of her synagogue (1994–97). One of her greatest gifts has been her dedication to Hadassah for thirty-five years, first as Oak Ridge chapter president (1969–72, 1990–92), then as president of the Southern Region of Hadassah (1981–84), and as a member of the National Board of Hadassah (1981–86). For years, Mira ran a "Passover store" out of the synagogue, providing "kosher for Passover" products to East Tennesseans, all benefiting Hadassah.

Mira's energies also extend beyond the Jewish community. From 1977 to 1979 she was president of the Oak Ridge Chapter of the American Field Service (AFS), and then, from 1979 to 1982 and again from 1984 to 1993, she was president of the United Nations Committee of Oak Ridge.

Oak Ridge and East Tennessee have shown their appreciation for Mira's dedication by showering her with recognition and awards. Since 1983, when she received the Sertoma Annual Heritage and Freedom Award, she has received seven more major awards: the Knoxville Women's Club Annie Selwyn Award for Teaching and Lecturing on the Holocaust (1987), the Oak Ridge Chapter of Hadassah National Leadership Award (1987), the Women's League Light of Torah Award (1992), the National Conference for Community and Justice Award for Religious Services (1997), National

Hadassah's Deborah Award for Hebrew Teaching (2000), the YWCA of Oak Ridge 2001 Women of Distinction Award in the category of religion (2001), and the Jewish Congregation of Oak Ridge Recognition Award for forty years of teaching (2003).

Mira not only teaches students prayers, the chanting of Torah and Haftarah, and how to lead services, she generously shares her time and talent with the congregation by participating in services herself and chanting the Haftarah (prophetic portion). For many years, she has chanted the Kol Nidre service (evening of Day of Atonement) for her congregation. If Mira in this book expresses her gratitude to Oak Ridge—Jewish and non-Jewish—Oak Ridge certainly has appreciated the contributions she and her family have made to the well-being of this community.

For nearly thirty-five years, Mira has taught and lectured on the Holocaust. Since her husband's death in 1990, hardly a week passes that she does not share her experiences with a group or class, not once but often twice. She has also traveled to other regions of the country for speaking engagements. We have indeed been blessed by Mira's commitment to "share her story," not only verbally but also in writing. Since the publication of Mira's first book, *Echoes from the Holocaust,* in 1997, the University of Tennessee Press has sold more than six thousand copies. All of the proceeds have gone to the Judaic Studies Endowment of The Fern and Manfred Steinfeld Program in Judaic Studies in the Department of Religious Studies at the University of Tennessee. In her generosity, Mira has likewise designated the proceeds from this volume to the same fund.

When we come to the end of a book in the Torah, we recite the phrase "Hazak, hazak, venithazek" (May you go from strength to strength). We wish you the same, Mira, at age eighty-one—strength and good health and good spirits.

GILYA GERDA SCHMIDT, PH.D.
DEPARTMENT OF RELIGIOUS STUDIES
THE FERN AND MANFRED STEINFELD PROGRAM IN JUDAIC STUDIES
THE UNIVERSITY OF TENNESSEE, KNOXVILLE

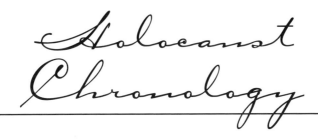

Holocaust Chronology

JANUARY 30, 1933
After the Nazi Party receives more than a third of the vote in a free election, Adolf Hitler becomes Reich chancellor.

FEBRUARY 27, 1933
The *Reichstag* building in Berlin is burned down and dissident elements are blamed. Nazis declare martial law.

MARCH 20, 1933
Dachau in a suburb of Munich is established as one of the first concentration camps for political undesirables.

APRIL 1, 1933
A boycott against Jewish stores in Germany is declared.

AUGUST 2, 1934
President Paul von Hindenburg dies. Hitler declares himself president and chancellor of Germany and henceforth is known as the Führer.

SEPTEMBER 15, 1935
The Nuremberg Laws go into effect, consisting of the Law to Protect German Blood and German Honor and the Reich Citizenship Law.

JULY 12, 1936
Preceding the Olympics, the concentration camp of Sachsenhausen in the Berlin suburb of Oranienburg is established.

JULY 16, 1937
The concentration camp of Buchenwald near Weimar is established.

1938
All Jewish businesses are Aryanized.

MARCH 13, 1938
Austria is annexed to Germany. This is known as the *Anschluss.*

JULY 6–15, 1938
Thirty-two nations meet at Evian on Lake Geneva to discuss the
Jewish refugee problem in Europe. Only the Dominican Republic
is willing to take in a sizable number of Jews (100,000).

AUGUST 17, 1938
Jewish women have to add the name Sarah, men the name Israel,
to their names.

OCTOBER 5, 1938
A red "J" is added to Jewish passports.

NOVEMBER 9–10, 1938
This wave of persecution against Jews in Germany and Austria,
including the Free City of Danzig (Gdańsk), is known as
Kristallnacht, or Night of Broken Glass. One thousand synagogues
are destroyed by citizen mobs, thirty thousand Jewish men are
arrested and interned in existing camps, one hundred Jews are killed,
and Jewish homes and businesses are ransacked and plundered.

NOVEMBER 15, 1938
Jewish children are excluded from German schools. Jews are no
longer allowed to frequent parks, movie houses, swimming pools.
In all, over four hundred laws forbidding Jews to participate in
German society are passed in this period.

MAY 13, 1939
The S.S. *St. Louis* departs from Hamburg, Germany, for Havana,
Cuba, with nearly one thousand refugees who have landing permits
for Cuba and in some cases hold visas for the United States. The
Cuban government refuses to honor the permits, and, while helpless

relatives watch, the passengers are returned to Europe (June 2), where most of them fall into the hands of the Nazis and perish.

MAY 17, 1939
The British government announces its new Palestine policy in a white paper.

SEPTEMBER 1, 1939
World War II breaks out when the German army invades Poland. Poland succumbs within three weeks. Warsaw and other Polish cities are destroyed.

SEPTEMBER 2, 1939
The Stutthof concentration camp is established.

SEPTEMBER 3, 1939
France and England declare war on Germany.

SEPTEMBER 17, 1939
Soviet troops invade and occupy eastern Poland.

OCTOBER 1939
Beginning of the Nazi euthanasia program. Over a two-year period, nearly one hundred thousand individuals with disabilities are murdered.

OCTOBER 8, 1939
The first Jewish ghetto is set up in Piotrkow-Trybunalski, Poland.

APRIL 1940
A concentration camp is established at Auschwitz (Oswiecim). From this time on, a total of nine thousand concentration camps for slave labor are established throughout Europe.

APRIL–JUNE 1940
France, Belgium, and Holland fall under German occupation, as do Denmark and Norway.

June 22, 1941

Germany breaks a mutual nonaggression treaty with the Soviet Union, and the German army invades the Soviet Union. *Einsatzgruppen* (mobile killing squads) follow invading troops and round up and murder all Jews that fall into their hands.

September 3, 1941

Germans experiment with gassing Soviet POWs with Cyclon B at Auschwitz. Nazis thus discover the primary method by which they will carry out the Final Solution.

September 19, 1941

German Jews are forced to wear the Star of David on outer clothing.

September 29–30, 1941

Rosh Hashanah 5702. *Einsatzkommando* kills 33,771 Jews at Babi Yar near Kiev.

December 8, 1941

Chelmno is the first of six death camps to be established and operative. Nazis begin deportation of Jews from Western Europe. 320,000 Jews are murdered here.

January 20, 1942

Wannsee Conference takes place in a villa located at the Grosse Wannsee in a Berlin suburb. Fifteen German leaders meet to discuss the Final Solution to the Jewish Question.

1942

Three more death camps are established—Belzec, Sobibor, and Treblinka. Operation Reinhard is set in motion. Auschwitz and Majdanek also begin operation. All but the Hungarian Jews are systematically rounded up and sent to concentration camps. The sick, the young, the old, and pregnant women are "selected" in ghettoes and concentration camps for immediate death. Only those capable of working may live as long as they are useful.

February 2, 1943

The German army is defeated in the Battle of Stalingrad.

April 19–May 16, 1943

Passover. The Warsaw Ghetto uprising begins. 265,000 Jews from the ghetto have already been deported to Treblinka and murdered. The remaining Jews rise up against the Nazis and with crude weapons fight for about a month until the revolt is put down and the ghetto destroyed.

August 2, 1943

Revolt occurs at Treblinka.

1943

By the end of the year, most European Jews have been murdered and the killing centers of Operation Reinhard cease operation.

March 19, 1944

Hungarian Jews are rounded up. Half of eight hundred thousand are deported to Auschwitz and murdered.

June 6, 1944

D-Day. Allies land at Normandy.

July 20, 1944

Assassination attempt on Hitler by Claus Schenk Graf von Stauffenberg and other German officers.

July 23, 1944

Soviets discover and liberate Majdanek. 360,000 Jews have been murdered there. Soviet military tries to tell the world what they found, but no one wants to listen.

August 1, 1944

Uprising in Polish Warsaw begins. This uprising is crushed in early October 1944.

SEPTEMBER 1944

Soviets discover and liberate Treblinka.

OCTOBER 7, 1944

Sonderkommando prisoners revolt at Auschwitz. Crematorium II is blown up; Crematoria III and IV are damaged.

JANUARY 19, 1945

Nazis retreat from the advancing Russian armies. They try to destroy evidence of camps and murder many of the surviving inmates. Auschwitz in Upper Silesia is evacuated. The Nazis send thousands of weak prisoners on death marches all over Europe toward Germany's interior, hoping that the victims will succumb to the harsh conditions.

JANUARY 27, 1945

The Soviet military liberates Auschwitz.

APRIL 11, 1945

U.S. forces liberate Buchenwald concentration camp.

APRIL 15, 1945

British soldiers liberate Bergen-Belsen.

MAY 8, 1945

V-E Day. World War II in the European theater comes to an end. All concentration and death camp prisoners are liberated. The world now knows about the horrors of the Holocaust.

JUNE 22, 1945

President Truman appoints Earl G. Harrison to investigate the needs of stateless displaced persons in Germany.

JULY 17–AUGUST 2, 1945

The "Big Three" (Truman, Churchill/Attlee, Stalin) meet at Potsdam, Germany, to discuss post–World War II logistics, culminating in the Potsdam Agreement of August 4.

AUGUST 6, 1945
Atomic bomb is dropped on Hiroshima.

AUGUST 9, 1945
Atomic bomb is dropped on Nagasaki.

AUGUST 15, 1945
V-J Day. The fighting in Asia ends as well.

NOVEMBER 13, 1945
Anglo-American Committee of Inquiry into Palestine is established by the British and United States together. It is their task to assess the viability of settling Jewish survivors in Palestine.

DECEMBER 22, 1945
The Truman directive that allows European refugees into the United States becomes operative.

MAY 14, 1948
David Ben-Gurion proclaims the State of Israel.

Part 1

Chapter 1

THE NEVER-ENDING PAIN

Liberation was not the end. What followed afterward was a different kind of suffering, a constant reminder of the horrors of the past. The effects are still with me, although more than half a century has passed since the moment of my rebirth.

"How can you live a normal life after what you have been through?" I have been asked this question over and over by those who hear me speak about the Holocaust. What is normal? And am I normal? When people look at me, they see only the "shell," the outside person. They do not see the other me, the one who is hidden deep inside me. This other me is still being tormented by the guilt of surviving, by endless nightmares, by many fears. Tears flow easily, at every emotional occasion. I cry watching a sad movie or reading a sad book. I cry at weddings or family events. I cry when I say good-bye to my children and grandchildren. I cry during our holidays.

Throughout the war years, I did not shed a tear. I was unable to cry, to show any grief or emotion. I was unable to mourn. One cannot bury tears and hide feelings forever, and mine exploded with a great force once the danger of the war years passed. For years after my liberation I did not attend funerals. Having lived with death for such a long time, I could not face death after the war. Death was something that had happened in ghettos and camps. In time of peace one should not have to face death. And I felt so guilty for not attending the funeral of our uncle Max Jacobs in Cincinnati. I told everybody that I was ill. Only my husband, Max, understood my fears. He knew that each death reminded me of my losses. I could not and would not enter a cemetery. "How can I go to a cemetery knowing that my dear mother, brother, grandparents, and members of my family have no graves?" These were the demons I had to struggle to overcome. Another fear was the fear of illness. I was frantic, I was hysterical when our children or Max became ill. Again I saw in my mind the sick who had no medical help, no medicine, no care. It took many years for me to overcome this problem.

I fear winters. To this day I am afraid of cold weather, recalling the harsh winters during the war. Snow and ice always remind me of the death march in January 1945, when we had to walk for miles in the coldest weather without warm clothing to protect us. And then there was the ever-present fear of hunger. I am now living alone in my house, with only one person to feed: myself. Two refrigerators and two freezers are filled to the brim. I probably have enough food to last one year, especially bread. My children joke about the danger zone when they have to open my freezers. Things are packed in—and falling out, if one is not careful. They do understand the reason for my hoarding of food, and nowadays we can joke about it. But my fear is genuine. "What if tomorrow there will be no bread available?" Bread meant life during the war years. To this day I think of bread as the most important food item. My hoarding of food is my security blanket.

Dreams and nightmares rob me of much sleep. When our sons were little, I woke up in the middle of the night to check if they were in their beds, if they were safe. Nightmares about Nazis taking our children away tormented not only me but also Max for a long time. Our constant fear for the safety of our children made us overprotective parents. I am sure that our sons sensed our anxieties and probably could not understand why we wanted to protect them as much as we did. This was our survivors' mentality and we had to struggle to overcome it. I stayed home, while Max was the breadwinner. I wanted to and felt it my duty to take care of our children, to protect them from harm.

I shall never forget one November day in 1952. Benno and I took the bus to go to downtown Cincinnati, and Benno suddenly disappeared. While I was paying for shoelaces (I still remember—at the Kresge Five-and-Dime on Race Street), he followed some lady and ran outside. This happened within seconds, and here I was without our son. He could barely talk, did not know his name. I alerted the store manager, and they in turn called the police. Fifteen minutes later Benno walked into the store flanked by two policemen. These were the longest fifteen minutes of my life. If anything had happened to our child, I would not have been able to go on living. Thank God this adventure ended well. But I shall never forget it.

For most parents, the end of a three-month summer vacation was a blessing—the children went back to school. I was the silly goose who cried her eyes out when our sons returned to school. Did I love them too much? Or did I need their presence so that I could protect them? Our family was the only security I had. I had to learn to let go.

Dreams, dreams, and more dreams. Not a night goes by without some dreams. Some are scary; some even come true. My survival depended mostly on luck, but also on premonition, and I developed a sixth sense. I am sure that many people's lives are guided by intuition, by a sixth sense. Only I feel it more often than others. All of my life I have enjoyed being with people. I have trusted my friends completely and have felt betrayed and hurt when my trust was abused. To this day I am oversensitive. Lack of sensitivity shown by people I consider friends hurts me deeply. Then I have to step back to distance myself from them in order not to get hurt again. I know that people do things without thinking, not realizing how much pain they are inflicting on others. And I forgive them. The many insensitivities that Max and I endured throughout the years are not easily forgotten. Today, I realize that people were not comfortable with us. They wanted to keep their distance from us because we were different. We were treated as if we were carrying some disease that they could catch by associating with us. This fear I notice today when people deal with someone who has cancer. Time heals; some of the wounds that were inflicted on us have healed. How grateful I am for the handful of friends to whom I can bare my soul and speak openly about my not-so-normal sensitivity. One does not need many friends. It is the quality and not the quantity that matters. I have been blessed with friends who are much more than friends; they have become my family.

Love and marriage were the anchors in my life. They helped me build a solid and steady foundation for the future. Max and I were as different as any two people could be. We were of a different temperament—Max did everything slowly but surely, while I was quick and impulsive. The age difference of fifteen years made Max much more mature, while I was still a child and quite immature when we got married. Max was not only my lover, my husband, and my protector, but also my best friend. For the forty-four years of our marriage I never hid any thought. I shared everything with Max. Our relationship was built on absolute trust and love. Max knew all my thoughts, and I knew his. By looking at each other we knew what was on our minds.

Max was very conservative. I was always a rebel, a liberal. We did not agree about everything. We quarreled and we made up. But we did respect each other's opinion. Max, who was raised in a strictly Orthodox family, was completely nonobservant when we met. I, on the other hand, was very traditional, observant, and believing. My faith helped me to survive. My religion was and is my moral and ethical stronghold. While Max was distrustful of people, I was naive and trusted complete strangers. Max was by nature much more realistic and a pragmatist. I was more idealistic. Max definitely knew whom he liked and disliked and openly voiced his opinions. He had certain standards, especially when it came to raising our sons, while I had a greater understanding of young people. Being a teacher I was more in tune with what American youth was thinking and how they were acting. Max was filled with deep anger when talking about his war experiences. There were moments when I sensed that he hated everything that reminded him of the Holocaust. He rarely spoke of it.

After having kept silent for twenty years, I was finally able to talk about my Holocaust experience. "Don't you feel hatred after all the suffering you endured?" I am asked repeatedly. I could never hate. Hate never entered into my feelings. Anger, yes. I was furious, I was angry and enraged. But I never hated. During the worst times I felt sorry for those who killed, beat, and dehumanized us. "They will have to live with their guilty consciences," I told myself. After the war I saw survivors take revenge; this never entered my mind. During all the bad times I saw a ray of goodness in people of all nationalities, people of different religions. I saw "righteous Gentiles" risk their lives to save a Jewish child. I saw complete strangers risking their lives to harbor Jews. I even saw Nazis trying to help us with a crumb of bread or a potato. There is good and bad in each of us. I have chosen to look for the good in human beings. To me the glass is always half full and not half empty.

Max and I came to this country empty handed and started to build our lives from the ground up. Neither of us ever accepted any charity; we both worked hard to make it on our own. We loved the freedom to move around; we felt secure. More than physical security, our souls needed emotional security. This had been denied us for many years. We felt different; we felt isolated. Both of us tried to lead as normal a life as possible, regardless of the scars that kept hurting. We recognized very early on that these scars would not fade away; it would take a long time for them to heal. The everyday fight to provide for our family was a diversion that kept the pain well hidden. Although we struggled financially, we were happy with whatever Max earned. We had seen money disappear in a minute; money was never a priority for us. We lived frugally, always content with what we had. Most of all, we were grateful for our children. We raised them in a home that may not have been normal, but they were raised with lots of love. Both my sons are hardworking, just like their father was. Both have wonderful families, loving wives, and each has two children. I hope that as children of survivors their lives do not bear scars.

Through the years I overcame my fear of death. I served as a volunteer in the *Chevrah Kadisha* (Jewish Burial Society). Each time I participated in the ritual of preparing the dead for burial, I thought of my dear ones who were denied this sacred service, the dignity of dying and being buried like human beings. I was present when our "uncle" Nathan passed away, my dear father died in my arms, and I was with my beloved Max while he was dying. And each time a part of me died, too. But there is no fear anymore.

There is still the hoarding of food and the fright of cold when winter comes. I am still petrified of illness and oversensitive when dealing with people. Does this make me abnormal, or can I qualify to be normal after all these years?

When the war ended sixty years ago, I was physically an adult. Emotionally I was still a child. Soon I became a wife, a mother, and now I am a mother-in-law and grandmother. Each day, when I rise, I am grateful to be alive. Each day I miss Max but feel his spirit in me. I thank God for the ability to work, to teach, and to function. But most of all I thank God for my family, my sons, daughters-in-law, and grandchildren. Although the pain and scars are still there, I know that they will never heal completely. I have learned to live with them, to keep them hidden deep inside me. Every person has to endure some kind of pain, everybody deals with it in their own way. I wish for my children and grandchildren lives filled with love, peace, contentment, and harmony, lives that will know only goodness.

Chapter 2

WHAT'S IN A NAME?

In the Jewish Ashkenazi (Middle-European) tradition, we give our children names after departed family members. In this way we honor our beloved departed relatives so that their memory lives on. My parents named me in Hebrew Miriam after my mother's grandmother Marien Szmant. Miriam is my Hebrew name, but I was always called Mira. Max and I named our two sons Benno and Gene. Benno's Hebrew names are Leib Benyamin (Louis Benjamin)—Leib for Max's favorite brother, who perished in Treblinka, Benyamin for my dearest brother, Benno, who was killed a few days before the war ended. Gene's Hebrew names are Yitzhak Efraim (Eugene Irvin). Yitzhak was Max's father's name, Efraim was the name of my paternal grandfather. Because we had no daughter, Gene's name reminds me of my beloved mother's name, Genia (Gitel).

Now we have a new generation. My sons have children of their own. Benno and Joy named their daughter Melanie Marie (in Hebrew Malka

Morit) for Max's mother and little daughter (Malka/Maryla), and Morit for my father, Moritz. Their son Michael Max is named in Hebrew Mordechai Moshe, for Benno's father and my beloved husband, Max, and my father (Moshe/Moritz). Gene and Caroline named their son Max Chambers; his Hebrew names are Mordechai Natan, for Gene's father, Max, and for "Uncle" Nathan. Chambers is Caroline's family name. Their daughter is named Eleanor Moore; her Hebrew names are Esther Gitel—Esther for my paternal grandmother, Gitel for my dear mother. We call her Ellie. Moore is Caroline's middle name and the maiden name of her maternal grandmother.

Except for Max's mother and father, all the Hebrew names that have been given to my children and grandchildren are of our dear ones who perished during the Holocaust or who survived and are no longer among the living. The stories of their lives will be told to Benno and Gene, to Melanie, to Michael, to Max, and to Ellie. I want them to know what's in *their* names.

Mira's grandchildren. *Left to right:* Michael, Melanie, Max, and Ellie.

What's in a Name?

Chapter 8

LIFE AFTER LIBERATION

Dear Benno and Gene,

Dad and I told you about our lives before the war and during the war. We never thought of how important it would be to share with you our lives after liberation, my life in the Bergen Belsen Displaced Persons Camp, our lives in Rötz after Dad and I got married. And then our new lives in the United States—first in New York City, then in Cincinnati, Ohio, where both of you were born. Some of these memories will be quite familiar; some you may have already forgotten. The last place I shall describe will be Oak Ridge, Tennessee, where we settled in 1964 and where I have spent the longest time of my life.

LIFE IN THE BERGEN-BELSEN DISPLACED PERSONS CAMP

Let me begin with Bergen-Belsen. I realized the significance of describing my life after liberation only when students frequently asked me, "What was your life like after you were liberated? You had nothing—no money, no clothes, no home." So let me begin with April 15, 1945, when the concentration camp of Bergen-Belsen was liberated by the Second British Army.

Once I was asked by a student at a school where I was speaking, "What was the first thing you wanted to do after you were free?" I had to reach back into my "memory bank," and the answer came back to me like a flash of lightning: I felt so dirty; I wanted to wash my hair. With my friend Anusch Katschinski from Danzig I walked to the empty barracks of the SS women (who had been caught and arrested by the British). I took a basin and washed my hair in cold water. For the first time in many months I felt clean (although cold water and no shampoo or soap gave me only the illusion of cleanliness).

We were sick, starved, infested with lice. The Medical Corps realized the weakened and hopeless state of our health and wisely imposed a diet on the emaciated former prisoners. They gave us powdered milk diluted with water, each day a stronger formula. Our bodies were not used to wholesome food, our intestines unable to digest rich food. Those who could not control their hunger and begged for chocolate, biscuits, or canned meat died minutes after they swallowed the food. And there was a typhoid epidemic among the former prisoners—to save the ill ones became the priority. For us, the liberated ones, war was over, the danger of being killed by the Nazis ceased to exist. Now we faced the danger of dying from typhoid, typhus, or dysentery.[1] Makeshift hospitals were created by the British in the now empty buildings that once housed the SS guards and officers. Before we were allowed to leave the camp to be taken to the hospital, we had to undergo disinfection. Whatever we wore was taken away from us and burned. The Medical Corps arranged portable showers in ambulances. First we were dusted from head to toe with an enormous amount of DDT powder; after a few hours we were given a shower with hot water. This was my first hot shower after many years. Even though I was weak and undernourished, when the British asked for volunteers to work in the hospitals, I volunteered. At that time I was immune to typhoid and typhus, having been ill with both of these dreadful diseases in the camps. I could not wait to get out of the filthy and infested former concentration camp. To work in a hospital seemed only natural for me. I wanted to be of use. At the time of my liberation I weighed only about eighty-five pounds. I had suffered from hunger for the past six years and had not eaten eggs, butter, meat, fruit, cheese, or sugar all these years. My diet consisted mainly of black bread, rotten potatoes, potato peels, and soup made of rotten vegetables, which smelled to high heaven. In other words, I was not a strong girl of twenty-one. Malnutrition had taken its toll. Yet I had inner strength, an urge to work, to help, not to be idle. I needed something positive to occupy my mind. My thoughts were constantly with my father and brother, whom I last saw at the gates of Auschwitz-Birkenau. Did they survive? Would I be able to find them? These painful questions occupied my mind, my heart.

Those of us who volunteered to work in the hospitals were given some used but decent clothes and were driven to the Belsen camp, where large brick buildings were transformed into hospitals. We, the "nurses," were given lodging on the top floor of the "hospital," in the attic. Each one of us had a clean bed, something that I had not had since 1942. I worked a twelve-hour day shift or night shift. Most of the patients on my floor were young girls, most came from Hungary. The work was hard; it was backbreaking. We were given nourishing food, which gave us the physical strength we needed. There was not much in medication to help our young patients. The doctors at first were all British, but soon they were joined by former prisoners who were physicians. Caring for the ill took all my physical strength. I was emotionally drained when my first patient—a beautiful young Hungarian Jewish girl—died. I collapsed. "How can such a young girl die after liberation? She survived Hitler's inferno and now she is dead. Why?" After living with death and the dying for almost six years, suddenly I could not face death. And I could not accept the death of this young girl. Somewhere in my mind I wanted death to disappear. Nobody should die after so much suffering. For years afterward I had a difficult time facing the loss of dear ones and could not enter a cemetery. How strange that the death of this young Hungarian girl haunts me to this day. Unfortunately, this was not the only person who died after liberation. Fifteen thousand former prisoners died in Belsen within the first month after they were liberated. For those unfortunate ones, freedom came too late.

The doctors ordered me to rest in bed as much as possible. While I recuperated, World War II ended on May 8, 1945. I can still hear the words of Winston Churchill announcing over the radio the capitulation of Nazi Germany. As soon as I got stronger, I tried to find traces of my family. At first traveling in postwar Germany was difficult and hazardous. Once I regained my physical strength, I volunteered to work for the British Red Cross. They needed people who could communicate in a few languages. Their aim was to reunite families. Many times I was asked to accompany children whose mother and father were in other parts of Germany. But we only traveled in the British zone of Germany. We were now living in a displaced persons camp and could not leave or enter without proper passes. These were issued in the office where I was now working. Whenever I knew of people who were leaving the camp in search of their dear ones, I gave them the names of my father and brother. Should they by chance meet them or anybody who knew them, at least they would know that I survived and was alive in Belsen. And whenever I heard of former prisoners coming into our camp, I sought them out in order to question them about my family.

The Medical Corps, the British Red Cross officers (all women) treated us, the former prisoners, with kindness and empathy, with understanding and fairness. Soon they gave complete autonomy to a newly created Jewish committee to administer the Displaced Persons Camp of Belsen. But the British always had the last word when it came to important decisions. In the city of Lüneburg, a thirty-minute ride from Belsen, the British military government set up court for the Nazi criminals. Many former inmates went to testify at the trials. The British court was swift and just. The worst criminals were sentenced to die; executions were carried out without delay.

The British military authorities ordered our camp to register each surviving ex-prisoner. This was done by country of origin. The Czech, Slovakian, Polish, French, and Russian prisoners were sent to their homes. Only the Jews had no place to go. Some Czech Jews returned to Prague, but most of the others from Poland, Hungary, Romania, Latvia, and Lithuania remained in the camp. Some tried to go back to their hometown to search for family; they soon came back. They found nobody; they were the only survivors. Lists were also circulated between our camp and other camps, and there were many of them. This way friends and relatives could find a familiar name, someone they were searching for.

The Belsen Displaced Persons Camp was divided into three camps: Camp II, Camp III, and Camp IV. (Camp I was the former concentration camp, which the British burned to the ground.) I resided in Camp IV, where the office of the British Red Cross and Welfare was situated. I was sharing one room with Eva Kolska and Diana Rubin, my close friends from the ghetto and camps. Our room was in Block L-12 (*L* stood for *Leutnant* [lieutenant]). At first all three of us worked as translators for the British; I gave it up for a job with the British Red Cross. Soon we had to vacate the building, which was converted into offices. Our next "home" was a room in Block S-3 (*S* stood for "sergeant"). My office was just a few minutes' walk from there in Block H-1 (*H* stood for *Hauptmann* [captain]). There was a camp kitchen with fairly good and adequate food; the kitchen was overseen by the Jewish Committee. Clothing, shoes, and blankets were sent to our camp by the British Red Cross and distributed fairly to all inhabitants. A post office was created; soon packages arrived from friends or relatives abroad. Most of the packages were opened; many never reached their recipients. Many months later I received a letter from my father's cousin in Northern Ireland asking me if I received the package with a winter coat, a suit, and a few dresses. They found out that I survived and wanted to help me. I never received this package. I do know that it arrived at the Belsen Post Office but never found out what happened to it. It was disappointing, as I desperately needed warm clothing for the approaching winter.

Besides the constant search for family members, people in displaced persons camps like Belsen yearned for a normal life. Young people were falling in love, marriages were performed, and babies were born. The camp gave us a sense of security. It was the only place where we felt safe; yet, we wanted to leave it. The Jewish Brigade from Palestine came to our camp to recruit young men and women for Palestine. The young Zionists were smuggled through Austria and Italy illegally. Many reached the Promised Land; some were caught and sent to Cyprus by the British; others in desperation returned to their hometowns in Poland hoping to find family members. Soon they came back with horror stories. Some returning Jews were mercilessly killed when they tried to enter their homes. The Hungarian Jews were torn by their wishes to find relatives in Hungary and the danger of returning to a Communist-controlled country. The same was true of the Jews from Czechoslovakia.

The Belsen camp included many Jews of diverse nationalities. The British and American zones of Germany saw a true *Völkerwanderung* (population migration) in the first year after liberation. Some flatly refused to remain in displaced persons camps and instead settled in German cities or towns.

In the first few months after liberation, my life was very busy. I was never paid in money, but I received rations of cigarettes, coffee, and choco-

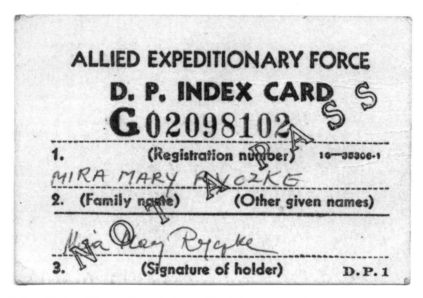

Belsen Displaced Persons Camp index card for Mira Mary Ryczke, 1945.

late. I did not smoke, so cigarettes became my currency. For cigarettes I could get butter, cheese, and meat. If I needed to have some of the clothes altered that were given to me, I paid with cigarettes. Soon schools were organized in the camp. People wanted to learn English and Hebrew, especially those who hoped to emigrate to Palestine, England, or the United States. Concerts and films as well as plays were performed in the camp. I recall a concert given by Yehudi Menuhin. What a thrill it was for us to listen to this famous violinist. It was important for cultural events to be brought to the camp.

Many of my friends went to Sweden. This country opened its gates to survivors of concentration camps and offered them a new home. Among them was my distant cousin from Lodz, Halinka Frydlender. When I found Halinka in Camp III, she begged me to leave with her for Sweden. Both her parents had been killed; her two brothers, Pawel and Rafal, had left Poland for the Soviet Union; and her husband was dead. She did not want to remain in Germany. As much as I wanted to be with Halinka, I was still searching for my father and brother. I would not leave the camp without finding out where they were. Traveling outside the camp was difficult, but I managed to go to other camps in order to search for my family. There were so many camps, where did one start? In the meantime, Halinka left for Sweden with her best friend from the ghetto, Luise Igler. It was the end of May 1945.

A few weeks later a young man with a slip of paper came to the office where I worked. He had asked for me and was told where I could be found. He handed me the paper with the following message: "I am looking for my daughter, Mira Ryczke, born September 17, 1923 in Zoppot, and for my son, Benno Ryczke, born the 24th of January, 1928 in Zoppot." The note was signed by my father. How can I begin to describe my feelings of bliss, my joy, my happiness when I read this small piece of lined paper. I recognized the signature of my beloved father. "My father is alive," I shouted. "He is looking for me and for my brother." Now I knew that I was not alone anymore. For a moment I was so overcome with joy I forgot that he was also looking for Benno. When were they separated? Where did they part? What had happened to Benno? There was a chance that my brother, too, would get a note like this. The young messenger told me that my father lived in Eggenfelden, in Bavaria, in the U.S. zone of Germany. He was liberated by the U.S. Army and he, too, was traveling in search of his children. He gave notes to everybody who traveled to different camps in the hope that in one of them his children would be found. The young man was returning to Eggenfelden; I told him that I would wait for my father here in Belsen and gave him a letter for my father. One month later, in July 1945, my father and I were reunited in Belsen.

It happened on a day when I was traveling to Flensburg to reunite a young Polish girl with her mother. When I returned to Belsen it was almost evening. My friend Rysia Lichtenstein saw me in the ambulance—we traveled for the Red Cross by ambulance—and she shouted to me, "Mira, your father is here. He is waiting for you." I ran home and fell into his arms. He was waiting for me in front of the building. There are no words that can describe our reunion. Both of us cried. These were tears of joy. Only a year had passed since we saw each other for the last time at the gate of Auschwitz. The year was like an eternity. Now we were finally together again. We needed time to be alone, to bond again. My father looked thin but well. His hair was very short (it had been shaved). We needed time to talk, to share our experiences, to allow the wounds to heal. Knowing that I had my father back made me feel like a child again. I could relax. He would take care of me, of our future.

Gendarmeriepoſt n Schönau
Landkreis Eggenfelden, Reg. Bezirk Niederb./Oberpfalz

B e s c h e i n i g u n g

Der Schutzhäftling Moritz R Y c z k e .... aus dem
Lager Auschwitz wurde heute wegen Auflösung des Lagers auf
Grund einer Anordnung der interallierten Kommission in seine
Heimat nach ...Danzig - Gdingen ········· entlassen.

Schönau, den 3.Mai 1945.

Jackel

Mit Lebensmittelkarten versorgt
vom
bis eine m.
E.-A. Abt. Pfarrkirchen

Moritz Ryczke registration after liberation in Eggenfelden, May 3, 1945.

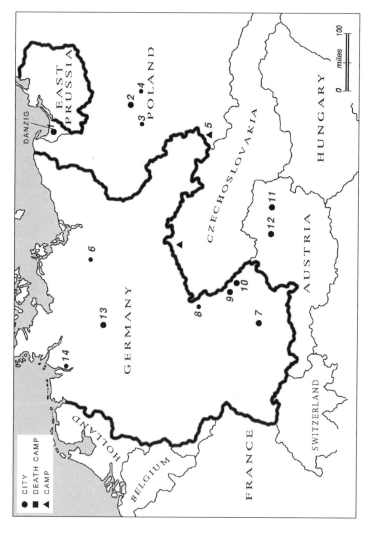

Moritz Ryczke's forced journeys during the Holocaust and travels thereafter: (1) Danzig (Gdańsk); (2) Warsaw; (3) Tomaszow-Mazowiecki (ghetto); (4) Blizyn/Majdanek (c.c.); (5) Auschwitz-Birkenau (d.c.); (6) Sachsenhausen (c.c.); (7) Dachau (c.c.); (8) Flossenburg (c.c.); (9) Kaufering (c.c.); (10) Eggenfelden; (11) Wien (Vienna); (12) Mauthausen (c.c.); (13) Hannover; (14) Bremerhaven.

Chapter 4

MORITZ RYCZKE (1897–1979)

Dear Melanie Marie and Michael Max,

You are my first grandchildren, and each one of you has two names. One of them is Morit in Hebrew and Marie in English, for my dear father, your great-grandfather, and one of Michael's Hebrew names is also for my father, Moshe (Moritz Ryczke).

Let me acquaint you with your great-grandfather, Moritz/Moshe Ryczke. Carrying his name entitles you to know as much as possible about him. With his name you also carry the memories of my father, the inheritance of our tradition that he left behind. I will try to do justice to my father's life, to the joys and pains that he and I experienced. Because you never knew your great-grandfather Ryczke, I shall try to tell his story as accurately as possible.

Moritz/Moshe Ryczke was born on February 1, 1897, in the small Polish town of Slupca, close to the German border. He was the second child of

Efraim and Esther Ryczke. His older sister was Rosa; his younger brother, Heinrich/Hersh. Efraim Ryczke, like his father, Benyamin, was in the grain business and traveled a lot. Moritz was his mother's favorite son and was quite spoiled. A highly spirited boy, he quarreled often with his older sister. When these constant fights did not stop, his parents sent him off to his uncle Aron Ryczke, Efraim's half brother, who lived in the nearby town of Kolo. Aron was a strict disciplinarian. He had six children of his own and knew how to keep them in check. Under Uncle Aron's watchful eye, Moritz settled down. He used to tell me how much he enjoyed living in Kolo—not because of Uncle Aron's discipline, which he hated, but because of his grandfather, Benyamin Ryczke, who resided in Kolo. The two of them took frequent walks, and grandfather Benyamin engaged Moritz in lengthy discussions. My father told me how impressed he was by grandfather Benyamin's knowledge of the Torah and Talmud and how he influenced his thinking. Grandfather Benyamin's Jewish spirituality made a great impact on my father.

After four years in Kolo, Moritz returned to his parents' home in Slupca. Now he was a handsome young man of sixteen who was popular with the girls. My grandmother Esther told me the story of how Moritz almost killed their horse. My father had a date with a pretty young girl. He wanted to take her for a ride but did not ask his parents' permission to take the horse and buggy. You see this was B.C.—before cars. He went to the barn, took out the horse, and hitched it to the buggy. The horse did not want to budge. What did young Moritz do? He went back into the barn, brought out some straw, placed it under the horse, and set the straw on fire. Well, you can imagine the rest. Grandmother Esther heard this loud noise outside and ran out just in time to save the horse from being burned. Moritz was not allowed to leave the house, and when his father returned that night he was severely punished. This was the kind of lad young Moritz was.

My father was a good student. He was especially good with languages. He attended the *Realgymnasium* for a few years and spoke fluent Polish, German, and Russian. He knew Greek and Latin. He spoke Yiddish and knew Hebrew. His father wanted him to go into the grain business and sent him to Breslau to attend courses in commerce. There he learned bookkeeping and found a job with the firm of Czerny. During World War I he was given a job with the German army in Warsaw at the *Armeeintendantur* (army supplier). There he worked until the war ended. He told me how he witnessed the disarming of German soldiers by twelve-year-old Polish boys in Warsaw on the last day of the war, November 11, 1918.

Poland regained its independence but soon was at war with the Soviets. The city of Danzig at the Baltic Sea became a free city, and my father decided to build his life there. At first he worked for a lumber company, then for a huge oil company. But my father was too independent. He did not want to have a boss telling him what to do, and he decided to start his own business. In the meantime his parents moved to the larger city of Kalisz. As self-reliant as my father was, he nevertheless respected and sought the advice of his father. In 1919 he went to Kalisz to discuss his future as a businessman with his father. While there, he visited a coffeehouse, where he was introduced by his cousin Kazik Bloch to Genia Hammer, my mother. It was love at first sight for both of them. Two years later, in 1921, they were married in Zoppot, the sea resort near Danzig. They rented an apartment, and both I and my younger brother, Benno, were born in Zoppot. From 1921 to 1928 my father commuted to Danzig by train, where he had his office. This became too time consuming, so we moved to Danzig. His business grew; our apartment was spacious and my father's brother, Heinrich, moved in with us. As busy as my father was, he always had time for his children. He was the smartest person I knew. He was quick, good looking, always elegantly dressed, yet not tall. He was an exciting person, and I adored him. He was full of life and enjoyed life to its fullest. Yes, he had a temper; yes, we were afraid of him—not of the punishment but of disappointing him. He was fair and loved us dearly. My mother was the opposite. She was calm, patient, and collected, while my father was dynamic and impatient. They made a perfect couple—both were chain smokers, both loved to dance and party, and both loved to play cards. In 1930 my father acquired another hobby. He learned to drive and purchased an old model T Whippet. From then on, Sundays were days when he took all of us for long rides into the Cashubian hills or to the many interesting places within the free city of Danzig. The car was dark green, and its license number was DZ 630. Moritz Ryczke became an excellent driver, and he loved to drive fast. And the faster he drove, the more we loved it—except for my poor mother, who was terrified. How we loved those Sunday drives! In 1934 he traded the old car for an English-made Hillman. It was requisitioned by the Nazis in 1939.

Mira, holding her father's hand, and Uncle Heinrich Ryczke in Zoppot in 1926.

Moritz Ryczke, Danzig, 1932.

Both of my parents came from traditional Jewish homes. Both knew the prayers and read Hebrew fluently. Naturally, they wanted their children to learn the sacred language. At that time only boys were obliged to learn Hebrew and to learn about their religion. I begged my father to allow me to learn as if I were a boy. My father hired an elderly man, Rav Deutsch from Zoppot, to teach me Hebrew. Mr. Deutsch was a lay rabbi. In his long black coat, black hat, and black beard, he commuted twice a week from Zoppot to Danzig to teach me Hebrew. He taught me Hebrew prayers, but I was eager to learn more than only how to read Hebrew. After one year with Mr. Deutsch, I transferred to Mr. Glückmann, a known Talmudic scholar. He opened a new world to me. Not only did I learn to read and translate the Hebrew Bible, Mr. Glückmann answered endless questions pertaining to God, religion, and Jewish tradition. And I had many questions. He always answered in a clear and honest way. Soon I became more observant than my parents. I questioned all Jewish rituals. I wanted to know the meanings of our prayers. Why suddenly all this interest in Judaism? The more exposed I became to anti-Semitism, the more I had to defend my being Jewish, and the greater was my desire to learn as much as possible about who I was.

While I was still attending the German Viktoria Schule, we the Jewish students had religious lessons with Rabbi Weiss from Langfuhr. When I was forced to leave the school and entered the Polish *Gimnazjum*, Jewish students were excluded from many activities. Jews could not belong to the Scouts [a Christian organization]. Jewish students also were excluded from certain school trips, like the one to Czestochowa to see the Black Madonna [a Christian site]. Yet we were given the opportunity to learn about our religion once a week after school. I recall two of the teachers we had—Mrs. Lurie and Dr. Lerchenfeld. Both were well-known Jewish educators. The trouble was that we did not want to stay in class and learn. We acted up, we joked, and our lessons were more fun than study. We drove our poor teachers crazy. My lessons with Mr. Glückmann continued and became more precious. With growing anti-Semitism in Danzig, Mr. and Mrs. Glückmann decided to leave in 1938. They received their visas to France and left Danzig to join their son in Paris. It was a sad day when my brother and I had to say good-bye to our dear teacher and mentor. I never forgot what he taught me. He truly inspired me to learn and study as much as possible. He kindled the light that made me search for my Jewish identity. We did not hear from the Glückmanns again. Did they survive the war? They will always live in my memory.

It was a special treat for me to attend services at the Orthodox Mattenbuden Synagogue in Danzig with my parents. Until the age of twelve I was permitted to be with my father on the ground floor, in the men's section. Later I joined my mother in the balcony. I can still see my father praying in his black silk top hat, his body covered with a huge woolen prayer shawl. Our home in Danzig was traditional. Religion and observances were important to us. As times became more stressful and walking to the synagogue more dangerous, it was faith and our tradition that gave us strength and determination to endure.

The political situation for the Jews in Danzig grew worse from 1935 on. The year 1938 was a crucial year for the Jews of Danzig. Slowly most of the ten thousand Jews who once resided in the free city sought a safe haven in other countries. Many who had families in Poland returned to Poland. Others left for England, France, the United States, Palestine, or South America. Most of my Jewish school friends had left. My parents rented an apartment in the Polish port city of Gdynia, only twenty-five miles from Danzig. Whenever danger lurked, we left Danzig for Gdynia but kept our apartment on Dominikswall. I still continued my education at the Polish *Gimnazjum*, until war broke out on September 1, 1939. Now little was left of Jewish life. Soon our family was forced to leave our apartment and Danzig. My world collapsed.[1]

Our accounts at the banks were blocked right away, and we had little cash on hand. In 1937 my parents took most of their jewelry to Rotterdam and placed it in a safety deposit box. Very little was left in Danzig. My father's money was invested in grain and seeds. The last big shipment went to Vancouver, B.C., on August 28, 1939, shortly before war broke out. All of a sudden we were poor. Ordered out of our apartment on 10 Dominikswall, we spent six weeks in a granary. All we had were the clothes on our backs and what each one of us carried in a small suitcase. My father still wanted to protect us, but now he was not in control. Our lives were never the same again, yet we still looked to my father for comfort, for protection.

In October 1939 we were deported to Warsaw. As refugees we arrived in the bombed-out city and found shelter with my aunt and uncle Lachman. My mother's illness and hunger and cold forced us to risk our lives and leave Warsaw for Tomaszow-Mazowiecki, where my father's parents, sister, and the rest of the family found a place to live. Happy to be with our beloved grandparents, soon we had to move into the ghetto. Life became a constant struggle; it was difficult to obtain food, fuel, and medicine. All of a sudden my father became a different person. He found ways to barter the few possessions we had to provide us with some extra food. He risked his life many times to smuggle potatoes into the ghetto for his family. His ingenuity knew no boundaries. I always knew him as generous, as selfless, but I never admired him more than during the times of need when he only had our well-being on his mind. Soon all Jews had to register their professions. My father gave his profession as "vehicle driver," knowing that as a businessman or merchant he would have little chance of finding a job. Soon the *Organisation Todt* (OT) was looking for drivers. My father was the only Jew in the ghetto who registered as one, and soon he was hired. His boss, Willy Feldhege, was the most decent and kind German. After he learned from my father that his family was starving in the ghetto, he sent each day a container with thick rice cooked in milk. We had not seen rice or milk in years. This extra food sustained us for the duration of our stay in the ghetto. We thanked God for this German who was so kind to us.

The year was 1942. My brother, who was fourteen years old, was six foot two inches tall. He grew rapidly but was very thin. He needed more and better food, and with the help of Willy Feldhege, he, too, found work at the OT, loading and unloading trucks. Now Benno could eat more and better food while at work. And working for OT saved his life. The ghetto was liquidated in October 1942. We lost my mother, grandparents, aunts, uncles, cousins. Willy insisted that my father escape to the Aryan side, yet my father flatly refused. He would never leave his children; he still was our protector, or father. As long as he was with us, we were not afraid; he always gave us hope. Soon the four of us who had survived the liquidation of the ghetto—my father and brother, my uncle Heinrich, and I—were sent to the Blizyn-Majdanek concentration camp. We became slaves working for the German war machine: my father and brother worked for a brutal SS officer nicknamed "Brillock" in the carpenter's shop; Uncle Heinrich worked in the leather shop; and, after first working in the laundry, I was later assigned to a knitting factory. Over three thousand Jewish slaves labored twelve hours a day or night for the DAW (*Deutsche Ausrüstungswerke*). Very little food, constant beatings, and infestation with lice made life in this terrible camp dreadful. My father, brother, and uncle slept together in the men's barracks, and I slept in the women's barracks. We were able to see each other once a day for a few minutes after the evening roll call. It was just enough time for us to embrace each other and to give courage and hope to one another.

A typhoid fever epidemic broke out. The first one to get sick was my father, then Benno, Heinrich, and then I. Covered with lice, we infected each other. There was no medication and no help to combat this feared disease. My father recovered but was so weak that he could barely walk. When Benno got sick and there was almost no food left, my father had his gold bridge removed by a dentist and bartered it for bread and some butter for Benno. When the four of us recovered, a miracle happened—"Brillock" needed a bookkeeper in his office. My father volunteered. Somehow this brutal SS officer took a liking to my father and left pieces of bread on his desk. This was a blessing. My father was able to bring us an additional piece of bread, which helped Benno and me to regain some of our strength. Uncle Heinrich in the meantime was sent away to another camp. We found out later that he was taken to the Plaszow camp and was killed soon after arrival.

In June 1944, my father managed to persuade "Brillock" to give my brother an easier job and to engage me in the office as my father's helper. One month later our camp was evacuated and we were taken to Auschwitz. Not knowing what to expect there, we planned on our last journey together to meet in Danzig when the war was over. At the gate of Auschwitz-Birkenau I saw my dear sixteen-year-old brother for the last time. He and my father went to the men's camp, and I went to the women's camp. From then on I was alone. I only had my friends who supported me. But I was confident that Benno would be protected by my father, that the two would stick together through thick and thin. Knowing my father, I was sure that Benno would be safe, that my father would sacrifice his life for his beloved son.

After my father and I were reunited in Belsen in 1945, the absence of my brother weighed heavily on both of us. The task of looking for him would become my father's mission. He could not wait to begin the search, but first he and I had to share our camp experiences. The need to talk was so great; we began the evening of our reunion. My father started telling his experiences. I recall every word:

"When Benno and I were taken into the men's camp in Birkenau, I desperately tried to find out what happened to you. I was told that the group of young women you were with had been sent away, and that these women, including you, were to work in a bordello. I was beside myself, hoping that what I was told was not true. Having Benno near me was consoling. I knew that it would be up to me to protect him, especially when I heard that young people between fourteen and seventeen had little chance to survive in Auschwitz or Birkenau. Luckily I had been chosen to work at 'Kanada,' the famous warehouses, where all possessions of incoming transports were collected and sorted. This was the 'best' place in which one could work in Auschwitz. It gave me the opportunity to 'organize' or steal some foodstuff for Benno. Each day I tried to take something nourishing for my son back into the camp. He was so thin; there was only skin and bones on this sixteen-year-old six-foot-two-inch boy. He stayed in our barracks. I had bribed the *Blockältester* (barracks supervisor) to keep Benno in the camp. Not only was I bringing food for my son, but I also had to bring cigarettes and liquor as a bribe to keep Benno safe. Each time when we entered the camp after twelve hours of work at Kanada, I risked my life. Prisoners who were caught smuggling food or other items into the camp were severely punished, even killed. But I had no other way to feed my son, to keep him alive. This lasted till October. One day, when I returned to camp with my *Kommando* and entered our barracks, Benno was gone. I was told that a group of young boys, including Benno, were selected for work in another camp. I was in shock. I questioned the *Blockältester,* whom I had bribed for over two months and who promised me to keep Benno safe. He just shrugged his big shoulders and told me that he tried to keep Benno out of the group, but, being so tall, Benno looked to the SS to be a good enough worker.

"You will understand my agony and the deep pain I felt. Benno was too weak to perform hard labor. He needed good food and I would not be there to help him. What could I do to find him? My first thoughts were to find out where these young boys were taken. This took more bribery. I found someone who worked in the office of the camp, and I promised him cigarettes if he could find out where Benno's transport was sent. After a few days, while I agonized about my son, I was told that these boys were sent to the concentration camp Sachsenhausen. Knowing this, my plan was to volunteer next time men would be chosen to be sent to Sachsenhausen. As you know, in concentration camps one never volunteered. One wanted to be seen as little as possible; we tried to become invisible. But I had a purpose; I had to find Benno to keep him from certain death.

"A few days later the SS were looking for men to be sent to Sachsenhausen. I volunteered. Our group arrived in this old-established camp and my search for Benno began. Soon I found out that these young men came here and were sent to yet another camp, to Mauthausen or Gusen in Austria. I was too late, Benno was now far away with nobody to look after him. In desperation I volunteered again to leave Sachsenhausen. There was no need for me to stay there. I hoped that maybe the next volunteers would be shipped to Mauthausen. No such luck. The next transport was sent to the Messerschmitt factories, to help build planes for the Nazi war machine.

"While in Birkenau, we were told to register our professions. Of course I could not put down that I was a merchant or businessman, Nazis did not need Jewish merchants. Just as a whim I put down *Feinmechaniker*, mechanic for precision work. Messerschmitt needed such mechanics; therefore, this was the place where I was sent.

"Thousands of prisoners worked in this factory. Food was in short supply; we were constantly hungry. During our twelve-hour day or night shift we were given tools to make parts for airplanes. One day I was looking at the tools I had to use, not sure what to do with them, when suddenly I felt a horrible blow to my head. This followed by yet more blows to my right ear, my back, and my face, and I could feel the blood covering my face. The hearing in my right ear was gone. The SS man who was beating me so viciously with his whip told me that they did not need Jews who could not use tools correctly. He asked for my profession. When I said, *Feinmechaniker*, I received another blow to my head. "You are a liar. You are not a *Feinmechaniker*." Then he told me to report to the man in charge of the factory. He would decide what to do with me. He might want to send me back to Auschwitz.

"I was in great pain. It was not only the physical pain that tormented me. I was scared to be sent back to Auschwitz. I knew what that meant. I would not have minded being sent to Mauthausen, but not back to Auschwitz. Dazed and petrified I went to report to the factory overseer. He looked at me, at my swollen face, at the blood running out of my mouth and ear and said, 'This beating was done by a specialist. Tell me, why were you beaten?' I had to tell him the truth. His next question was, 'You evidently are not a mechanic. Tell me honestly what was your profession before the war?' Now I had to invent another lie. I could not say that I was a merchant, a businessman, in Danzig. I did go to bookkeeping school in Breslau in 1915, so I told him, 'I was a bookkeeper.' 'I can use a good bookkeeper,' was his reply. And this is what saved me from being returned to Auschwitz. Each morning I reported to my new boss, did all his bookkeeping and other office work. One day he said to me, 'I do not know why, but I trust you. In my private office I have a radio. We are not allowed to listen to stations other than the German ones. Each day at noon the BBC reports news. I will disappear each day at noon and will leave the door to my office open. I want you to go into the office, turn to the station that I set—it will be the BBC. I want you to listen to the news. Remember what was broadcast, do not write anything down. In the evening, before you return to camp, I will call you into my office and you will report to me the BBC news. If you are caught, it is your head. I will not be able to save you. I will have to deny that I knew anything about your listening to the forbidden station.'

"I was stunned. Here was this Nazi bigshot trusting a Jew to tell him the true political situation. We in camp lived on rumors; we only knew what the Germans told us. Now I had the opportunity to listen to the outside world, to find out what was actually happening on all fronts. Whatever I heard on the radio, I reported to my boss. But I also had the chance to share all news with my fellow prisoners. Here I had to be very careful. Nobody knew that I was ordered by a Nazi to listen to the BBC. I only told them that I saw the radio and secretly tuned to the BBC. A few times a week I dared to share the news about the war. I had to be so careful; otherwise, it would be the end of me.

"Not only did my boss trust me with the news, but each day when I went at noon to tune in to the BBC, there was a sandwich on his desk for me. As a German he was forbidden to give the Jewish prisoners food. Yet he did it. To survive physically we desperately needed more food, but our spiritual and emotional survival could only be assured by hope. These daily BBC broadcasts allowed me to give hope to my fellow prisoners. Ultimately, to be able to share the news with my friends in the barracks was more important than an extra piece of bread.

"After two months at the Messerschmitt factory, a group of us were sent to Dachau. I hoped that some transports would go to Mauthausen. I never had this opportunity. I landed in so many other camps, never in Mauthausen."

My father continued: "From Dachau they evacuated us to Flossenburg and finally to Kaufering. We learned from the SS guards that the Americans were not far away, and we prayed to be free soon. The weather was warm. It was the latter part of April 1945. Now there were no more trains to evacuate us and we had to walk. We were in Bavaria and the march was difficult. We were weak and hungry, yet the SS were forcing us to walk fast. Those who were too weak, those who could not keep up with the march, were shot. This was our death march. The column was long, the roads were curved. I walked together with a French and a Polish prisoner. The constant shootings and the brutality of the SS guards terrified us. The three of us decided to escape during the march. We discussed the best way of leaving the marching column and speculated that the best way would be to run into the woods as the column turned at a bend in the road. We also had to find a spot with an embankment. A few hours later the Pole left the column and jumped over an embankment. The SS guards began shooting, but the column had to walk on. I was the second one to leave the march. I jumped into a ditch, lay low, and then ran into the woods. I heard shots, but luckily was not hit. The French prisoner was last. All three of us waited for hours until we met in the dense forest. We removed our prisoner garb and buried the clothes under dry leaves. And then we waited. That night we spent shivering, covering our bodies with leaves and branches. The next morning the Pole decided to walk to the nearest village. Maybe the Americans would already be there. After a few hours he came running back to us, 'The Americans are here; come and follow me, we are free now.' And this is how I was liberated in lower Bavaria on April 28, 1945. The Americans took us to the nearby town of Eggenfelden. We received new clothes and a room in the house of former Nazis. After we regained some strength and the war was over, the Frenchman returned to France and my Polish companion to Poland.

I remained in Eggenfelden. I had to begin the search for my children, for you and for Benno.

"In order to obtain food, I borrowed a bicycle and went to the nearest village to get some eggs and butter. When I returned to Eggenfelden, my landlady told me that while I was away I had a visitor. A man with a mustache asked for Moritz Ryczke and told her that he was my brother-in-law. He left his name and address and said I should visit him. She handed me the note. It was signed 'Ludwik Turkiewicz' and gave an address in Plattling. I had never heard of Ludwik Turkiewicz. I had never had a brother-in-law by that name. Curious to find out who this man was, the next morning I bicycled to Plattling to meet this mysterious person. You will never guess who he was—it was Uncle Heniek Hammer, your mother's brother. He survived the war as a Pole; his papers were in the name of Ludwik Turkiewicz. I met his wife Franka, who also survived as a Pole. We spent the day together, exchanging stories about our lives during the war. Heniek lost his first wife, Rozka, and only son, Jasio. Franka lost her husband. Now they were living in Plattling and Heniek was president of the small Jewish community. I told them about my goal to find my children and that I would be in touch with them.

"In the meantime, lists of survivors from different concentration camps were being distributed all over Bavaria. I looked at each one of them, desperately trying to find your and Benno's names. On one list, from Belsen camp, I found the names of Eva Kolska and Diana Rubin. I knew that you were good friends and that you were together in Auschwitz-Birkenau. But I did not find your name. So I decided to give a note with your and Benno's names to people who were traveling north. And this is how you received my note, and I received yours. Now I knew that soon we would be reunited."

When my father mentioned the lists of survivors, it occurred to me that I did type up lists of people who were in Belsen. I must have forgotten to put my own name on the list.[2] Thank God that my father remembered the names of my friends and assumed that they would lead him to me.

It took me hours to recover from my father's story. I could feel his pain, his desperate wish to save his son. I was grateful that he shared his experience with me, his heartache, his helplessness.

After a few days in Belsen, my father became restless. He had to find Benno. On the way to Auschwitz we promised to meet in Danzig after the war. We hoped that my brother had remembered this promise. A pass to travel to Danzig, now Gdańsk, was issued to my father in search of his son. This would be a dangerous trip, as he had to travel through the Soviet zone of Germany and then across the border to Poland. But Moritz Ryczke was a brave man. He promised to return in a few weeks. With the pass in his pocket, he left Belsen. Now I had to wait again. Anxiously I waited for four weeks for my father's return.

By the middle of August 1945 my father was back. He did not find Benno in Gdańsk. Physically and mentally exhausted, he rested for a week, then he wanted to return to Gdańsk a second time. "If Benno got to Danzig after I left, he might have heard that I was looking for him." And so he left Belsen again in search of his son. I wanted so much to go with him, but he explained that for a young woman it would be too dangerous to cross the border, especially with Soviet troops guarding it. My father spoke fluent Russian and would know how to deal with the Soviets. Disappointed, I remained in Belsen, where I continued to work; there was so much to do, I could not be inactive. A whole month was gone, and I began to worry, imagining that my father was caught crossing the border and that maybe he was somewhere in jail.

It was the end of September when I saw my father again. The news he had was devastating. He did not find my brother in Danzig. Then he decided to return via Austria. Maybe he could find traces of Benno in one of the camps there. The largest camp was Mauthausen near Linz. There, in the camp register, he found Benno's name. He was registered as Benno Ritschke (the German spelling of our name), date of birth: January 24, 1927, born in Zoppot—tattoo number 3536. Now my father knew for sure that his son had been in Mauthausen. He even found his Mauthausen number: 133856. What happened to him? Where was he sent from this camp? He met many survivors who were in camps near Mauthausen. Among them he found a young man who was with Benno in Anstetten, a camp not far from Mauthausen where prisoners were repairing the railroad tracks. When the U.S. army was getting close and Anstetten was evacuated, he was with Benno on this last march out of the camp. It was another death march, and Benno was too weak to walk. This man told my father that he saw Benno being shot during the march. A few days later the prisoners were liberated by the Americans. For Benno it was too late. Here was an eyewitness who saw my dear brother's death, yet my father would not believe it. He would not accept the fact that his seventeen-year-old son did not survive the war. For years he was putting ads into newspapers in Germany, Israel, and the United States searching for his lost son. Deep in my heart I knew that Benno was not alive. I mourned his loss for many years; he was my best friend, and I still miss him terribly.

After learning about the death of Benno, plans for the future had to be made. My father was against settling down in Belsen; he did not want to live in a camp anymore. "I had enough camps during these past six years. Now I want to live a normal life. I want to live in a city." The closest city was Hannover, south of Belsen. It was not even an hour's trip by car. He rented a room from a German family on Beekestrasse in Hannover. We spent some weekends together in Belsen. Sometimes I went to him; Hannover had a good opera house, and both of us loved to attend performances.

My father and I discussed my future. I was now twenty-two years old, and I really wanted to continue my interrupted education. I took my final high school examination in the ghetto, but this was in 1941. The university I wanted to apply to was Heidelberg, and I wanted to study law.

My father and I also applied for visas to the United States. My father's only living uncle resided in Cincinnati, Ohio. He explained to me that we had lost all our relatives; the only one who was still living was his mother's brother, Uncle Max Jacobs. Therefore, we should try to be with the only family we still had. Among the papers that I had managed to save was also my father's address book with Uncle Max's address. After my father and I were reunited, we resumed the correspondence with our Cincinnati relatives. We wrote to Uncle Max in November 1945, letting him know that of the entire family, only my father and I were alive. Soon we had a reply from his daughter, Rose Roth. She wrote that in order to sponsor my father and me they would have to ask someone in the family to help who was financially better situated. Uncle Max had worked all his life as a presser and now he was retired. Rose's husband, Sam, worked in a tailor shop and did not earn enough to sponsor us. She promised to let us know as soon as the necessary papers would be issued. Time went by and we did not expect to hear from our relatives in Cincinnati soon.

My father's plans were to start his own business, the same seed business he had before the war in Danzig. But first he wanted us to travel to Bochum, where Willy Feldhege, his former boss from the OT in Tomaszow, lived.[3] Willy extended an open invitation to my father and me. It was close to Christmas, and the Feldheges invited us to spend a week in Bochum. I planned to travel to Heidelberg after we returned from Bochum. I never did. Education lost out to Max Kimmelman.

Chapter 5

MEETING MAX KIMMELMAN (1908–1990)

LIFE IN RÖTZ, GERMANY

Dear Benno and Gene,

Let me pick up where I left off in chapter 3. When we returned from Bochum to Belsen on December 27, 1945, I met your daddy. This was a turning point in my life. Ten days later, Max Kimmelman, your daddy, asked me to marry him. All this happened so suddenly, my father was not prepared for the shock. His plans for me were to get a college education. "I have only my daughter left. I want you near me, and I want you to go to university," were his words. Your dad understood the dilemma. He knew how much I loved and respected my father. We had to play the waiting game, to make my father realize that he was not losing a daughter, he was gaining a son. It took months and bitter tears until my father gave in and faced reality. In April 1946 he gave me the blessing to marry Max Kimmelman. More than I wanted a law degree, I wanted to be with the man I fell in love with and to start a family. I could not pursue an education and have a family. I did not have the strength for both. And I never regretted the choice I made. This short and wonderful courtship resulted in our marriage on May 19, 1946, in Rötz, Oberpfalz, where your dad resided. My father and I left the British zone and, after a lengthy train ride, arrived in the American zone, in Rötz.

Rötz had a population of about three thousand, a truly small Bavarian town. The population was 100 percent Catholic. No Jews lived here before the war, and we were told that the majority of the population were staunch Nazis. While we lived there, everybody denied ever being a party member, everybody was suddenly against Hitler. Dad came to this town mainly because of his dear friend "Uncle" Nathan, who left the even smaller town of Stamsried and found Rötz to his liking. Dad and Uncle became close friends in the camp of Schlieben and wanted to live as close to one another as possible. In the small town of Stamsried many former Jewish concentration camp prisoners were liberated; some of them moved later to Rötz. For the first time there was a Jewish presence in Rötz; they even had a Jewish community center for the thirty-plus Jews. Jews were given lodging among the German population, which created an anti-Jewish climate. Dad was assigned two rooms; his friend Danek Frenkel moved in with him. The landlady, with her two spinster daughters, occupied the rest of the house. There was little contact between the local Germans and the Jews. The United Nations Restitution and Rehabilitation Administration (UNRRA) supplied the Jewish survivors with food and cigarettes. As in Belsen, cigarettes were bartered for fresh eggs, chicken, or milk. Like the German population, we were issued ration cards. We could only get bread, flour, potatoes, and vegetables for the cards. Everything else had to be obtained by bartering items received from UNRRA. Dad and I used to walk once a week to villages surrounding Rötz in order to get something nourishing to eat. Food was a problem. We did not starve but constantly struggled to obtain meat, eggs, or butter. It was quite different from living in a displaced persons camp, where we did not have to worry about food.

I can only testify to life in the British zone around Hannover and the American zone around Rötz. The differences were significant. The British occupation treated the former concentration camp prisoners fairly; it was the population that made our lives difficult in both zones. Most of the Germans resented us, especially now that we were supported by UNRRA or the American Jewish Joint Distribution Committee, while there was deprivation in the country. Black marketing flourished; when some of the former concentration camp prisoners were caught, they were severely punished and jailed. This was true in both zones. Needless to say, the occupation forces contributed to the black market. Cigarettes became the most valuable commodity. For cigarettes the British and U.S. soldiers were able to obtain jewelry and art objects. It was a vicious circle. Most of the local population traded food for cigarettes, as well as clothing.

After Dad and I were married, my father returned to Hannover. While we were waiting to hear from our relatives in Cincinnati, my father found some old German friends who once lived in Danzig. With their support he was able to start a small seed business. It was very difficult. There were anti-Jewish feelings among some of the established German firms, and they resented that my father opened a business. It was rough sailing, but my father never was a quitter. Gradually his business was growing. He purchased a small used car, a Hannemag (two-cylinder car), and after our marriage in May of 1946 he drove the seven hundred kilometers from Hannover to Rötz quite often, and we always looked forward to his visits.

One month after Dad and I were married, my father received a letter from cousin Rose telling him that an affidavit had been issued for my father and me and that soon we would be called to present ourselves to the American Consulate in Frankfurt. The affidavit was for Moritz and Mira Ryczke. I was now Mira Kimmelman and a married woman. My father right away found an answer to our dilemma. He telegraphed his cousin telling her that I was now married and that he would like her to change the affidavit to Max and Mira Kimmelman. He wanted us to emigrate to the States first, and he would follow later. We had no idea how long it would take for the changes to be made. In the meantime, we settled into life in Rötz while my father continued to live in Hannover and expand his business.

Living in the home of the unfriendly German women in Rötz became a challenge. Dad and I occupied the two rooms on the ground floor. Dad's friend Danek had left for Sweden soon after Dad met me. But the landlady would not allow us the use of the kitchen. Only two hours in the morning were we allowed to enter the kitchen, to cook something, to fetch some water. This situation made my life miserable. Finally Dad decided to complain about it to the U.S. military government in nearby Waldmünchen. We went together; I spoke English and explained our situation. They promised us that someone from their office would come to Rötz and speak to the lady of the house. The following day a uniformed U.S. officer rang the doorbell. He asked for the three women and, in perfect German, informed them that "from now on Herr and Frau Kimmelman have full use of the kitchen. If you need to enter the kitchen, you will have to ask permission. From now on the kitchen is theirs, and if they have more complaints, you will have to vacate the house." With these words, he left us. The women were in shock. Of course we let them use the kitchen to cook their meals. Soon they decided to make one of their many upstairs rooms into a kitchen. They could not stand asking us for permission to enter the kitchen. We were barely tolerated, we were strangers, we were Jews. Knowing that all this was only temporary, that we would be leaving that "loving" town soon, we tried to endure all these unpleasant episodes. In other words, Rötz was no paradise.

In the nearby village lived an elderly woman by the name of Anna Bücherl. Before the war Anna worked as a housekeeper for a Jewish family in Berlin. When the family was deported, Anna returned to her village in the Oberpfalz. One day she came to us asking if she could be of some help. She needed to earn some money and could not exist on the allotted rations. We had so little but decided to help Anna after we heard her story. By now the American Jewish Joint Distribution Committee took over supplying survivors with extra food and some clothing. By bartering our allotment of cigarettes, we could "hire" Anna. She came every morning for a few hours to help clean the kitchen and dust the rooms. Sometimes we paid Anna with part of the coffee or tea we were receiving from the Joint Distribution Committee. Anna Bücherl became part of our family. She stayed with us from November 1946 until June 1948, when we left Rötz. We never forgot her. Once we arrived in the States, we sent Anna packages with coffee, tea, and chocolate. All this she could barter for items she needed. Anna, in turn, sent us embroidered pillows, tablecloths, and later knitted sweaters for our children. We exchanged long letters. In one of them she wrote that people in Rötz told her that once the Kimmelmans were in America, they would forget about her. When the packages started to arrive for Anna, the "good" people in Rötz were perplexed. Anna suffered a stroke in 1968 and could not write anymore. Some friend then wrote letters for her. We sent packages to her until she passed away in 1970. I still have very fond memories of our Anna, a devoted and good woman.

The denazification of Germany began in 1946. Life in Rötz was full of intrigue; there were constant rumors about the behavior of some local people during the war. When the denazification began in Rötz, we soon learned the truth about the locals. Naturally, most denied that they had ever been Nazis. Among those whom we suspected to be Nazis were the three women in whose house we lived. We already knew how they hated and detested Jews from the way they treated us.

Our dear friend Uncle Nathan lived next door to us, on Böhmerstrasse. He was renting a room from a war widow. Soon people in town were spreading rumors that "the widow of a German soldier is living in sin with a Jew." She was the kindest woman, taking care of Uncle Nathan, who was not well. She cooked and watched over him. People in Rötz stopped talking to her; she was ostracized by the local population. When Uncle Nathan left Rötz for the United States in fall of 1949, his landlady became ill. She died of cancer in 1952. They buried her under a fence in the only cemetery in town. Even in death, they would not allow her to receive a decent burial place. Nobody came to the funeral; she was punished for living with a Jew. We were told about it by Anna Bücherl in one of her letters. This was another picture of the town of Rötz with its righteous citizens.

When Dad and I were notified in May 1948 that the affidavit for our departure for the United States was waiting for us at the American consulate in Munich, we took the train first to Regensburg and from there to Munich. There we presented ourselves at the American consulate. Each of us was asked to enter the office of the consul separately. Afterward, we shared the conversations we had with the American consul. Dad said, "He asked me if I was really Jewish. When I answered in the affirmative, his second question was: 'Maybe one of your parents was not Jewish.' Again I assured him that both of my parents were Jewish. His next question was, 'How about your grandparents?' I had to smile and told him that all my relatives were observant Jews. Then he got up, shook my hand and wished me good luck in the United States."

When I walked into his office, his first question was, "How did you get your birth certificate from Zoppot? Today this is Poland—you must have crossed the border illegally." I told him about my father's search for my brother, about our promise to meet again in our hometown. I told him that my father traveled with a pass from the British authorities to Gdańsk to find my brother, and while there he went to Sopot (Zoppot) to obtain copies of my brother's and my birth certificates. I told him the facts. I told him the truth. The consul got up, shook my hand, and wished me all the best. Dad and I recalled the visit to the American consul in Munich many times. We joked later about this encounter.

Now came the waiting period. We would be notified as soon as our visas arrived. We returned to Rötz. Each day seemed like an eternity. We had to prepare for our journey to America. The only suitcases we could get were made out of cardboard. Our bedding would have to be packed into a canvas bag. During the two years in Rötz, I saved all the feathers from the chickens, ducks, or geese that we consumed. Therefore, we were fortunate to have enough for two pillows and a featherbed. We learned from our wanderings during the war years how important bedding was. And we would leave Rötz with the comfort of knowing that we did have something on which to lay down our heads, something to cover ourselves with. Whatever we had saved in cigarettes, now was the time to barter it for items we might need in the New World.

By now Israel had been reborn, and we had a Jewish state, a safe haven for those of us who suffered so much and had no place to go. I was terribly torn. All my life I had been a Zionist.[1] I had belonged to the Zionist Youth Movement since I was ten years old. Both my parents were Zionists, and here I was preparing to leave for the United States instead of Israel. My father's words, "We should be where we have family," still rang in my ears. Yet my heart said, "You should go to Israel." But it was not my decision to make. Dad always had the dream of going to America. He was not raised in a

Zionist family, and it took years for him to develop the love for Zion. There was also another reason. Israel had been invaded by her neighbors and was at war. Dad was petrified of war and would never move to or visit a country at war. When we finally visited Israel in 1971, he fell in love with the country and with its people.

Voyage to America

In June 1948 we were notified to report to Munich, to Funk Kaserne, from where we would be transported to Bremen and later board a boat to the United States. After saying our good-byes to friends in Rötz, especially to Uncle Nathan, we left Rötz for good on a cool June morning. Until now we lived in a place where we were familiar with the language and the culture even though we had to suffer discrimination. Optimistic and full of hope we looked forward to a new country, new customs, a friendly environment. I knew the language; Dad would have to learn it in the States. Yes, we were scared; our relatives in the United States were strangers to us. We hoped that our new lives would be filled with love and kindness, that we would be accepted and allowed to live our lives free in a friendly and positive atmosphere. What we were leaving was a hostile place, a place where we were not wanted. Although I grew up with German culture and German was my first language, I felt out of place in Germany. The poison injected by Hitler into the German people was obvious. It would linger for generations. Dad and I could not and would not stay there—we had to leave. There was no hate, but we felt uncomfortable.

My father met us in Munich, he wanted to spend our last days in Germany with us. He brought a bottle of good cognac and we toasted our future in the unknown world. My father would wait for his affidavit to arrive and promised to join us soon.

Most of the survivors who were at Funk Kaserne had small children; some were single people. We were the only couple without children. Dad and I were approached by a representative of the American Council of Churches. She asked if we would volunteer to safeguard twenty children on their voyage to the United States. We gladly consented to chaperone the ten boys and ten girls all the way to New York. We were told that most of these young people—between the ages of ten and seventeen—were traveling to America to meet their families. Most were German; there were only a few Holocaust survivors among them. They needed supervision during the ten-day voyage. Many families had been approached, but they refused the responsibility. Without even thinking twice, both Dad and I agreed to take care of these young people. It was a volunteer job and we felt good that we could be useful. Together with the boys and girls we boarded the train for Bremen. My father saw us off; I parted from him with a heavy heart and many tears. The following day we arrived in Bremen and were driven to the harbor, to Bremerhaven, from where the ships were leaving. But first we were taken to barracks, to primitive housing, men separate from

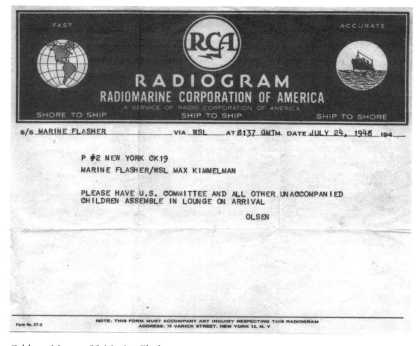

Cable to Max on SS *Marine Flasher.*

MEETING MAX KIMMELMAN

women. The ship that was to sail the following day was the army transport ship *Marine Flasher*. But there was a problem—the ship was already full, with no place for us. We were told that our wait for the next ship would be a fortnight. Dad and I were quite upset. Here we were with twenty young people in a situation that was not conducive to supervision. Suddenly we heard over the loudspeaker that Max and I were to report to the office. It turned out that the organization in charge of the children heard about the difficulties and ordered that we with "our" twenty children were to board the *Marine Flasher*. Now we were on the way to the New World, to a new a life.

In a nutshell, after my liberation I lived for a year in the Belsen Displaced Persons Camp, got married and lived for over two years in the unfriendly town of Rötz, Oberpfalz, and for the last few weeks of our stay in Germany lived in Funk Kaserne in Munich and in Bremerhaven. Now we were off to a brand-new chapter in our lives.

On the *Marine Flasher* most of us occupied the very bottom of the ship. The journey was filled with adventures. Just keeping track of "our" children was enough to keep us busy. Some were sixteen- and seventeen-year-olds who wanted to have a good time. We had a hard time tracking them down, especially at night. This meant many hours on the deck of the ship acting as chaperones and being responsible for young people. As we had no children of our own, we did not know how teenagers behaved. Many times frustration set in, but we knew that we had a job to do and had to do it right. Among Dad's ten boys was one fourteen-year-old Jewish survivor from Hungary. He had lost one leg in a streetcar accident in Munich shortly after liberation. He was tall and heavy and had to walk on crutches. To get around on the ship he needed to climb steps. Dad was actually carrying him up and down steps, to the dining room and to the deck. Dad took the job of caring for this young boy seriously; he became very fond of this special boy. There were a few other survivors: from Austria, Germany, and Poland. All of them were sponsored by relatives in the United States. The remaining young people were German, not Jewish. Their relatives lived in the United States already before the war and, knowing the economic conditions in postwar Germany, sponsored them. It became our task to watch over them and deliver them safely into the hands of the church organization.

Dad and I spent the days on board the *Marine Flasher* together; we had our meals with "our" children. The food was excellent by our standards. We had fresh oranges and bananas daily, fruit that we had not seen for many years. On days when the ocean was choppy, many of the passengers became seasick and did not come into the dining room. Then we were given extra fruit, extra pastry, and for the first time we tasted Coca-Cola. On days when the ocean was truly rough, the dining room was empty. Dad and I never got seasick. We never missed a meal.

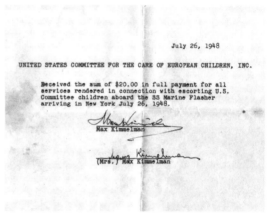

SS *Marine Flasher* baggage tag for Mira Kimmelman.

Receipt for payment for escorting twenty children aboard SS *Marine Flasher*, July 26, 1948.

There were moments of doubt, times when we were afraid of the future. Did we have the right qualifications for America? How would we be able to support ourselves? Except for our personal belongings, our bedding, and some dishes, we had nothing. Yes, my father gave us $250 in Munich, money that he saved so that we, his children, would not be penniless. Dad was holding on to this money, and we promised ourselves not to touch it. Being optimists, we said, "We have to make it on our own. This money we shall return to my father untouched." Dad was unable to communicate in English. He knew the textile business, but would there be a place for him in Cincinnati? I, on the other hand, spoke English but had no other qualifica-

MEETING MAX KIMMELMAN

tions. "Maybe I could work as a clerk in an office or in a store," I thought. Our family was sponsoring us (or rather some stranger who was doing them a favor, as we later found out). We knew nothing about our relatives except that Uncle Max was the brother of my grandmother, Esther Ryczke. The person who corresponded with us was his daughter, Rose Roth. We knew that she and her husband, Sam, had a daughter, Faith. We studied the map of the States to find the city of Cincinnati. This was to be our destination, but we knew almost nothing about the place. All these thoughts were tormenting us in spite of our optimism. At night I could not sleep. I had no one to talk to. Dad was sleeping in the men's section, and I felt very alone. Many nights I cried myself to sleep during our voyage to America. Yet on the following day, when I saw Dad, when the sun was shining bright and the ocean looked so peaceful, all my doubts vanished.

As the eighth day of our journey approached, people were receiving telegrams from family members or friends. "We have no one who would send us a message," said Dad. No one would be meeting us when we arrived in New York. Then, on the last day of our journey, while sitting on deck of the *Marine Flasher,* we heard our names called. We approached the purser and were given a cable. The organization in charge of our children would be sending representatives to meet us in New York. At that time, we were to hand over the twenty children. It felt wonderful to know that we, too, would be met by somebody in the New World. On this last day we docked first in Halifax. The next stop was New York.

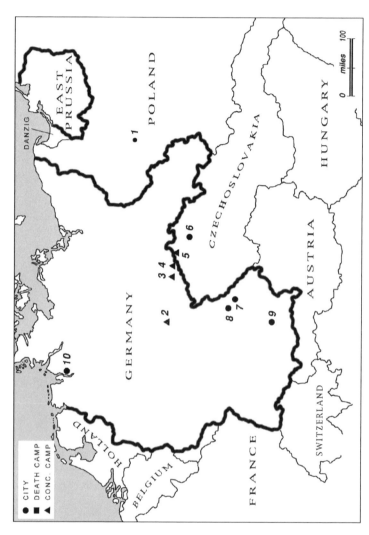

Max Kimmelman's forced journeys during the Holocaust and travels thereafter: (1) Piotrkow-Trybunalski (ghetto); (2) Buchenwald (c.c.); (3) Schlieben (c.c.); (4) Bautzen (c.c.); (5) Nixdorf (c.c.); (6) Prague; (7) Stamsried-Opf; (8) Rötz-Opf; (9) Munich; (10) Bremerhaven.

Chapter 6

Max Kimmelman

Dear Michael Max and Max Chambers,

You never knew your grandfather, or Opa (this is what you would have called him). Opa Max Kimmelman was born on March 25, 1908, the tenth and last child of Yitzhak and Malka Kimmelman. Opa died February 25, 1990, and both of you bear his name. You, Michael dear, were born nine months after Opa's death, and you, Max, seven years later. I wish Opa could have shared with you the story of his life from early childhood on. I will have to do it for him, quoting Opa's words as he told them to me.

"My mother told me how upset my father was when his youngest child turned out to be a boy. He did not want another *Fahnenträger* (flag carrier). What my father meant was that he had just lost his oldest son, Yechiel, who was the organizer and leader of the Jewish Socialist *Bund's* self-defense group. He organized strikes and headed up the most courageous actions. Arrested for his involvement in the assassination of a czarist policeman who was known for his cruelty toward political prisoners, Yechiel refused help from his friends to escape. He was first sentenced to death, but after our mother appealed to the czarina (wife of the czar), to lifelong hard labor in Siberia. There he died two years later. I was born the year Yechiel died. My parents were still mourning the loss of their firstborn son when I arrived. Ours was a large family: Regina, Leon, Eva, Hela, and Moshe (Michael). It was a busy household; my mother was in charge of our restaurant located on the ground floor. She not only supervised the cooking but also took care of the business part. With the sentencing of Yechiel, the alcohol license for the restaurant, which they had had for years, was taken away. And then there were all the children who also kept my mother busy. My parents hired a nursemaid to take care of me, their baby. I remember my mother telling me that she noticed, when I was a few months old, that I never cried and that I slept quite a lot. She worried that I was sick and started to question my nursemaid. At first there were no answers to her questions; finally, after she asked her over and over, the nursemaid confessed. She was an alcoholic, and whenever I started to cry she put a few drops of vodka in my mouth. This made me stop crying and also made me very sleepy. For months this was going on until my mother became suspicious and worried about my behavior. First of all my mother took me to our family physician and told him about the alcohol I had consumed for months. When he heard the story he told my mother to continue giving me drops of vodka, but to decrease the dosage gradually until my sleeping pattern and crying normalized. I think that this early introduction to alcohol did something to my system: later in life no matter how much alcohol I drank, I was never affected by it, I never got drunk. Did my nursemaid (who was fired after this episode) make my system immune to strong alcohol? Who knows. This story was told to me by my mother when I was a young boy.

"I was closest in age to my brother, Michael, but adored and admired my oldest brother, Leon (Leib). Our parents used to dress us, their three sons, in navy suits with sailors' collars; they called us *Die Drei Matrosen* (the three sailors). I must have been three or four years old when my oldest brother, Leon, who was already fifteen or sixteen years old, left our home for the United States. Together with a friend he traveled to New York to seek adventure in the New World. My parents did not encourage him, but Leon was strong willed and did not heed the advice of our parents. I was too young to remember all the details. All I remember is that one year later Leon came back. He told us that the summer in New York was unbearably hot; he had to work hard and could not stand conditions in the United States. His friend remained. Many times during the war I reminded Leon of his sojourn in the United States. Had he remained like his friend, my brother would have been alive. I almost forgot about this episode until our son, Benno, was born in Cincinnati. The newspaper, the *Cincinnati Post,* ran the birth announcement and one day we had a strange telephone call. The caller wanted to know if I, Max Kimmelman, had a brother by the name of Leib Kimmelman who left Europe for the United States before World War I. The caller, Mr. Joskowicz, was my brother's friend and companion to the United States. He resided in Cincinnati and happened to see the birth announcement. I was in shock. I never knew my brother's friend's name, and now after forty years I was talking to him. We invited him to come and visit us. The next Sunday afternoon he rang the doorbell; with a box of Whitman Sampler chocolates in his hand he entered our small apartment. Mr. Joskowicz was a slim and small man in his early sixties. He told us that in America he learned to be a roofer and that he was still employed. Not only did he bring us sweets, he brought with him a photograph of himself with my brother Leon. This picture was taken before these two young lads left Europe for the United States. I was overwhelmed. This picture, and the stories that Mr. Joskowicz told me about my favorite brother, were so precious. Life is full of surprises. We came to live in Cincinnati, and so did my brother's friend. If not for the fact that the birth of our son was announced in the local newspaper and that Mr. Joskowicz happened to see it, we would never have met. We kept in touch with him for many years. Mr. Joskowicz had a married daughter in Cincinnati; her husband was a pharmacist who worked in a drugstore that we frequented. One day the pharmacist told us that his father-in-law was killed while working on a roof. He evidently lost his balance and fell off the roof to his death. I felt so sad; I had lost the one person with a link to my dear brother Leon.

"My father died when I was twelve years old. He was much older than my mother, but so in love with her. I recall a letter to her that he gave me when he went on a business trip. It was a love letter to my mother. I read it out of curiosity; I know I should not have done it. But my father's letter to the woman he was married to for so many years was so moving, so full of love and adoration that its words have stayed with me to this day. The customary Kaddish is said for close departed family members or parents for eleven months. I went with my older brothers each morning and evening to say Kaddish for my father. I recall quite vividly my mother's words: 'Who will say Kaddish after I die?' She may have been wondering, but I took it seriously and never forgot these words.

"We were an Orthodox and very traditional family. My mother's grandfather was a rabbi. She wore a beautiful black wig (like all orthodox married women do). I loved to walk with her. She was tall, distinguished, and very good looking. I was her favorite and youngest child, and she did spoil me. Many of my school friends envied me for having such a beautiful mother. It was not only external beauty; she was also the kindest and most generous person. She was beautiful inside, too. But years of hard work, of losing a son and three infants, took its toll. She was diabetic and died at the age of fifty-seven. I was in my last year of the gymnasium when I lost my dear mother. She was such an important part of my life, I could barely think of life without her. At the funeral, all the poor people to whom she had given food and alms for so many years walked behind the hearse and cried. They, too, would miss my mother's kindness and generosity. After the funeral, my mother's words came back to me: 'Who will say Kaddish after I die?' She had said these words after my father's death. For eleven months I got up at dawn, went to the small synagogue not far from where I lived, said Kaddish, and then went to school. I returned again in late afternoon to the synagogue to say Kaddish. It was not easy, especially getting up at the crack of dawn. It was something I had to do for my dear mother and for myself. My brothers by now were grown men and did not live with me anymore. It was my sister, Regina, who took me under her wing. She took my mother's place in the restaurant and ran the business. My brother Leon was an accountant, and Michael moved to Berlin, where my father's younger brother resided with his family. Michael went to dental school and became a very good dentist.

"After my graduation from the business gymnasium, my dream was to study in Switzerland. I applied to the higher business school in St. Gallen and was asked to come for an interview. The year was 1926. Excitedly, I packed a suitcase and took the train to Berlin, where I wanted to stop for a few days to see my brother Michael. To my dismay, Michael talked me out of studying in Switzerland. 'Why don't you stay here and go to a good dental school like I did? Or why not go to a textile college?' I never continued my trip to St. Gallen and returned home confused and disappointed. I did take Michael's advice to study textiles. By 1930, I met a lovely girl, fell in love, and we were married. Her name was Roma; she was a year older than I. In 1934, our first and only child was born, our daughter, Malka (Maryla). She was named after my beloved mother, and this beautiful girl became the center of my life. I was hired by the large textile mill Piotrkowska Manufaktura in the city of Piotrkow and moved with my family to the factory housing, where nice apartments were available for the employees. We lived there from 1937 until the beginning of the war.

"In September 1939, war broke out and the Nazis occupied half of Poland, including Piotrkow. My job was gone. With my family I had to move into the ghetto, the Jewish quarters. The very first ghetto in occupied Poland was established in Piotrkow-Tribunalski in October 1939. Soon followed endless restrictions for the Jews. Maryla was five years old; the following year she would have to attend school. Makeshift schools were created in the ghetto and Maryla was able to attend nursery school, kinder-garten, and first grade until the tragic day of the liquidation of the Piotrkow ghetto. October 1942 was the saddest time of my life. The Nazis announced the liquidation of the ghetto. Only the employed and young ones would be allowed to remain in a much smaller ghetto. All of us—old and young, women and children—had to report to the marketplace. We were sur-rounded by the SS and Ukrainian SS volunteers. A selection took place, and the SS pulled out of the crowd all able-bodied men and women. But no women with babies or children were allowed. This is when I found myself separated from my wife, Roma, and my darling daughter, Maryla. I tried to leave my side and join them, but the SS pulled me back and threat-ened to beat me with a whip. There was no choice; I had to watch how my family was marched away with over twenty thousand Piotrkow Jews. Taken by train to the death camp of Treblinka, all were gassed to death. My child was only eight years old. Why did she have to die? For weeks I cried after the loss of my family.

Max's daughter (right), Maryla (Malka), at age six in Piotrkow-Trybunalski, 1940.

"By this time most of my siblings were gone. Regina died suddenly of a stroke in 1938. Leon was married and, like our oldest brother, Yechiel, was very much involved in the Jewish *Bund*.[1] Sought by the Gestapo, he and his wife, Gucia, managed to escape to Warsaw. They, too, met their deaths in the Treblinka death camp when the Warsaw ghetto was liquidated. Michael, with his German wife and two children, was forced to leave Berlin in 1938 and come to Piotrkow. At first he and his family were allowed to reside out-side the ghetto (because of his Aryan wife), but by 1942 they were ordered to move into the ghetto. His wife was advised by the Gestapo to take the children and return to Germany and to leave her Jewish husband behind. She was told in no uncertain words that this was the only way to save her children. Very reluctantly they parted from Michael and returned to her par-ents in Germany. Michael was now alone, but not for long. A young and very attractive widow, Ewa, fell in love with him. She had a small daughter, Elizabeth, and after the liquidation of the ghetto wanted to save her child by all means. Being resourceful and energetic, she obtained Aryan papers for herself, her daughter, and for Michael. They left the ghetto for the Aryan side and survived the war.

"Michael's escape got me in trouble. The Nazis punished family mem-bers when someone close to them escaped. They came at night to get me, and I was sure that like others I would be shot for my brother's escape. Luck had it that with the Gestapo was a young Jewish policeman who knew me. He told the Gestapo man that my brother and I were not even on speaking terms (he made it up to save me), that I had no knowledge of my brother's escape. My life was spared thanks to this young man. Later I found out that he worked for the Gestapo.

"Like all the remaining Jews, I was now in forced labor. Ironically, the place to which I was assigned was the factory at Bugaj, where I worked before the war. Not a textile mill anymore, it became a factory that produced tents for the German army. I was given the job of overseeing the production of a small group of workers. Each time we left the factory, each time we reentered the small ghetto, we were searched by the SS. One day they found a few nails on two young men I was overseeing. This meant sabotage and the penalty was death. The directors of the Bugaj forced labor camp were Fischer and Dietrich; both were SS officers, both brutal sadists. 'The overseer step out,' they shouted. I stepped out of the column. Knowing what was awaiting me, I was petrified. For the first time in my life I could feel my heart in my mouth. Suddenly, Fischer stepped forward, pointed to me, and said, 'I need this man, take other Jews in his place.' Under no circumstances did I want inno-cent people to die in my place, and I said so to Fischer. What happened next is hard to believe. Fischer ordered that nobody should be shot; the 'thieves' were punished (they were whipped), but nobody died. We returned to the ghetto, and I never forgot this incident and how close I was to being killed.

"In November 1944 our ghetto was being evacuated. We were shipped to the concentration camp in Buchenwald. The only relatives left were my sister Eva's son, Abram Tuszyner, and my cousin, Joseph Weinberg. My sister, Eva, died in the ghetto in 1941; her husband, Shaya, was killed in Treblinka. My youngest sister, Hela, was helped by her boyfriend Piotrowski to escape as an Aryan. Piotrowski was a Catholic Pole; he was in love with Hela and wanted to save her by sending her to his sister, who lived in Krosno. From the moment we left Piotrkow, I took care of Abram; he became like a younger brother to me. When we arrived in Buchenwald it was night. The *Kapos* told us that all our valuables, all money, and jewelry would be taken away from us the following morning.[2] For the night all of us were put into huge empty barracks, with ditches nearby to relieve ourselves. In all my life I have never seen so much money, gold, and jewelry being dumped into the cesspool. 'Better to throw it away than give it to our enemies,' people were saying. I had a problem. Maybe some of the money would come in handy to bribe a *Kapo.* I had five twenty-dollar gold coins and two diamonds—one in a platinum ring, the other one a loose stone. I knew that I could always throw everything away, but I had a different philosophy. I wanted to find the best way to save what I had. Luckily I had with me a bottle of vodka from Piotrkow. Keeping it hidden under my coat, I approached one of the *Kapos* who looked trustworthy to me. I handed the bottle to him and all I asked him was, 'What do the SS return to us after we are taken to the baths?' He looked at me and said, 'Only trusses (people who have a hernia wear them) are being returned.' Now I had to think. Whom did I know with a hernia? I recalled a young boy from the Piotrkow ghetto who I knew wore trusses. Instead of sleeping, I searched for the boy and found him. He was asleep. I woke him up and said, 'If you let me borrow your trusses for an hour, I will return them to you; and I will share whatever food I will be able to obtain with you.' He understood and gave me his trusses. There was little time to waste. Abram was a tailor by profession. He had with him scissors, needles, and yarn. Both of us went into a corner while most people were asleep. I told Abram to open a seam in the truss. We put the gold coins and jewelry deep inside the padding of the truss and Abram sewed it up again. Then I returned the truss to its owner. Early the next morning we were led into the camp and to the bathhouse. Everything we wore, everything we had, was taken away from us. Our heads were shaved, and we went into the showers. Then we were handed striped prisoner's garb. Most of the items we were given did not fit. So we tried to exchange the small ones with shorter people, the larger ones with larger people. I was given a pair of leather shoes instead of wooden ones, but they filled with water every time it rained. The trusses were returned; I looked for the one my young friend was getting back. As soon as possible, I asked him again for his truss. Abram opened the seam, removed what we put in, sewed up the truss, and I gave it back to the owner, saying again, 'As long as we are together, you will not go hungry.' The gold coins I hid in my shoes; the jewelry Abram hid in his ears (he had unusually large ears). The first coin I bartered for bread; the truss owner received half of it. During my stay in Buchenwald I shared with him bread and other food. He did not go hungry.

"By the middle of December 1944 the SS were sending prisoners as slave laborers to munitions factories. Abram and I were selected and sent to the town of Schlieben, where the famous *Panzerfaust* (antitank grenades) were being produced. Situated near the town of Bautzen close to the Bohemian border, the Schlieben camp was hell on earth. A very sad episode took place as soon as we arrived in Schlieben. Among our group from the Piotrkow ghetto was an older man, in his early fifties. He was highly respected in the ghetto and became our mentor. Seeing how depressed and miserable we were, he held a pep talk, trying to boost our morale. 'You can and will survive. Think positively. The war will be over soon,' were his words to us. We all felt better. Mr. Zajaczkowski gave us the hope we needed; he boosted our low morale. We went to sleep and as we entered the washroom the following morning, the body of Mr. Zajaczkowski was hanging from the rafter. After giving us the strength, after encouraging us to go on, he took his own life. All of us were shattered by this tragic event; we lost a dear friend and often talked about him.

"We worked in Schlieben under horrible conditions, exposed to poisonous sulfur with which we had to fill the *Panzerfaust*. Our skin became yellow; our stomachs could not handle the terrible camp food. Our barracks had dirt floors; the walls were covered with snow and ice. Our food consisted of a small piece of black bread, some black liquid—the so-called coffee—in the morning, and for lunch and dinner a horrible smelling soup made out of rotten vegetables. One evening, when we returned from the factory and were given this foul soup in the barracks, prisoners refused to eat it. The containers were sent back to the kitchen. It did not take long for the SS to find out that in our barracks prisoners were 'revolting' and refusing to consume the soup. It was already night when the SS entered our barracks. There were two SS men and three Jewish camp policemen. 'Who does not want to eat the food?' one of the SS officers barked out. There was complete silence. The men were petrified. I got off my bunk and told the SS, 'These men and I came from the same ghetto in Piotrkow, where all of us worked hard. Here in the *Panzerfaust* factory we work to exhaustion exposed to the sulfur. We came back to camp hungry, but the soup was so bad that we could not eat it.' As soon as I was finished, one of the SS hit me in the face. 'Take him away to the bunker (a place for punishment),' he shouted to the camp police. I left the barracks, led by the three camp policemen, who were called *Lagerschutz* in Schlieben. In complete silence they took me to the bunker. One of them beat me very hard on my head, face, and back. My ears were bleeding, the pain was excruciating, yet I remained silent. They wanted me to give them the names of those who refused to eat the soup. I told them, 'You can beat me as much as you want. I will not give you the names of my comrades.' The beating stopped. They led me out of the bunker to their private rooms—light, warm, clean, and comfortably furnished with beds, blankets, and pillows. What a contrast to our miserable barracks. In the middle of the room was a table set up with sandwiches, sausage, cheese, plenty of white bread. 'Eat, you must be hungry,' one of the *Lagerschutz* said. I was starved, but said, 'I refuse to eat or take anything from prisoners like you who are beating up other prisoners.' They stood dumbfounded. Here was a prisoner who had not eaten all day, and he refused to take their food. Then one of them said, 'You have guts. You are brave and we admire you for it. Return to your barracks and forget what happened to you tonight.' I was led back to my barracks. The men were sure that by now I was dead. The following morning when I entered the factory, the German *Meister* (overseer) asked me, 'Who the devil did such a professional job on you?' My face was swollen. One could not see my eyes. I had a hard time opening them. I was bruised and aching. I told the *Meister* what had happened. He had no idea what kind of food and how much of it the prisoners were receiving. This was a revelation to him.

"A few weeks went by. One evening, while I was ready to go to sleep, two of the *Lagerschutz,* who weeks earlier had taken me to the bunker, appeared. They called my name and ordered me to follow them. Once we entered their living quarters, they said, 'We were so impressed by you, by your solidarity with your fellow prisoners, we want to help you. We need another *Lagerschutz;* if you agree to join us, you will have a clean bed and all the food you can eat.' My answer was, 'I refuse to be a part of the camp police that harasses, beats up, and tortures other prisoners.' 'And if we promise you that your only duty will be to guard the kitchen and the storerooms, will you agree to do it?' one of them asked. Now I had to do some thinking. If I accepted the job as a guard and had the benefit of plenty of food, I would be able to help my nephew Abram, my cousin Joseph Weinberg, and other people, too. 'If you give me your word that my only duty will be to become a guard, then I will agree to your offer,' I told them. They gave me their word and poured a glass of vodka for each of us to toast our agreement. They brought to the table the best meat and plenty of white bread—things that I had not seen or tasted for a long time. I ate and ate until I was full. Again they toasted their promise to me, and I became part of the *Lagerschutz* in Schlieben.

"They kept their promise. Indeed, my only duties were to guard the kitchen, the clothing storeroom, and the canteen. Daily I took extra bread, sausage, and cheese to my old barracks and asked Abram to help me distribute this God-sent food. Abram and my cousin Joseph received daily bread, sausage, and other delicacies for as long as we were in Schlieben. This way I could ease the hunger of my relatives and friends just a little bit, making it possible for them to go on, to survive.

"One day, while standing guard in front of the kitchen, I noticed that two SS men were leading away the son of an old friend of mine from Piotrkow. The young man recognized me and shouted, 'Go to my father, tell him that I was arrested for sabotage.' Right away I realized the danger this young man was in. Sabotage was punished by death. I ran to find another *Lagerschutz* to stand guard, told him about this young man who needed help, and went to search for his father, Yechiel Kurnentz. As soon as I found him and told him of his son's predicament, he said, 'Please try to save him. Please save my son's life.' My only hope was to speak to one of my *Lagerschutz* colleagues who was in good standing with the SS. After I told the *Lagerschutz* about my friend's plight, he told me to go back to the father. 'If he has any money, foreign currency, gold, or jewelry, bring it to me. I will have to bribe the SS in order to save this young man,' he said. I went back to Yechiel Kurnentz and delivered the message. Somehow he was able to find enough jewelry and money, which I took back to the *Lagerschutz.* By evening young Kurnentz was free. We met again in Israel in 1982. His father had already died. Young Kurnentz (now Yechieli—a Hebrew surname) was now married and a father of three children. He hugged and kissed me and could not thank me enough for saving his life. 'I shall never forget that thanks to you I am alive,' he told me in Israel.

"In the spring of 1945, camps all over Germany were being evacuated. Prisoners were sent in cattle cars or had to walk to other camps. The SS did not want any of us to fall into the hands of the Allied armies. Abram with a group of other men was sent to the Theresienstadt camp. The rest of the Schlieben prisoners, many of them my old friends from Piotrkow, were marched by foot, pulling wagons with weapons, uniforms, and food that the SS wanted to save. We were the horses and, like horses, slept standing up. The long march took its toll. Many perished or were shot when no longer able to walk. The march ended in the Sudetengau, part of Bohemia. The SS made an appeal to those prisoners who were Aryan Germans but were sent to camp for their political beliefs. They were told that if they would now join the German army, they would be free. Among them was one of the *Lagerschutz,* the one who had beaten me in the bunker. Not one of the German prisoners answered the appeal. They decided to stay with their fellow prisoners, their comrades.

"The place where we stopped was a small town by the name of Nixdorf (now it is called Miculasovice in Bohemia). I became very ill with diarrhea and knew that I might not survive. For days I could not eat anything and saved the small pieces of our allotted bread ration. 'If I die, I do not want to die hungry,' I said to myself. The barracks where I stayed had a small stove that prisoners kept feeding with wood, garbage, twigs, anything that would burn and keep the barracks a little warmer. It was the end of April 1945, and it was still chilly. I got off my bunk, went to the stove, and warmed up the stale bread that I had collected for the past week. I ate every crumb of it, drank some of the black liquid, and went back to my bunk. 'I am full, now I do not care if I die.' These were my thoughts as I went to sleep. When I woke up after a few hours, no more diarrhea—I could not believe that the danger had passed. The bread did the trick. But I was extremely weak. One day, when I was trying to get off my bunk, I fainted from hunger and weakness. Near me slept a good friend of mine from Schlieben. He revived me. Our friendship started in the camp and lasted until he died. His name was Nathan; he became 'Uncle' Nathan, an important member of our family.

"All of the prisoners knew that the end of the war was near. We heard rumors from the SS guards that Hitler was dead and could hardly believe it. But for us the war was not over. One day the SS was placing dynamite around our camp, and the danger of being blown up was real. Fortunately, the SS did not succeed.

"The Polish-Russian army liberated our camp on May 9, 1945. Now the war was over. I was finally free. But free to do what? Here I was in the small Bohemian town of Nixdorf. My family was no more, and I had only Nathan, who was like an uncle to me. I started to call him 'Uncle.' After liberation he was in a deep depression and did not want to live. Uncle had lost his wife and two children, and he also lost hope. After that, I promised him that wherever I would go, he would be with me, we would always be together. We left Nixdorf together for Prague, the capital of Bohemia. The Czech people opened their hearts and homes to concentration camp survivors. We stayed in Prague until July 1945. The Czech government insisted that all strangers not born in the Czechoslovakian republic return to the country of their birth.

"With Uncle and another friend, Danek Frenkel, we boarded a train for Germany. I loved Prague and wished I could remain there, but this was unfortunately not possible. We ended up in Munich. Here we met other survivors who lived in displaced persons camps. Neither Uncle, Danek, nor

I wanted to return to camp life. Taking a chance, we boarded a train going north. We came to Regensburg in lower Bavaria but could not find lodging. Next, we traveled to a small town in the Oberpfalz by the name of Stamsried—a quiet place, beautifully situated between forests and hills. We were given lodging—Danek and I in one house, Uncle in another building. Our German landlords were suspicious of us; they did not trust survivors. This changed in time, and soon they became friendly. Stamsried had a small concentration camp during the war; the liberated prisoners decided to remain in town. All of us were allotted food coupons, mostly for bread, potatoes, and marmalade. To obtain butter, cheese, or meat, one had to barter clothing, cigarettes, or coffee, which we did not have. I still had the treasure I saved from Buchenwald and bartered another gold coin for food. We saw no future in Stamsried. One day Uncle borrowed a bicycle and rode to explore greener pastures. He returned late at night and informed us that he found a small town, Rötz, not far from Stamsried. He liked the place; it was larger than Stamsried. He even found lodging in this new town and decided to move there. I remembered my promise to Uncle, to be with him wherever he or I would live. After a long discussion with Danek, we, too, followed Uncle and went to Rötz.

Left to right: Max Kimmelman, Nathan Laznowski, Danek Frenkel, Rötz, Oberpfalz, 1945.

"With a population of about three thousand, Rötz had more cows than people. We needed a place to live. Uncle told us that next to him there was a nice villa at 210 Böhmerstrasse. He heard that three women occupied the house and advised us to try our luck. Danek and I knocked on the door. An elderly woman opened the door but would not let us in. We asked if she would be willing to rent one or two rooms to us. The answer was a sharp 'no.' She shut the door in our faces and left us standing outside. I decided to seek the help of the American occupation forces (Rötz was located in the American sector of Germany) located in the town of Waldmünchen. We presented our case to the American authority and soon were driven in a jeep to Rötz in the company of an American officer. When we arrived at 210 Böhmerstrasse, the officer did not knock politely but shouted, 'Öffnen' (open up). This time a younger woman opened the door and let us in. The officer told her that by order of the military authority Max Kimmelman and Danek Frenkel were to be given two rooms in their house with the use of the kitchen. Then he added, 'If I hear any complaints from these two gentlemen, the whole house will be requisitioned.' We thanked the officer as he left us in our new 'home.'

"Traveling in postwar Germany was difficult and risky. Trains were few; railroad tracks were still damaged from Allied bombings. Yet many survivors traveled from one town to another, from one camp to another, in search of family or friends. From one survivor I heard that my nephew, Abram, was alive and lived in the DP camp of Feldafing, not far from Munich. We parted in Schlieben, and I had not heard from him until now. Mail was slow but efficient. I contacted Abram and found out that my sister, Hela, survived as an Aryan in Poland in the town of Krosno. She was hidden by a noble Polish Catholic, Stefan Pruc. After the war she married him and raised his young son, Jozio. This was still a dangerous time for Jews, especially in Poland. Jews in many cases were being killed when they ventured back to their home-towns. Jews were afraid to admit to being Jewish. Hela lived in Krosno as a Catholic until she died in 1965. Only her husband and adopted son knew that she was Jewish. I also learned from Abram that my brother Michael with his friend Ewa and her daughter, Elizabeth, survived and resided in Lodz. How did Abram know all these details? When Uncle, Danek, and I left

Prague for Germany, Abram went from Theresienstadt to Poland. He was searching for his family and went to Lodz, where he resided before the war. There he met his uncle Michael, who in turn told him about Hela. Abram also found his only brother, Heniek, in Lodz. Heniek was an ardent Communist before the war and survived in the Soviet Union. When he returned with the victorious Soviet army to his hometown, he was a high-ranking Soviet officer and a clerk for the Secret Service. All this was not to Abram's liking; he had nothing in common with his only brother. With anti-Semitism everywhere, he decided to leave for Germany. He landed in Feldafing.

"Now I knew that, of my entire family, I still had a brother and a sister as well as two nephews. The trouble was that most of them lived in Poland. My heart would not let me return to the place where I suffered so much sorrow. I had to be satisfied to keep in touch with my family by mail. After the war, my brother Michael divorced his first wife and officially married Ewa, who saved his life. He now lived under his Aryan name, Leon Sroczynski. As a dentist he became an officer in the Polish army, where nobody knew about his Jewish origin or that his wife, Ewa, and his adopted daughter, Elizabeth, were Jewish.

"In November 1945, Danek Frenkel found out that his sweetheart from the ghetto, Krysia Zajaczkowska (it was her father who committed suicide in Schlieben), was well and alive in Sweden. He loved her dearly and decided to travel to Sweden and marry her. Danek also learned that his parents and brother survived the war and lived in the DP camp of Belsen in the British zone of Germany. To reunite with his family, he would first travel to Belsen, from there to Sweden. Danek did not want to make the trip alone. He convinced me to go with him. I might find some friends in Belsen, and if I wanted to, he would love for me to go to Sweden. 'No way,' I said. 'I may go with you to Belsen, but I will return to Rötz. I will not leave Uncle alone.' My promise to Uncle was sacred. In December 1945, Danek and I were ready for the new adventure—to travel by train to Belsen. The trip took almost five days. Trains were overcrowded, with no place to sit, so we traveled standing up. Every few hours the train would stop because of repairs to the tracks. Tired and dirty, we finally arrived in the city of Celle and took a bus to Belsen. Danek's parents were overjoyed to see their son. They fed us and offered me a place to sleep. In the camp I found old friends from Piotrkow. One of them, Aron Geisler, who was a barber, suggested that I stay in the building where he lived. He had a friend who had a small room but was away with her father to visit their German friends in Bochum. He led me to the room and opened the door (Aron had keys to all rooms in the building). It was a narrow, small room, but cozy. Then I noticed a photo near the bed and asked Aron, 'Who is this girl?' He told me that this was the girl whose room we were now in. I fell in love with the girl in the photograph. Nothing like this ever happened to me. Will I be able to meet her? I wanted to know all about her. Aron told me that she worked in this building in the office of the British Welfare and that she would be returning to Belsen after Christmas. Guess who this girl was—your Oma. I also found out that her name was Mira, and that she and her father were the only ones from her family to survive the Holocaust. I could hardly wait to meet her, to get to know her.

"Then came the day when I would meet Mira—December 27, 1945—a gloomy, drizzly day in Belsen. I stayed with Danek's parents; I did not take Aron up on his offer to sleep in Mira's room. I needed a haircut badly and walked over to Aron's building. I knew Aron from the Piotrkow ghetto, knew that he lost his wife and small daughter just like I. In this building in the Belsen camp he had his barber's room, which was totally equipped for him. As he was cutting my hair, a young girl walked in asking for the keys to her room. Immediately I recognized Mira, the girl from the photograph. Aron introduced me to her, but she was in a hurry, and we barely spoke. I was disappointed. How will I be able to see and talk with Mira? An idea occurred to me. 'What are you doing for New Year's Eve?' I asked Aron. 'My wife, Ella (whom he married in Belsen), and I did not make any plans. What do you suggest?' said Aron. I knew what I wanted—a small party arranged by Aron. 'Could we celebrate the evening together in your place? Would you also invite Mira? I will provide all drinks if you and Ella could prepare some food.' I waited a few seconds for Aron's reply. He agreed to have a small party but had to make sure that it would be all right with his wife, Ella, since she would have to prepare the food. The following day he told me that the party was on, that I could bring the drinks. The next three days seemed like an eternity.

"I arrived early at Aron's place on New Year's Eve. Mira had not yet come. When she finally entered the room, a middle-aged man was with her. She introduced him to me as her father. Aron had a few records with music to dance to. I danced with Mira the entire evening, and I knew that I wanted to be with her forever. I was so in love and already loved everything about this girl whom I barely knew. From then on we saw each other every day until I left for Rötz. On January 6, 1946, I asked Mira to be my wife but did not receive an answer. She wanted to talk to her father, who was all she had left and whom she adored. A few days later I left Belsen but wrote each day a letter to Mira and was beside myself when I didn't receive a reply right away. Four weeks later I was back in Belsen. I had to be near the girl I loved. This time Mira promised to marry me, but not right away. She wanted her father's blessing. It was agreed that she would leave the DP camp and come live with me in Rötz. We were married on Lag b'Omer, May 19, 1946, in my rented room in Rötz.[3] My happiness was complete. I found a new purpose in life: I had Mira as my beloved, as my companion and friend. Uncle, too, approved of my choice; he and Mira became friends right away.

"Mira's goal was to leave Germany. She had a great-uncle in Cincinnati, Ohio, and in June 1948 we were able to leave Rötz for good. Uncle promised to follow us. He left Rötz one and a half years later and settled in Louisville, Kentucky. In spite of my misgivings about America, both of us were ready to start a new life in a new country, in a free society."

Chapter 7

LIFE IN THE UNITED STATES

NEW YORK

Dear Benno and Gene,

It was a July morning when we saw the Statue of Liberty greeting us as we entered the port of New York. The day was foggy, but the sight was unforgettable. This statue, the symbol of liberty and freedom and hope, brought tears to our eyes. We all shared in this incredible emotional experience. Dad and I were instructed not to leave the boat. We gathered our twenty children and waited patiently for all to disembark. The children wore name tags, and so did we. Soon two ladies approached our group. They introduced themselves, called out the names of the young people, and thanked us for our efforts. We had become attached to some of the young people and they promised to keep in touch. After we embraced and kissed them, we said good-bye. One of the ladies handed a twenty-dollar bill to Dad, one dollar per child. This was the first money we earned in America. We never anticipated we would be paid, yet it felt good to be thanked this way. After both of us signed the release papers, the ladies with the twenty young people left the boat. Now we too could disembark.

As I walked down the plank, I spotted among the waiting people a familiar face. It was Clara Weiner, a dear friend of my parents' from Danzig. She had waited for us for hours with a bouquet of flowers and could not understand why we were the last ones to leave the ship. I was so moved and thrilled to see Mrs. Weiner. The last time I saw her was in our Danzig apartment in July 1939. Now it was July 1948 and many things had changed in our lives. She apologized that her husband could not meet us, too, but he was working at his cousin's chocolate factory and could not afford to take off. Shea Weiner, Clara's husband, was a dear friend of my father's for many years. The Weiners left Danzig in the summer of 1939 shortly before the outbreak of World War II and went to Poland. My father was still in Danzig when the American consul in Danzig was searching for the Weiners. Their visas had arrived but nobody knew their whereabouts. Luckily my father had their address and notified the Weiners about their visas. They returned to Danzig soon after hostilities against Poland stopped. We were already gone, deported to Warsaw, when the Weiners came to claim their visas. They first traveled to Berlin; from there they left for New York in 1940. We corresponded with them until 1941. I still have two postcards my father wrote to them, which Mrs. Weiner gave me when we were reunited in 1948. After the war, when my father reestablished contact with them, they tried to help us as much as they could. But they were elderly, and though they both worked very hard they were not able to sponsor all of us. However, they did sponsor my father, after they learned that my relatives sponsored Max and me.

Mrs. Weiner called a taxi. We loaded all our possessions and drove off to the Hotel Marseilles, where the Hebrew Immigrant Aid Society (HIAS) was placing us until our departure for Cincinnati.[1] The hotel was an old, tall brick building at the corner of 103rd and Broadway. The heat was unbelievable, and here we were wearing our heavy woolen European clothes. Nobody ever told us that summers in New York (and Cincinnati) are so hot and humid. We were assigned a tiny room on the tenth floor of the hotel. Mrs. Weiner told us that her husband would visit us after work and she returned home. Alone in our tiny hotel room, we looked out of the window and saw a jungle of tall buildings. The sky was hardly visible, but the heat was torturous. Both Max and I were drenched with sweat. We washed up and decided to walk the streets when it got a little cooler. Fascinated by the night life on Broadway, we spent most of the nights of our stay in New York walking the streets. It was astonishing for us to see shops and stalls open all night. We guarded the twenty dollars we earned, but the sight of fresh peaches was too tempting. At a fruit stand we bought three pounds of the prettiest peaches, sat down on a bench, and ate them with delight. Years later we recalled the delicious taste of our first peaches on Broadway.

Little by little some of my father's friends from Danzig visited us. First came Mr. Weiner with a huge box of chocolates. The next day came his brother-in-law, Max Feuerstein, who had also been in the seed business in Danzig. From him we received as a gift our first box of Barton's candies. People who were in our hotel, and who were with us on the boat, were being picked up by their sponsors or by their relatives. The young Hungarian boy without a leg was met by his ultra-orthodox relatives. His parting from Dad was quite emotional, but we never heard from him again. I had my best school friend living not far away, on West End Avenue. Gala Ebin—along with her sister, Ima, and her parents—came to the United States on the *Batory,* the last Polish liner to leave Gdynia before war broke out. Gala and I attended the Polish *Gimnazjum* together; we sat on the same bench. When Gala found out that we were in the ghetto, her family sent us packages. Only two of them arrived, but they provided us with food to barter. After the war, when I wrote to Gala, she sent CARE packages to Rötz; again we had special food that was good for bartering. Dad and I walked to the Ebins' residence on West End Avenue—a huge apartment building with a doorman. We had to identify ourselves before being allowed to enter the elevator. Mr. Ebin received us with great warmth. His daughters Gala and Ima were vacationing in Europe; his wife was in their summer house in Long Beach. The three of us talked for many hours. Mr. Ebin wanted to hear about my life during the war. We also told him that our affidavit had been issued in Cincinnati, that in a few days we would be leaving New York. Without hesitation he offered Dad a job. He was positive that New York would be a better place for us. But we could not accept his offer, although it was very tempting. Mr. Ebin and his brother had a chicken canning factory and Dad would be well paid. We had to decline politely. Then Mr. Ebin invited us to come to Long Beach the next Saturday to spend the day with his wife and with him. He gave us directions how to get there and we promised to come.

The excitement and stimulation of life in New York provided us with insight into the making of this fascinating city. We were on a high. I did notice a pain in my right knee. Walking became more and more painful. Finally, Dad asked where we could find a doctor to examine my knee. We were sent to one nearby who diagnosed a severe inflammation of the knee. In Germany, where we lived on the ground floor, I never had to climb steps. On the boat I lived in the hull, and the steps were steep and made of metal. The strain of walking many times up and down the steel steps of the ship evidently caused the inflammation. The doctor gave me pills and told Dad to keep me from walking too much. He also issued a certificate that would allow us to remain in New York a little longer, until my knee felt better. "Your ligament needs time to heal. Do not try to climb steps." We thanked the doctor, glad that we would have a few more days in this city.

From Gala's letters, I found out that another of my Danzig school friends lived in New York. Tula Dlugolecka was a dear friend of mine. I knew her before I met Gala. The two of us were very close. Tula was a Polish Catholic girl from a very liberal family. She and I used to sit together in school, until the priest called her and forbade her to sit with me, a Jewess. It was painful for both of us. We continued our friendship outside of school and saw each other daily in each other's homes. Gala wrote me that after the war Tula married a Mr. Panski in Poland, who was sent by the Polish Communist government to represent the Polish trade mission. I had Tula's telephone number from Gala and called her. She and her husband lived in Brooklyn and she wanted us to come and visit them right away. Tula picked us up with a taxi and took us to their apartment. She told me the story of her family during the war years. She, her father, and her two sisters, Kazia and Krysia, resided in Gdynia. When the Nazis entered the city in September 1939, they escaped to Kraków. Her father and Kazia were killed during the war, only she and Krysia survived. Tula met her husband and they were sent to the United States. Krysia remained in Poland. When we arrived in Brooklyn, we met Mr. Panski. A distinguished looking gentleman in a smoking coat, he looked quite pompous. Very reserved, at least ten years older than Tula, he spoke little. Dad tried to engage him in conversation, but it was like pulling teeth. Tula took me into another room and asked, "What can I do for you? How can I help? What do you need?" All I said was, "Tula, I want to take a bath. I want to wash my hair with the best shampoo you can give me." I told her about the tiny room in our hotel, without a tub or shower, with only a small sink to wash up. She gave me a plush, thick towel and wonderful smelling soap and shampoo and showed me her bathroom. It was a thrill, an unforgettable experience, to indulge in the luxury of taking a much desired bath and washing my hair. I was forever grateful to Tula for this luxurious bath. After we returned to our hotel, Dad mentioned to me that he thought Mr. Panski to be of Jewish origin. He never asked him, but his way of speaking, his avoiding of any conversation, made Dad almost sure of it. He told me that he knew a Panski family in Piotrkow-Trybunalski. A prominent and assimilated Polish-Jewish family, they were the owners of the largest printing press in Piotrkow. Could Tula's husband be related to them? Many years later, while in Israel in 1993, I met a Miss Panski at a concert. She and her family fled Poland for Sweden in 1968, when Polish anti-Semitism was at its peak. She told me that one of her relatives by the name of Panski once worked in the United States as an attaché (like Tula's husband). Could this have been Tula's husband? Dad may have been right. Tula and I kept in touch. I received her last letter in Cincinnati in 1950. In it she mentioned that her husband had been recalled to Poland. They were stopping first in London and from there they would return to Poland. This last letter was posted from London. I never heard from her again. Her husband, as a government attaché, may have been removed from his post for political reasons. We wondered many times what happened to Tula and her husband. She would have written to me, but maybe she was afraid. I shall always cherish her friendship and the memories of the years of our youth in Danzig and Gdynia.

One day, while Dad and I walked along Broadway, suddenly someone called out, "Max, do you remember me?" Dad turned around startled. He recognized the man from the camp in Schlieben, where he worked as a *Lagerschutz*. The two of them met in Schlieben in strange circumstances.[2] Dad was delighted to see his comrade from Schlieben. He gave Dad his address and asked us to visit him. His apartment was not far from the Hotel Marseilles. The following day we went to visit him, his wife, and their baby boy. They lived on the third floor. I can still feel how painful it was for me to walk up the stairs. Dad actually carried me part of the way. The apartment was small, dark, and very crowded. His young wife looked quite unhappy. He asked us to sit down on an old, uncomfortable couch and began telling us his story. "When the Schlieben camp was evacuated in April 1945, you, Max, went to Nixdorf, while I ended up in Theresienstadt. After the war ended, I decided to return to Poland to look for my family. Nobody was left. My wife and children dead, I was alone. I was desperate. I did not want to live. But life was stronger. I returned to Germany to start a new life. I met my future wife, and we got married. But some of the former prisoners from Schlieben recognized me and started to make my life miserable; I went into hiding and eventually was able to take my family to America." Dad told me later that this man had a bad reputation in camp; he did hit some prisoners, but he was not a killer. We wondered how he came to the United States; he probably took another name. We never heard from him again and never found out if they remained in New York. Unfortunately, he had to suffer the consequences of his behavior during the war.

Back in our hotel room we made a telephone call to Cincinnati to let our relatives know about our arrival in Cincinnati the following Monday morning. Cousin Rose told us to take a taxi from the train station and come to their house on Lexington Avenue. Needless to say, we were disappointed. Was this an American way of greeting relatives? Why could they not meet us? We had a similar experience with the wife of Dad's first cousin Leo. Leo's wife was the daughter of a midwife in Piotrkow, and she and Max had known each other as young people. Rose left Poland for the United States in the mid-twenties and worked in a laboratory as an X-ray technician. While on a visit to Poland, she stopped in Berlin and met Dad's cousin Leo. They fell in love and were married. Leo and Rose lived in Forest Hills, New York, and had a son, Jerome, and a daughter, Helen. Rose sent pictures of the family to us in Rötz and wrote warm letters. When we notified her about our coming to America, she insisted that we call her as soon as we arrived. Well, we did. Dad spoke with her. He hoped to be able to see Rose and Leo and meet their children. It was not to be. Rose told Dad that they were busy and could not come to the city to meet us. From then on Dad never called and never heard from them. It was painful and disappointing to both of us. We never learned of the reason why all of a sudden Rose turned away from us. Her letters had been so warm, so comforting. Well, we shall never know the answer.

Destination Cincinnati, Ohio

After one week in New York City, Dad and I had to depart for Cincinnati. The weather in New York was steaming hot on Sunday, August 1, 1948, when we left the Hotel Marseilles in Manhattan for Penn Station. A taxi took us plus our two suitcases and one canvas bag (these were all our material possessions) to catch the evening train to Cincinnati. Our family there had been alerted about the time of our arrival. All our travel expenses had been paid by HIAS, for which we were most grateful.

For the first time we traveled on an American train. The Pennsylvania Railroad in comparison to German trains after the war was quite luxurious. Traveling coach, we had clean and comfortable seats; even the conductor was surprisingly friendly and helpful. While riding the train, we realized for the first time the vastness of the country, how great the distances between cities were. Our ride lasted overnight, almost twelve hours. It was Monday morning, August 2, when we arrived in Cincinnati. After we got off the train, we were directed to the Travelers' Aid office. There we were told that our relatives called and that we should take a taxi to their home. We did, and we arrived on Lexington Avenue in Avondale, where my relatives resided. It was a lovely suburb north of Cincinnati, with a lot of greenery and quiet neighborhoods.

Driving to our relatives through the streets of Cincinnati we noticed how much smaller this city was than New York City. There were just a few skyscrapers, many trees and flowers, and benches on which people could sit. It was very different from the hustle and noise of the big city. The ride from

Union Station to Lexington Avenue took about twenty minutes. The taxi stopped in front of the house, and we could hardly wait to meet our American relatives. All we had was a photo of my cousin Rose Roth with her daughter, Faith. She sent it to us in Germany while we awaited our visas. I had no idea what my uncle Max looked like but soon found out. On the steps of the house where we stopped stood a slim man of medium height. He came down to greet us, and I couldn't get over how much he resembled my grandmother Esther Ryczke. I knew right away that this must be Uncle Max. He hugged and kissed me, and Dad and I loved him from the moment we met. After we took our luggage into the house, we met Aunt Yetta and Cousin Rose. Aunt Yetta was short and stout with white hair. Rose looked exactly like she did in the photo she had sent us. She resembled her father and was petite and slim with a twinkle in her eyes, just like my father had. She introduced us to her only child, Faith, who was about twenty years old.

The house was a nice-looking two-family dwelling. Uncle Max and his wife lived with their daughter, Rose, and her husband, Sam, and their daughter, Faith, on the first floor. We were given the solarium as a temporary home and were happy to be among family. From now on Cincinnati would be our home. No more displaced persons camps; no more temporary residences. Here in this city Dad and I would begin to build a new life for ourselves. Knowing that we had family here would make life easier. Luckily, Uncle Max, Aunt Yetta, and Rose spoke not only English but also Yiddish, and Dad could converse with them. I spoke English so that Faith could understand our conversation. She knew almost no Yiddish.

Who were our relatives? Uncle Max was born Mordechai Cyruliczak-Jakubowski in Slupca, Poland. This was where his family came from, and this was the small town where my father, too, was born. His father was the owner of a flour mill in Slupca and was well off. In the 1890s Uncle Max was a young man who loved to gamble. His parents decided to send him to America, where some of their friends from Slupca established a home. These former Slupca friends resided in Cincinnati, and Uncle Max came to them. Here he met his future wife, Yetta, and soon they were married. They had three children: two sons, Isidore and Philip, and a daughter, Rose. Uncle Max joined his new relatives and worked in a tailor shop as a presser. He was never wealthy but earned enough to raise a fine family. Uncle Max changed his last name to a more American one. He became Max Jacobs instead of Mordecai Jakubowski. All his children were married: Isidore to Bessie; they had a daughter, Lillian, and one son, Don. Philip was married to Jenny and had one son, Harold. Rose married Sam Roth and they had one daughter, Faith. None of them had a car, and they all led modest lives. Before the war my father had corresponded with his uncle Max. It had been my father's wish that one day I would go to the United States to be with his family. But, as I already mentioned, I had other ideas: I was a Zionist and wanted to emigrate to Palestine. The outbreak of World War II changed all our lives, changed all plans.

Once we arrived in Cincinnati, my cousin Rose told us the true story about sponsoring us. Financially, nobody in the family had enough assets to bring us over and to guarantee that they could support us. They turned to the people who owned the tailor shop where Uncle Max and Sam Roth worked and asked for their help. We knew the names of our sponsors and told Rose that Dad and I would like to meet them and thank them in person. Cousin Rose told us: "You cannot meet them, they do not want to meet you. We had a gentlemen's agreement that they would only sponsor you under the condition that they would never have to meet you. They did us a favor by sponsoring you." We were shocked but had to accept this fact. We never met them, we never had to ask them for help, and we could never say thank you.

Our first meal in the home of our relatives was a lavish lunch. We felt so welcome and admired how warm a relationship there was between the three generations that lived under one roof, in one apartment. Uncle Max asked me many questions about his family. He remembered life in Poland at the end of the nineteenth century and remembered many details from his early years in Slupca. Over and over he asked me if I was sure that only my father and I had survived. He knew that he had one nephew, Heniek Jakubowski, who went to Palestine. But all relatives that lived in Poland during World War II perished. Then came the strangest question: "What happened to all the money and jewelry that belonged to my parents?" His mother died in 1910, and his father remarried, had another child, and died in 1920. All I could tell him was that if there was money or jewelry, his parents must have given it to their children and that I had no knowledge about this. Dad told him that the Nazis stripped the Jews of all their material possessions before they killed them. This Uncle Max did not know.

Both Dad and I were anxious to find work. We did not want to be a burden to our family and wanted to earn money as soon as possible. Rose told us that the Jewish Federation in Cincinnati had been notified of our arrival and they had already begun looking for jobs for us. "Once we find work, we shall also look for a place to live," I assured my family. They had opened their modest home to us and had been so warm and kind. We did not want to impose on their hospitality. While waiting to hear from the Jewish Federation, Rose and Uncle Max took us on a tour of the city. We traveled by streetcar from their neighborhood in Avondale to downtown. Rose told us that Cincinnati had about half a million inhabitants, twenty thousand of whom were Jews. She also told us that there were neighborhoods in Cincinnati where Jews could not rent an apartment or buy a house. These were the "restricted" neighborhoods. We also found out that some companies did not employ Jews. This came as a shock to us. We never thought that we would have to experience discrimination and anti-Semitism in the United States. How can this be true in such a free country, a country that welcomes refugees? Nobody ever mentioned this to us in Europe. This was truly an eye-opener.

The four of us got off the streetcar and walked the streets of downtown. Rose took us to the largest department store, Shillito's. She wanted to show us the abundance of goods. She also wanted to get some material to make a dress for me. Dad and I arrived in heavy woolen clothing, not knowing how hot and humid it would be in Cincinnati. Rose saw my few dresses and decided to sew a cotton dress that would be more comfortable in the Cincinnati heat. She asked me to select a color. I chose blue. The following day Rose went to work, and I had my first brand-new American dress: a blue shirtwaist. I was deeply touched by cousin Rose's gift. She was an accomplished seamstress and made all clothes for herself and her daughter. Dad and I talked about this trip to Shillito's and about my first dress many times, especially when the thermometer hit one hundred degrees Fahrenheit and more.

While we were exploring Cincinnati, the Family Service of the Jewish Federation called and told Aunt Yetta that they had found a job for Dad. He was to report to the place that offered the job for an interview. Dad put down on his job application his profession in textiles, and the federation found a place for him with the Adler Company, a factory that produced hosiery for men. Uncle Max got up early the next morning to take Max to his interview. The Adler Company was located on Queen City and Harrison Avenue. They had to take two streetcars and one bus to get there. The interview took place on Thursday, August 5. With Uncle Max as an interpreter, Dad's interview did not last long. Fortunately, one of the vice presidents of the Adler Company, Harry Groban, was present, and he asked Dad if he spoke Yiddish. Mr. Groban took a liking to Dad right away and hired him. Dad's background was as a textile engineer. He worked before the war in a large textile factory in Piotrkow, Poland. Here he was hired to work as a laborer in the shipping department. His pay would be sixty-three cents per hour, with the opportunity to work overtime. Dad was to report for work the following Monday.

When Dad returned with Uncle Max, I could hardly wait to hear the good news. Dad was elated. He had a job and would soon be earning money. "What about me?" I asked. The Jewish Federation soon found an office job for me. I would be working downtown in the office of an accountant who, too, was from Europe. On Monday, August 9, 1948, both Max and I joined the workforce. Dad had to leave Uncle Max's house at 6 a.m. to get to the Adler Company. I left after 8 a.m. to get downtown to the accounting company. A new life with new experiences was in store for us.

We asked Rose and Uncle Max to look in the classified section of the newspapers for a furnished room or apartment for us. We did not want to burden our family much longer. They assured us that we were no burden and told us, "You are staying with us until we find something suitable for you." They were gentle and kind to us.

My job consisted of entering bills into ledgers, filing, and other office work. My boss and his wife both were from Vienna. They escaped Hitler in 1938 and came to Cincinnati. Here they opened a bookkeeping and accounting office and were doing fairly well. Both were excellent bookkeepers and seemed to be very nice. They hired me because the federation asked them to. My wages were fifteen dollars per week, five days a week, eight hours a day. When they came to the United States, they had a very Jewish sounding name, which they soon changed into a "French" one. They were childless and told me that as long as I would work for them, they would always help me and Dad with advice. We were green, we knew nothing of America, and they already had years of experience in this country. All this sounded nice and generous to us.

Until now we had had only a few minor surprises since our arrival in Cincinnati. Nothing had prepared me for what was to follow. The summer of 1948 was exceptionally hot. The office I worked in had no air-conditioning, and I had to wear sleeveless or short-sleeved blouses to work. My boss's wife noticed the tattoo on my left arm and right away told me, "You cannot work here unless you cover this tattoo." I asked her, "Why should I cover it? I am not ashamed of it." "People will think of you as a criminal, they will not understand." I still remember how hurt I was by her words. It is hard for me to describe my feelings of pain and anger. This tattoo had been inflicted on me and other Jews as a mark of shame. To me it was a constant reminder of our suffering. Now it would become a mark of Cain in the United States. I should have left this place right away, but I was so new and needed a job desperately. From then on I covered the tattoo each morning with a Band-Aid, which I removed when I came home. Dad could not believe his ears when he heard my story. Next I was told by my boss never to answer the telephone: "You have an accent." Yet both of them spoke with a European accent, which they claimed to be French. I dreaded each day when I had to go to work, never knowing what to expect next. Each day was an ordeal, and I could not understand that all this emotional suffering was being inflicted by Jews who fled Europe ten years earlier and came to this country as refugees as I did. I only shared my feelings with Dad. I did not dare talk about them to my relatives. I suffered quietly, hoping that things would improve in time.

Two weeks after we started to work, Uncle Max found an ad in the newspaper about a furnished room with a kitchen and bath. Rose called them up and walked with us to inspect the place located on 418 Rockdale Avenue. The landlady, Mrs. Kraus, took us upstairs to the second floor, where we found a modestly furnished bedroom with a small kitchen and bathroom.

Her first question was, "Do you have children? Because I do not rent to families with children." Another shock—we never heard in Germany or Poland that children were unwelcome. The rent was $50 a month. This place looked fine to us; Dad and I told her that we would take it. But Mrs. Kraus asked for a $50 deposit, which we did not have. We asked her for twenty-four hours, so that we could come up with the deposit. All we had was the $250 my father gave us before we left for the States, and we had promised ourselves not to touch this money. The following day, Dad went to see Mr. Groban and told him about our dilemma with the deposit. "How much do you need?" Harry Groban asked Dad. "If I could borrow $50 and each week pay back part of it, we could rent this apartment," Dad told him. Right away Harry Groban instructed the office to give Dad the money and the same evening we walked over to hand the $50 to Mrs. Kraus. Dad paid back the borrowed money within two months, and we were fortunate to be able to move into our own place. By the end of August we packed our few possessions and moved out of our relatives' home, forever grateful for their hospitality, for their good hearts.

The only person we knew who had a car was an old friend of my father's, Gertie Cohn. She knew my father when he was a young boy in Slupca. Gertie came to America to marry a man much older than she. He had passed away and now she was a widow looking for a husband. She helped us move into our first American apartment. The apartment had a bedroom with one bed, a night stand, and a chair with three legs. A brick served as the fourth leg. The kitchen had a small table with two chairs, a stove, and a refrigerator. And the bathroom had a bathtub, where I washed all our clothes. There was no shower. To us this place was paradise; we were happy. Both of us were working, and Dad worked overtime most days. From each paycheck we decided to put away some money and we opened a savings account in a bank close by. While I had been subjected to mental cruelty at work, Dad had to struggle with hard physical labor. He was working ten to twelve hours a day pushing bales of wool or cotton that weighed six hundred pounds. He had to carry heavy boxes with finished hosiery, tying them with metal bands, with steel strips. His hands were swollen and bleeding when he came home. Dad was by nature an optimist. He never gave up. But this was more than he could take. "Let's leave and return to Germany," he told me in a moment of despair. "In all my life I never had to work that hard, not even in the camps," Dad said. I had to calm him down, give him encouragement that things would be better once he learned to speak the language. The inability to communicate in English made Dad's life so much harder. There was no time for him to attend evening school for newcomers because he worked too many hours. In time we weathered our difficulties. What mattered was that we were together. We had each other. Under no circumstances would we return to Germany. Our goal was to make it here, in the United States, no matter how hard the beginning was. I was confident that in time things would turn out for the best.

It was September and the High Holy Days were upon us. Shortly before our holidays, we were visited by two ladies from the Jewish Family Service. They came to offer us financial help so that we could purchase new clothing and food for the holidays. We thanked them politely and declined their offer. "We are both working. We earn enough and do not need money." We never accepted charity and never would. Both of us felt offended. We understood that their intentions were good. They wanted to help us. We told them how glad we were to be in this country, that we appreciated the fact that the federation helped in securing jobs for us, but we would never accept any money. Then they asked if they could help with medical expenses, should they occur. Again, we declined their offer. What troubled us was the fact that the Family Service was solely interested in material help. Not once did they ask about our spiritual and social needs. We were so lonely. No one ever invited us into their homes. The only homes we had been to were the homes of my relatives. As newcomers, as refugees, and as Holocaust survivors, we were not accepted by the American Jewish community. This was painful and many times we felt like outcasts. Only many years later did we understand that people were apprehensive about getting close to us, did not know how to talk to us—maybe were afraid to offend us.

The holidays came and we were alone. Mr. Groban asked Dad if we would like to attend High Holy Day services. He had secured two tickets for us from Tom Adler, the president of the Adler Company. The Adlers were Jewish and belonged to the largest Reform Temple, the Rockdale Temple.

Their forefathers came from Germany in the nineteenth century, and the Adler family never attended religious services. The Rockdale Temple was across the street from where we lived. Most of the members were descendants of German Jews and were quite wealthy. Needless to say, Dad and I felt out of place in the temple. But we attended services; both of us needed the spiritual and religious uplift at this solemn time of the year. I recall how much both of us cried during these holidays.

In the meantime my left arm became sore from the daily removal of the Band-Aid. Soon the wound became infected. The physical pain was not as great as the shame and anguish. Through some German refugees I met a girl my age who came from Bielefeld and had spent years in the Riga ghetto and camps. She came to Cincinnati after the war and married her school boy-friend. Inge Friedemann became my first good friend in Cincinnati. She worked for the Union of American Hebrew Congregations, and by October I decided to confide in her about the abuse I had to endure at work. I also asked her if there was a possibility of getting a job with UAHC, the place where she worked. Inge told my story to her boss, and I was asked to come for an interview. During my lunch hour I walked over to the offices of UAHC on Sixth Street, had the interview, and was hired on the spot. When I returned to my office, I told my boss that I was leaving at the end of the workday. I was showered with verbal abuse, with the most coarse words. "You are the most ungrateful person. You did not appreciate what we did for you by giving you a job. We hired you out of pity. Go now. We never want to see you again." Without saying a word, I left the office and never saw or spoke to them again. I never forgot the humiliation and mental anguish of my first job. Both of them died of cancer ten years later.

Thanks to Inge Friedemann I began work at UAHC in October 1948. It was a clerical job. The pay was not great, but the people I worked with were warm and kind. We printed and distributed books and other educational material for Hebrew Union College as well as for all Reform congregations. I had ample opportunity to read all of the books that I could lay my hands on. I stayed in during my lunch hour to read and learn. It was now over two months since Dad and I had come to Cincinnati—time to apply for our first papers, the first step to becoming American citizens.

Papa was still in Hannover, Germany, and he, too, was planning to join us in America. We never wrote him about our difficulties, our struggles. We did not want him to worry about us. He knew how kind our relatives were to us. We wrote to him that each of them had invited us to dinner. We described our apartment and our Sunday walks to Fleischmann Gardens. We never complained in our letters, and we even sent packages with sweets to him. Except for Inge and her husband, Werner, we had no social contact. They invited us to a gathering at the Gate Club, a social club established by German refugees who escaped Hitler's persecutions. They were all well established and assimilated into American life. Not one of them ever invited us into their homes, as though they were afraid to get close to us. Again and again Dad and I were told not to speak about the war years, not to mention our experiences in the camps. "Forget about it. Now you are in America," we were told. We kept silent for almost twenty years.

We also met two families who knew my parents before the war—the Potters (their name once was Piotrkowski) and the Flax family. Both families came before or during the war. Both were settled and had businesses. They were my parents' age, and I felt a kinship with them. For the first two years even they did not invite us into their homes, always claiming to be too busy. Dad and I felt like pariahs. Our first American holiday, Thanksgiving, was spent in our small furnished apartment alone. At that time we did not know any other survivors in Cincinnati, and when in 1949 the first families arrived, we made sure to invite them for holidays and to keep our home always open for the newcomers. They became our friends and our extended family throughout our stay in Cincinnati. Although not all of them became close, we shared a common past and could talk openly about our problems. Because we were socially not accepted, we had to create our own close-knit environment where we felt comfortable, where we could live with dignity.

In August 1949, my father left Germany and came to the United States. He was sponsored by his friends the Weiners, from Danzig. In order to meet my father in New York, I took a week's vacation without pay (paid vacation was given only after one worked a full year) and took the Pennsylvania Railroad to New York. The boat my father came on docked in Boston, and from there my father took the train to New York. At midnight on August 29,

Mr. Weiner and I met my father at Penn Station. I was so happy to see my dear father, so thankful that he decided to come to the United States. The Weiners invited him to stay with them and gave him a room so that he would have his privacy. The following day my father and I went shopping. Like us, he arrived in heavy European clothes. The heat and humidity in New York were unbearable; my father needed to get proper clothes. At Macy's we found lightweight slacks and a jacket, as well as short-sleeved shirts. He only had long-sleeved shirts, as in Europe even in summer men wore long-sleeved shirts. The next item was a typewriter. My father loved to correspond, and he typed all his letters. We found a Royal portable typewriter cast in iron. To this day I am using this vintage typewriter; it is manual and by now ribbons are hard to come by. Wherever I go, I search for ribbons so that I can continue using the typewriter my father bought in New York in 1949. It is old but it is still reliable, and whenever I type, I think of my father and hear him typing. In September 1949 I was to celebrate my twenty-sixth birthday, and my father wanted to get me something nice. He knew that Dad and I earned very little and that I did not spend any money on myself. At Macy's Little Shop he purchased a black silk taffeta dress for me and a little black velvet hat. I still have both, and the dress still fits me!

My father did not want to impose on the Weiners and found a room with a family from Danzig. I helped him move and returned to Cincinnati, being assured that for the High Holy Days my father would visit us. Two weeks later Dad and I met him at the Cincinnati Union Station. We wanted my father to meet his only living uncle, his mother's brother, Max Jacobs. When they met, everybody was astonished how much Uncle Max and my father resembled each other. Because my father did not speak English, it was Yiddish that was spoken between uncle and nephew.

In the meantime Dad and I had moved out of our small apartment and rented a three-room furnished apartment next door to Mrs. Kraus. Knowing that my father would be coming, we needed a place for him. The new apartment had a living room with a sleeping couch, a bedroom, a kitchen, and a bath. Our new landlords were Jack and Fay Stoll. They, too, wanted tenants without children. Our rent was now sixty-five dollars, which was steep for us. Although our lifestyle was very modest, we never skimped on food and

Mira in a little black dress and hat from her father in Cincinnati, September 1949.

we saved a few dollars each week. Someday we wanted to be able to buy our own furniture. In the meantime, we were able to welcome my father into a pleasant apartment at 422 Rockdale Avenue. The first impressions my father had of our place were not too positive. "You are living like poor people," were his remarks, while to us our place was a palace. He was comparing our modest furnished apartment to the apartments that I grew up in before the war. He soon realized that we lived within our means and that we were happy. My father was astonished when Dad returned to him the $250 he had given us before we left Germany for a rainy day. We did not touch a penny of his money, but were grateful that he meant well and did not want us to be penniless. We knew very well that my father would soon need this money. He had some, but not much. The seed business that he had started in Hannover after the war did not bring in a lot. He had money from the sale of the Opel car, which he sold to Willy Feldhege, his friend and former boss during the war, before leaving for the United States. Now he also had the money he had given us.

We spent the High Holy Days together and were invited to Uncle Max's for dinner. After two weeks in Cincinnati my father said, "Cincinnati is too provincial for me. The city is too small. I like New York, where I have friends from Danzig. Here I feel like a fish out of water." Knowing my father, I was certain he would not change his mind. He needed to be in a city where he would have people of similar background, stimulation, and a social life. We knew from our own experience that he would be terribly lonely and unhappy in Cincinnati. He was still young. I knew that he wanted to marry again and there was no chance for him to find someone who would suit him in Cincinnati. Dad had a hard time understanding why he did not want to live close to his only child. But I understood and wanted my father to be happy. He returned to New York City, and long letters describing his adventures followed. Then came disappointments. Without a lot of money he had no chance to start a seed business in New York. The friends he had counted on were giving him a lot of advice and telling him to forget about going into business. One of his old friends felt sorry for him and asked him to make a business trip to Germany for his firm. In the spring of 1950 my father returned to Germany. He found anti-Semitism everywhere and was glad to return to New York. Dad and I met him for Memorial Day weekend in New York. We had wonderful news: I was pregnant and our baby would be born in January 1951. I think that my father was shocked. He felt much too young to be a grandfather, yet he was so pleased. Dad and I were filled with so much happiness. We wanted to share it with my father. We talked about our baby. We worried that the Stolls would not let us stay in the apartment. Both of us decided that "there will be no negative thoughts. Everything will turn out for the best." And we were right.

In the meantime, the Weiners tried to be matchmakers for my father. They introduced him to several ladies but to no avail. A widow from Danzig was interested in my father. Mrs. K. and my father knew each other from Danzig, where she and her husband had a cigar, cigarette, and tobacco store on the corner of Holzmarkt and Dominikswall. My mother often sent me as a young girl to their store to purchase "Derby" cigarettes, the brand she smoked. My father saw Mrs. K. a few times in New York but said, "She is too old. I would prefer a younger woman." In the summer of 1950 he went for a week to the Catskills and met a younger woman, Bella Goldenberg. He fell in love and in March 1951 he and Bella were married.

By the end of 1950, Dad and I had saved up enough to purchase our own bedroom furniture. The excitement was indescribable when the furniture arrived and when we slept for the first time "in our own beds." By the end of the year I left my job. I was now in my ninth month. The Stolls became such good friends that they did not object to having us stay with our baby. Before I left my job, my coworkers and friends gave me a baby shower. This was something very new and unknown to me. There are no showers given in Europe. This was an American custom and a very nice one. All the beautiful baby clothes were put away until the arrival of our baby. Next we were preoccupied with finding a proper name for the child. Our doctor assured me that "your baby will be a girl." Naturally we believed him and were looking for girls' names. There was no doubt in our minds that our daughter would be named after Dad's mother and after my mother. After a lot of searching we came up with the names Gloria Mae (Gloria for Gitel, my mother; Mae for Malka, Max's mother). When my father arrived shortly before my due date and heard about the names, his response was, "You must be kidding, I never heard of such stupid names." We quarreled every evening, and we came up with different names each day. And we laughed a lot, because whatever names we suggested, my father opposed them. It was like a comedy, and we never forgot the search for our daughter's name.

My labor pains started the evening of January 29, 1951. It was snowing and bitter cold outside. The Jewish Hospital was one mile from our apartment and we decided to walk. The three of us walked in snow and ice to the Jewish Hospital on Burnet Avenue while Dad was having terrible stomach cramps. He was in worse shape than I. Our baby was born at 4 a.m. on January 30, and our daughter was a *son*. We did not have a name for him; we only had names for "her." But Dad had a dream shortly before our baby was born. He saw his favorite brother who told him, "my name, my name." Our son was named in Hebrew Leib Benyamin (Louis Benjamin in English). We called you Benno. My father saw in you the son he lost; he adored you, Benno. For us the birth of our first son was the happiest moment in our lives.

When you, Benno, were two years old, we had to look for another apartment. The Stolls decided to sell the house. Luckily we found a two-bedroom apartment across from Fleischmann Gardens, on Washington Avenue. The house was once a mansion, with marble walls on the staircase, in the kitchen, and in the bathroom. This apartment was not furnished and now we were forced to use our savings to purchase additional furniture. Dad still had to take two streetcars and one bus to get to work. Somehow he got used to it.

When you, Benno, were three years old, Dad and I decided that one child was not enough. You needed a brother or sister. We wanted another child. On December, 14, 1954, our second son was born. This time there were no arguments about names. We named you in Hebrew Yitzhak Efraim (Eugene Irvin in English), and decided to call you Gene. You, Benno, were delighted to have a little brother; our family was now complete.

In 1955 we purchased our first car. Dad and I took driving lessons, passed the test, and bought a used Oldsmobile. A dark green, shiny used car, it looked great, and we were so proud of our new acquisition. Unfortunately we knew nothing about cars and paid dearly for our naive trust in the car dealer. The price of our car was six hundred dollars. Within a year we paid twice as much for repairs. We learned a bitter lesson, but the car made Dad's life easier. By now he was earning one dollar per hour. Instead of working physically, he worked as a shipping clerk. A few years later the West German government began to pay reparations to survivors of ghettos and concentration camps. Together Dad and I received the sum of four thousand dollars, which for us was a fortune. The following year the house we lived in was sold. This time we decided to look for a house of our own. Twice we had to move because the places we lived in were sold. It was time to find a small house where we could live with our sons for a long time. In the summer of 1956 we found a twenty-year-old small brick house in Golf Manor, a suburb north of Avondale. The four-thousand-dollar restitution was the down payment for the house.

We had no qualms about accepting German restitution. The word in German is "Wiedergutmachung," which means "to make good again." It was Germany's way to "make good" all the bad things that the Nazis had done to us. What we received was only a token compared to what was taken away from us and the suffering we endured. Restitution money enabled us to purchase our first American home and made our lives easier.

Benno and Gene in front of their home in Cincinnati, August 1964.

Located at 6422 Stover Avenue, our new home was within walking distance of a public school, one block to the bus stop, and shopping was just around the corner. Soon a synagogue was built on our street and we joined the Orthodox Golf Manor Synagogue. Since we had arrived in the United States we had never borrowed money, never had any debts. To purchase a house we had to take out a fifteen-year mortgage, and both Dad and I had sleepless nights. Until now we had paid for whatever we had bought. For our house we had to borrow money and this bothered us. In time we adjusted to the idea that in America people take out a mortgage, that this is no shame. "When in Rome, do as the Romans do," we were told. Slowly the American way of life infiltrated our lives, too. Some assimilation was natural, but we did not want to lose or forget our background, our culture. At home we spoke Polish or German, outside the home we spoke English. By now Dad had become comfortable with the English language and had no difficulty expressing himself. You, Benno and Gene, were used to hearing two foreign languages. We wanted you to understand when we spoke Polish or German. Except for our relatives and next door neighbors we had absolutely no contact with Americans.

Our first American friends were our next door neighbors on Stover Avenue—Marge and Floyd Sherrick. They became an integral part of our lives, just like family. To this day Marge and I are close friends; Floyd passed away many years ago. Uncle Max and his wife were old and died. Now we saw little of our relatives. I spoke to them over the phone, but we saw them seldom. The Flaxes and Potters invited us from time to time. They were our only link to my parents. Pola Flax made sure that we kept close contact. You, our children, played mostly with children of other survivors until you started school. Now you also found friends among the American children you went to school with.

Eventually, Cincinnati had a good number of survivors. Like many other groups of people, the survivors were not homogeneous. They differed among themselves. It was not often, but it did happen that some of them tried to hide their Jewish background and claimed to be either Polish or German. There were some who shied away from other survivors and did not want to associate with them. Some tried to assimilate into American culture to forget their past. They became more American than Americans. Goals differed among survivors. For some the quest for financial security dominated their lives. To make as much money as quickly as possible was important to some. They felt that only wealth would help them to find the right place in American society. All these trends were probably typical of immigrants. For Dad and me the well-being of our children and their education was our priority. Most of our friends shared our goals; they were wonderful friends and part of our extended family. We shared not only a common past but also common goals and ideas. And we needed each other for moral support.

Mira with her two sons, Benno, four years, and Gene, four weeks, Cincinnati, January 1955.

After my father and Bella were married, he bought a small chicken farm in Estell Manor, New Jersey. From the time you, Benno, were half a year old, we spent at least two weeks each summer on my father's chicken farm. You both loved to visit Papa on his farm. He tried to keep his grandsons happy by taking us to see the enchanting Longwood Gardens, to explore our capital in Washington, D.C., and to visit the United Nations in New York City, the beaches of Atlantic City, Ocean City, Wildwood, and Cape May, New Jersey. I know you have fond memories to this day of the trips you took with Papa. Each summer we also had the opportunity to visit my only surviving uncle, my mother's brother, Heniek Hammer. He, too, settled on a farm, not far from Estell Manor, in Vineland, New Jersey. He loved you both, and you were fond of him. A chicken farmer's life was not easy. My father worked every day of the year and his health started to fail. He did manage to come for a day or two to visit us in Cincinnati. What worried us most was that his marriage was not a happy one.

You have your own memories of what follows, dear Benno and dear Gene, so I will address this part of our family history to the reader. In 1962 Benno finished Losantiville School in Cincinnati and was admitted to Walnut Hills High School there. The next year he began preparing to become a Bar Mitzvah. At first Max and I wanted a very small celebration only for the few relatives we had and for our closest friends. Benno's Bar Mitzvah in 1964 turned out to be our farewell to Cincinnati. The Adler Company was sold to Burlington Industries; production and shipping were moved to Rockwood, Tennessee. We had no choice but to go where Max had a secure job. He was fifty-five years old with very slim chances of finding another job. Knowing that we would leave Cincinnati soon, Benno's Bar Mitzvah was the last time we were together with our relatives and friends. The idea of leaving Cincinnati was most depressing for Benno and for me. He had his good friends, a wonderful school, and his baseball team. For me Cincinnati was the place where I now felt at home. I had friends and a feeling of security. Besides, I knew nothing about Rockwood or Tennessee. Max was already commuting to Rockwood. When I asked him, "What is Rockwood like?" he said, "It is a small town, beautifully located between mountains, but has only one Jewish family." The closest town with a Jewish population and a synagogue was Oak Ridge, Tennessee, some thirty-five miles from Rockwood. I had written to the rabbi in Oak Ridge and found out that indeed there was a synagogue, a religious school, and a vibrant Jewish community.

In June 1964, while Max was already working in Rockwood, Benno, Gene, and I took the Southern Railway train from Cincinnati to Rockwood. From there we drove to explore Oak Ridge. Compared to Cincinnati, Oak Ridge was different. It struck me as a typical company town, with the plants subsidized by the government. One missed the cultural stimulation, the presence of a "city." It was like suburbia without the "urbia." Oak Ridge had only shopping centers. There was no city. Knoxville was the closest city to it. It was much larger than Oak Ridge but fifty-seven miles from Rockwood. The choice was a hard one. On the one hand, there was a larger city with a well-established Jewish community and a temple and synagogue; on the other hand, there was Oak Ridge. Max would have to do all the driving, the daily commuting.

We decided on Oak Ridge. At that time there were a few houses for sale on Stover Avenue in Cincinnati. Because we had just painted and put new lighting fixtures in our home for Benno's Bar Mitzvah, the house sold within one week. We lost some money but were glad that the sale went through. Max came home for the weekend and could hardly believe that our house had sold so quickly. We all drove to Oak Ridge in search of a house. My heart was heavy. I did not want to leave Cincinnati, the place where I lived longer than anywhere else. I was unhappy and afraid to face the future in a new place. "Again we will be strangers in a place where we do not know anybody. Will we be accepted or will we have the same pain of being outsiders?" I knew that I was being unfair to Max, who really had no choice but to work in Rockwood. It was he who was willing to make the sacrifice and commute so that our sons could be in a Jewish community and I near a synagogue.

There were not many houses for sale in Oak Ridge. Financially we were limited and had to look for a house we could afford. After weeks of looking, we found a beautiful brand-new house in the western part of Oak Ridge. It was much more expensive than the house we sold in Cincinnati. Both of us worried whether we would be able to make the monthly payments. The only way this was feasible was to take a long-term mortgage. To make our monthly payments affordable, we took out a thirty-five-year mortgage. Max jokingly said, "In the year 1999 this house will be ours." Max's wages were never high, yet we managed to live within our means. We were always content with what we had.

We left 6422 Stover Avenue on a sunny Tuesday, August 25, 1964. We left behind a community where we had started to grow new roots. We certainly did not leave Cincinnati willingly. As a Polish song explains it best, "Dla chleba Panie, dla chleba" (for the sake of bread, God, for the bread). We left a way of life that was comfortable and stable for the unknown. What kind of life was waiting for us? Whatever it would be, we were together, and deep in my heart I knew that we would adjust to a new life. As a family we would support each other and together build a new future.

"Welcome to Oak Ridge, Tennessee"

What did we know about Tennessee? Very little, almost nothing. The hills, mountains, and lakes looked enchanting. Our new house was located on top of a ridge amongst hundreds of trees (their leaves became an annual nightmare each autumn). In Cincinnati nobody knew anything about Tennessee, and our friends felt sorry for the Kimmelmans, who were leaving a city filled with culture for an unknown place "somewhere in Tennessee." But once we came here, this became home.

Only after we moved to Oak Ridge did we learn the history of this "secret city." All we were told was that it had plants where cancer and other research was being conducted. Little by little did we find out that in Oak Ridge components for the atomic bomb had been produced during World War II. This came as a shock. Both Max and I abhorred war. We had seen too much suffering and hoped for a peaceful future. A bomb that caused mass destruction among civilians in Japan or anywhere in the world was something we did not feel comfortable about. We came to Oak Ridge simply because it had a Jewish house of worship and could provide our sons with a Jewish education, and the distance to Rockwood was shorter than from Knoxville. Once we were here, we had to accept Oak Ridge's past.

Scientists from all over the United States and the world worked in Oak Ridge, with the largest ratio of Ph.D.'s per capita in the country. The plants operated first under the direction of Union Carbide, later Martin Marietta and Lockheed, and were government funded. This unusual city had a population of over seventy-five thousand during the war years. Once war was over, it became an open city. But it always depended on government funding for the operation of the plants.

I am writing this chapter in August 2000, thirty-six years after Oak Ridge became our new home. Looking back at the good and the sad times I have experienced in Oak Ridge, it was not important what size city it was—its people are what is most important. And we do have a variety of cultural attractions—concerts, plays, ballet, lectures. We have a science museum and a wonderful children's museum. Oak Ridge has an art center and many gifted artists. Most of all, it has one of the best school systems in the country. We have numerous civic organizations, colleges, and adult education programs. One can be busy every minute of the day in Oak Ridge. Things have changed during these past thirty-six years, but life changes in big cities, too. Our largest shopping center was torn down to make place for a mall; now the mall has more vacant stores than occupied ones. Funding for the three plants in Oak Ridge has been systematically cut by the government, and people are retiring early or forced to look for jobs elsewhere. When we came to Oak Ridge, the Jewish religious school had close to 150 children. Now we have 23 in the entire school. There is no influx of young Jewish families; the older people are the ones who support almost all activities. Only time will tell what the future of Oak Ridge will look like. One thing I know for sure: the friends and the neighbors are as devoted and as helpful now as they were years ago. This has not changed. It is the people who make Oak Ridge what it is, not the houses, streets, or shopping centers. In Oak Ridge we are like one family, sharing each other's happy and unhappy moments. I doubt if there is another community like Oak Ridge in all of the United States. Now I have to pray for good health so that I can continue my teaching and community involvement in this wonderful city.

Max was by nature superstitious. "If we move, it has to be on a Tuesday," he said. According to something he heard as a child, for Jews Tuesdays are lucky days. And so we left Cincinnati on Tuesday, August 25, to arrive in Oak Ridge the same day. Our furniture would arrive a day later, so we had to spend the first night in the Holiday Inn. But there was one thing we had to do: affix the mezuzah to the doorpost of our new home on West Outer Drive. My very first friend in Cincinnati, Inge Friedemann, gave us as a going-away gift a mezuzah, which we affixed to the doorpost of our front entrance.

When we arrived, the population of Oak Ridge was approximately twenty-eight thousand, with about eighty Jewish families. Right away we joined the Jewish Congregation and enrolled our sons in religious school. Benno, who was thirteen and a half, would only attend religious school on Sundays. Gene, at nine-and-three-quarters, had to go three times a week— on Tuesdays, Thursdays, and Sundays. Since we were without a car during the week, friends would pick up Gene. On Sundays I had the car and drove other children as well as our sons to religious school. No sooner did they begin their religious education than I was approached by the education chairman, Sig Lindenbaum, and asked to teach religious school on Sundays. "We do not pay much, but it would cover gasoline expenses," were his words. I accepted gladly.

Max remained in Oak Ridge until our furniture arrived and began his commuting to Rockwood, Tennessee, on Thursday, August 27, 1964. This left the boys and me without a car. We had only the one Dodge Lancer, which Max drove to and from work. Oak Ridge had no public transportation, and we lived four miles from the nearest grocery store. Luckily, our neighbors were fabulous and most helpful. The boys needed to be registered in school and neighbors offered to drive us. Gene was stung by a wasp and we needed medical help, another neighbor drove us to the emergency room of the Oak Ridge Hospital. I could not get over the kindness of people to whom we were complete strangers. None of the people who offered help were Jewish, something that we had not experienced in Cincinnati, except for the Sherricks. There most of our friends were Holocaust survivors—all were Jewish. Were we dreaming? Were we going to be treated like normal people in this mysterious city of Oak Ridge? The outpouring of hospitality from Jews and non-Jews was mind-boggling. Neighborhood coffees and dinners to meet people on our street followed. Being so new in Oak Ridge, I wanted to get involved in the life of the community. I am still teaching, this being my thirty-seventh year.

Once Benno and Gene started school (there were school buses, so no transportation problems), they made friends and were invited to friends' houses. It was hardest on Benno, who hated leaving Cincinnati and had to leave good friends behind. For Gene, Oak Ridge became a new adventure, a new challenge. Both our boys had been good students. In Oak Ridge they had to compete with the children of scientists, who excelled in the sciences. Our sons had to work harder to keep up with their peers. Schools in Oak Ridge were very good and among the best in Tennessee. Benno attended Robertsville Junior High, and Gene went to Linden School. Both adjusted to their new environment, although they still talked about their old home, Cincinnati. For them, coming to Oak Ridge was culture shock.

No sooner did we settle down than my father and his wife came for a visit. They wanted to see where we were living. My father enjoyed the long drive; he came via the Blue Ridge Parkway all the way from New Jersey. They loved our home, but most of all the beauty of our surroundings. With the approaching High Holy Days, we wanted to make sure that Papa and his wife, Bella, could attend services with us. I called to ask where we could purchase tickets for them and was told, "In our synagogue we do not sell tickets, everybody is welcome to worship with us." This would have been unheard of in Cincinnati, where one could not enter a synagogue on the High Holy Days without purchasing a ticket. My father was greatly impressed, and all of us went together to Rosh Hashanah (Jewish New Year) services. As soon as services were over, we were invited to an open house reception at the home of Ernest Silver, the president of the congregation. It was the most heart-warming experience. From the beginning, Oak Ridge felt like home.

The rabbi at that time was Alexander Gelberman, a widower born in Hungary who came to the United States many years before World War II. He became our trusted friend. Sensitive to aesthetics, he felt that the synagogue should be a place of beauty. The building was built out of blocks by the congregants; the sanctuary walls, too, were made out of cinder blocks. Not very pretty, but the building was functional. It was Rabbi Gelberman who initiated the beautification of the sanctuary. To this day, whenever I look at the marble-lined ark, the paneled walls, I have to think of Rabbi Gelberman. His three years in Oak Ridge were not always happy. Rabbi Gelberman had his own heartaches. He raised two children by himself who were nearing college age. When he left our community after three years and went to Newcastle, Pennsylvania, we were without a rabbi for a few years. Rabbi Gelberman wrote to us. In his first letter he wrote that his colleague from the Reform Temple was Rabbi Ivan Grün from Danzig. I knew Rabbi Grün and his daughter well; they left Danzig in 1939, shortly before war broke out. Just by chance I found another thread to my Danzig past.

In the summer of 1966 our dear friend Uncle Nathan moved to Oak Ridge. He had lived in Louisville, Kentucky, since coming to this country in 1950 but was spending all the Jewish holidays with us. Uncle was getting on in age, and his health was not the best. He needed to be close to us so that we could take care of him. And so in August 1966 we rented an efficiency apartment for him within walking distance of the synagogue. He was still spending every Friday evening and Saturday with us.

The time was also nearing for Gene's Bar Mitzvah. With no rabbi, he had been trained and prepared by two lay leaders, Joe Spector and Ernest Silver. No catered affair, Gene's Bar Mitzvah was celebrated by the entire Jewish community with everybody helping, everybody baking. Our Oak Ridge extended family helped us celebrate this joyous occasion. From Cincinnati twenty-three of our friends arrived in Oak Ridge; they were speechless at the friendliness of our community. Yet, it was a bittersweet day. We had no blood relatives attending Gene's Bar Mitzvah. My father had just undergone surgery and was not able to travel. Only Uncle Nathan, our adopted relative, was present. And poor Gene was sick with pneumonia and poison ivy (someone burned leaves in the neighborhood). He conducted the entire service, but I could hear his wheezing and breathing. Again I had to think of the family we did not have, of my brother's Bar Mitzvah in the ghetto, of the aunts, uncles, and cousins my children never knew.

Max and Gene at
Gene's Bar Mitzvah,
December 23, 1967, in
Oak Ridge, Tennessee.

As we adjusted to our quiet life in Oak Ridge, Max had the burden of commuting. He never was a good driver. The distance from our house to Rockwood was thirty-five miles, and Max had to leave at 6 a.m. Many times the fog was so dense early in the morning that he could barely see anything. And in winter he had to fight snow and ice to make it to work. Winters were not severe, but we did have ice storms and some snow. It was sheer hardship for poor Max, yet he never complained. He loved Oak Ridge and our many good friends and social life. For the first time since coming to the United States, we were not "the green ones," the refugees, the survivors. We were accepted and respected by our friends and for the first time felt like normal people. In all the years that I lived here I never encountered anti-Semitism or any kind of discrimination. This can be attributed to the fact that most of the people we came in contact with were highly educated. Many of them traveled abroad and had been exposed to people of other religions and nationalities.

Besides teaching religious school, I became involved in other organizational activities. There was the Oak Ridge High School PTA, the American Field Service, Jewish Congregation, Hadassah, Sisterhood, and the United Nations Committee. Many friendships were formed while working with different people, and we cherished all of them. There was no driving problem anymore. We purchased a used Corvair, the one Ralph Nader called "unsafe at any speed." This gave me the freedom to move around. Benno was now driving, too, and soon we were thinking of his going off to college. Hardworking, Benno wanted to go east to study. He applied to many colleges to which he was accepted; he chose Yale. Scholarships and loans helped pay his tuition. We missed him terribly when he left home. We still had Gene, who was more interested in sports than in studies. "I do not have to be like Benno. I do not have to be the best," he used to say. Gene wanted to enjoy life. He wanted to have fun. Once Benno left, Gene became very close to Uncle Nathan. In 1968 Uncle was diagnosed with cancer. We did not tell Uncle about his condition because that would have frightened him to death. After surgery we brought him to our house to recuperate. He bounced back in no time; his physical strength was unbelievable.

In 1972 Gene applied to become an American Field Service (AFS) exchange student and was accepted to live in Denmark for a year. Although we knew how much we would miss him, we were happy for him. In October 1972, while Gene was in Denmark, Uncle Nathan passed away. He died peacefully in our home. We mourned him for a long time, especially Max. They shared memories from their incarceration in the Schlieben concentration camp. Uncle was like an older brother to Max, and he missed him terribly. He was liked and respected by many. To this day people stop me on the street and tell me how much they had liked Uncle. My children still recall jokes and stories that Uncle used to tell them. He was their beloved uncle.

While Gene was in Denmark, I was asked by Catherine Ledgerwood, a teacher at the Oak Ridge High School, to come and speak to the students about my experiences in World War II. She knew that both Max and I were in concentration camps during the war. This was the beginning of my lectures on the Holocaust to schools in Oak Ridge, East Tennessee, and beyond. Soon civic groups and churches invited me to speak to them. The demand did not diminish; more and more schools have incorporated Holocaust Studies into their curriculums. But what about our own religious school? To my dismay, I was asked by parents not to teach their children about the horrors of World War II. Their children should not have nightmares. We were without a rabbi; I had nobody to turn to and ask for advice. I was asked to teach Jewish history, yet not allowed to teach about the Holocaust. When we hired a new rabbi, I shared with him my concern. Rabbi Robert Marcus was young; we were his first congregation. A son of a rabbi, a scholar, and a wise man, he understood the problem. Slowly he incorporated Holocaust lessons into our curriculum, and he did one more thing: he introduced the observance of Yom Hashoah—Holocaust Remembrance Day—to our congregation.[3] This day had been observed throughout the United States for many years, but not in Oak Ridge. Unfortunately, very few people attended the observance. "We do not want to think of those terrible times" or "we cannot take the pain of coming and listening" were some of the comments made by our friends. We could not blame them; it certainly was not a pleasant way to spend an hour or two. They were our friends, and we were hurt by their absence. We felt sad but grateful to those who came to help us mourn our losses. To this day, Yom Hashoah is observed in our community, thanks to Rabbi Marcus's initiative. And we continue to teach in our religious school the "lessons of the Holocaust."

In March 1973, Max retired after twenty-five years with Burlington Industries. His first and only job, he had worked hard and looked forward to some time of leisure. With my father in Israel and Gene in Denmark, we decided to visit both of them. We had the opportunity to meet Gene's Danish family and spent a week with them. Gene (and we) were the first Jews they had met. Both parents were teachers and very fond of Gene. Knowing that Jews do not eat pork, they went to great expense to get chicken for us. It was very touching to see how much they cared to make us feel comfortable. They knew about the suffering of the Jews under Hitler, and they knew how their own people risked their lives to smuggle the Jews of Denmark to Sweden. Spellbound they listened to our stories; some of them Gene had to translate into Danish.

When we returned to Oak Ridge, Max became restless. He was sixty-five, too young to sit back and do nothing. He found a "job" watching the teenage children of our friends. Max loved children, loved being with them. He also had time now to become involved with the Jewish community and was elected to the board. He served a total of eight years—first as membership chairman, then ritual chairman, cemetery chairman, and finally as treasurer. Max also became a salesman for Amway products. This was not very profitable, but it helped him meet new people.

Our older son, Benno, graduated from Yale Law School in 1975. He had achieved his goal; he now was a lawyer. It was a long and hard road. We had to take out loans for both of our sons to enable them to pursue their dreams. Max was making a fraction of what our friends in Oak Ridge were earning. We lived according to our means, trying to save for our sons' education.

When Max retired, he had no pension plan. The textile industry had almost no safety net for its employees; the stock that was given to Max in lieu of a pension was worth one-half of its original value when we sold it. Yet we always felt rich; we had our two wonderful sons, I had my father, and we had each other. Our sons may have missed some of the luxuries their peers had, but they understood that "their parents came with empty hands to this country and had to begin from scratch."

Chapter 8

FOR THE LOVE OF OUR CHILDREN

One of the most frequent questions people have asked me is, "How did you and your husband raise your children after what you two went through?" I, too, have asked myself this question many times. A lot of self-examination and self-criticism will help me to answer this question. And I will have to reach back into my memory to find some of the answers.

Max and I were married in May 1946, one year after the war ended. Both of us were still bearing deep scars of our Holocaust experiences and were physically as well as emotionally recuperating. Whenever we talked about the future, we always talked about the child or children we might have one day. Why did we not start having children right away? From the moment we met, both of us decided to leave Germany. I knew that our relatives in the United States were in the process of sponsoring my father and me. As it turned out, right after our wedding my father was notified that papers for him and for his daughter (that meant me) had arrived. There was no hesitation on my father's part. He replied asking that instead of his name, the name of Max, who was now my husband, be entered on the application for visas. Each day Max and I expected to hear from the U.S. government. Little did we know that the waiting period would last almost two years. During this time both of us knew that to emigrate with a baby would cause a lot of hardship. We knew that both of us would have to work to create a new life for ourselves as well as for the children we would have someday. To be quite honest, we wanted our children to be born in a country that was free of hatred and discrimination. In our eyes the United States always embodied freedom. This would be the country where our children would someday be born.

Ketubah for Max and Mira Kimmelman, Rötz, May 19, 1946.

FOR THE LOVE OF OUR CHILDREN

We arrived in the United States in July 1948. We came to Cincinnati and started working right away. After almost two years in our jobs, Max and I decided that no matter how little money we were earning, it was time to think of starting a family. I was terrified that maybe I would not be able to have children, knowing how many of my friends from the ghetto and camps were unable to conceive. What if I, too, would be unable to bear a child? I shared my thoughts with Max, who understood my anxieties and assured me, "You will see, we will have a child." Fortunately, my fears did not materialize and Max's optimism prevailed. In May 1950, I became pregnant with our first child. Our son Benno was born on January 30, 1951. To both of us the birth of our first child was like a miracle; both of us realized how blessed we were. Jubilation and bliss filled our hearts. Max marked the calendar for January 30 HOLIDAY! This was the beginning of our family, the beginning of the future.

While Max had to work, I was left alone with our new baby. There was no one to guide me, to advise me how to handle the baby. Unable to nurse, I was a frustrated new mother. "How I wish my mother would be alive. How I wish I had a sister or sister-in-law to turn to for help and advice," I used to pray in silence. But I was alone and had to learn everything "the hard way." From our Cincinnati relatives we were receiving names of pediatricians. All of them were Americans, and we had a hard time dealing with them. It was not because we could not communicate in English—my English was near perfect. They just could not understand our fears, our concerns. We felt misunderstood and quite unhappy. Finally we turned to Dr. Martin Abraham, our family doctor, for advice. He came to the States from Germany years before World War II and suggested Dr. Bruno Leichtentritt, a colleague of his who also came from Germany. A famous pediatrician from Breslau, where he had his own clinic, Dr. Leichtentritt became our pediatrician. He came to Cincinnati in 1938 with his German (non-Jewish) wife. While he was studying for admission to the American Medical Board, his wife worked as a ladies' room attendant in one of the large department stores in Cincinnati. The Leichtentritts were childless and immensely devoted to each other and to the children the doctor treated. The moment we met Dr. Leichtentritt, Max and I felt at ease and trusted him completely. The poor doctor had to put up with my numerous calls, some in the middle of the night. "Our baby is crying constantly. He must be ill," I said many times. He always reassured me with gentle answers, never admonished me. Dr. Leichtentritt understood my fears and helped me to cope with them. A cautious and excellent physician, he became a trusted friend. When on December 14, 1954, our second son, Gene, was born, I was already an experienced mother and much more relaxed in dealing with our second baby. While Benno was fairly healthy, Gene was born with many allergies and had frequent infections. Not once during the thirteen years while Dr. Leichtentritt treated our children did he prescribe medicine over the phone. He always insisted on seeing the child first. While growing up, Benno only once had a penicillin injection. Dr. Leichtentritt did not believe in giving children antibiotics each time they were sick. How right he was. Yet Gene needed them often, and until the age of three, when he underwent a tonsillectomy, Dr. Leichtentritt had him on antibiotics. He guided and cared for our sons wisely and cautiously from infancy until we moved to Oak Ridge. We were always grateful for the guidance and the advice he gave us.

Throughout the years when our sons were growing up, both Max and I had nightmares and constant fears about our children being taken away from us. The reflexes of our Holocaust experiences were returning again and again. Max was waking up screaming, and so was I. There also was the constant consternation about the health of our sons. The fear of losing our children to illness, to some strange disease, was causing us to be overprotective. As parents we were overbearing, too cautious, too shielding. For Max and me our children were our lives. We loved them more than words could ever describe. They were our future, and to think that something bad could ever happen to them made us "different" parents. Unconditional love for our sons sustained us.

After the physical well-being of our sons came their upbringing. As Europeans, as old-fashioned Jewish parents, we tried to raise our sons as best as we knew how. Each of us reached back into our own childhoods as we remembered them; these memories became our guidelines. Max and I grew up in very different times, in different environments. Max was the youngest of ten children, born when his father was already in his late fifties. Being the baby in the family, he was the darling of his parents and siblings. Pampered and spoiled, he was barely twelve when his father died. Max adored his mother. He always talked about the high respect and love he had for his parents. I, on the other hand, grew up in a highly disciplined household. Being the older of two children, I had to behave and perform to the high expectations of my authoritarian father. My younger brother was given much more tolerance. My mother, who was quite lenient and very understanding, never disciplined me; this she left to my father. In spite of his strictness, I adored my father just as much as I loved my mother for her wisdom and tolerance. When our children were born, Max left the disciplining in my hands. I was at home, Max was at work. He left the house at 6 a.m. while the children were still asleep and returned many times when our sons were already in bed. And so I became the disciplinarian, not by choice but by default. Whenever our boys misbehaved, it was I who had to be the "bad one," the one to reprimand or punish them. Today, in retrospect, I realize that maybe I expected too much of our sons (like my father expected too much of me). Maybe I was too strict. I acted according to the only standards I knew. When Max was told about some of the disciplinary problems, he always supported me. He knew how important the proper upbringing of our sons was. He also knew that he had to work and was not home to act or react to our sons' misbehavior. Both Benno and Gene were good children, and their misbehaviors were the usual ones for boys. Our household had rules. Both Max and I felt strongly that our sons should adhere to these rules. We made it clear to our children how much we loved them, but expected them to grow up with high moral standards. The values that we tried to instill in them and teach them were the values both Max and I grew up with. Sometimes we had the feeling that we were fighting a losing battle.

In Cincinnati our children grew up among children of survivors like us. The neighborhood we lived in was a mixed one, but most of their school friends were Jewish. Except for children of survivors, most of their friends came from upper-middle-class families. Some lived in spacious homes with two or more cars, with maids and gardeners. It is normal for children to compare their own surroundings to those of their friends. Max and I never tried to hide the fact that we had to struggle in this country, and we let our children know that we wanted to provide them with a safe and good home. They understood and accepted these facts. We were members of an Orthodox synagogue, and our children attended services and religious school. Our home was traditional. We tried very hard to have a good Jewish home. We stressed in our sons the importance of religion, tradition, and heritage.

Once we left Cincinnati we were faced with different problems. When we came to Oak Ridge, Tennessee, in 1964, Benno was thirteen and Gene was nine. All of a sudden we were in a place with less than 1 percent Jews. Now most of our sons' friends were not Jewish, and none of our neighbors were Jewish. Jewish education for our sons became a priority. We were living in the Bible Belt, and our sons needed the security of a Jewish home and Jewish education more than ever. Our children made wonderful friends and were welcome in their homes. Yet our home was not typically American. We spoke Polish and German, and I still prepared European dishes. Both Max and I spoke with European accents. All this must have been very different for our sons compared to the homes of their friends. Max and I understood that, like all children, our sons wanted to blend in. This was true with each wave of immigrants to this country. But we were not only immigrants and refugees; we were survivors of the Holocaust.

Both Benno and Gene were good students, and both were active in school, in sports, and in extracurricular activities. They had many friends, and we noticed how differently the American young people behaved. We were especially struck by their lack of respect for their elders. Their parents were much less demanding and much more permissive. We hoped that these negatives would not influence our children. From the time they were little, we emphasized punctuality in our home. Our meals were eaten together and on time. It was important for us as a family to partake of our food together. "None of our friends have to be home at a certain time," we heard our sons say. Max used to answer, "We do not run a restaurant. We eat together at a given time." We also explained to our children the need to know if for one reason or another they could not be home on time. "We worry about you. Please call us should you be late," we told them. Indeed they called us whenever they could not be home on time. Punctuality did not only mean "to be on time," it meant also respect for our rules.

Life in Oak Ridge was also different from what we had known in Cincinnati in other respects. In Oak Ridge, the emphasis was on education, not on material things. What one knew rather than what one possessed was more important. We had stressed education from early childhood. Both of us wanted our sons to seek the profession they wanted, to go into the world and become independent. As painful as it was to see them leave the nest, I wanted them to leave the small town of Oak Ridge and experience life in the real world. For Max our sons' departures were traumatic. He wanted them close by. But in order for them to grow, they needed to find themselves, to expand and seek their own purpose in life. There was also the problem that Oak Ridge had such a small Jewish population. Our sons were dating, but there were too few Jewish girls their age. From early on they had heard Max and me talk about the importance of marrying someone Jewish, the significance of Jewish continuity. "I want my grandchildren to be Jewish," he used to say. Max was much less traditional than I, yet he was adamant about his sons marrying somebody who shared their religion. He spoke about it openly and frequently. Our sons grew up in a Jewish home and were aware of their heritage. We were well aware that now we lived in the United States with an open society and a lot of assimilation. Both of us were as liberal as people can be. Yet for us, Judaism was our past, present, and future, an integral part of our lives. Our sons understood and respected our feelings.

Max lived to see his older son, Benno, married under the chuppah. He danced at Benno and Joy's wedding in June 1986, elated that he was able to partake in their happy union. How happy he would have been to be at the wedding of Gene and Caroline in September 1991. They were married one and a half years after Max passed away. Caroline became Jewish by choice. She and Gene were married by our rabbi, Victor Rashkovsky, from Oak Ridge in Caroline's grandmother's backyard. Max was missed terribly, but his spirit was present.

Wedding of Benno and Joy,
June 15, 1986.

Gene and Caroline at their
wedding, September 22, 1991.

It is impossible for me to tell how much our sons have been influenced by our past. From early childhood they heard us say, "One does not waste food. We eat what has been put on our plates." They heard the word *hunger*, but fortunately they never knew what that meant. They were never starving. They were always well dressed, because to Max and me first impressions mattered. We knew from past experiences that people are judged by the way they look. The German saying "Kleider machen Leute" (clothes make the man [and the woman]), expresses it best. Our children were never deprived of important things, but we lived modestly and instilled modesty in them. We had learned to appreciate and cherish everything that life had bestowed on us and tried to teach this to our sons. Not only did they learn not to waste food and to be frugal, they learned to save for the future. As I had been taught *tzedakah* (righteous giving and living) from my parents, we taught

For the Love of Our Children

our sons the significance of sharing with those less fortunate. My father used to say, "It is better to give than to receive."

Whenever people ask me, "How and when did you tell your children about the Holocaust?" I have to admit that I have no easy answer. Max and I never hid the fact that we were in ghettos and concentration camps. Our sons saw the tattoo on my left arm and as soon as they were old enough to understand, I told them what it meant. We did not dwell on it, did not go into details. Max and I were fearful that our children might be hurt by what they heard from us. We actually wanted to wait until they were more mature. Of course Benno and Gene heard us talk among ourselves, heard us discuss some of the past with other survivors. My father used to share with them some of his Holocaust experiences, and so did Uncle Nathan. Not until our sons started to ask us questions did they have the whole picture. They must have been in their teens when the first questions about the Holocaust came up. At that time we told them about our years of persecution and anguish. Nobody knows how difficult it was to talk to our children about these painful events. Max especially had a hard time and never really could talk to his sons about his suffering. Each time he tried to talk he broke down and cried. It was agony for him and must have been agonizing to our children. The most painful moments of his life he never shared with our sons. Somehow it was easier for me to share my life, although it was tearing me up inside. Both Benno and Gene read books and took college courses on the Holocaust. The more they read, the more details they wanted to hear from us. Those opportunities presented themselves when I was speaking in school or to a group—when I was speaking to strangers.

In 1973, when I was invited to speak at the Oak Ridge High School about my experiences during World War II, Benno was home from college for spring break. I asked Benno if he would come with me, warning him that this might be a painful experience. He came and sat down in the back of a large room, where over one hundred students in the Combined Studies class were assembled. As I spoke to the students, I had to think of my son sitting in the back of the room listening to his mother's Holocaust experiences. How much pain did I inflict on him? How would he handle all the gruesome details? I did not dare to look in his direction, afraid to see his pain.

This must have been a terrible experience for him, but he never said a word. All I knew was the excruciating pain in my heart. But now Benno knew many more details about my life.

Gene heard a great deal about World War II and the Holocaust while spending a year in Denmark. In his senior year of high school, while he lived as an AFS exchange student with a family on Fyn in Denmark, he learned that one of their relatives had been directly involved with the saving of Danish Jews during World War II. The relative lived in Copenhagen and drove a taxi. When in October 1943 the Nazis wanted to deport all Jews from Denmark, the Danish underground organized a rescue operation to save the Danish Jews. This man was driving Jews at night in his taxi to the seashore, where boats were waiting to smuggle them to Sweden. Almost six thousand Jews were rescued by courageous Danes. Decent people, like this taxi driver, risked their lives to save complete strangers. When Max and I were in Denmark in 1973, we stayed overnight in the apartment of the widow of the taxi driver. "Aunt Ewa" told us many details about the rescue operation. Her husband never mentioned this to her until the war was over. He did not want to endanger her if he should be caught by the Nazis during the rescue operation. Upon his return, Gene accompanied me to the Oak Ridge chapter of the Lion's Club, where I had been invited to speak about the Holocaust. This is how he learned details about my Holocaust experiences.

When our sons were young, most of their friends were also children of survivors; very few of them had grandparents, uncles, aunts, and cousins. Once Benno and Gene made friends in school, they saw another picture. Their friends had many relatives, while they had only my father and my uncle. Max and I felt the need for family deeply. That is why we adopted Uncle Nathan. There was a vacuum in our and our children's lives. This we felt during holidays and celebrations. At Benno's and Gene's Bar Mitzvah we missed our family. There were too few to share happy moments with us. How did they feel? We told them what had happened to our families. I told them that my father had lost not only his parents but also his wife and his son, his sister and brother. They knew that Uncle Nathan had lost his wife and two children. They were directly affected by these losses, by the Holocaust.

Friends had to compensate for family we did not have; friends became our extended family. Maybe Max and I felt the loss of our family members much more than our children who never really knew them. With love we tried to fill this gap, showing our sons how grateful we were for our "small" family.

At home, our children were taught to be tolerant, to respect people who were different. They were told of the many non-Jewish men and women who had risked their lives during the war to save a Jewish child, woman, or man. They heard us speak of Max's sister, Hela, who owed her life to a Polish Catholic, Stefan Pruc. We tried to instill in our sons the same ethical and moral values that our parents instilled in us. Our wish was for our sons to grow up as decent and good human beings who would carry on our tradition. We hoped that both Benno and Gene would emerge physically and mentally "whole" in spite of growing up in the shadow of the Holocaust. We were so lucky that both of them had the inner strength to live meaningful and productive lives.

It is not for me to praise my children. My dear mother used to say, "The praise should come from other people." But I know that Benno and Gene are devoted sons. They are both caring men, respected and loved by their families as well as friends. Max would have said, "Each of my sons is a mensch." I am counting my blessings for having such a loving family, for having lived to enjoy my four grandchildren. Each time I look at them, I think, "If only Max could have lived to see them grow up, to love them and enjoy them as much as I do."

Chapter 9

MORITZ RYCZKE—FOREVER YOUNG

Dear Melanie Marie and Michael Max,

In chapter 4 I told you about Papa's youth, Holocaust experiences, and liberation. Now let me tell you a little more about Papa's adventures after he left Germany in 1949.

When we, your Oma and Opa (Grandma and Grandpa), left Germany for the United States, my father, Moritz Ryczke, remained in Germany. He had a business to run and was in no great hurry to leave Hannover. Opa and I arrived in the United States in July 1948; my father arrived thirteen months later. In September 1949 he came to Cincinnati for the High Holy Days and met for the first time his uncle Max Jacobs and his cousins Rose, Philip, and Izzy, as well as his aunt Yetta.

My father was fifty-two years old, full of vigor and bursting with energy. Ready to start a new life in the United States, his first steps were to locate his old Danzig business friends who emigrated before the war. He was thinking

Max Jacobs and his wife, Yetta, Cincinnati, Ohio, 1946.

of going into the business he knew best—the seed business. But in the United States the seed business was predominantly in non-Jewish hands. The few Jewish merchants acted mainly as agents. My father was told, in no uncertain terms, that without a large amount of money and without the knowledge of the English language, he had no chance to succeed. To my father this was a blow. "I should have remained in Germany," he told us. "There at least I was in my environment, had my own business, and could communicate with people."

In May 1950 he returned to Hannover, where he soon realized that Germany was not the place for him. Germany was now flooded with German refugees from the East who needed help more than Jews. My father liquidated his firm in Hannover and returned to New York. My father's friends, the Weiners, took good care of him. Most of all they wanted him to find somebody; they wanted him to get married. Mr. and Mrs. Weiner spent a few weeks each summer in the Catskills. In July 1950 Mrs. Weiner got sick and asked my father to go with her husband to the Catskills. It would give him an opportunity to meet more people. He needed to relax; he needed a change of pace. Lo and behold, he met a chic divorcee and fell head over heels in love. Her name was Bella. She was born in the United States but raised in Germany. Her parents came to the United States from Romania, found life here too difficult, and returned to Berlin. She and my father could speak German with each other; they had a similar cultural background. We received a long letter in which he told us all about Bella and enclosed a snapshot. Both of us were delighted that he had finally found someone to love, to share his life. But first he had to find a way to earn a living. With no prospects to go into the seed business, he started to look for other possibilities. One thing was certain—he would not go to work for somebody. He was still too independent and wanted to be his own boss. There was no compromising. Moritz Ryczke had not changed; he had to be in control.

My father was in touch with my uncle Heniek Hammer (they had come to the United States on the same boat) and learned that Heniek had settled on a chicken farm in Vineland, New Jersey. My father bought an old Plymouth in New York and drove with Bella to Vineland. For many Jewish immigrants, chicken farms provided a modest income. My father was a city man; he loved the excitement of large cities. Would he be able to live on a farm? After visiting his brother-in-law, he wrote us a long letter. "If I decide to become a chicken farmer, I will not have to worry about the language. I can speak to the chickens in German, Polish, or even Russian. And I would be my own boss. If Heniek Hammer can be a chicken farmer, so can I." We did not know enough about the egg business to advise him. It would have to be my father's decision. He returned to New Jersey to look for a small farm. He would invest the money that he made in his business in Germany in a chicken farm. While driving near Vineland, he found out that an old friend from Danzig, Adam Engel, had a chicken farm in Risley, New Jersey, near Estell Manor, twenty minutes from Vineland. He and Bella visited him and his wife, Lena, in Risley. Adam Engel mentioned to my father that not far from his place was a small farm for sale. It had a two-story house and an old chicken coop. He took my father to the owner, and my father purchased the farm. The property consisted of five acres, space enough for raising chickens. Because it was not in a city like Vineland, the price of the property was much lower, and this too was one of the reasons my father agreed to purchase it. He did not have too much money to spend. Bella, too, looked forward to a quiet life, after living in New York for many years.

The farm in Estell Manor was purchased in February 1951, a few weeks after your daddy, our first son, Benno, was born. On March 16, 1951, my father and Bella were married in Trenton, New Jersey, and soon after they moved to Estell Manor. My father, the city dweller, became a chicken farmer. Once he made the decision to be a farmer, he became a model farmer. He put all his energy into making his place efficient. Little did he know what was involved. A new coop had to be built. Hatchlings had to be purchased and raised under special lamps. Once the chicks were large enough, they had to be inoculated and transferred into coops. When they started to lay eggs, he had to collect, wash, sort, and pack them. My father was getting up at 3 a.m., and his work was not finished until 10 p.m. He had no free day—there were no Sundays or holidays. Dealing with living things required every minute of his time year round. With no outside help, work on the farm was very hard. But my father did not complain. From the very beginning Bella told him that the farm was his business and that the household was her responsibility. She would not help with farm work. When I came to Estell Manor with my six-month-old baby in August of 1951, I hardly recognized my father. This once dashing and elegant man looked like a *muselman* in a concentration camp.[1] He had lost so much weight that one could see his ribs sticking out. With little sleep, and worried about his chickens, who quite often got sick, he was physically exhausted. Max and I decided that he could not go on like this. He had to hire someone to help him with the farm work or the farm would be sold. My father would not hear about selling the farm, so we started to look for someone who would live in the little house on the property and help my father with the work. Within a few days we found Ralph. He worked for my father for many years. Never again would we allow my father to do all the physical work. Another problem developed. When my father bought this farm in 1951, eggs sold for one dollar per dozen. When his chickens started to lay eggs, prices dropped to seventy cents, then sixty cents, and by the end of 1952 to fifty cents. Feed prices remained the same. Financially the situation did not look good. Every dollar from the sale of eggs had to be reinvested. Coops needed constant repair, and soon feed prices began to rise while egg prices fell. My father would not give up. He found a way of feeding his chickens with the right combination of mash and other products. His chickens started to "produce" huge eggs. This method was written up in a New Jersey poultry magazine under the title, "Moritz Ryczke Is a 'Big Egg' Man."[2] His farm was immaculate and the coops were clean. The former seed exporter from Danzig became a model chicken farmer. Once a perfectionist, always a perfectionist.

By 1960 most of the chicken farms were losing money and were being sold. But my father would not quit. Being deep in debt, he was on the verge of bankruptcy. The feed merchants demanded money and would not wait. My father would never declare bankruptcy. We lent him the money to pay off his feed debts. When Uncle Heniek sold his farm to a land developer in Vineland, my father had to be realistic. In 1964, after thirteen years of farming, he sold the farm. Every penny he got from the sale went to pay off debts. His only income was now the monthly restitution pension from Germany. Now friction between Bella and my father grew. After the sale of the farm, they rented a beautiful apartment in Vineland. But Bella wanted to move to Florida; my father did not. My father wanted to leave the United States and live in Israel; Bella did not want to leave the United States. I was getting desperate telephone calls from my father about their marital problems. I did not want to get involved, hoping that they would somehow solve their problems. What I did not know was that my father had changed. He was taking so much medication that many times he was overdrugged. Driving with him became hazardous. He was also a chain smoker and that affected his heart. His doctor ordered him to give up cigarettes, and my father stopped cold turkey. He always had tremendous willpower. But he also suffered from the years in concentration camps, and Bella could not understand his changing moods. He often became depressed and then took more drugs. It was a vicious cycle. We saw my father at least once a year. I did not know my father anymore. I loved him with all my heart and wanted to help him, but I was helpless. He became jealous of Opa. I was caught in the middle between my father and my husband. My father was now seventy-two years old. He had angina and had developed prostate problems. Surgery was necessary. He told Bella that she did not have to come with him to the hospital in Philadelphia; his daughter would take care of him. Not wanting to hurt his feelings, Opa and I agreed that I should fly to Philadelphia and stay with him. I left my husband and our two young sons in Oak Ridge in order to be with my father. The nurses in the hospital were telling me stories that were hard to believe. My father, who was always impatient, would not wait for nurses to bring his food. He got dressed, left the hospital, and went shopping for things he liked to eat. When surgery was scheduled, he demanded that it be on time. If he had to wait, he would get off the operating table and return to his room. And he did. When he finally had his surgery, there were complications. Unfortunately, the surgeon, a well-known urologist, had developed arthritis in his hands.

In 1970 my father went to Bad Nauheim in Germany. He suffered with angina, and the doctors told him to rest for a few weeks. The German restitution paid for the treatments in Germany, and so he went, leaving Bella, his wife, at home. When he returned, Bella was gone. Their marriage had been on the rocks for many years. Bella could not understand the pain and suffering my father experienced. She could not accept his survivor mentality, as she called it. And so she divided all their possessions and left him. This was a terrible blow to his ego. I left for Vineland, New Jersey, to help him decide what to do next. Opa and I asked him to come to Oak Ridge, where we could take care of him. My father sold everything he had and we drove together to Oak Ridge. But this city was too small for him. He needed excitement and stimulation. He wanted some social life.

Papa was always an adventurous person. He decided to go to Israel and establish some kind of life there. My father never did anything halfway. To go to Israel, one needed to know Hebrew. At the age of seventy-five, he enrolled in an Ulpan (intensive Hebrew language school) in Israel to learn the modern language. My father spent two semesters there, and this must have been the happiest time for him. I do not know how much Hebrew he actually learned, but he made friends, had a full social life, and was falling in and out of love. He finally obtained his religious divorce *(get)* and was traveling and enjoying life. He still came for the holidays to Oak Ridge and entertained us with his stories of adventure.

By nature my father was the most generous person. He always showered on us the most beautiful gifts, especially on his two grandsons, Benno and Gene. My father had a special relationship with Gene. With Gene he shared many of his war experiences. My father was a great storyteller. Gene loved to listen to the many stories he told him.

After my father moved to Israel in 1971, Gene visited him twice; this was a special time for both of them. Opa and I visited my father in Israel in 1973 and found out that he had planned to marry his landlady. Unfortunately, she died suddenly. Again he was alone. His last visit to Oak Ridge was for Passover in 1978. He was in love again and wanted us to invite his lady friend. They met in Switzerland. She came from Germany and resided in Florida. To please my father we invited her to stay with us for a week. They were happy and planned to travel to Switzerland together. My father left Oak Ridge in July to meet his friend in Europe. Something went wrong between them and he returned to Israel. She did not want to live in Israel; he did not want to live in Florida. It reminded us of the dilemma with Bella. He soon found another love in Israel, but his health declined.

In January 1979 my father came down with shingles and asked me to come to be with him. In February, Opa and I traveled to Israel. We found my father pale and in constant pain. But still he wanted to be in control of his life. He wanted me near him at all times. We did not leave him alone in the apartment for a minute. I truly felt that it was my duty, my obligation as his daughter, to take care of him, to make him feel comfortable. Opa and I understood only too well how frightened and how lonely he felt. He was planning a trip to Switzerland for the summer; this gave him something positive to think about. When his doctor suggested that he might want to move into a retirement home, we took a taxi and went to Kfar Saba to visit some homes. "I will never live among old people. My mind is still young and so is my spirit," was my father's reply after we visited one of the homes. There was no retirement living for my "young" eighty-two-year-old father. He knew what he did not want. When we suggested that he return to Oak

Ridge with us, he refused at first. One day later he said, "I think that if I could find an apartment in Oak Ridge with a view of the mountains, I would consider moving to Oak Ridge." I was elated. I knew that he was thinking of the Garden Apartments, where one could see the Cumberland Mountains. In Oak Ridge, Opa and I would be able to take care of him.

On March 12, 1979, the Monday before Purim, the three of us, Papa, Opa, and I went to a special bakery in Tel Aviv to purchase my father's favorite pastries. He was a connoisseur of good wine, cognac, and sweets and wanted the very best stuff for Purim. While we walked on Allenby Street, he had to stop frequently. He was experiencing chest pains, yet he continued to walk and did not want us to call a taxi. When we passed a dress shop, my father said to me, "I want you to go in and find a white wool suit, just like the one your mother used to have." He wanted me to be as elegantly dressed as his wife (my mother) had been. This was not the time for shopping; the streets were crowded with children, Purim was in the air. In the evening we sat down to consume the tasty pastry and drink good cognac. Suddenly my father said, "Why am I alive? Why did my seventeen-year-old son have to die? Why could I not protect my Benno?" The thoughts and memories of his son tormented him; he never stopped thinking of him.

Tuesday, March 13, was Purim; the three of us looked forward to a festive day. Early in the morning I heard my father leave his room for the bathroom. A few minutes later he was back in his room and called for me. My father was standing near the window clasping his chest. I knew right away that he was in pain; I gave him his nitro pill and led him to his bed. As my father lay down, there was again a strong pain to his chest. I called out to our landlady to telephone for an ambulance. Another sharp pain followed. I held him in my arms and suddenly I heard a rattling noise. He wanted to say something but could not. I was still holding on to him when his breathing stopped. Opa and I took turns administering mouth-to-mouth resuscitation. There was no sign of an ambulance; it was Purim, a semi-holiday, and they took their time. When we were unable to restore his breathing, we realized he was gone. I was in utter shock, but my beloved father did not die alone. He was surrounded by those who loved him. The many years of suffering took their toll; his heart gave out. I wanted to be alone with him for the last

MORITZ RYCZKE—FOREVER YOUNG

time. I had to say good-bye, I had to kiss him one more time and ask for his forgiveness. If I ever hurt him in any way, I never did it intentionally. I loved him much too much. I knew his strengths; I also knew his shortcomings. And I will always remember him for the loving, selfless father he was. He left behind a good name.

There is another thing I need to mention about Papa, my father. In August 1971 our son Benno was visiting my Danzig school friend, Janka Waril, in Stockholm. He wrote to us the following words: "Janka [Waril] told me that she knows a man here named Joseph Bornstein who told her that Papa carried him on his back near the end of the war when he was unable to walk. He asked Janka if she knew Papa from Danzig and Janka told him that she did. Mr. Bornstein is close to fifty years old and remembers that Papa saved his life. He may call up here before I leave."

Our Benno never met Mr. Bornstein, but I did in 1991 when I was in Sweden. He told me how my father carried him; he told me that without his help he would have been shot during the death march in April 1945. My father never mentioned it to me until I told him about Benno's letter. He said that this young man reminded him of his son; maybe somebody would have done the same for his son. Mr. Bornstein never forgot "Mr. Ryczke from Danzig who saved his life."

Your great-grandfather, my father, Moritz Ryczke, was a man with a big heart, a man of integrity, a man of courage and guts, generous and most charitable, witty and entertaining, for whom family always came first. Wise and intelligent, daring and sometimes reckless, an optimist all his life, he also was uncompromising and opinionated. Strict but fair, he loved to be in control and the center of attention. A man of perfection who expected others to be perfect, too, he had a brilliant mind but sometimes misjudged situations. Quick-tempered, he quickly calmed down. Respected by family and friends, unconditionally loved by his wife and children, Moritz Ryczke was a good and loving person.

Chapter 10

Malka Kimmelman (1868–1925)

Dear Melanie Marie,

Your birth was one of our greatest joys. When your daddy, Benno Kimmelman, called us early on April 3, 1988—it must have been 5 a.m.—to tell us that we had a granddaughter, your Opa and I were ecstatic. We had two sons, and now we had lived to become grandparents of a little girl. We were thrilled that you were named after your Opa's mother, Malka, which in Hebrew means "queen." Your parents have chosen a very beautiful name, Melanie, with the middle name of Marie (in Hebrew, Morit) after my father. Malka was also the name of Opa's little daughter, who perished with her mother during the Holocaust.

Your great-grandmother Malka Kimmelman was born in 1868 and died in 1925 on the last day of Passover. You were born on the second day of Passover. Malka Kimmelman came from a rabbinic family, Weinberg. I know only what Opa told me about her. She married Yitzhak Kimmelman in 1883; he was fifteen years older and she was his second wife. His first wife died, and he was left with a young daughter. As Opa told me, "My father and mother were very much in love. He was traveling and always sending love letters to my mother." Malka and Yitzhak had ten children. As previously mentioned, the oldest, Yechiel, born in 1888, died in Siberia in 1908. Next came a daughter, Regina, born in 1889, who died in 1938. She never married. The next child was another daughter, Chava (Eva), born in 1890; she died in the Piotrkow ghetto in 1941. She was married to Shaja Tuszyner; they had two sons: Heniek and Abram. Heniek survived the war in the Soviet Union; he lived later in Poland and died in 1996. Only Abram is still alive; he resides in Tel Aviv. There were a few babies born who did not survive. Then came a son, Leib (Leon), after whom your daddy is named. Born in 1895, he and his wife, Gucia, perished in Treblinka in 1942. In 1900 a daughter was born, Hanna (Hela). She escaped from the Piotrkow ghetto in 1942, helped by a Polish friend by the name of Piotrowski, and survived as an Aryan. She died in 1965. I visited her grave in Krosno in 1990. After Hela, another son was born, Moshe (Michael), in 1902. Michael died in Toronto, Canada, in 1974. He, too, survived on Aryan papers. The last and tenth child was your Opa, Mordechai Kimmelman. He was Malka's baby, her favorite child. And he adored his mother. Opa used to tell me how proud he was when he walked with his mother, who was tall and very beautiful, to the synagogue each Shabbat. Malka Kimmelman was a devout Jewess; she wore the traditional "sheytel," a wig worn by Orthodox Jewish women after marriage. Covering the hair with a sheytel was a sign of modesty and was widely practiced by Orthodox women in prewar Eastern Europe. Opa used to tell me how he watched his mother comb her gray hair (she became gray early in life), before she put on her sheytel.

He loved everything about her, and when she died at the age of fifty-seven he was only seventeen years old. He felt her loss for many years. Opa used to tell me that for eleven months he went to the synagogue early in the morning before school to say Kaddish for his mother. And in 1934, when his little daughter was born, he named her Malka, after his beloved mother. And now you bear this meaningful name. Opa saw in you the mother and daughter he loved, and all this love he transferred to you. Melanie dear, I wish

I could tell you more about your Opa's mother; I am trying to recall all I heard from Opa. She was the one who kept the business going after her husband died. She kept the family together and instilled in all her children the importance of family. After she died, Regina took over the family restaurant. She stepped into her mother's shoes and took care of Opa. She, too, died at an early age; she was only forty-nine.

Opa used to tell me that at his mother's funeral crowds of poor people who had been helped by her walked to the cemetery. They lost in Malka a most generous and kind benefactor. You bear the name of a beautiful and honorable person.

Opa's daughter, Malka (Maryla), was much loved by her parents. And, as an only child, she was pampered and had a loving home. Opa tried in vain to save her when the threat of ghetto liquidation and deportation became a reality. Malka looked too "Jewish"; she had black hair and black eyes, which would have given her away. Nobody wanted to hide her. Opa never really got over the loss of his daughter; it haunted him to his dying days. With your birth, this little girl's memory is honored—Opa saw in you his little girl.

You are my oldest granddaughter, my first grandchild. In your name, Malka, I see the continuation of two lives, lives of people that your Opa loved. Their memories will live on, because your dear parents were wise and thoughtful to give you this beautiful name. The day of your naming was one of the most important days for Opa. He was already ill. In order to travel to New York the doctor gave him a blood transfusion to boost his diminishing strength. He gathered every bit of stamina to make this last trip to be present at your naming, to be called up to the Torah during Shabbat services and hear the name Malka given to his first granddaughter. Physically and emotionally he relived this moment many times. He talked about it with great happiness. Yes, my dearest Melanie, you gave your Opa many happy moments. How proud he would have been of you, his little Malka, who grew up to become a kind, thoughtful, and beautiful young woman.

So now you know a little about the women you were named after. The story of the life of your great-grandfather, Moritz Ryczke, I have written down in my letter to you and your brother, Michael.

Chapter 11

ESTHER CYRULICZAK/JAKUBOWSKI RYCZKE (1872–1942) AND GITEL/GENIA HAMMER RYCZKE (1897–1942)

Dear Eleanor (Ellie) Moore,

You were born on Monday, March 1, 1999. It was the eve of the happy Jewish holiday of Purim, a holiday in which children especially delight. When I held you in my arms for the first time and looked at your beautiful face, my joy was endless. I was grateful that your dear parents carried on the tradition and made you the bearer of two good Hebrew names, Esther and Gitel. First, let me introduce my grandma Esther.

ESTHER CYRULICZAK/JAKUBOWSKI RYCZKE

Esther Cyruliczak/Jakubowski Ryczke was born in 1872 in Slupca, a small Polish town. At that time this part of Poland was under Russian rule. Her parents were Moshe Avram and Rosa Cyruliczak; Grandma had three younger brothers. In the town of Slupca lived also a Polish Catholic family by the name of Cyruliczak. Esther's grandfather, Jacob Cyruliczak, encountered many problems because of the other Cyruliczak. Officials in this small town constantly mixed these two men up. He decided to change his and his family's name to Jakubowski. So Esther's family in Slupca was known as Cyruliczak/Jakubowski. Not until 1918, when Poland regained her independence, was the family name officially changed to Jakubowski. At the end of the nineteenth century, Grandma's oldest brother, Max (Mordechai), came to the United States and changed his name to Jacobs. This was the English version of Jakubowski. It was the family of Uncle Max Jacobs who brought Opa and me to the United States in 1948.

Grandma Esther was eighteen when she met a handsome, tall man. She was a petite woman. His name was Efraim Ryczke; they were married in Slupca in 1892. Efraim was a grain merchant just like his father, Benyamin, and my father later. He lived in the nearby town of Kolo and came to Slupca on business. The young couple lived for some time in Slupca, in the house of Grandma Esther's father. Two of their three children were born there— their daughter, Rosa, and my father, Moritz (Moshe). The youngest son, Heinrich (Hersh), was born in Poznan (Posen) in 1907. They later moved to the city of Kalisz.

Here my memories of Grandma Esther begin. From the age of six, I and my younger brother, Benno, visited my grandparents each year during the Passover holidays. Both sets of our grandparents resided in Kalisz, but we always stayed with our paternal grandparents. My first memories are of Grandma's kitchen. She always allowed me to participate in the preparations for the holidays. Grandma's cakes were the best. I can still see her sitting on a tall stool with a huge bowl in her lap. She was beating a large amount of egg whites for the traditional Passover sponge cake. There were no electric beaters; Grandma was using two forks. As she was adding sugar to the egg whites, a foaming white mountain emerged, yet it never ran over the rim of the bowl. The best thing was the licking of the bowl; my brother and I could hardly wait to taste the sweet mixture. Grandma allowed me to set the table; she included me in many holiday activities. It was Grandma who explained why certain dishes are served; she was my first teacher. She was never too busy to answer my questions, and I did ask many of them. Being with Grandma Esther was fun; it was fascinating and I felt always welcome.

For the Purim holiday, when it is customary among the Jewish people to exchange gifts of sweets, Grandma Esther sent boxes filled with cakes and goodies to us in Danzig. One of her specialties was a pastry filled with layers of apples, raisins, nuts, and preserves. She called it "flooden." I can still remember the taste of this delicious Purim treat.

Left to right: Unknown, Efraim Ryczke (father of Moritz), and Moritz Ryczke, in Bad Reinerz, 1929.

Grandpa Efraim traveled extensively and visited us in Danzig often. He was tall, over six feet, and had blond hair and light blue eyes. A big man, he towered over Grandma, who was not quite five feet tall. Grandma had dark brown eyes and black hair. Grandpa and Grandma were observant and very traditional. As a child I watched Grandpa pray each morning before breakfast. I was fascinated by the ritual—his large woolen prayer shawl and the black boxes with leather straps that he tied around his left arm and forehead. I asked Grandma for the meaning of this fascinating ritual; she told me that these small black boxes contain prayers and that what Grandpa was doing was very traditional for Jewish men. Only much later did I fully understand the deeper meaning of what I saw Grandpa practice. Grandpa suffered from asthma. Whenever he came to visit us, my father took him to see our family physician, Dr. Hans Bing. Both Grandpa and Grandma were his patients; they trusted him completely and followed his orders. I can still remember the medicine Grandpa took; it was called "Felsol." Every year when we traveled to Kalisz for the holidays, we took a large supply of Felsol for Grandpa.

My most memorable experiences were in the summer of 1933, when Grandma and Grandpa Ryczke invited me to spend a month with them. They were planning to spend some time at a resort in Wlodzimierzow, near Lodz. I was not quite ten years old and felt privileged to be invited. My grandparents also invited my uncle Heinrich Ryczke and his wife, Anni, who lived in Danzig. I traveled by train with them. Once we arrived in this beautifully secluded wooded resort, we were met by my grandparents. We were also joined by Aunt Rosa Ryczke Przedecka and her two daughters, Halina and Gina. My two cousins were older than I. They spoke only Polish and tried to teach me this difficult language. At home and with my grandparents I only spoke German. I only understood Polish phrases and spoke little. Speaking the language was hard. My accent was German, and I had a difficult time pronouncing certain words. Everybody made fun of my German accent; Grandma always defended me. The weeks went by quickly; I loved being with my family. Watching my older cousins dress up and flirt with the boys was new to me. I, too, wanted to be grown up.

One day Grandma Esther asked me if I would like to travel with her to the small towns where the Ryczke family came from. She knew how much I always wanted to know about our family; now I would have the opportunity to meet some of the family members. I would learn firsthand about the Ryczke family and would have Grandma all to myself. We left Grandpa with

Esther Ryczke and Gitel Ryczke

Spa guests in Bad Reichenhall, 1930. Esther is in the back row, fourth from right; to her right is Efraim Ryczke.

the Przedecki family in Wlodzimierzow and Grandma and I went off to explore the small Polish towns.

We traveled by bus. The first stop was Slupca, the birthplace of Grandma and of my father. It was much smaller than Kalisz and had unpaved streets and bleak-looking houses. In my mind I tried to compare it to Danzig, my hometown. How different this small town looked. Yet it fascinated me. As in Kalisz, I had noticed men in black coats with small black caps. I knew they were Jewish because I had asked about their attire already in Kalisz. Here in Slupca all the Jewish men looked alike. Both my grandfathers wore regular clothing. They wore a hat while outdoors, and in the house, as a sign of respect for God, they wore skullcaps. We came to the house where Grandma grew up. It was a large, gray, two-story building. The only people living in it were Grandma's stepmother, Teresa Jakubowski, and the house-keeper. As we entered the house, Grandma introduced me to her step-mother. She was seated in a large velvet armchair, in a dark room with the drapes drawn, and I could hardly see her features. She looked ancient to me. I kissed her cheek while Grandma told her who I was. They spoke in Yiddish, a language derived from Middle High German mixed with Hebrew. Because so many words sounded German, I could follow some of their conversation. Once we left the room, I wanted to know more about Teresa. Grandma told me that her own mother died while she was still a young girl; her father had married Teresa, his second wife, and they had one son, David. I also wanted to know why Teresa was sitting in a dark room. Grandma explained that Teresa's eyes hurt when she was in a room with a lot of light.

We stayed in Slupca for two days. Grandma showed me around town. She took me to the flour mill that belonged to her father. After his death, his son, David, managed the business. He later sold it. Our next visit was to Konin. Located at the Warta River, Konin, too, was a small town. The houses were larger, the streets wider than in Slupca. We stopped at a cousin's house. Grandma called her "Aunt Andzia" (*Ciocia* Andzia). She lived in a small one-story house near the bridge and had a millenary business. I was intrigued by all the hats that Aunt Andzia had in her shop. She even allowed me to try some on. Here I was not quite ten, looking at myself in the mirror wearing fancy hats. When our relative saw I liked hats, she gave me a royal blue beret. This was my very first hat (I still like wearing hats); I wore it during the entire trip with Grandma, until I arrived home. I felt so grown up, I could hardly wait to show the beret to my parents and brother.

After one day in Konin we proceeded by bus to Kolo. Again, it was only a short bus ride from Konin. All these small towns are in close proximity. Kolo was my grandpa's birthplace. His father, Benyamin Ryczke, had been dead for many years; his mother died while he was a small boy. Benyamin Ryczke married a second time and had another son, Aron. Grandma wanted me to meet Uncle Aron Ryczke and his wife, Hela. They had six children: three sons and three daughters. None of them were in Kolo when I visited them. Most of the children moved to Warsaw. Kolo was a little larger than Konin; it looked well kept. While visiting Uncle Aron, I was told that my father, as a young boy, had lived with them for a few years. Now I recalled my father telling me that he had lived in Kolo for some time while his grandfather Benyamin was still alive. He always spoke of Uncle Aron and Aunt

Hela with great respect; he especially recalled his grandfather Benyamin with fondness.

Grandma and I stayed in Kolo for a few days before returning to Danzig. We rode the train from Poznan to Danzig and talked about the many impressions, the places and people I met. She always answered my questions; some must have been quite childish. Her patience, kindness, and understanding made me love her very much. She was my friend and did not treat me like a child. Whenever I hear the names of the towns Slupca, Konin, and Kolo, I have to think about Grandma Esther.

In 1937, Uncle Heinrich and Aunt Anni divorced. It was painful for me; I loved both of them. A year later my grandparents Ryczke decided to move to Lodz, the large city where their daughter, Rosa, lived with her family. Uncle Heinrich, too, moved to Lodz. In 1938, my brother and I spent the last Passover holidays with them in Kalisz; soon afterward my grandparents left for Lodz.

When the Nazis entered the city of Lodz in September 1939, everything in the lives of the Jewish population changed. The Nazis were merciless; they beat and killed Jewish men in the streets. One day Uncle Markus Przedecki was caught while walking in the street. That night he returned home with open wounds on his back and head. He could neither sit nor lie down. Grandma Esther was afraid for Grandpa. She would not let him out of the house, not out of her sight. Soon Lodz was incorporated into the Reich—Germany proper—and the name of the city was changed to Litzmannstadt. New orders regarding Jews went into effect; Jews had to wear the yellow Star of David on their outer clothing. They were robbed of their freedom to walk the main street, to use any public transportation. Next, a ghetto was to be declared in the city of Lodz. This meant Grandma and Grandpa as well as Aunt Rosa and family would be forced to leave their apartment. At this point my grandparents decided to leave Lodz illegally. Together with Aunt Rosa and her family they rented an open wagon with a driver and, taking only a few of their possessions, left Lodz for the city of Tomaszow.

Tomaszow-Mazowiecki was not in the Reich; it was already part of conquered Poland called the General Government. Here Grandpa had business friends, and the family hoped to be able to live peacefully in this smaller city. They rented a three-room apartment and settled down. One month later, my family escaped from Warsaw and joined them in Tomaszow. After we were expelled from my hometown, Danzig, and the hardships in Warsaw, I was so happy to be again with my grandparents. They took us into their apartment, fed us, and kept us warm. In times of stress the closeness of family makes life easier. I felt safe, but not for very long.

In autumn of 1940, the Nazis created a ghetto in Tomaszow. We were separated. My grandparents, with Uncle Heinrich, moved to Poludniowa Street; my aunt and uncle Przedecki, with my two cousins, to Polna Street; and my family, to Zgorzelicka Street. With each day life in the ghetto became more difficult, more dangerous. I could see the changes in my dear grandparents. They were not even seventy, but they looked much older. Both were getting very thin. Grandpa's asthma attacks were getting worse; there was no medicine in the ghetto. There was constant hunger. I knew they did not have enough to eat; most of their possessions had been used to barter for some extra food. Yet every time my brother and I came to see them (we went as often as possible), Grandma always had a slice of bread for us or a boiled potato. This good-hearted woman would go hungry, but for us she always had a treat. My grandparents were always most generous and showered us with gifts before the war. Now, in such a difficult situation, their good character showed—they still were loving and giving.

My father and brother had been forced to work for the Germans outside the ghetto. They were told that their families would be protected in case of a resettlement. We were told that all Jews living in the ghetto who were not employed would be sent east to work. Grandma knew that Grandpa was too ill to do any hard work; she asked my father to find some work for her. She did not realize that the Germans only took young people to work.

The Tomaszow ghetto was to be resettled on October 31, 1942. The evening before, my whole family went to say good-bye to Grandma and Grandpa. I shall never forget that evening. We sat with our grandparents; they and my parents were crying. Nobody knew what to expect. When I embraced my grandma, she and I cried bitter tears. Would we see each other again? Where would the Nazis send us? Maybe we would meet soon and work hard until the war was over? It was a heartbreaking evening. This was the last time I saw my grandparents. To the last minute Grandma believed that even if she and Grandpa were sent away to work, she would be willing to work hard as long as she could protect Grandpa. She was the most devoted wife, mother, and grandmother. And my father had such high hopes that by working for the Germans he would be able to protect his family. His hopes were shattered the following day.

Not only was my father unable to protect his dear parents; he could not protect my mother either. Their fate had been sealed by the Nazis. With almost twenty thousand Jews in the Tomaszow ghetto, they were ordered to march to the railroad station. In crowded cattle cars they were sent not to work but to the death camp of Treblinka. As we later learned, within twenty-four hours all of them were gassed to death, their bodies burnt. Nothing but ashes remained of my beloved family. Only by sheer luck did I and Uncle Heinrich escape deportation. We were taken out of the columns to work. My father and brother, too, were spared, because they were at work outside the ghetto. We, the four remaining members of my family, were devastated. To see my dear ones disappear was too painful to describe. The pain was excruciating; I could not believe or understand what was happening. All that remained were memories of those I loved.

GITEL/GENIA HAMMER RYCZKE

Dear Ellie,

Let me now tell you about my beloved mother. Gitel/Genia Ryczke was born in Kalisz in 1897, the middle daughter of Shlomo and Sarah Hammer, my maternal grandparents. Her older sister was Golda/Gucia, the younger Haya/Hela. She also had two brothers: Stasiek, born in 1898, and Chaim/Heniek, born in 1906. The Hammer family resided for many generations in Kalisz, one of Poland's oldest cities. Located close to the German border, the Jews constituted 30 percent of the general population. At the time when my mother and her siblings grew up, Kalisz was in the part of Poland governed by the Russians. With its closeness to the German border, my mother spoke not only Polish and Russian but also fluent German. At home she spoke Yiddish or Polish.

As early as I can remember—I must have been six years old—my mother told me a true story about her war experiences. "I hope that we never have to live through a war. I certainly do not want to go through such experiences. When World War I broke out, I was seventeen years old. I had finished school and enjoyed a carefree life. My father was the owner of a lace and embroidery factory in Kalisz, and I had learned to do beautiful embroidery. As soon as the German army entered Kalisz in August 1914 at the outbreak of war, the city of Kalisz was set on fire. People fled the burning city, and so did my family. My parents gathered all five of us, in a hurry took a few of our possessions, and, in an open, horse-drawn wagon, the family escaped from Kalisz. We were seven; not much space was left in the wagon for our most important possessions, our bedding. I and my brother, Stasiek, were chosen to return to Kalisz at night, to retrieve pillows, blankets, and featherbeds. The nights were cool, and we had nothing to cover ourselves with. One night Stasiek and I returned to the city that was now occupied by German soldiers. What if we were stopped by a patrol? Stasiek was the brave one and dismissed my fears. When we arrived at our home at Piskorzewie Street, Stasiek went upstairs while I remained outside on the wagon. He began to throw pillows, featherbeds, and blankets out of the window while I caught them and arranged the bedding on the wagon. We had to work fast and leave the city as quickly as possible while it was still dark. As soon as the wagon was loaded, Stasiek drove our horse-drawn wagon through the city I knew so well. Many houses were still smoldering; even in darkness we could see the ruins of the burned-out houses and factories. The horrible smell of fire was everywhere. To avoid the German patrols, Stasiek took us through back streets and soon we were outside the city. My parents were happy to see us; they too were worried about our well-being, our safety. I shall never forget this night, this frightful ride to and from Kalisz." This story was embedded in my memory; I can still hear my dear mother telling it to me.

After a few weeks, the Hammer family and other inhabitants of Kalisz returned home. The factory was gone; it had been destroyed by fire. Only the house on Piskorzewie Street remained. As a young girl I wanted to hear more about my mother's life. "Once we lost the factory," she said, "my parents had to find some other source of income to support our family. Because I had learned to embroider, my father took orders from factories that had escaped the destruction. I worked hard many hours a day to help support my family. My father tried other business ventures; he never again had enough money to start manufacturing lace and embroideries.

"In 1915, my older sister, Gucia, met her future husband, David Lachman. They were married the same year and moved to Warsaw. I fell in love with a young Jewish man who was serving in the German army, and we were engaged to be married once the war was over. During the campaign, he was away quite often. By 1918 I learned that he had fallen in battle. I was devastated by the death of my boyfriend. In November 1918 Poland regained its independence. At home my parents were struggling but somehow managed to keep us as comfortable as possible. Some of my father's ventures met with success, others did not.

"One day in 1919, while I was sitting in a coffee house in Kalisz with my friend Karola Szajniak, her fiancé, Kazik Bloch, came to our table with a dashing young man. He was dark and handsome, of medium height, and elegantly dressed. Kazik introduced him as his distant cousin Moritz Ryczke. This is how I met your father. It was love at first sight. Your father had fiery black eyes with a twinkle, wavy black hair, and a mustache. He loved to dance and invited me out to wine and dine me. He was such a gentleman; I loved being with him. One day we went rowing. Kalisz was on the Prosna River, and the river ran through Kalisz's famous park. People were renting boats there, and your father and I planned to spend some time rowing along the river. When I tried to enter the rowboat, I missed it by a fraction and fell into the Prosna River. I did not know how to swim; your father, who was a good swimmer, saved me from drowning. From then on I was afraid to step into a rowboat." My mother never learned to swim, although we lived only minutes from the Baltic Sea in Zoppot. But she made sure that both I and my brother, Benno, learned to swim at an early age.

While living in Zoppot, my mother used to take me to a skating rink in the winter. She loved to skate; I did not. In the winter of 1927 the two of us went sleigh riding in Zoppot. The hills were covered with powdery white stuff; my mother led the sleigh, I sat behind her. Suddenly, on the way downhill she lost control and we were thrown out of the sleigh. I landed in the soft, fluffy snow, but my mother hit her head against a pole. Her forehead was bleeding. I was crying when I saw my mother hurt. She was taken home, and a doctor came to take care of her wound. It was only a cut, and in a few days mother was all right. That was the last time mother and I went sleigh riding; this incident left her too afraid.

My father left Kalisz for Danzig in 1919. At that time my parents were engaged, and in 1921 my mother followed him to Danzig. They were married in Zoppot in September 1921, where I was born two years later.

When I was a little girl of four, I loved to watch my mother getting dressed up. She had an exquisite taste for clothes, and it was a thrill for me to look at her in her beautiful dresses. My mother was tall and had a full figure. Pitch-black hair, brown eyes, very shapely legs—she was a picture of a lady. Mother was nearsighted but did not like to wear glasses. She and my father loved to go dancing at the Zoppot Kasino-Hotel, and I sat at the table and watched and admired my parents. I also remember my mother's addiction to roulette at the Zoppot Kasino. She used to go there in the afternoons, while I took walks with my nanny. Sometimes she won, sometimes she lost. I recall one evening, I must have been four years old. Mother returned from the casino in tears. She had lost a substantial amount of money. My father, who was commuting by train from Zoppot to Danzig, where his office was, found my mother crying when he came home that evening. He did not say anything. All he asked mother to do was to tear up her casino membership card. She never entered the casino again. But she did find another source of entertainment—cards. She learned to play bridge and became an avid bridge player. I remember card parties in our home—men played with men, women with women. Men played mostly poker, while the women played bridge.

In January 1928 my brother, Benno, was born. Soon afterward we moved from Zoppot to Danzig. I was five and soon started school in the big city. We still spent our summers at the seashore in Zoppot and took boat rides and explored the Kashubian hills. During the summer of 1930, mother and I took a boat ride to the Hel peninsula. I still remember the name of the boat, *Jadwiga*. It was a sunny Sunday. Father decided to stay at home with my little brother while mother and I went for a pleasure ride. It was an ideal day for a boat ride. We left in the morning and would be back in the afternoon. This ride is still quite vivid in my mind. While we were one hour at sea, a storm broke out. Lightning and thunder and a strong wind kept our boat rocking. The waves were becoming huge, water was reaching the upper deck. I became hysterical and cried out, "Ich will nicht sterben" (I don't want to die). Mother tried to comfort me, but I knew that she too was petrified. I was sure our boat would capsize. After four hours at sea, we finally reached Hel. As soon as we left the boat, my mother telephoned father to tell him about the storm, about my fear to return by boat. Finally mother and I took the train from Hel to Danzig; it took us six hours until we were safely at home. I shall never forget this excursion. Many times my mother and I recalled how terrified I was, how much I was afraid to die. Later, whenever I was afraid of something, she used to say, "Do you remember Hel?" And she made me laugh.

When I was ten, mother took me to a piano recital. Two of her cousins, Celina and Harry Szmant, were playing piano at the recital. She was so impressed by the students and teacher that one week later I began to take piano lessons from Lucie Jung.

As I was getting older, mother took me to concerts and to the theater; we went together to see movies. I loved to dress up in my mother's formal dresses and put on her high-heeled shoes. I continued to watch her when she dressed up to go to parties.

All this changed once the Nazis came to power. By 1934 many of our Jewish friends were leaving Danzig. We did not go to Zoppot for the summer months; instead we rented a house in nearby Orlowo. Orlowo was in Poland just outside the border of the Free City of Danzig. After our cousins from Warsaw and Lodz graduated, we invited them for the summer months. My mother's younger brother, Heniek, with his wife, Rozka, and their infant son, Jasio, also joined us at the seashore. These were happy times. Mother had many friends; she loved people, and people loved her. I never heard her say a loud word; she never raised her voice. Wise, levelheaded, reliable, and loving, she was my role model. Raised in a traditional Jewish home, she was the embodiment of a traditional Jewish mother. An excellent cook, she loved to set the table for holidays with elegance and style. Our apartment was comfortable; furniture was in the best of taste, nothing was gaudy. During the Jewish holidays, I walked with my parents and brother to the Mattenbuden Synagogue in Danzig. I still recall my mother's seat in the balcony— it was seat number 14.

Above: Genia (Gitel) Ryczke, Danzig, 1935.

Left: Benno Ryczke, age six, Orlowo, 1934.

By 1938 the Nazis began to arrest Jewish businessmen. My mother feared for father's safety, and we left Danzig for Gdynia in Poland but kept our Danzig apartment. Mother begged father to emigrate. I recall her words: "I lived through one war—I do not want our children to be here when war breaks out." Yet father was an optimist and did not believe that war was imminent. While we lived in Gdynia, I contacted a group of young Jewish pioneers who were training to become fishermen in Palestine. I wanted to leave. They helped me in contacting the agricultural school in Ben Shemen, Palestine, and in applying for an affidavit and permit to be accepted. Only mother knew about my plans; I did not tell my father. Mother was my confidante, my friend. She wanted me to leave even if my father was against it. I needed her support and encouragement. She understood me; she wanted to help me get away.

In spring of 1939 we returned to our apartment in Danzig, and the situation became calmer. In retrospect it was a lull before the storm. Young Jewish children ages five to fifteen were being sent to England on the *Kindertransport* (children's transport). Mother begged my father to let us go. He felt that we should stay together as a family.

In August 1939 I received a letter from Warsaw to prepare to come and pass an exam in Hebrew. I was accepted to the agricultural school in Palestine. I was beside myself. Mother was happy for me, but I had to face my father now. It was dear mother who took it upon herself to tell him about my dream to go to Palestine, about the acceptance to the school. Well, father was not happy. At first he categorically refused to allow me to leave. But mother somehow calmed him down and told him that she wanted me to leave, to get away from the danger of war. Finally, father consented. Mother and I took the train to Warsaw—this was the last happy trip we took together. In Warsaw she went with me to the Europejski Hotel, where the exams were given. I passed. I had to leave my passport and other papers and was told to return home, pack, and be ready to leave by the beginning of September. The following day Poland was mobilizing; war was imminent. We returned to Danzig. Two days later, on September 1, 1939, World War II broke out. The world that we knew collapsed.

We were caught in Danzig with no hope of escape. Mother was right all the time; my father's optimism failed us. From now on our lives were engulfed in the Holocaust. Expelled from our home in Danzig, we became refugees from the moment war began. With very little we left our home, then were deported to Warsaw. In 1940 we escaped the harsh conditions in Warsaw and came to Tomaszow-Mazowiecki. My dear mother got sick with pneumonia. She never regained her former health. Mother was a chain smoker. We begged her to give up smoking. "This is the only pleasure I have left," she used to say. And we exchanged bread for cigarettes to give her this pleasure.

While we were in the ghetto in Tomaszow, with very little food, my mother concocted the most amazing recipes—soup without meat or potatoes, noodles made without eggs, tea made without tea leaves. She learned to make soap, a very expensive commodity in the ghetto. Some of the broken pieces we used to wash our bodies and clothes; the bigger ones she sold for bread. By 1941 my mother's beautiful black hair turned white; she lost weight and looked older than her forty-four years. Yet she still had her elegant posture, still looked like the lady she was. But we constantly worried about her failing health.

By 1942 we heard rumors in the ghetto that all Jews who were not employed by the Germans would be resettled "east." Father and my brother were at forced labor outside the ghetto; the rest of our family was not working. My father was told that all families of workers were protected from resettlement, that wives, children, and parents of those who worked for the Germans would remain in the ghetto. Mother, I , and my grandparents felt safe—but not for long.

On the morning of October 31, 1942, the ghetto was surrounded by the SS. The men and women who worked for the Germans were allowed to go to their jobs. Mother was getting washed when the knock at the gate was heard. We, the ones who remained, were told to get dressed in warm clothes, wear heavy working shoes, and march to the railway station. We dressed in a hurry, putting on layers of clothing so that we would not have to carry much. There was very little that we still had. All our valuables—money and jewelry—had already been bartered for food. All my mother had was her wedding band. We left the building and marched in columns with the other people. The day was sunny and exceptionally warm. Although almost twenty thousand Jews walked in columns, no noise was heard. Everybody was very quiet, walking to an unknown destination. While the column passed in front of a little white church, I was ordered to step out by an SS officer. My mother walked on—we had no chance to say a word, to embrace each other, to say good-bye. It never occurred to me that we would not see each other again; I was sure that after some time we would meet at the railway station. This was the last time I saw my dearest mother. After my father returned from work, he desperately tried to have mother return to us. By the time his German boss reached the station, mother was already in a cattle car. We could not save her. The destination of the train was Treblinka. The name meant nothing to us. Much later did we learn that it was a death camp; that within twenty-four hours the transport of Jews from Tomaszow, including my dear mother and fourteen members of our family, were gassed to death, their bodies burned.

At work my father got hold of an illustrated German magazine. In one of the pictures he swore that he recognized my mother. "She must be in Germany working," he said. He wanted so desperately to believe that my mother was alive and safe. All I have left of my dear mother are memories, precious childhood memories, memories of a loving and devoted mother. There is no grave, no place to mourn. Only ashes remained from our dear ones, ashes and memories.

Not a day goes by that I do not think of my mother. Did she feel abandoned by me? Did her intuition tell her that this was the end, that she would never see us again? How did she survive the horrible journey in the cattle car? There is no end to my feelings of guilt. If I had not obeyed the order of the SS man, he would have shot me in front of my mother. I hope that my mother understood my predicament, that she forgave me. She knew how much we loved her, how much I adored her. Much too young to die, she left me with the legacy of her exemplary life. Once I had children of my own, I always wanted to be like her. Her image is always before my eyes, especially at times of family gatherings and holidays. This is when I miss her the most. Gitel is a good name; it means "the good one."

But now I have something more—you, my dear Ellie, will carry the names of those I loved. In you the names of my dearest mother and grandma will be memorialized forever.

Chapter 12

"Uncle" Nathan Laznowski (1893–1972)

Dear Max Chambers,

In our Jewish tradition we name our children and grandchildren after those family members who were very dear to us, after those who passed away. You have been given two Hebrew names: Mordechai, after your grandfather Max, and Natan (Hebrew spelling), after our adopted uncle Nathan. You will also be able to read the story about your grandfather Max Kimmelman, but now I want you to get acquainted with Uncle.

Who was Uncle Nathan? I heard about him from Max when we met in Belsen, a displaced persons camp. He told me how he met an older man in the camp of Schlieben, where both were concentration camp prisoners at the end of 1944 until their liberation in May 1945. Uncle, like Max, came to Schlieben from Buchenwald. Here they suffered deprivation, hunger, and cold. Uncle was working as a wood chopper, Max in an armament factory that produced *Panzerfausts* (antitank grenades). Their friendship grew stronger when Uncle revived Max. Max never forgot that it was Uncle who saved his life. When they were liberated by the Soviets on May 9, 1945, they promised to stay together. This story Max told me after we met in Belsen.

Nathan Laznowski was born on January 30, 1893, in Dzialoszyce, Poland. A small town not far from the city of Kielce, it was under Russian rule while Nathan was growing up. His parents were observant Jews and had four sons. Nathan was the oldest. The family owned land that included a forest. They were supplying wood for buildings. Nathan grew up surrounded by nature; he loved to go into the forest where workers were chopping down trees for lumber. He was physically strong and as a young boy learned how to chop wood. This skill later helped him to survive when he was in the Schlieben concentration camp and the Nazis needed men who could chop wood.

Uncle was a wonderful storyteller. I recall one of the stories that he told our sons Benno and Gene. It was a story about a Polish soldier from Dzialoszyce at the time of the Kosciuszko revolt (end of the eighteenth century). The soldier tried to hide from the Russian army and climbed inside a hollow tree but was unable to get out again. His petrified body was found by Nathan when he went into the woods as a young boy to watch the workers cut down trees. Our sons were fascinated by this story. They asked Uncle over and over to tell it to them.

The only formal education Nathan received was his religious education. Like all Jewish boys at that time he was sent to *cheder* (Jewish religious elementary school). Like his parents, he was quite observant. Two of his younger brothers left Dzialoszyce after World War I. They went to Breslau, Germany. Nathan and his youngest brother remained with their parents. In 1927 Nathan married his first cousin Rosa Laznowski and soon they, too, moved to Breslau. Nathan joined his two brothers in the tannery and hides business. His job was to travel to small villages and purchase hides. These he brought back to the tannery in Breslau. His brothers managed the administration, production, and sales parts of the business. In Breslau, Nathan and Rosa became parents of two children; their son was named Jacob (after Nathan's father) and was born in 1930. Their little daughter was named after Rosa's mother, Rebecca, and was born in 1932. Because Nathan was born in Poland, he and Rosa remained Polish citizens.

In October 1938 the Polish government issued an order for all Polish citizens living abroad to return to Poland; otherwise their passports would become invalid. The Nazis did not want the Polish Jews in Germany. That month, throughout Germany, approximately 20,000 Jews holding Polish passports were expelled from the country. They were allowed to carry one suitcase and were sent by train to the city of Zbaszyn near the Polish-German border. This is how Nathan, his wife, and their two small children were forced to leave their home in Breslau. All their belongings were left behind. His two brothers and their families managed to escape to France, where they survived the war.

First Nathan and his family stopped in Dzialoszyce. His father was dead, and his mother and youngest brother had moved to Lodz, where both perished during the war. Their next stop was Warsaw. They lived through the three terrible weeks of bombardment in September 1939 after the Nazis invaded Poland. In the winter of 1940 they left Warsaw and returned to Dzialoszyce. In the summer of 1942, the Nazis began the liquidation of ghettos throughout the General Government (occupied Poland). Dzialoszyce was not spared. Late in the summer of 1942 most of the Jews from Dzialoszyce were taken to the death camp of Belzec. Rosa and Nathan's two children died there. The Jews who were spared and survived the liquidation of the Dzialoszyce ghetto were taken to Kielce. Among them was Nathan. In 1943 Nathan and other surviving men and women were sent to the forced labor camp in Skarzysko Kamienna. Here Nathan worked hard in quarries. By winter 1944 some of the prisoners were sent to the Plaszow concentration camp near Kraków; Nathan was among them. When the Soviet army was pushing westward, the Plaszow camp was evacuated and Nathan came to Buchenwald. He arrived there in August 1944 and was given the prisoner number 67988. In December he was sent to Schlieben near Leipzig, where he and Max met. They went together to Bautzen after Schlieben was evacuated and were together on the long march to Nixdorf.

The day of their liberation was bittersweet. Yes, they were alive, but they were alone. Both had lost their families. Uncle was Max's senior by fifteen years. He became depressed and talked of suicide. This was the moment that Max told him, "You are going to live; you will be my uncle, and wherever I go, you will go, too. We will be together from now on." Max kept his word. They were liberated in the Sudeten part of Bohemia in the little town of Nixdorf (Mikulasovice) and traveled from there to Prague. In the summer of 1945, Max, Uncle Nathan, and another friend, Danek Frenkel, left Czechoslovakia and came to Germany. Danek was a handsome young man, about ten years younger than Max. First they settled in the small Bavarian town of Stamsried in the Oberpfalz, then they moved to Rötz. Danek was very attached to Max, and when Uncle asked Max to leave Stamsried for Rötz, Danek came along.

Now the "three musketeers" were happily settled in furnished rooms. Other surviving Jews followed them, and soon Rötz had a small Jewish community of thirty.

After the war, Germany was divided into four zones: American, British, French, and Soviet. By the end of 1945, Danek had heard that his parents and brother had survived the war and were living in the displaced persons camp in Belsen. Rötz was in the American zone; Belsen, in the British. Traveling was not easy. The railroad tracks were in disrepair, trains were not running on schedule, and the cars were unheated and terribly overcrowded. Yet Danek wanted to see his parents and brother, and even more impor-

Uncle Nathan Laznowski in his prisoner's jacket after liberation in Nixdorf, May 1945.

Bavaria 1945. Nazis digging graves for Nazi murder victims under U.S. Army supervision. These victims were found in mass graves on the road from Stamsried, Oberpfalz.

tant, he wanted to be reunited with his girlfriend, Krysia, in Sweden. Danek did not want to leave Rötz without Max. The two ventured from Rötz to Belsen. Once in Belsen, Danek found his parents. He also made plans to join Krysia in Sweden. Max found some old friends from the ghetto, and, what was more important, Max met me. I can say that thanks to Danek Frenkel, Max and I found each other.

Your Opa Max knew that he wanted to marry me. He returned to Rötz to tell Nathan the good news. He wanted to share his happiness with his uncle. I later learned that Uncle tried to dissuade Max from marrying me. "She is too young for you" (Max was fifteen years my senior), and he was afraid to lose his friend, his adopted nephew. Once Max made up his mind, even Uncle could not change it. Max returned to Belsen in February and March 1946.

We were so much in love but lived hundreds of miles from each other. "You have to come to Rötz," Max insisted. After discussing it with my father, we decided that he and I would visit Max in Rötz in April for the Passover holidays. Indeed, my father and I arrived in Rötz in early April 1946. I knew it was a small town, but I did not imagine it to be so small. Everybody knew everybody; the town was full of gossip. Yet it was picturesque. The Böhmerwald was so peaceful and beautiful. What I loved most was being near Max. Now came the time for me to meet Uncle. From the moment we met I knew that he and I liked each other, that we would be like family. Right away Uncle told Max that he approved of me and that we should get married as soon as possible. Uncle sensed that he would have a friend in me and that he had nothing to fear—he would not lose Max.

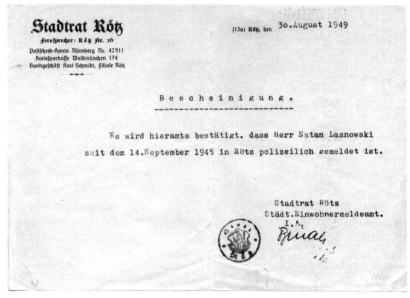

Nathan Laznowski's Rötz police registration, September 14, 1945.

On May 18, 1946, Uncle walked with us to the *Bürgermeister,* where we were married in a civil ceremony. The following day he was one of our witnesses when we were married by a rabbi in a religious ceremony. Uncle's signature is on our *ketubah* (Jewish marriage contract).

As much as I enjoyed the natural beauty of Rötz, I wanted to leave Germany. At first we talked about emigrating to Palestine, but we had no rel-

"Uncle" Nathan Laznowski

atives there. The only relations we had lived in the United States—my father's uncle and family. We wrote to our family and in spring of 1948 were notified that our visas were waiting for us in Munich. Uncle was terribly upset. We promised to help him come to the States; we knew how terrified he was to remain alone. When we were already in Cincinnati, Ohio, a new law went into effect allowing displaced persons to enter the United States without sponsors. Right away we notified Uncle, who registered for emigration to the United States. He arrived in winter of 1950 in New York and was sent to Louisville, Kentucky. For Passover 1951, Uncle visited us in Cincinnati. It was but a few hours' bus ride, and from then on he came to us for every Jewish holiday. It was only natural that Uncle Nathan should be with us for the holidays.

Uncle worked very hard in Louisville. His first job was with a furrier, then he worked for a chemical company. Because he was afraid that he might be too old to find work in America, he gave his age as ten years younger than he really was. When he retired early, at the "official" age of sixty-two, he was actually seventy-two years old. When Max and I moved with our family from Cincinnati to Oak Ridge, Tennessee, in 1964, Uncle followed us and came to live in Oak Ridge in 1966. He wanted to be close to us, especially as he was getting older.

Uncle Nathan Laznowski (*front*), Oak Ridge, Tennessee, November 1967. *Left to right:* Max, Mira, Benno, Gene.

Max and Mira Kimmelman, 1967

As much as Uncle loved us, under no circumstances would he move in with us. He wanted to be independent; he wanted a place of his own. We rented for him an efficiency apartment with a small kitchen and bath, conveniently located within walking distance to the synagogue and to a restaurant, where he took his meals. On Friday afternoons I picked up Uncle so that he could spend Shabbat with us. At Passover time, he stayed the whole week with us; it was such a pleasure having him around. He and Max teased each other often, but there was true love and friendship between them. Uncle made friends in Oak Ridge quickly. He had nicknames for everybody. With his dry humor and sharp mind, he became an integral part of the Jewish community. Uncle had a special talent for seeing people for what they are. In German we call it *Menschenkenner* [one who knows the true person]. He was a quiet, unpretentious man with a keen sense of humor and a great deal of common sense. He was a father/grandfather figure to us.

Uncle loved to smoke, especially good cigars. In 1967 he developed sores in his mouth. I took him to our dentist, Dr. Cross, who right away sent him to the hospital for tests. It was cancer. We never told Uncle; he was terrified of this disease. He underwent surgery, and for a few months things were all right. Then Uncle developed a growth on his back. The cancer was spreading. One surgery followed another, but Uncle always recovered. He also suffered from Parkinson's disease. This was treated by Dr. Lyon. In his poor English, Uncle told the doctor many jokes; it was hilarious to listen to him. I remember Uncle asking Dr. Lyon before Yom Kippur if he could fast on this Holy Day. Dr. Lyon told him that if Uncle promised to take his pills with water, he could abstain from food. Reluctantly Uncle agreed to this compromise. Many years after Uncle passed away, Dr. Lyon still remembered this conversation.

Uncle turned seventy-five in January 1968. Max and I decided to give a party in his honor. Planned in advance, we did not tell Uncle about it. It was a Saturday and Uncle was at our house. He found out when friends started to arrive. It was a surprise and he was so happy. This must have been the only time in his life that a party was given in his honor.

The many pills that Uncle was taking daily began to confuse him. Sometimes he took too many, sometimes he forgot to take them at all. There had to be a better way for him to remember. Each week I prepared little envelopes with his pills for breakfast, lunch, and dinner. On the outer envelope the day of the week was written. We checked during the week to see if he took them correctly. This did not always work. One night he called me around midnight and said it was morning and he could not find his pills. We woke up Gene, who drove to Uncle's apartment to make sure that he was all right. He was now having trouble distinguishing day from night.

In 1970, after his wife left him, my father moved to Oak Ridge. At first he stayed with us. He was depressed and needed our care. Now Uncle had to share us with my father. The two were as different as day and night. In order to keep peace, we had to be careful not to hurt the feelings of either one. At times the rivalry became almost funny, especially at Passover, when each one wanted to lead the traditional Seder. Again we found a compromise: my father would lead the first night, Uncle the second night (thank God we had two Seder nights). Each one was jealous of the other; each one felt we were paying too much attention to the other.

My father became restless. Oak Ridge was too small a city for him. He decided to travel to Israel and study Hebrew at an Ulpan. This brought some relief for Uncle; he would not have to compete with my father during this time. It was the year 1971, the year when Max and I would be married twenty-five years. My father returned before Passover. He and Uncle were present when our dear friends, the Rossmans, gave Max and me a surprise second wedding at their home. The ceremony was conducted by our dear friend Rabbi Robert Marcus; again Uncle was asked to sign a "funny" *ketubah*.

There were more surgeries for Uncle in 1971, but he bounced back quickly. He never asked the reason for the operations, and we never discussed it. Deep down he may have suspected that he had cancer. Each time when he went into the hospital, he took his prayer book with him. Uncle was deeply religious; his faith sustained him throughout his difficult life.

In 1972 my father returned to Israel, and Gene left for Denmark. Benno, who had been away since 1968, graduated from Yale University in 1972. Uncle missed both boys, especially Gene, who watched over him. He always called Gene "Eisenhower," because of Gene's love for golf, just like the former president's. When Benno told Uncle that he would study law, Uncle called Benno "Your Honor."

In October 1972 we found Uncle on the floor of his room. He was taken to the hospital, where he stayed for a few days. The doctors said that there was nothing they could do, no more surgery. The cancer spread; Uncle was getting too weak and a nursing home would be the best place for him. They gave Uncle six months to live. After hearing the news, Max and I spent a sleepless night. How could we put Uncle into a home with strangers, where nobody would understand him? He spoke mostly Yiddish and German but no English. We decided to bring Uncle to our home. We would take care of him for as long as he was alive. We prepared for him one of the bedrooms (it was Benno's study), and put railings on the bed to keep him from falling out. We brought him to our home by ambulance. Uncle knew where he was; he was safe. Max took care of Uncle during the night, and I cared for him during the day. We fed him, bathed him, changed his dressings. Uncle was always gentle and good-natured; he never complained. After ten days I noticed that his breathing became loud and I called the doctor. David Stanley was a surgeon and our good neighbor. He knew Uncle and he knew the situation of his illness. He came over and told us that Uncle was dying. "He may last twenty-four to forty-eight hours." This was on Friday, October 27. Right away we called Benno and asked him to come. When Benno arrived on Saturday evening, Uncle was still alive. He heard Benno greeting him and motioned with his hands. A few minutes later he died peacefully. His five-year-long battle with cancer was over. He died after the Sabbath was over, surrounded by his family, the people he loved and who loved him. The date was October 28, 1972, exactly thirty-four years after he and his family were expelled from Breslau. Uncle was buried in the Jewish cemetery in Oak Ridge on Sunday, October 29, with the entire Jewish community paying their last respects. Everyone loved and respected this quiet man. He lived and died like a *tzadik* (righteous man), and he left a good name. May his memory be for a blessing.

Like most survivors, Uncle was troubled by many fears and anxieties after the war. In 1955, when the German government began paying restitution to the survivors of ghettos and camps, Uncle put his restitution payment into his savings account. A few years later he petitioned for additional money to compensate him for his poor state of health. I took care of all the applications and wrote many letters to the German authorities. But whenever a letter from Germany arrived and Uncle saw the German stamp, he became terrified. He was shaking all over and would not open the mail from Germany. Uncle's fear and anxieties and sleepless nights got worse as he became older. Finally he decided that he did not want to receive anything from Germany. He did not want to subject himself to the suffering and trepidation that would be associated with restitution. For his sake we decided not to pursue this matter further. We just dropped it.

As Uncle was getting on in age, he talked more and more about his years as a young man. He remembered so many details, had so many stories. His father died in the 1920s; his mother and youngest brother, in the Lodz ghetto. He lost his wife and two children in the death camp of Belzec. He would never let people know the pain that was in his heart. With his wit and dry humor he covered his pain. More than anything, he wanted to have some close contact with his brothers in France. Once, while he was still in Rötz, one of Uncle's brothers from Paris visited him. He came for twenty-four hours; this was the only time Uncle saw his brother. This pained Uncle a great deal. Like other Jewish survivors just after the war, Uncle was supported by the United Nations Relief and Rehabilitation Administration (UNRRA) and the American Jewish Joint Distribution Committee ("Joint"). We had nothing—no jobs, no income. Nathan was now the poor relative; his brothers in Paris had their families and their business. For years Uncle Nathan suffered emotionally because his brothers were so cool toward him. He was ashamed to tell people that he had two brothers. From time to time he received a letter from them and even tried in 1964 to visit them. He had his passport and his plane ticket ready. Then came a letter from his brothers that he should not come. They were planning to be on vacation, and the timing was not right. It was a blow from which Uncle did not recover. He never saw his brothers or their families again.

Uncle was honest to the core and he was quite frank. When he disliked someone, he let it be known in a very gentle way. His honesty was tested right after the war when Uncle was still in Nixdorf. A German asked him to hide his box (it was a cigar box) filled with jewelry for a few days. After the war was over, Russians were searching the houses of Germans and robbing whatever they could. After a few days things calmed down and Uncle returned the box to the German without opening or touching the contents. Uncle had nothing, was poor as a mouse. Many people would have been tempted to take some of the jewelry, but not Uncle. In gratitude the German gave Uncle a silver pocket watch (a Schaffhausen), which he wore all the time. This watch is hanging on the wall of our den. Whenever I clean it, I think of Uncle and of his honesty.

Even today, many years after his death, we recall how funny Uncle's English was. He never really mastered the language; he translated everything he said more or less literally from the German. One of his favorite sayings was, "I never no see it" (ich habe so etwas niemals gesehen), which meant, "I never saw anything like this." To this day Benno and Gene repeat some of the things Uncle said. They loved and adored him, although he was not a blood relative. He was much more; he was chosen by us. Even today, when we sit down to the Seder at Passover time, we sing the songs the way Uncle liked to sing them. And we still marvel how fast he could read Hebrew without vowels (vowels help us pronounce Hebrew); Uncle knew what he was saying.

And now Uncle's name lives on in you, dear Max. You were born on October 27, 1997, almost twenty-five years to the day after Uncle's death. By giving you Uncle's name, your dear parents made sure that the memory of the person we loved is kept alive.

Chapter 18

Max Kimmelman—The Valiant Fighter

Dear Michael Max and Max Chambers,

Now it's your Oma's turn to continue about Opa. One year after Papa passed away, Opa's health started to fail. He had suffered with high blood pressure since the end of the war. For years we were watching his diet. He underwent bypass surgery in summer of 1980. Opa was a fighter. He wanted to get back on his feet; he wanted to be able to travel some more. Next followed kidney failure. Now we were faced with another diet, and Opa followed it religiously. He wanted to be well, he wanted to live.

As long as I could keep him well, we continued to travel. Both of us knew that time was running out, that dialysis would be the next step. We managed to travel to Israel. Opa wanted to visit my father's grave. On the way back we stopped in London, where Opa met Lusia Krakowska Arendt, my school friend from Danzig. He also had the opportunity to see again one of my surviving cousins, Gutek Krzewin, now Tony Gorbutt (see chapter 17). Opa had met my other cousin, Michael Lachman, in Israel many years before (see chapter 16). Both of these cousins were the remnants of my family. In 1986 we traveled to New York to be at the wedding of our oldest son, Benno, and his wife, Joy. They were married shortly after Opa and I celebrated our fortieth wedding anniversary. My school friend Janka Krakowska Waril from Sweden came to the wedding, and one year later Opa and I traveled to Stockholm to be at her daughter's wedding.

In April 1988, our first grandchild, your sister, dear Michael, and your cousin, dear Max, was born. Benno and Joy named their first child Melanie Marie, Malka Morit in Hebrew, after Opa's mother and my father. Opa was ecstatic. He lived to be a grandfather. Now we were planning to see our grand-daughter, to be at the naming ceremony. This was to be Opa's last trip to New York. How proud he was to be able to hold his granddaughter in his arms, to be present at her naming. Not only was she bearing his mother's name, but also the name of his little daughter who was killed during the Holocaust.

Max and his first grandchild, Melanie Marie Kimmelman, on the day of her naming, New York, April 22, 1988.

We had to cut our visit short, and Opa was rushed to the hospital as soon as we arrived in Knoxville. The next day he began dialysis. He was losing weight and strength. We still tried to live as normal a life as only possible. This handsome man, who had weighed almost 180 pounds, was now down to 130 pounds. But Opa never lost his humor, never lost his will to fight, to live. Unable to travel, our children were now visiting us quite frequently. Every two months Benno and Joy were bringing Melanie for Opa to enjoy. How he loved his darling little girl.

In spring 1989, Opa had more complications. Lack of circulation in both legs was causing him terrible pain. Soon there was no choice—both legs had to be amputated. Opa was so brave; he never complained. Both of us moved into a nursing home, so that he could get physical therapy and I could learn how to help him. He wanted to return to his home. In early February 1990 I brought him home, but our happiness did not last long. After ten days he had to be rushed to the hospital; he had cardiac arrest. Opa recovered and joked with the doctor that he had survived Hitler and would survive this too. Our children, Benno and Joy and Gene, came to visit and Opa joked with them. Shortly before Opa died, our nephew Dr. Michel Kady (the husband of Elizabeth) came from Toronto to be with us and to give us comfort.

Finally on February 25, 1990, Opa lost his battle. He died with the four of us at his bedside: Benno, Gene, Michel, and I. We all believed in Opa's strength; we wanted him to live, but his time ran out. I lost the best husband one can have. My sons lost a father who loved them more than life itself. Melanie lost her beloved Opa.

Heartbroken, we returned home, where Joy and Melanie were waiting for us. It was so much easier to bear the pain with my sweet granddaughter near me. No words can describe the outpouring of support and love that was shown to me and my children during Opa's illness and after his death. All my friends, all my neighbors, Rabbi Victor Rashkowsky, and the entire Jewish community went out of their way to show their support, their love, and to help us.

Now I was a widow and would have to face life alone. How would I go on living without Opa? With the help of friends and the love of my children,

I adjusted to my new life as a widow. Without their physical and moral support I do not know how I could have survived the period of grief and mourning. The nights were the worst time. For years I barely slept four hours. No matter how exhausted, how tired I was, I could not sleep. And so my nights were now occupied by writing down my memories. I began writing in 1980 after visiting the Danzig exhibit in Atlanta, Georgia. But with Opa's illness, I had to stop. Now I had the long nights before me, the quiet time to put my thoughts and memories on paper. Days were filled with teaching and organizational work. And there were constant demands to lecture to students about the Holocaust. Keeping busy was my salvation.

Both my children lived far away from me, Benno and his family in New York City, Gene in Washington, D.C. I knew that I could always count on their moral and physical support, but they did not exactly live around the corner. My Oak Ridge friends were right here. I could call them in the middle of the night if I needed help. Throughout the years some moved away, some passed away. Since Opa's death, life has never been the same, yet I knew that I had to adjust to go on. My family and my friends became the foundation of my existence. Keeping occupied and involved kept me sane. I needed to be busy, to be completely exhausted at the end of each day. Eventually my sleep returned after many years of sleepless nights. Loneliness was overcome by keeping occupied, despair by remembering happy moments in our lives.

Opa and I had shared forty-four wonderful years. We knew each other's thoughts. To this day I still speak to Opa. When faced with a dilemma, when in a difficult situation, I ask myself, "What would Opa do?" Pretty soon I find the answer. This spiritual communication with Opa has helped me in many instances and is most comforting. Another important factor in my survival is my religion. Attending services and praying has helped soothe the pain, lift me spiritually, and allow me to appreciate life. Judaism has always been a part of me. Its traditions, its spirituality have sustained me throughout my life. Was this not the main reason for our choosing Oak Ridge as our home? I needed the presence of the synagogue not only for myself but also for my family. Friday nights were always special for Opa and me. We always tried to attend services. Since Opa's death, however, I wanted to be at home on Fridays—but not alone. And so a new tradition evolved. I invited friends to share Friday night meals with me. Either friends came to spend Shabbat eve with me or I was invited to be with them in their homes. I never had to face a Friday night alone. "Only in Oak Ridge," Opa would say, "could we feel so much at home."

Nine months after Opa's death, Joy and Benno became parents to a little boy. That's you, dear Michael. Your parents named you Michael Max. And so on November 19, 1990, another Max was born. You were named in Hebrew Mordechai (after Opa) and Moshe (after my father). I rushed to New York to meet my new grandson. At your *Brit Milah* (circumcision) all I could think of was how much Opa would have loved this beautiful baby boy. I thanked God for you, for this boy who carries on Opa's name.

Before Opa passed away, Gene was already dating a lovely girl. What a pity that Opa never had a chance to meet Caroline Chambers. I met her for the first time in May 1991 when she and Gene came to Oak Ridge to be with me on what would have been our forty-fifth anniversary. They did not want me to spend this day alone. Gene, who went first to Brown University and later graduated from the University of Virginia Law School, met Caroline in Washington, D.C., where both were working. Gene was a dedicated consumers' advocate, first for Ralph Nader, then for the Consumer Federation of America, later in the Senate, and finally for Consumers Union. He and Caroline were very much in love and had much in common. There was only one problem: Caroline was not Jewish. I knew for years that Gene had a very unconventional approach to Judaism. He disliked "organized religion," as he called it. He did know how deeply Opa and I were steeped in our heritage, our tradition, and our religion. Gene spoke about it to our rabbi and friend, Victor Rashkovsky, who became his spiritual adviser. Both Caroline and Gene felt very comfortable with Victor, and in July 1991 Caroline embraced Judaism. They were married by our rabbi in September 1991.

What kind of a person was Opa? Brave, loyal, loving and caring, honest to the core, friendly, handsome, and full of life. He could talk tough, but he was a gentle man. Opa loved to tell stories and sometimes stretched them a little. He loved life and people, and he worked hard and was always fair. But family came first. He loved his sons and cherished what he had. With Melanie's arrival he talked daily about her, worried about her well-being.

Benno and Joy brought her to us as often as possible, so that Max could be near his little Melanie. Only I know how much he would have loved all of his grandchildren—you, dear Michael, Max, and Ellie. Opa will always live in our memory. His high spirit will always be with us.

Well, now you know Opa's story, know the person whose name you carry. I hope that both of you will grow up to be as good, decent, brave, and honest as your Opa, Max Kimmelman.

Part 2

Chapter 14

In Search of Remnants

Once World War II ended, those who survived began the agonizing search for family members. Everyone hoped to find parents, siblings, grandparents, uncles, aunts, and cousins. Unless we had witnessed the death of our dear ones, we continued our searches, which sometimes lasted for years. We traveled to different camps; some crossed illegal borders to find even a distant relative. So great was the need for family that nothing stopped survivors from endangering their lives in search of relatives.

My father and I were reunited in July 1945. Soon afterward he left on a dangerous trip in search of my brother. Not once but twice did he cross the illegal borders of East Germany, Poland, Czechoslovakia, and Austria hoping to find traces of his son. Then we learned about the tragic death of my beloved brother, Benno. For many years my father would not accept the fact that his son had been killed. We all were in denial about the loss of dear ones, and it took me years to accept the deaths of my mother, brother, grandparents, and other close relatives.

While my father stopped in Lodz on his way to Gdańsk to find his son, he learned of the deaths of his only sister, Rosa Przedecka, and her two daughters, Halina and Gina. My father's only brother, Heinrich, who had survived the ghetto liquidation, was killed in the Plaszow concentration camp. On the Ryczke side of the family only my father and I remained. The only hope was the maternal side of my family, the Hammers. I knew from my father that my mother's only brother, Heniek Hammer, was alive. He survived on Aryan papers as Ludwik Turkiewicz and settled after the war in Plattling, Lower Bavaria. When Uncle Heniek and I were reunited in March 1946, he told me the sad fate of the Hammer relatives. Neither of us knew the fate of my only two remaining cousins, Mietek Lachman, the son of Gucia and David Lachman, and Gutek Krzewin, the only child of Hela and Zygmunt Krzewin. We knew that Mietek Lachman escaped first to Bialystock, then to the Soviet Union at the start of World War II, and Uncle Heniek told me that Gutek Krzewin left the Warsaw ghetto in 1943 with Aryan papers. I hoped that both were alive and that somehow I would be able to find them.

When I was growing up in my hometown, Danzig, my mother's uncle and aunt, together with their two children, also resided in the city. Uncle Leon Szmant was my maternal grandmother's brother. His wife, Tilly Szmant, was the sister of my maternal grandfather, Shlomo Hammer. Their children, Celina and Harry, were older than I; both graduated from the Polish *Gimnazjum* in Danzig, which I, too, attended. In 1946 I met a man in Hannover who survived the Lodz ghetto. I mentioned to him that I was from Danzig and had relatives by the name of Szmant who left Danzig for Lodz. He remembered the name Szmant, especially my cousin, Celina, who had worked in the ghetto office for some time. He told me that neither she nor her parents survived the ghetto. He was not sure if they died there or were deported to the Chelmno death camp. This left only Harry, who left Danzig in 1937 and went to the United States.

My father found out that three of his first cousins from the Ryczke family had indeed survived the Holocaust. They were the children of his uncle Aron Ryczke and aunt Hela. Aron was my paternal grandfather's half brother. He and his wife had six children, all born in Kolo. Of the six, three survived the Holocaust: Adam Ryczke, who spent the war years in the Soviet Union, and Bronka and Cesia Ryczke, who both survived on Aryan papers. Adam left Poland in the 1950s for Israel; Cesia went first to France and then to Israel; and Bronka went to England. In the late 1950s, while on a visit to see her mother's brother in Chicago, Bronka was killed in an automobile accident in Canada. Adam Ryczke met his future wife, Mala, in Israel. She had lost her first husband in France and survived hidden with her little son, Daniel Kolodner. Adam and Mala had a son, Ronnie. They named him after Adam's late father, Aron. All of them are gone now.

My father was corresponding with his cousin, Adam Ryczke, and in one of his letters Adam mentioned that, while playing cards, someone mentioned the name Lachman. Adam knew that we had relatives by this name. He went to see this Mr. Lachman and found out that it was Mietek Lachman, my first cousin from Warsaw. Right away he gave him our address and I began my correspondence with Mietek. From him I also learned that our other cousin, Gutek Krzewin, was alive. The two met by chance in Italy after the war ended. Gutek was now Tadeusz Podkulecki; he kept the name from his Aryan papers. They parted in 1945. Gutek/Tadeusz went to England, and Mietek went to Canada and from there to Israel. And so it happened that many years after the war ended, I was lucky to find two of my first cousins alive.

While I was recuperating after liberation in the Belsen camp, I found my distant cousin Halinka Frydlender, the daughter of my mother's second cousin Mina (see chapter 19).

When I wrote about my family, of all my relatives who miraculously survived the Holocaust, only Mietek Lachman, Ronnie Ryczke, and Halinka Frydlender were alive. Now only Halinka Frydlender remains. Mietek Lachman and Ronnie Ryczke both died in Israel in 2001.

FAMILY TREE OF MIRA'S MOTHER (HAMMER)

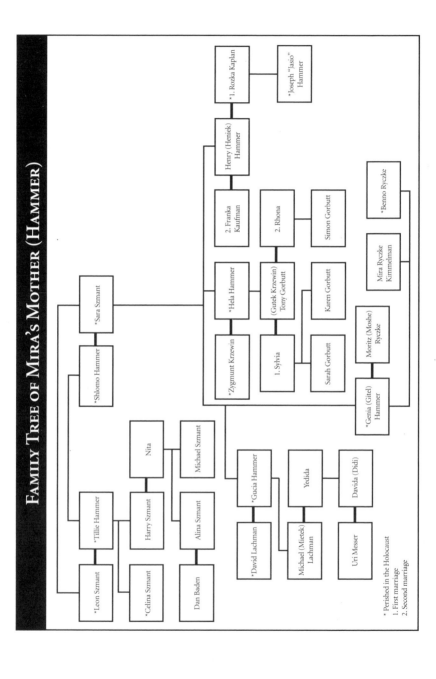

* Perished in the Holocaust
1. First marriage
2. Second marriage

Chapter 15

RECONNECTING TO MY MOTHER'S SIDE OF THE FAMILY—HENRY (HENIEK) HAMMER (1906–1989)

Heniek was the youngest child of Shlomo and Sarah Hammer, my maternal grandparents. My mother's brother, he was the only one of her siblings who survived the war. He had three sisters—Gucia (Lachman), who lived in Warsaw; Genia (Ryczke), my mother, who lived in Danzig; and Hela Krzewin, who lived in Kalisz before the war. His older brother, Stasiek, died in 1922 in Vienna.

Heniek Hammer was born in Kalisz on March 25, 1906. The Hammers resided in this city for many generations. Before World War I, grandparents Hammer had a lace and embroidery factory there that was burned down at the start of World War I. Heniek finished his schooling in Kalisz and enlisted in the Polish army. What a striking and handsome young man he was. I can still see him in his uniform; he was my favorite uncle. In 1933 he married

Rozka Kaplan from Konin. From our family, only my mother went to their wedding. It was winter; I wanted to go, too, but I would have had to miss school. My mother later told me that on the day of the wedding it was raining; there were puddles and the ladies were in high heels and long dresses. Uncle Heniek was physically very strong—he carried each lady to the hall where the wedding took place. Their first child, a son, was born in 1934. They named him Jasio (Joseph), after great-grandfather Joseph Hammer. In 1938 their second son was born prematurely. They named him Theodor (Teos). He died at age six months; we all grieved at his loss. The Hammer family lived on No. 9 Targowa Street in Kalisz and resided there until World War II broke out. Grandparents Hammer also lived in the same house on the ground floor.

Heniek worked in Kalisz for the leather factory Sawacki. He became their main traveling salesman for the district of Pomorze, which brought him often to Danzig. I saw Heniek at least once each month; he always stayed with us over the weekend. Heniek's wife, Rozka, was very fond of my mother. In the summer of 1935 we rented a summer house in Orlowo for the whole season, so that Rozka, Jasio, and Heniek could spend the summer with us. They even brought their maid with them, so that Rozka could have more free time. Heniek always had some strange ideas (strange to me as a teenager). He never believed in paper money and changed it into gold coins. Naturally he brought his coins to Orlowo and hid them between the bedding. One day he had been looking for the gold and could not find it. He right away suspected their maid. And, sure enough, she admitted taking the gold and burying the coins under a tree in the forest behind our house. All of us went to retrieve the buried treasure; it was quite an adventure. The maid found the place right away. The money was buried under a marked tree (the tree trunks were painted so that the people would not get lost in the forest). The thief was sent home right away. I never forgot the episode of the buried gold coins.

While Heniek visited us in July 1938 in Orlowo, he received the telegram that his little son, Theodor, had died. This was the first time that someone I had known, a baby that I had held in my arms, had died. Heniek left right away to bury his infant son. When, one year later, on September 1, 1939, war broke out, Heniek was drafted and went to fight with the Polish army. Rozka and Jasio were on her parents' estate at Glinka near Konin when the first German bombs began to fall. Jasio fell while running to the shelter and broke his leg. Rozka had one sister living in the city of Lodz, and she decided to take her son there. When they arrived at her sister's house, they were told that her sister had left for Warsaw. In desperation Rozka came to my paternal grandparents Ryczke, who resided on 49 Zawadzka Street in Lodz. They took her and Jasio in and nursed the child for four weeks. When Rozka's sister returned from Warsaw after the city's capitulation, Rozka and Jasio went to live with her. Heniek had no idea what had happened to his wife and son. He was defending Warsaw. After the capitulation of the city, he changed into civilian clothes and returned to Lodz, where he was reunited with his family.

When Lodz was incorporated into Germany and became Litzmannstadt at the end of 1939, Heniek decided to take his family to Warsaw, where by now most of the Hammers lived—the Lachmans, the Krzewins, and his parents, Shlomo and Sarah Hammer. They all rented rooms or apartments on 19 Nowolipki Street, where the Lachmans had lived for years. Only the Krzewins found a place around the corner, on Karmelicka Street. My family arrived in Warsaw in October 1939, and Aunt Gucia gave us one room. We stayed until the end of January 1940. This was the last time I saw the family— my grandparents Hammer, the Lachmans, and Heniek and his family. My family left for the city of Tomaszow-Mazowiecki, the rest of my mother's family remained in Warsaw.

When I saw Heniek again in March 1946 in Hannover, he told me the story and fate of the Hammer family members.

"With the closing of the Warsaw ghetto at the end of 1940, it was hard to support the family. One by one I bartered away the gold coins that I had saved. Then I sold our fur coats and any clothing we could spare. From time to time I was called to work and earned extra food. Jasio we sent to a preschool, so that he could be with children his age. In 1941 my mother (Grandma Sarah Hammer) died after a stroke. We buried her in the Jewish cemetery, which was costly. Most burials in Warsaw were now in mass graves. In June 1942 my father (Grandpa Shlomo Hammer) was shot by an

SS man. He was mortally wounded; I took him to the hospital in the ghetto. There I met a former school friend, Dr. Joziek Goldstein. When he saw my father, he gave him an injection of morphine, so that he could die in peace. The problem was how to bury him. I went home and fetched my sister Gucia and some men's clothes. We rented a rickshaw, came to the hospital where we "dressed" my father and almost carried him to the rickshaw. We had to pretend that he was alive to get him out of the hospital, into the rickshaw, and to the cemetery. I did not want my father's body to be dumped into the mass grave. We had to find somebody who for money would bury him in a single grave. We were lucky—a cemetery worker took two hundred dollars from us, and we stood by as the grave was dug and our beloved father was buried.

"On July 22, 1942, the deportations of Jews from the Warsaw ghetto began. We were told that the people were being sent east to work. At first nobody had any doubts; some even went voluntarily and were given extra bread and marmalade for the trip. The Jews of Warsaw were being deported to Treblinka. Soon the horrible truth became known to us, as some of the deportees escaped and returned to Warsaw. At first nobody believed them. The stories they told about people being gassed, about their bodies being burned, were just too fantastic. We did not want to believe it; all of us were in denial. The first ones to be picked up were David Lachman, Marysia Lachman and her two-year-old son, and Marysia's husband, Mietek. My sister, Gucia Lachman, went into hiding with relatives of her husband, the Perlmutter family. The next ones to be taken to Treblinka were my wife, Rozka, and our beloved son, Jasio, age eight. Now I was alone. My younger sister's husband, Zygmunt Krzewin, was working outside the ghetto at the *Baustelle* (construction site). He took his young son, Gutek, and me to work with him. When Zygmunt, Gutek, and I returned home on Yom Kippur Day in September 1942, Gucia, who had joined us, and my sister Hela were gone. The Nazis took them while we were at work. The three of us who were left behind were in total despair. It was time to think of escaping. I, too, decided to leave the ghetto and had asked Zygmunt's Polish friend Jan Morek for papers for myself. Soon I, too, was lucky to obtain papers and became Ludwik Turkiewicz. All this was costly; it was quite expensive to obtain

Polish papers. The first one to leave was Zygmunt. With Zygmunt gone, Gutek and I decided to leave. Gutek was the next one to leave. I was not so lucky. On January 18, 1943, I was taken to the *Umschlagplatz* (collection point), from where Jews were sent to Treblinka. It was no secret anymore what Treblinka meant, and I had no intention of becoming another victim of the Nazis. While standing with a multitude of Jews at the *Umschlagplatz*, I overheard a Jewish policeman saying to a man next to me, 'Say *Werterfassung*.' I did not have the vaguest idea what this word meant, but when it was my turn to walk toward the cattle cars, I said with a loud voice, '*Werterfassung*' (collection of valuables). Right away I was released and sent back to the ghetto. This one word saved my life. As I found out, *Werterfassung* was situated at the Tlomackie Synagogue in Warsaw and became a depot for Jewish valuables, clothing, bedding, household items, and furniture. The Jews who worked there were exempt from deportation.

"After this close call, I left the ghetto. There was nobody left—my wife, my son, both my sisters, and their families were gone. Only Gutek was now safe on the Aryan side. First and foremost I had to find a place to hide. My boss from Kalisz, Sawacki, had a nephew in Warsaw. His name was Bolek Niewiarowski. I remembered his address and turned to him for help. I recalled Bolek from before the war, and the fact that he was a socialist and friendly toward Jews. When I told him about my predicament, about the loss of my family, Bolek agreed to hide me. In his apartment he was also hiding two other Jewish men. Our hiding place was behind a huge tile oven in Bolek's living room. The three of us were hidden there during the day; only late in the evenings were we allowed to leave our hiding place. For one solid year I spent my life behind the oven—from January 1943 till January 1944. I knew quite well the consequences if I should get caught. I had with me a pistol and a hand grenade, in case the SS or Gestapo should approach my hiding place. The danger for the Niewiarowski family was just as great. The penalty for harboring Jews was death. There were frequent searches in Polish homes, and the two Jewish men who were hiding with me decided to leave the apartment and find a safer place. Bolek and his family were planning to leave their apartment; they were afraid that someone might denounce them for hiding a Jew. They moved into a suburb of Warsaw and left me alone in their apartment. Bolek was such a decent person, such a good friend, that he came a few times a week to the apartment where I was alone now, bringing me food and water so that I would not starve. He really risked his life every time he entered the apartment. I realized soon that I, too, would have to look for another place to hide; I could not allow Bolek to sacrifice his life. But where to go? Suddenly I remembered something. While Bolek and his family were still living in their apartment and I was hiding behind the oven, I overheard something. Bolek and a few friends were playing cards. One was a man by the name of Janoszewski, another was an engineer from Kraków. They were talking about their nannies. The engineer mentioned that he was visiting his nanny from time to time; she now lived in Praga (the town across the Vistula River) near Goclow, by the railroad station. While in hiding, your hearing becomes much sharper; I was aware of every noise and remembered many things I overheard. Now I remembered details about the nanny and decided to try my luck. I left the apartment early the next morning, carrying nothing with me. I took the tram to Praga hoping to find the nanny. While standing on the platform of the tram, I recognized an old school friend from Kalisz. Should he have recognized me, it would have meant death. I could not take any chances now and jumped off the tram. I decided not to take another tram and walked all the way to Goclow. Finally I was able to locate the nanny. I introduced myself as a friend of the engineer and gave her his best regards. I am sure that she sensed that I was Jewish. She asked me to come inside. When I asked her to allow me to stay at her place, she reluctantly agreed to hide me for a few days only. Everybody was afraid to harbor a Jew; I understood her fear. I stayed with her a few weeks and then went to find other places. This was January 1944. Until the outbreak of the Warsaw Uprising I had two more hiding places, always grateful to the Poles who helped harbor me.[1] When the uprising collapsed, Poles were ordered to leave Warsaw and Praga. I too left. With other Polish men I was taken to the railroad station and sent west, to Gleiwitz. I lived under constant fear of being recognized by fellow Poles as a Jew. The danger was great; I saw myself denounced every minute. Yet I had to play my part, the part of a Polish schoolteacher from Warsaw. The

HENRY (HENIEK) HAMMER

most dreaded moments were when we were taken to the baths. I was circumcised; Polish men were not. Should they notice my circumcision and tell the SS, I would be shot right away. What should I do? Finally I decided to use a lot of soap while taking a shower. I lathered my private parts so that nobody could see anything. Some of my Polish friends had noticed that I was using so much soap and asked me the reason. I told them "in confidence" that I was embarrassed because of the lice I had noticed, and wanted to get rid of them by intensive lathering of this sensitive spot. They believed me and did not ask me again. The fear of undressing, the fear of being recognized as a Jew, was constant.

"In Gleiwitz, some men were working in German factories. I was left in the camp. Our camp housed Polish men; across from us, separated by a wire, were Polish women. Most of the women were employed in the camp. With nothing to do, and always hungry, I used to walk by the kitchen barracks, where women were busy peeling potatoes. I hoped to secure some potato peelings or maybe a potato. While observing the women, I noticed one in particular. Somehow she reminded me of my sister, Gucia. I was watching her carefully and saw how clumsily she was peeling potatoes. She took much more skin off than the other Polish women. "Could she be Jewish?" I thought. It was too risky to just ask her. I waited a few days and approached her one day. "My intuition tells me that you're Jewish," I said to her. She denied it right away and avoided me. I understood that I had scared her. One day, against my better judgment, I decided to tell her that I was Jewish. I told her about the loss of my family, the loss of my only son. To this day I cannot understand why I revealed my identity. But I was lonely, I needed someone to talk to, and my heart told me that I could trust this woman.

"My heart was right. Finally she admitted that she, too, was Jewish. Her name was Franka, maiden name Kaufman. She was a widow. She and her husband were hiding in Warsaw, but not together. She lived under the Polish name Anna Wielgus. While in hiding, her husband became ill and died of typhus. She could not even attend his funeral. Franka/Anna was most anxious to find out why I suspected her of being Jewish. I told her what a bad potato peeler she was, that this gave her away. This became a standing joke between us for many years to come.

"Franka/Anna lived with a young Polish girl, Stachula. They were inseparable. Of course Stachula did not know that Anna Wielgus was Jewish. After a few months in Gleiwitz, we could see that the Germans were losing the war. It was time for us to get away, because rumors were that we would be evacuated. It was the beginning of January 1945. I spoke to Franka/Anna about leaving for Czechoslovakia. She agreed, but under the condition that Stachula would come with us. To plan our escape, we needed some outside help. I had noticed that a man in a fez was walking close to our camp. One day I asked him if he would be willing to purchase three railroad tickets for me; I would give him the money. The man was very pleasant and agreed to get the tickets for us. He spoke with a strange accent; I was sure he was a Turk. The day of our escape came; we left the camp carefully and met at the railroad station. The "Turk" was already waiting for us with the tickets. When the train stopped, and we got in, the "Turk" leaned over and whispered to me, "A broche of eych," which means in Yiddish, "a blessing on you." He blessed us; he, too, was a Jew who lived disguised, and I had mistaken him for a Turk. God protected us in so many ways; we were helped by so many good people.

"We left the train in Pusary, Czechoslovakia. There we had to change homes often. The Czech people were suspicious of us; the Germans were still in charge. Our ordeal ended in April 1945 when the American army liberated this part of Czechoslovakia. Once we were free, we confessed to Stachula that Franka/Anna and I were Jewish. She was in shock; she could not believe it. Stachula returned to Poland in May 1945, while Franka/Anna and I left for Germany. We settled in a small Bavarian town, Plattling, close to Passau. Many camp survivors had also settled there; most of them were the only survivors of their families. They took Franka and me for Poles, until we told them our stories. Soon they elected me to become the president of the Jewish Committee of Survivors in Plattling.

"More than anything else Franka and I wanted to find out who of our families survived. Lists of survivors were circulating from town to town.

One day I spotted the name 'Moritz Ryczke' on such a list. 'This must be Genia's husband,' I thought right away. There was an address in Eggenfelden, not far from Plattling. The next morning I borrowed a bicycle and went looking for Moritz Ryczke. After arriving in Eggenfelden I found the house, but Mr. Ryczke had left for the day, said the landlady. I left a note which said, 'Your brother-in-law was here looking for you,' gave my address and signed it Ludwik Turkiewicz. I as well as Franka still carried our Polish names. The following day your father, Moritz Ryczke, arrived in Plattling. I was overjoyed. It was so good knowing that he had survived. The first thing he said was, 'Why did you sign the note Ludwik Turkiewicz? I never had a brother-in-law by that name and only came here out of curiosity.'

"We spent the day together, exchanging and sharing news about the families we lost. We cried together over the loss of our dear ones. Your father told me that his goal was to find his children—you and your brother, Benno. He was planning to leave Eggenfelden in search of the few family members he hoped had survived. We parted, and Moritz promised to keep in touch with me.

"In the meantime an American garrison settled in Plattling. One of the officers by the name of Kaufman became very friendly with us. He and Franka/Anna soon became close friends, especially since her maiden name was Kaufman, too. I was eager to find some work and to earn some money. Captain Kaufman made it possible for me to become a trustee (*Treuhänder*) of a large leather factory near Plattling. The owner was a former Nazi; now I was given the leadership of the factory. Because I knew the leather business from Kalisz, I was able to manage the factory and make it prosperous.

"In February 1946, I received a letter from your father, from Hannover. In it, he told me about his two journeys to Danzig in search of Benno and about finding you alive in Belsen. He still had not given up hope of finding his son. But this letter had another purpose. Moritz, your father, wanted me to do some research. He mentioned that you had met a certain Max Kimmelman, and that you two planned to get married. Your father asked me to find out details about the background of Max Kimmelman. Evidently quite a few people from Piotrkow resided in Regensburg, and Moritz asked me to go there and ask people about Max. How could I refuse? I know your father had your best interest at heart; he wanted to make sure that you married the right person, a decent and good man. Well, I went to Regensburg. All I heard were superlatives about Max Kimmelman. With the good news I traveled to Hannover. And here I see you again after many years."

This was the story told by Heniek. I was so grateful that Heniek and I had the opportunity to be together and for him to share the horrors and miracles of the war years. Heniek was definitely on my side when it came to marrying Max. He was eager to meet him and suggested that my father, Max, and I come to Plattling for Passover. I, too, wanted for Max to meet my only uncle. I left the displaced persons camp of Belsen the beginning of April 1946, joined my father in Hannover, and traveled by train first to Rötz, where Max lived, and then to Plattling. By then my father agreed to our marriage and we contacted a rabbi in Regensburg. The date was set for Sunday, May 19, the Jewish holiday of Lag b'Omer. In the meantime Heniek told us that Franka was pregnant. This was her first pregnancy. She had no children with her first husband. Franka was almost thirty-six years old, and both she and Heniek were afraid that she might be too old to bear a child. Her pregnancy was terminated, and Heniek regretted it all his life. At our wedding we had only my father and Heniek as family members; Franka was too weak to attend. Although this was the happiest moment of my life, when Max and I were united in marriage, all of us shed many tears. Our thoughts were with those members of our family who would have been at our wedding but who were gone. Suddenly we realized how few of us were left.

While Max and I were planning to leave Germany for the United States, my father had managed to open a small seed business in Hannover and was not thinking of emigrating. Heniek and Franka were corresponding with Franka's uncle in Philadelphia; they, too, were planning to go to the United States. In the meantime, Heniek developed an infection in his left eye. Soon the doctors discovered that there was severe damage to this eye, and it would have to be removed. The years of hiding, especially the year behind the stove, caused great damage to his eye. The trauma of losing the eye severely influenced Heniek's life. Before he and Franka applied for visas to the United States, they changed their names to their original ones. They were

HENRY (HENIEK) HAMMER

now Henry Hammer and Franka Hammer. He continued to work as a trustee in the leather factory until the papers for the United States arrived. Max and I had already left in July 1948. One year later Heniek and Franka came to the United States. By then my father, too, decided to leave Germany; he came on the same boat with Heniek and Franka to Boston. It was the end of August 1949. I waited for my father in New York City; Franka and Heniek went to Franka's family in Philadelphia.

Henry Hammer and his second wife, Franka, in Plattling, 1947.

Heniek could not speak English and became restless. He wanted to start some business and decided that New York would be a better place for him and Franka. They moved to New York City, where my father, too, settled. Heniek found out that many Jewish immigrants had settled on chicken farms in New Jersey. He and Franka took the bus to Vineland, New Jersey, to investigate the possibilities of getting into the egg business. They met a family by the name of Nagler who owned a chicken farm on East Chestnut Avenue in Vineland. Heniek liked the idea of becoming a farmer and suggested a partnership to Mr. Nagler. Sure enough, Mr. Nagler agreed, and Heniek began to learn the egg business, how to raise chicks, and how to operate a prospering chicken farm. Soon he and the Naglers parted; he paid them their part of the value of the farm. Now he and Franka were sole owners of a large chicken farm. A few years later egg prices began to fall, and the chicken farmers were slowly losing money. But Heniek was lucky. His farm was located on a large parcel of land near the Vineland High School. Builders were eager to purchase land to build housing for a growing population. Heniek sold almost all the land, which was parceled off. All he and Franka kept was the lot where their comfortable house stood. He never had to worry again about egg prices; now he and Franka could enjoy a leisurely life. Both of them loved reading, and both cherished a quiet lifestyle. My family used to see them every summer when we visited my father on his farm in Estell Manor, New Jersey.

I knew Heniek before the war; I knew him as a young man full of life, a man who always was the life of the party. Heniek Hammer after the war was a different person. He and Franka became loners. They did not have many friends. Heniek lived in constant fear; he did not trust anybody. He would not permit a stranger to help with housework; Franka did everything herself. Heniek was still reliving his months of hiding; he was still hiding. These were some of the post-Holocaust syndromes. They never traveled; Heniek seldom left the house. Both of them became recluses. Neither of them came to our sons' B'nai Mitzvah. People in Vineland could not understand their behavior, but we knew that they lived haunted by their past.

It was Sunday morning, October 2, 1983, when I received a telephone call from Heniek. He never called. I was quite startled when I heard his voice. "Franka died this morning," he said. "Soon I will be picked up by the limousine from the funeral home and taken to the cemetery." I was shocked. We did not know that Franka was ill; we had no idea that there was anything wrong with her. Because Heniek hung up after notifying me about Franka's death, I waited a few hours to call him. There he was all alone burying his beloved wife, not willing to share the grief with me, who was his only relative in the United States. When I called him and asked why he never let me know about Franka, he just said, "I had to deal with it alone, I needed to mourn alone." Franka was a devoted and loving wife for thirty-seven years. She nurtured and cared for Heniek through many operations. Now she was gone, and Heniek was all alone. From then on I kept calling him every few days and promised to come to Vineland for the unveiling of Franka's tombstone. In June 1984 I went to the unveiling.

In March 1986 Gene, Max, and I drove to Vineland to celebrate Heniek's eightieth birthday. Heniek was still driving his car and looked well. Two years later he had a stroke. He now lived in a nursing home in Atlantic City, New Jersey. I kept calling him; many times he did not know who I was. At the nursing home he told people he was never married; his memory was gone. I spoke to him for the last time at 3 a.m. on July 10, 1989. On July 13, I received a telephone call from the nursing home telling me that Heniek had died peacefully in his sleep. The last child of Shlomo and Sarah Hammer was gone. Heniek, the survivor of the ghetto and of many hiding places, had lost both his parents, his three sisters and their families, his first wife, and his only son. He suffered years of indignation, inhumanity, and deprivation. To me his death was a terrible blow, a great loss. I could not attend his funeral because Max was on dialysis and could not be left alone. Our sons Benno and Gene were the only relatives to accompany Heniek's body to his eternal rest. May his memory be for a blessing.

Heniek Hammer survived against all odds. By overhearing a word, he was saved from deportation to Treblinka. Through the good-heartedness of Bolek Niewiarowski and the nanny he did not know and other Poles, he survived in hiding. Jan Morek made it possible for Heniek to live with Aryan papers as Ludwik Turkiewicz. His alertness and keen sense of intuition guided him through years of imminent danger. So many factors, so many good people contributed to Heniek's survival. He lived and relived these years of danger all of his postwar life; they all contributed to the different person and personality Heniek became. The burden of survival is a heavy one to bear for all survivors. Some became more affected than others. Heniek remained a victim of the Holocaust until he died.

Chapter 16

MICHAEL (MIETEK) LACHMAN (1916–2001)

On November 24, 2000, my only living first cousin, Mietek Lachman, celebrated his eighty-fourth birthday in Israel. The son of David and Golda (Gucia) Lachman, he was born in 1916 in the city of Kalisz. His mother was my mother's older sister.

In 1915 Gucia Hammer married David Lachman, whose family came from the nearby towns of Turek and Kolo. The young couple moved to Warsaw from Kalisz. Gucia became pregnant and when it was time for her to give birth to her first child, she came back to Kalisz to be near her mother. Mietek was born at the end of November 1916 at Piskorzewie Street in Kalisz. Soon mother and son returned to Warsaw and settled at 19 Nowolipki Street, apartment 21. David worked as a salesman and distributor of fine cutlery for the firm Gerlach in Warsaw, while Gucia took care of their child. In 1920 their second child, Marysia, was born. She and I were given our Hebrew names after our great-grandmother Marien (Miriam) Szmant, the mother of grandmother Sarah Szmant Hammer.

Both my cousins Mietek and Marysia Lachman graduated from their respective *Gimnazjums*—Mietek in 1934, Marysia in 1938. While my family resided at that time in Danzig, for the three months of summer we rented an apartment or cottage near the seashore in Zoppot or Orlowo. As a graduation gift to Mietek, my parents invited him to spend a month with us in Orlowo in 1934. It was exciting and fun to have my older cousin with us. Mietek was an athlete and an excellent swimmer. He loved swimming in the Baltic Sea and impressed many young girls by showing off his diving talents. He was full of vigor and constantly flirted with pretty girls. I am sure that he broke many hearts. I still recall his coming home to our cottage in the wee hours of the morning. Because he did not want to awake his aunt Genia, he entered the room through an open window. He was young and charming, and my mother always forgave him for his unorthodox behavior.

In Warsaw, Mietek studied to become an agricultural engineer. When World War II broke out, he joined the Polish army in the defense of Warsaw. After the surrender of the capital of Poland, he was helped by the Polish underground and crossed over the new border to the Soviet-occupied part of Poland. Upon the outbreak of German-Soviet hostilities in 1941, he joined the newly formed Polish army in the Soviet Union, under the command of Gen. Wladyslaw Anders.[1]

Gucia, David, and Marysia Lachman remained in Warsaw. In the meantime, Marysia married a young man also named Mietek; his family name was Lauterstein. When we were expelled from Danzig in October 1939, my family found refuge in the apartment of Gucia and David, where we stayed until the end of January 1940. Marysia stayed with her husband at his parents' apartment and in 1940 gave birth to a son. The Nazis ordered the liquidation of the Warsaw ghetto on July 22, 1942. Mietek's family perished in Treblinka.

In the meantime, Mietek Lachman traveled with General Anders and his Polish army first to Iran and from there to Italy, where he fought with the Polish army against the Nazis. He was stationed in Anconia, Italy, when World War II ended. Here by sheer chance he was reunited with his cousin, Gutek Krzewin, now Tadeusz Podkulecki. From Gutek he learned about the liquidation of the Warsaw ghetto and the tragic loss of his entire family. He was devastated and decided to leave Europe after being discharged from the army. While Gutek moved on to England, Mietek left for Canada. He did not stay long. Some time later, after the Jewish state was created in 1948, Mietek decided to leave for Israel.

There he met his future wife, Yedida, and they married in 1951. When their only child, a daughter, was born, she was named Davida (Didi), after Mietek's father, David. Mietek served for many years in the Israeli army as a lieutenant colonel and later worked for the Ministry of Defense. The Lachman family traveled extensively in Europe. Didi Lachman graduated from law school and in 1976 married another attorney, Uri Messer. Both of them visited us in Oak Ridge in May 1978 when they toured the United States. They are parents of three lovely children—a son, Alon, born in 1980; a daughter, Yael, born in 1982; and another son, Dan, born in 1988. Yedida Lachman passed away in May 1992.

Wedding of Mietek Lachman's only daughter, Didi, to Uri Messer, Tel Aviv, November 1976. *Left to right:* Mietek Lachman; his wife, Yedida; Mira's father, Moritz Ryczke; Didi; Uri Messer; Tony Gorbutt (formerly Gutek Krzewin).

Mietek Lachman moved into a retirement community in Kfar Saba, sharing his life with an old friend, Klara. They traveled together and enjoyed life.

In early February 2001 Mietek Lachman called from his home in Israel. My first question was, "Are you already in Switzerland?" For the past five years, he and his companion, Klara, had been spending a few months of winter in Switzerland. "No," Mietek answered, "I am calling from home and I have bad news. Before our annual trip abroad I went to the doctor for a check-up and all was okay. But before I left his office the doctor wanted me to take another blood test. A few days later he called me with the bad news that I have leukemia and only frequent blood transfusions can keep me alive." I could not believe what Mietek told me. Here was a youthful eighty-four-year-old frequent traveler, a man who swam daily, who was trim and slim. At first I thought that maybe Mietek exaggerated, but when he said, "I am not allowed to travel outside the country [Israel], these are doctor's orders," I knew that it was serious. His next question was, "When are you coming to Israel?" Usually I traveled there every two or three years; my last visit was in November 1998. I knew right away that I had to go soon. The timing was not the best. The second intifada, with many suicide attacks, kept people from traveling to Israel. I knew that I had to see Mietek before he got too ill and too weak, and I made my plans to go to Israel in May. This time I would fly with the Israeli airline El Al for security reasons.

Upon my arrival, I called Mietek. I needed to know when we could see each other. He had just returned from the hospital, where he was given another blood transfusion. "I am now strong again, I was given another dose of 'instant strength,'" were his words. We met for dinner the day after I arrived. Every day counted; I came to Israel for seven days only. Mietek, Klara, and I spent a beautiful evening having dinner in a new restaurant in Herzliya overlooking the Mediterranean Sea. Mietek looked pale and tired quickly. But his spirit was good. Now he was worried about Klara, who was scheduled for surgery on Wednesday (this was Monday night). She reassured him that she would be fine. Mietek and I spoke a few times daily, and he called me immediately after Klara was out of surgery. My last time with Mietek was on Friday, May 25. His daughter Didi picked me up at the hotel and took me to Kfar Saba. Klara was still in the hospital; Mietek and I had a few hours to ourselves. This last visit was filled with nostalgia. He and I shared so many childhood memories. We spoke about our annual visits to our grandparents Hammer in Kalisz. He came from Warsaw, and my brother Benno and I came from Danzig. Mietek and I saw each other at least once a year, and we shared some wonderful memories. Mietek recalled that when he graduated from the *Gimnazjum* in 1934, my parents invited him to spend the summer with us at the Baltic Sea. Mietek was the last link, my only link, to many childhood memories. As he now sat in his leather chair, he wanted to share these memories with me. Then he took out his photo album and showed me pictures of his latest travels with Klara. Unhappily he said, "Without these trips life is meaningless to me. Now I am living from one blood transfusion to the next. I do not want to live like this." When I told him not to give up, to fight, he said, "I already lived longer than any member of my family. I do not want to fight. I do not want to live." These words were coming from a man who was always so full of life, who went through many hardships in Siberia during World War II, who fought as an officer in Anders's Polish army and who was a lieutenant colonel in the Israeli army. I realized that I was not sitting with the same Mietek I had known all my life. Here was a man who was tired of living and had no wish to go on. It was time for me to leave. Mietek presented me with a charming silver necklace with turquoise stones: "This is a gift from Klara and me." Our eyes filled with tears when we said our good-byes. I knew that I would never see Mietek again. We spoke for the last time on July 20. When I called one week later, he was in the hospital and Klara prepared me for the worst. On August 1, 2001, Didi called and told me that her daddy just passed away. He died peacefully surrounded by his loved ones. May his memory be for a blessing. I shall miss Mietek, his Polish jokes, his humor. But most of all I shall miss the telephone calls before each holiday. He used to call early in the morning (our time) to wish me "Chag Sameach"—happy holidays. To me he was like an older brother, a caring and loving relative. He was blessed with a loving daughter, son-in-law, three wonderful grandchildren, and a devoted companion, Klara.

Chapter 17

The Survival of Gutek Krzewin (1927–1986)

In 1960, fifteen years after the end of World War II, I learned that my first cousin Gutek Krzewin had survived and was alive. A miracle—I had found another close member of my family. The first one was Michael Lachman, who recently died in Israel. It was Michael who wrote me that Gutek had survived, and gave me his address in London.

Gutek Krzewin was the only child of my mother's younger sister Hela (Haya) Hammer and her husband, Zygmunt Krzewin. Hela, born in Kalisz in 1902, met her future husband in 1923, and they were married the same year. Their son, Gutek, was born in 1927. The family resided in Kalisz until the outbreak of World War II.

Both of Gutek's parents were good looking—his mother tall and very attractive, his father dark, tall, and handsome. Zygmunt was a printer and owned a printing shop in Kalisz. An ardent socialist, he always fought for the rights of the working class. He was an atheist; there was no religion in the

Krzewin home. Hela tried to earn a little money to supplement Zygmunt's income. An enterprising woman, she learned to be a manicurist. This profession was not too successful. She had a good friend, Jan Morek, a Christian Pole who owned a car. She and Jan formed a partnership and each summer they drove vacationers to many summer resorts near Kalisz. Again, this was only a summer business. She was a most enterprising woman; she always found ways to earn additional income for her family. Jan Morek was a devoted family friend, always ready to help. He was very much in love with Hela, and I think she loved him too.

I remember Gutek from the time when he was a two-year-old boy. He and his parents always came to my grandparents Hammer to celebrate the second Seder. In April 1930 the whole Hammer family had a picture taken in Kalisz by Engel, a photographer who had a studio in the Kalisz park. In that picture Gutek and my brother, Benno, both age two, were seated on little chairs. When Gutek was older, around six years old, Uncle Zygmunt provided us with free tickets to movie houses. As a printer, he was printing all the tickets for five movie houses in Kalisz and was given free tickets. These he gave us each time when my brother and I came to Kalisz for Passover. The three of us, Gutek, Benno, and I went each day to see another movie. We had such a good time together. I saw more movies in Kalisz than I can recall. But there was one that I still remember; it was a scary movie with the title *The Black Cat.*

The next time I saw Gutek was in Warsaw in October 1939, when my family was forced out of Danzig. Here I was reunited with Gutek; we saw each other frequently. By the end of January 1940, when conditions in Warsaw became unbearable, my family left for Tomaszow-Mazowiecki. Then I saw Gutek and his family again in May 1941. My father and I came to Warsaw so that I could take the final exam for high school, which was given in total secrecy. The Krzewins had moved to Sienna Street, and at that time we spent two nights with them. This was the last time that I saw Hela and Zygmunt Krzewin.

The liquidation of the Warsaw ghetto started on July 20, 1942. The first members to be taken to the death camp of Treblinka were Uncle David Lachman, his daughter, Marysia, her husband and their two-year-old son, then Uncle Heniek Hammer's wife, Rozka, with their eight-year-old son, Jasio. Aunt Gucia Lachman, who was hiding with other relatives, decided to join Hela, Zygmunt, Heniek, and Gutek and moved into their lodging. After Gucia and Hela were taken away, Zygmunt started to doubt the safety of any one of them in Warsaw and wanted to protect the life of his son, Gutek. He got in touch with Jan Morek, their old family friend from Kalisz, who lived outside Warsaw. When he learned from Zygmunt that Hela Krzewin was gone, he provided Gutek with Polish papers in the name of Tadeusz Podkulecki, born in 1925. These papers were authentic, and it was important that the age was close to Gutek's. Now I am quoting Gutek's words from the letter he wrote to me in 1964: "My father decided to escape. He looked like a Pole and was planning to run away before the column returned from the *Baustelle*. While [Uncle] Hammer and I returned to the ghetto, my father escaped. I never saw him again; I was told that the Nazis caught him and that he was killed. It was time for me to leave, too. I had the papers Morek gave me and left after work and went to Morek's sister. She was hiding me for some time. Morek came every day; he was so good to me. He also provided Uncle [Heniek] Hammer with Polish papers in the name of Ludwik Turkiewicz. Morek gave me some money; the few valuables my father gave me were gone, I do not know what happened to them. Morek insisted that I sign up for work as a Pole outside of Poland; this would be safer for me. At first I did not succeed. On the second try I managed to be sent to Graz, Austria. There I had to work outdoors in the coldest weather from 8 a.m. to 8 p.m. As a Pole I was paid for my work and managed to save enough money for a ticket to Vienna. Here I enlisted in the International Camp as an auto mechanic, knowing that Opel had a factory in Vienna. Thanks to a Polish secretary at the Opel plant, I found work for nine months. In winter of 1943 I escaped with a group of Polish workers and we went to Berlin. I never felt safe in one place. While working for OT (*Organisation Todt*), a German supply outfit that also built and repaired roads and bridges, our group stole uniforms as well as papers. Dressed in these uniforms we traveled to Italy. I came to Rimini, where I went into hiding until the Germans left this part of Italy. I later joined the 2nd Corps of the British Army unit stationed in Italy.

"I traveled with the British outfit to Anconia, where by sheer luck I ran into my cousin, Mietek (Michael) Lachman from Warsaw. After spending years in the Soviet Union, Mietek came to Italy with the Polish Anders army. He knew nothing of the fate of his family; I told him the sad news about his parents, his only sister, and her family. Mietek was also the sole survivor of his family. After a few days we parted and I left for England. I was dismissed from the British army in 1947."

The rest of Gutek's story I learned from talking to his daughters, his first wife, and to Gutek himself. Gutek/Tadeusz found a new home with a Catholic family in England. They had many children and gave him the warmth and love he so desperately needed. He never told them that he was Jewish, only that he was a Pole from Warsaw. In 1950 Gutek changed his name again; this time he became Tony Gorbutt. First he was Gutek, then Tadeusz, and now Tony. He fell in love with one of the daughters of his new family. They married and soon became parents to two beautiful girls, Sarah and Karen. Gutek had a hard time adjusting to normal life. To help support his family he had to learn a profession and became an optical technician. He could not hold a job for long. Soon he became restless and went through periods of depression. His next job was as supervisor and later director for a kosher catering outfit in London. Gutek inherited his parents' good looks; he was extremely handsome. Unfortunately, he began to drink and smoke more than was good for his health. All this had a negative effect on his home life. His wife became ill; she was troubled by manic depression.

In 1977 Gutek met an attractive young woman and they fell madly in love. Soon Gutek and his first wife were divorced, but they always remained good friends. Throughout his life Gutek cared for her, and he was a devoted father to his much beloved daughters.

In April 1982 Gutek and Rhona, his new love, were married; in December 1983 their only son, Simon, was born. They were a happy family, although Gutek continued to be driven by demons.

Gutek and I had not seen each other since 1941. We were in touch and had corresponded since 1963. My family was planning a journey to Israel for the unveiling of my dear father's tombstone in November 1979. I wrote to Gutek, asking him to "please come to Israel to meet my family and to reunite with me." He and Mietek Lachman in Israel were my only living cousins, the remnants of our families. Gutek complied, and we met again after thirty-eight long years. The occasion was a sad one, at the grave of my father. But it brought us together and formed a family bond. Gutek asked Max and me to stop in London on our way back to the United States to meet his two daughters. The visit to London was memorable. Gutek waited for us at the airport. By now he was working as manager for a tourist-oriented company with many night clubs and entertainment. He picked us up in a Rolls Royce (compliments of the company). This was the only time in our lives that we rode in such a prestigious car. We were staying with my old school friend from Danzig on Harley Street, Lusia Krakowska Arendt, and her husband, Jurek. She and I had not seen each other since 1940 and had so much to share, so much to catch up on. Gutek invited my friends and us to night clubs; he wined and dined us. And we had the pleasure of meeting his two lovely daughters, Sarah and Karen. It was amazing how much the two girls resembled Gutek's father, Zygmunt. We also met Gutek's divorced wife, Sylvia, a warm and lovely person. Yet I was troubled. I saw the extent of Gutek's drinking and became worried. He was living in the fast lane. His daily schedule was such that he slept most of the day; work started at nightfall and lasted until morning. He certainly enjoyed what he was doing. Gutek loved people and was well liked by all. His good looks certainly were an asset.

I saw Gutek again in June 1985 when Max and I were returning home from Israel. Gutek wrote me that he was not well and that he would like to see me. We were guests of Gutek, Rhona, and little Simon, who was sixteen months old. Rhona was young, beautiful, kind, and a perfect hostess. Simon was an adorable toddler, and I could see how much Gutek loved this child. Gutek looked tired, drawn, exhausted. He stopped working and was on painkillers. Gutek had a cancerous kidney removed in the winter of 1985 and was in constant pain. This was not the same Gutek I knew. Most of the time he just sat in his favorite chair and watched old movies. Rhona was taking such good care of him, but Gutek was often irritable and moody. He and I talked a lot. I had to remind him of periods in our lives when we spent time together in Kalisz. His memory was not the best, but he did recall many events. He would sit and talk with Max for hours. Max was for him a father figure, the father he had lost as a young boy. One day Gutek asked me if I would prepare gefilte fish just like Grandma Hammer used to make. I went to the fresh fish market and was able to obtain fresh salmon and white fish. They chopped and prepared it for me, and I cooked for Gutek his favorite dish, a reminder of his childhood. The next day he asked me to cook chicken soup. I made a huge pot so that Rhona could freeze some of it after we left. These little things were Gutek's reminders of his childhood, of his Jewish heritage.

Mira and Tony Gorbutt in London, June 19, 1985.

THE SURVIVAL OF GUTEK KRZEWIN

A few weeks later we left London. Gutek, Rhona, and Simon took us to the airport. At that time Max, too, was not feeling well; he, too, had kidney problems. I saw Gutek at the airport in London in August 1985 for the last time. Rhona called me in January 1986 to inform me of Gutek's death. He was too young to die; he was only fifty-eight years old. Rhona was with him to the last minute. She had his body cremated and buried the ashes in the church yard. Rhona was devastated. Now she was alone with a two-year-old son. She and I stayed in touch, and when she met someone a few years later and married I was delighted. After years in London, Rhona and her husband left England and settled in southern Spain, where they reside to this day.

As previously mentioned, growing up in a home with an atheist father and an assimilated mother, Gutek had no Jewish upbringing or Jewish education. He knew almost nothing about his heritage. When the war ended, he really did not want to remain Jewish and never told his first wife about his origin. Yet most of the places where he worked were Jewish. He loved Jewish food; this was his only link to his past. When his daughters were older, he did tell them about his background. Gutek was only fifteen years old when he lost his parents. Too young to cope with the tragedy, he tried to forget; he drank to forget. Depression followed. He never wanted to talk about his past, except to me. He asked me to tell his children about his parents, about his grandparents. All this was too painful; he could not do it. He was haunted by the loss of his parents; he lived in perpetual pain. How much he would have loved to see his grandchildren and his beloved son, Simon, grow up. Gutek was a loving person and will be remembered by all who loved him. He, too, was a victim of the Holocaust.

Addendum

In August 2000, out of the blue sky, I received a telephone call from Rhona, Gutek's widow. Remarried and residing in Spain, she called to ask if she, Simon (Gutek's son), and her husband could visit me. I was delighted and quite excited to see her after fifteen years. But most of all to see Simon, who was sixteen months old when I saw him last. The three of them arrived on Sunday, August 20. Rhona was still as attractive and pretty as I remembered her. Her husband, Charles, was a most pleasant, witty, and smart man. And Simon, now sixteen years old, was 6 feet 2 inches—a good-looking, slim, dark, and charming young man. I only wished that Gutek could have seen his son. Rhona had done an excellent job raising him, giving him all the love and affection a child can ask for. To become reacquainted with Rhona and Simon was wonderful.

I felt that Rhona needed to read my chapter about Gutek's life. She knew some of his experiences, but Gutek never wanted to divulge details about his past. When Rhona came to the place about Gutek's escape from Vienna to Berlin, she mentioned to me what Gutek had told her shortly before they were married. "With a few Polish men I left Vienna. I do not know why, but we were stopped by some German soldiers and told to strip. It was very cold, and I was sure that this would be the end of me. If they noticed my circumcision, they would shoot me. I do not know if it was the bitter cold or a simple miracle, but they never noticed that I had been circumcised. I think that somebody in our group must have suspected that a Jew was among us and reported it to the Germans. But it ended well, although I could have paid with my life for the inspection. When I had a physical checkup not long ago, the doctor mentioned to me that my circumcision was not a very good one. I told him the story of my escape during the war and about the inspection. The doctor said, 'The *mohel* (person who performs Jewish circumcisions) saved your life. He did a poor job; therefore the Germans let you go. Only an expert would have seen the circumcision.' Well, now I knew why I passed the inspection. The cold plus the faulty job done on me saved my life." I was glad that Rhona disclosed this incident, that she remembered it and was able to recall Gutek's words. She cried while reading about her beloved Tony and insisted that Simon read the chapter, too. His only memories of his father are what Rhona or I have told him.

ANOTHER ADDENDUM

While in England for the Ryczke family reunion in 2002, I wanted to see my family on my mother's side, too—the Hammer side. I had met Tony Gorbutt's (Gutek Krzewin's) two daughters, Karen and Sarah, many years ago, and I wanted to see them again. For a few days before the Ryczke reunion, I stayed with Gutek's beautiful daughter Karen, her companion Matthew, and their adorable daughters, Jessica and Helena. I also had a chance to get reacquainted with Sarah and her two children. This time I had the good fortune to get to know better Gutek's first wife, Sylvia. She poured out her heart and talked at length about meeting Gutek and their marriage. And then an unexpected bonus: Rhona (Gutek's second wife) and their son, Simon, flew in from Spain to be with me. How nice of them—I was very touched. And so we had our small family get together. Gutek would have been so proud to see his three children all grown up, all very precious young people. He would have loved his four grandchildren, the youngest one was named after his dear mother (Hela Krzewin) of blessed memory. And so my journey to London served two purposes: a Ryczke family reunion and a reunion of the Gorbutt (Hammer) family.

Tony Gorbutt's children, London, 2002. *Left to right:* Sarah, Simon, and Karen, with Mira.

Chapter 18

HERMAN (HARRY) SZMANT (1918–2000)—
THE LONE SURVIVOR OF THE SZMANT FAMILY

The only close relatives who resided in Danzig while I was growing up were Leon and Tillie Szmant and their two children, Celina and Harry. My earliest recollections of the Szmant family were from 1929. Uncle Leon and Aunt Tillie resided then at 26 Milchkannengasse, while we lived not far from them on Brotbänkengasse. Aunt Tillie was the sister of my grandfather Shlomo Hammer, my mother's father, while Uncle Leon was the brother of my grandmother Sarah Szmant Hammer. The Szmant family moved to Danzig from Kalisz in 1921 with Celina and Harry. They were my mother's close relatives, and I saw them quite often.

Celina, born in 1911 in Kalisz, attended the Polish *Gimnazjum* in Danzig and graduated in 1929. A very talented and capable young lady, she had a special gift for languages. She and my mother were close, although she was much younger. I remember Celina calling my mother in 1933 and inviting us to a piano recital given at the Danziger Hof restaurant. At that time we were living at 10 Dominikswall, very close to where the recital took place. I went with my mother, and at the age of ten was greatly impressed by the students who played piano during the recital. Celina and Harry were part of the recital. Their teacher was Lucie Jung, a close friend of Celina's. Miss Jung, too, lived on Milchkannengasse and was a neighbor of the Szmants. My mother was introduced to Lucie Jung, and the next thing I remember is that my parents purchased a black upright piano, a Sommerfeld piano, so that I could study music with Miss Jung. After three years of lessons, Miss Jung, who was German, was told to stop teaching Jewish students. Nazi rules were already in effect in Danzig. By 1937 I had a Jewish piano teacher, Mrs. Slotowsky, from Budapest. She came to Danzig to escape Hungarian anti-Semitism. Her stage name was Feher. She and her family left Danzig in June 1939 for northern Manchuria. I vividly remember going to her home with my brother to say good-bye.

In 1934 the Szmants moved to 27/28 Holzmarkt. Harry (whose Hebrew name was Chaim, after his maternal grandfather) attended the Polish *Gimnazjum* and graduated in 1936. We often walked to school together, as he had to pass my house on the way to school. Of course he was much older, and I was proud to be seen in his company. This was the time in Danzig when most Jews belonged to some Jewish Zionist organization. Many organizations thrived in the city. My parents both belonged to the Zionist "Verein." My mother was active in the Zionist women's movement, WIZO. We, the youth, had many choices—*Habonim, Blau-Weiss, JJB (Jung-Jüdischer Bund), Akiba,* and the right-wing *Betar.* I belonged to *Habonim* (The Builders) as well as to the *Turnverein Bar Kochba (Bar Kochba* Gymnastics Society). We had an excellent instructor, Herr Radischewski, who was an ardent anti-Nazi. It was in the Zionist youth organization that I became acquainted with modern Hebrew. How different it sounded from the Ashkenazi pronunciation of the prayers I had learned. I loved to sing the Hebrew songs and to learn modern Hebrew. We were also exposed to Jewish history and the history of Zionism. Soon Theodor Herzl became my hero. And so I became immersed in Jewish life outside of my everyday school life. Anti-Semitism only strengthened our desire to protect our Jewishness; the Zionist movement and Jewish studies were my defense against the rising

Nazism. Harry joined the religious-Zionist organization of *Akiba*. Harry was a great influence on my young brother, Benno, who too was considering which organization to join. Harry became his mentor, and Benno also joined *Akiba*.

Uncle Leon and Aunt Tillie insisted that Harry study abroad. The situation for Jews in Danzig was deteriorating, and in 1937 Harry left for the United States. He was admitted to the University of Cincinnati. His sister, Celina, at that time was working for the Spanish consulate in Danzig. In 1937 she got married and moved with her husband to the city of Lodz in Poland. In early 1938 Uncle Leon and Aunt Tillie left Danzig for good. They, too, settled in Lodz. I saw them for the last time walking the main street in Zoppot during the summer of 1937.

During the war Harry's parents and sister were in the Lodz ghetto. They did not survive. All I know is that they perished during the Holocaust. That left Harry as the sole survivor of the Szmant family.

When my husband Max and I came to Cincinnati in 1948, I contacted the University of Cincinnati in order to trace Harry. All they knew was that before the war he was on a student visa. He had to leave the United States to request permanent residency, and he had two options while his request was being processed—to go to Canada or to Cuba.

Harry had chosen Cuba. After two years of writing, I finally was given an address in Santiago de Cuba. I wrote to Harry and received an immediate reply. At the time (1956) he was teaching at the university in Santiago. He was married to a Cuban native by the name of Nita and was the father of two children—a daughter, Alina, and a son, Michael. This was the only letter I received from Cuba. It took many years until we connected again. This, too, happened by chance. While reading *Life* magazine, I noticed on the cover among other names the name Alina Szmant. She was one of many scientists working at La Jolla in a marine biology lab. I only knew of one family named Szmant. She must be Harry's daughter, I thought. The year was 1970. I tried to contact Alina through the University of California San Diego at La Jolla. After trying to get in touch with her and leaving my telephone number, I had to leave for New Jersey to be with my father. Alina got the message and called our home. She spoke to our son, Gene, and gave him the address of her parents. Harry was now teaching chemistry at the University of Detroit.

He wrote me about their flight from Cuba, about the many places he had been since I had heard from him last. He and his wife, Nita, became ardent orchid collectors and were attending conventions all over the United States. He mentioned that the next one, in 1971, would take place in Knoxville, Tennessee. This was a perfect chance for Harry and me to be reconnected. I invited them, and they came to visit in October 1971. After thirty-four years, I saw Harry again. He was the spitting image of his father, Leon. Harry came with Nita, and we spent a wonderful day together. My father was staying with us at that time, and together we reminisced about the years when we lived in Danzig. I was amazed that Harry had forgotten almost all his Polish and German. The languages he had spoken for the past thirty-some years were English and Spanish. But he could understand when my father spoke to him in Polish. Harry promised to remain in touch.

In 1979, after my father passed away, I tried to collect Danzig memories from my old Danzig friends and relatives. I sent Harry a questionnaire asking him to fill it out and return it to me. There was silence. I received no answer from Harry. Finally I called him and asked why he did not answer my questions. Harry did not wish to speak about the past.

When, in 1991 and 1993, I traveled to Gdańsk and went to see our old *Gimnazjum,* I had to think about Harry and Celina. From an old school friend of Harry's, Leon Lendzion, I heard that Harry had moved to Florida. He gave me the address, and again I began writing to Harry. This time he answered every letter. He was retired and lived with his wife on Sanibel Island, Florida. I wrote him about my visits to Danzig, about seeing his old school friend Leon. Harry wanted me to visit him on Sanibel Island, but they soon had to move again. His wife, Nita, needed constant help, and Alina decided that they should move closer to her, to Miami. We spoke on the telephone from time to time, and I was planning to go and see him soon. The opportunity presented itself in October 1995. I contacted Alina and told her that I would be in Miami to attend a meeting. Right away she invited me to come for a few days and stay with her and her family. I accepted. She and Harry met me at the airport. I was delighted to meet Alina and later her husband, Dan, and their daughter, Kaitlin. I spent the whole next day with Harry. I wanted to utilize every minute to be with him. Nita was in a wheelchair; she did remember me from her visit to Oak Ridge in 1971.

Harry Szmant with his daughter Alina Baden, Miami, October 20, 1995.

Harry seemed depressed; I thought the reason was his wife's illness. But there were deeper reasons for his depression. At first he did not want to talk about the past. But suddenly the past came alive. He could not stop talking. He regretted that he never returned to Danzig after the war; he tried to blot out the past. "But I can still do it, and Alina will come with me," he said. I shared with Harry my visits to our hometown, told him about my visit to his friend, Leon Lendzion. We also spoke about religion. Both his parents had belonged to the same Orthodox synagogue my parents belonged to, the Mattenbuden Synagogue in Danzig. Harry belonged to the religious Zionist youth movement *Akiba*. He told me that when he learned about the death of his parents and only sister, he lost all faith in God. He never embraced another religion and said, "If my religion could not save my family, then there is no God, and I do not believe in anything anymore." He certainly was not the only one who distanced himself from religion after the Holocaust. I tried to tell him that faith gave me the strength to survive, but his was a different opinion. We parted, hoping to see each other again. His physical and mental state deteriorated; Alina had help for him and her mother twenty-four hours a day. Harry soon did not respond to Alina; Alzheimer's disease took its toll. Harry Szmant passed away on July 10, 2000, with his wife, Nita, and daughter, Alina, at his side. He was eighty-two years old. Another link with my past was gone; only memories remain.

All her life, until she was eighteen years old, Alina only heard her father telling her about his young years as a Pole; he never mentioned to his children his Jewish origin. Harry wanted so much to be Polish, to erase his Jewish religion and heritage. In the eyes of his children he was Polish. Unfortunately, in Europe Jews were first and foremost Jews; their belonging as citizens to a country came second. I believe that Harry hid the pain of losing his parents and sister behind the mask of the Pole Harry Szmant. Like all of us who have lost dear ones, he, too, lived with feelings of guilt—guilt for being alive while our dear ones died. These feelings haunt most of us who have survived. Although Harry had spent the war years free from persecution, he, too, became a victim of Hitler's war against the Jews. He saw no need to give his children any direction when it came to religion; religion simply did not exist for him. Alina confided in me that she would have liked to know more about Jewish culture and traditions. What little religious education Alina received was as a Catholic during the years the family lived in Cuba (1956–61), continuing after they moved to Puerto Rico. But she, too, ended up rejecting religion, and like her father became an atheist by the age of eighteen. Her husband is Protestant, but they are raising their daughter without any religious training and allowing her to choose her own direction.

I wondered many times if Harry would have relinquished religion, tradition, and his heritage if there had been no Holocaust.

HERMAN (HARRY) SZMANT

Chapter 19

HALINKA FRYDLENDER GELLES—
A DISTANT COUSIN

Once the war was over and we were free, everybody was looking for surviving family members, close or distant. Where I was living in the displaced persons camp in Belsen I luckily found a relative of mine, Halinka Frydlender. Halinka and I had common great-great-grandparents named Ader. Our mothers were second cousins, our grandmothers first cousins. To me Halinka was a relative and a friend.

Before the war the Frydlender family resided in the city of Lodz (which was called the Polish Manchester because of its textile industry) on Limanowskiego Street. The family house was on the premises of their textile factory. Halinka's parents, the late Stasiek and Mina Frydlender, born Przygorska, had three children. Halinka had two older brothers, Pawel, born in 1910, and Rafal, born in 1917. Halinka and I were almost the same age; both of us were born in 1923. She and I became close friends in 1938 when I was visiting my paternal grandparents Ryczke after they moved from Kalisz to Lodz. Halinka, being the youngest child, was adored by her parents and brothers. She was loved and spoiled, especially by her brothers, whom she worshiped. When World War II broke out in September 1939, her brothers were in the Polish army and left Lodz. After the fall of Poland they managed to cross the eastern frontier and remained on the Soviet side.

By the end of 1939, Lodz was incorporated into Greater Germany and became a part of the German Reich. When a ghetto was being established in the oldest and most dilapidated part of the city, Halinka and her parents managed to escape to the nearest town in the General Government (Poland proper), to the city of Piotrkow-Trybunalski. Although at the time of their arrival Piotrkow already had a ghetto, conditions were better than in Lodz. While the Frydlenders lived on Szewcka Street in the Piotrkow ghetto, my family and I were only thirty-three kilometers away from them in the Tomaszow-Mazowiecki ghetto. I found out about Halinka's whereabouts from people who came to our ghetto from Piotrkow, and she and I corresponded via ghetto mail for a short while until 1941.

When Halinka and I were reunited in Belsen in early May 1945, I spent one night with her and she told me about her life in the ghetto. "While I lived in the Piotrkow ghetto with my parents, I met a fine young man by the name of Kuba Szlesinger. Kuba was the nephew of the president of the ghetto *Judenrat,* Szymon Warszawski," Halinka began her story. "In 1942, before the liquidation of our ghetto, my parents purchased false Polish papers and tried to leave for the Polish side. I was to follow them a few days later. Unfortunately my parents were caught and brought back to the ghetto and jailed. Through bribery it was still possible to save them and I used money and jewelry that we had to bail them out. Those Jews who were caught with Aryan papers but had no one to pay for their release were either shot in the synagogue where they were kept as hostages or taken to the Rakow Forest outside of Piotrkow and killed there. Four times my parents were taken to the synagogue; four times I was able to bail them out. Then the money ran out. I was told that if I would get married, my parents would be allowed to

HALINKA FRYDLENDER GELLES

be present, they would be released from the synagogue. Kuba and I immediately agreed to be married so that my parents could be freed. They were
present when Kuba and I became husband and wife. A few weeks later the
Gestapo arrested fifty people: forty-three men and seven women. My parents
and I were among them. I was separated from my parents. Soon I learned
that forty-eight of the fifty Jews, including my dear parents, were taken to
the Rakow Forest and shot. I shared the cell with another young woman, a
friend of mine, Franka Kenigstein. For four months I was in jail. I was tor-
tured by the Gestapo for four months, subjected to indescribable humiliation, physical pain, and mental cruelty. I was only twenty years old, but I still
bear the scars. By some miracle only Franka and I escaped execution."

When the Piotrkow-Trybunalski ghetto was liquidated in November
1944, Halinka, with most of the women, was taken to the Ravensbrück concentration camp. Her closest friend throughout the time in the camps was
Luise. She became like a sister to her, sharing food and shielding Halinka.
After the war the exhumed bodies of the victims of the massacre in the forest of Rakow were buried in the Piotrkow Jewish Cemetery, which I visited
in 1990 and 1993. On the monument it says, "In memory of the 50 victims
arrested and shot by the Gestapo in 1943." This means that Halinka and
Franka were counted among the dead.

I told my father about Halinka's survival and how glad I was that she
did not succeed in persuading me to leave with her for Sweden. During my
father's odyssey to Poland in search of my brother, Benno, he stopped in
Lodz, which became after the war a center for Jews who returned from camps
or from the Soviet Union. There he learned that Rafal Frydlender, Halinka's
younger brother, lived in the city. He found his address and spent the night
at his apartment. They talked about their experiences during the war,
exchanged news about relatives and friends who survived and who did not.
While they talked, my father asked Rafal, "When did you hear from your
brother, Pawel, the last time?" Rafal was separated from Pawel while fighting the Germans and did not know what had happened to his brother. My
father told him that Pawel was alive in Palestine. Rafal was elated. Pawel was
alive and he would contact him right away. When my father left Rafal the

next morning, he returned a few minutes later. He said to Rafal, "It occurred to me that if you did not know about Pawel, you may not know that your sister, Halinka, is alive and well in Sweden." And so Rafal Frydlender learned from my father in August 1945 that his brother, Pawel, and sister, Halinka, survived the war. A few years later Rafal left Poland for Israel.

The next time I saw Halinka was in Tel Aviv in May 1971 when Max and I traveled to Israel to celebrate our twenty-fifth wedding anniversary. Halinka's brother Rafal resided there with his wife as well. Her brother Pawel had died in 1970. All of us met at the home of Diana Rubin Adler, my dear friend from Tomaszow. What a spectacular and happy reunion this was, seeing Halinka after twenty-six years, and her brother after thirty-two years. Luise, in the meantime, moved to the United States and married Salek Gotthelf, who was in the camp of Majdanek/Blizyn with me. Salek, his father Alexander, and younger brother Jozek came to our wedding in Rötz in May 1946. Alexander Gotthelf was a good friend of my husband's older brother Leon. His signature is on our *ketubah* as one of the witnesses. Now Luise is a widow; Salek died very young. We see each other every time I visit my children in New York.

Halinka left the Belsen camp in 1945 for Sweden. In 1946, she met and married a German Jew, Werner Gelles, who had come to Sweden in 1943. Born in Essen in 1915 (making him eight years older than Halinka), Werner Gelles moved to Hamburg with his family when he was a small boy. The name Gelles is Hungarian. Werner's father had come to Germany from Hungary. His mother's family was from Poland. In 1939, Werner, who was a member of the Zionist youth organization *Blau-Weiss* for many years, left Hamburg for Denmark. As part of *Hechalutz* (another Zionist youth organization), he and other young Jewish people came to Denmark to be on *hachshara* (a course preparing young Jewish people to work the land and become farmers in Palestine).

Erna Schwartz, a dear friend of mine from Danzig who was my leader in *Habonim,* also left for Denmark. Saved in Sweden, she moved to what is now Israel after the war. I found Erna's whereabouts in winter of 2003 and telephoned her often. In Israel she had married a young man from Berlin; Erna and her husband had three children. Erna died in May 2003. I spoke

HALINKA FRYDLENDER GELLES

to her the last time two days before she died. She was the only one who called me "Mirachen," just as my parents did.

While Werner left for Denmark in 1939, his parents left Hamburg for Brussels. In 1943 they were sent to Auschwitz and perished there. Werner and his friends were sent to a farm on the island of Fyn, to Kyferndruk, forty kilometers from Odense. It so happened that I knew this part of Denmark because our son, Gene, spent a year on Fyn. When the Germans came to Denmark on April 9, 1940, life for the Jewish youth became more difficult. There were twenty young Jewish men and women working on Danish farms learning to milk cows and to work the land from 6 a.m. till evening. The Danish people were very good to them, and until his death Werner was in touch with the children of his friends on Fyn. Werner and Halinka sent gifts to them for Christmas and visited them every year in Denmark.

The year was 1943. On October 1, the Nazis wanted to round up all Jews living in Denmark and deport them to Auschwitz. A German by the name of Georg Duckwitz, who worked as an attaché for the German merchant marine in Copenhagen, shared this news with Hans Hedtoft, a Danish social-ist who warned the Jewish leaders about the forthcoming "Aktion." The Danes helped to organize a rescue operation for the Jews. Werner and his friends helped to flee from Fyn to Copenhagen. Here Danish students took them to the *Statshospital* (state hospital). The young people slept on straw on the roof. On a certain day in October 1943, all were taken at noon from Copenhagen and brought to the seashore. At night, in small fishing boats, their rescuers took them ten kilometers across the sound to Sweden. Almost six thousand Jews were taken out of Denmark to Sweden and their lives were saved.

In Sweden, Werner first went to a summer camp for one week. Then he and his friends worked on a farm in southern Sweden for six months and later up north on a farm near Eskestona. By 1945 Werner found a job in a tex-tile factory. The owner was Jewish and was very kind to him. Werner remem-bered that when he was taken to the factory, he was given a coat for winter.

After meeting and marrying, Werner and Halinka first settled in Malmö, then in Eskestona, and then they moved back to Malmö. This is where I met Werner for the first time in summer 1991 upon returning from my first trip to Danzig. Having taken a job as manager in a textile factory in 1945, Werner continued that work after he and Halinka were married. Then they moved to Eskestona and opened a store with quality fruit and vegetables. They had no children of their own, so they adopted a Swedish girl, Margarita. The little girl had already been in three foster homes and was an abused child. Werner and Halinka gave her all the love and care they could, but it was not easy. She is now a grown woman with two sons of her own. Halinka visited her brothers in Israel quite often; she wanted to be close to them. There was a time when she wanted to move to Israel, but Werner refused. He did not speak the Hebrew language; Sweden was now his country. Being older than Halinka, he had no strength to start life from scratch. Halinka lost her brothers—both Pawel and Rafal died at the age of fifty-six. She missed them more than she missed her parents and mourned their deaths for years. Her brothers were her life, her strength. And now their children visit Halinka in Sweden. She sees her brothers in them.

For many years Halinka and Werner spent the winter months in Spain. Shortly after they purchased their home in Costa del Sol, during one of their trips to Spain, Werner suffered a stroke at the Madrid airport. He was partially paralyzed and used a wheelchair to move around the house. Yet he was able to drive the car. What struck me was Werner's humor. He had the sharpest mind and a remarkable memory. For every situation Werner had a joke and a story. He loved to share his stories, especially when he could do it in his native tongue of German.

Halinka was a perfect wife. She took excellent care of Werner and catered to all his wishes. But she, too, was getting older and suffered from arthritis. Many times she was in great pain, yet she never let Werner know.

In January 1999 Halinka called with the sad news that Werner had passed away. She was left alone and did not know where to turn. First she wanted to move to her daughter's. After being near her for a few weeks, she returned to her house. Then she wanted to move into a retirement home. This, too, did not materialize. Finally she decided to remain in her house. She would hire somebody to help with the housework. No more planting roses, no more garden. With Werner gone, she turned to some of the friends

Halinka Frydlender Gelles, Malmö, August 1991.

she had neglected for many years. Halinka's spirit had been broken during the war years. She had suffered so much humiliation, so much pain. Now Halinka would have to make a life for herself, and I was sure that her friends would help her. Luise and I call her from time to time, and I keep writing to her. She does need every bit of moral support, and we shall continue to give it to her. We have invited Halinka to come and visit us in New York or Tennessee, but I doubt whether she will travel such a distance alone.

The few of us who are still alive—friends and relatives—know how little time there is left and how precious each moment is. And so we try to use every moment to be in touch, to talk or write to those who are so dear to us.

FAMILY TREE OF MIRA'S FATHER (RYCZKE)

Yetta

Rose Jacobs Roth

Faith Roth

Max (Jakubowski) Jacobs

Sam Roth

2. Bella Goldenberg

XX *Ester Cyruliczak- Jakubowski

Moritz (Moshe) Ryczke

*Benno Ryczke

XX *Efraim Ryczke

*1. Genia (Gitel) Hammer

2. Mira Ryczke Kimmelman

Caroline Chambers

Eugene Irvin "Gene" Kimmelman

Max Chambers Kimmelman

Eleanor Moore Kimmelman

Malka Weinberg

Max Kimmelman

Joy Noveck

Yitzhak Kimmelman

*1. Roma Basior

Louis Benjamin "Benno" Kimmelman

Michael Max Kimmelman

Melanie Marie Kimmelman

*Hela Zawacka

Mala Kolodner

Orly Gutfreund

*Aron Ryczke

Adam Ryczke

Ronnie Ritchke

*Maryla (Malka) Kimmelman

* Perished in the Holocaust
1. First marriage
2. Second marriage
XX Transliteration of Hebrew spelling

Chapter 20

DISCOVERING THE RYCZKE FAMILY

THEO RICHMOND

It was November 1995 and I was spending Thanksgiving with my children in New York City. While breezing through the *New York Times,* I came upon an article about *Konin,* a book written by Theo Richmond, a British author. The word *Konin* rang a bell. This was the small town in western Poland where part of the Ryczke family once lived. With my paternal grandmother, Esther Ryczke, I had visited Konin in 1933. I was not quite ten years old, but I vividly recalled my visit to Konin, a small town compared to my hometown, Gdańsk. Sixty years later, in 1993, with my older son, Benno, we drove through Konin and I told him of my visit as a ten-year-old girl. What a change: in 1993 Konin was a thriving city. During World War II deposits of natural gas had been discovered near Konin, and after the war Konin became a supplier of gas to heat water carried to all parts of Poland. The gas lines are visible everywhere.

After returning to Oak Ridge from my Thanksgiving visit, I ordered the book *Konin*. It took three weeks until the book was in my hands. Needless to say, I did not put it down until I finished it. While reading the book I found out that Theo Richmond's father was a Ryczke who changed his name to Richmond upon his arrival in England. A few days later a friend showed me the newspaper *Forward* where, in their book reviews, they mentioned the book *Konin* and that the Richmond name was originally Ryczke. Right away I had to recall the words of my dear father of blessed memory (Moritz Ryczke), "There was only one Ryczke family, and all of us were related." Now I was determined to get in touch with Theo Richmond. I obtained his address through his publisher and wrote him a long letter, explaining my family background.

In the meantime I found in the *Konin* book a chapter about Henry Kaplan, whom Theo interviewed for the book. Henry Kaplan was the brother of my aunt Rozka Kaplan Hammer. In the chapter Henry described the beginning of World War II, when bombs were falling on Konin and how he and his family members ran to a shelter. Anxiously I awaited Theo's reply. I wanted to know how we were related. A lengthy letter arrived from Theo. He was unable to shed light on our family relationship. But he did mention that he had a first cousin, David Richke, living in Israel. He thought maybe David could help answer my questions. My father lived the last five years of his life in Israel; he mentioned once that he heard of a certain Ryczke living there, but he never had a chance to meet him.

By sheer luck I had a chance to meet Theo in person in September 1996 while I was in New York for the High Holy Days and Theo was there for the publication of the paperback edition of *Konin*. We had breakfast in the hotel where Theo was staying, and from the moment we met there was an amazing bond between us. We felt like soul mates, as Theo said. We shared stories about our lives, about our families. And we promised to stay in close touch.

In November 1998, I traveled to Israel via London to be at my father's grave. Theo and I spent the day together during my stopover in London. I visited his house in Richmond-on-Thames and had the pleasure of meeting his lovely wife, Lee. At that time I still did not know how we were related.

David Richke

I wrote to Theo's cousin David in Israel. Not hearing from him, I telephoned him. David spoke perfect English. He told me that his father is buried at the Holon cemetery, the same one where my father, too, is buried. David told me that he noticed the grave with the name Ryczke, but he did not know who Moritz Ryczke was. Again I had no luck—David did not know how we were related. It was up to me now to search for our common roots.

In the meantime David did meet another Ryczke, my cousin Ronnie Ritchke in Ramat Aviv, Israel. When I visited Israel in 1998, Ronnie and I drove to Kfar Saba so that I could meet David Richke.

Grave of Moritz Ryczke in Holon, Israel.

Ronnie Ritchke

Ronnie's father, Adam Ryczke, was my father's first cousin. Our grandfathers were half brothers. Both had the same father, Benyamin Ryczke. Ronnie was very dear to me, like another son. He was a year older than my younger son, Gene, and two years younger than my older son, Benno.

Ronnie's life was not easy. Both his parents were not young when he was born. His mother, Mala, lost her first husband during the Holocaust and survived in hiding with her small son Daniel in France. They came to Israel, where they met Adam Ryczke. Adam, a handsome bachelor, fell in love with Mala. Some time later, Ronnie was born. He adored his older brother, Daniel. Unfortunately, in the Six-Day War in 1967, Daniel was killed, leaving a young wife with a child. The loss of this brother was devastating for the whole family, especially for Mala and Ronnie. Adam Ryczke tried to mold his only son into the man he was. Adam Ryczke was the son of a very authoritarian father, Aron Ryczke (I knew him well). Like father like son, Adam, too, was quite strict. Ronnie rebelled many times, but he loved his father and tried to please him.

I stayed with Ronnie many times while visiting Israel, and during my visit in 1998 he told me that he had melanoma. Surgery was performed and the doctors gave him a clean bill of health. In the meantime the cancer recurred in 1999. Ronnie underwent all possible treatments, and the disease was arrested (so we hoped). In April 2000 Ronnie married Orly. They were so much in love; they were such a beautiful couple. But there were more treatments necessary, more chemo, more radiation. I spoke with Ronnie at least twice a month, and he always assured me that he was fine.

When I called him in April 2001 to inform him about my coming to Israel, he sounded great and told me that I could stay with him and Orly, that he would wait for me at the airport. Well, things did not turn out this way. To catch my El Al flight, I had to fly to New York. I spent a few days with my children (Benno and family), then, one day before my departure, Benno had a call from Orly that Ronnie was very ill. He was in constant pain and too weak to leave the house. I right away made reservations in a hotel, and I knew that this journey to Israel would be a very sad one. I was going to see my only two cousins for the last time—Mietek and Ronnie—to assure them of my

Ronnie and Orly Ritchke, Tel Aviv, 1998.

love and give them my support. Although my children wanted me to cancel my trip, my heart told me that I had to go. I knew how ill both of them were.

Ronnie wanted to live; he never gave up. Orly was by his side day and night. And they had so many good friends who took turns to watch Ronnie, to help him to get to the hospital.

While I was sitting near his bed, Ronnie asked me, "What do you know about the Ryczke men?" I told him how all of them tried to discipline their children. I was speaking from my experience with my own father. "And they did it out of love," I said. We discussed with Ronnie how difficult it is to grow up in a strict household, but, on the other hand, whatever our parents did, was done out of love. David Richke was present during our discussion. He was of great moral support, and he visited and helped Ronnie as much as he could. In David, Ronnie had a devoted relative, a loving person. I understood that Ronnie was searching for the reassurance of love from his parents. He always disliked authority; as a child he had too much of it. But there was so much goodness, so much giving and love in Ronnie. He gave it to his parents, to his friends, to all of us who were close to him.

Seeing how little time there was left for forty-eight-year-old Ronnie, David and I talked about getting the Ryczke family together. Both of us realized that time was running out for all of us, and if we wanted to have a family gathering, we could not delay. This was a dream we wished to realize.

Ronnie also had a special bond with my older son, Benno. They loved each other like brothers. Benno flew to Israel to be with Ronnie after Adam Ryczke, his father, died. And he flew there to be at Ronnie's side when Orly called him to say that Ronnie wanted to see him.

I spoke with Ronnie every week after I returned home from Israel. When I said to him, "I wish I could take some of your pain away," Ronnie answered, "Each time you call, you are easing my pain." We spoke for the last time two days before he passed away. I told him how much I loved him. His voice was quite weak, but he wanted to speak to me. "Thank you for all your calls, I love you, too," were his last words to me. On November 6, 2001, Benno called me with the sad news that Ronnie had passed away peacefully. In his home, surrounded by his loving wife, Orly, and by relatives and friends, Ronnie Ritchke (Ryczke) died at the age of forty-eight. Ronnie was the last link of the Ryczke family who once lived in the town of Kolo. He died exactly one and a half years after Orly and he were married. My heart goes out to this beautiful young woman. The love that filled her and Ronnie's lives was strong. They cherished each moment they were together. Now memories of this love and close friendship will have to strengthen and sustain Orly.

I still did not know how Theo, David, Ronnie, and I were related to each other. With all our fathers gone, we had no one to ask questions. Back in Oak Ridge, I told a dear friend of mine, Ruth Gove, that I had to find out about the Ryczke family. Luckily, she, too, was doing genealogical research for her family and told me about the microfilms on file in the Mormon Church.

Right after World War II the Mormon Church sent people to Poland to copy the Jewish files on births, deaths, and marriages in many small towns and cities. These were microfilmed and reels were available for research. At first I rented reels from Kolo, Konin, and vicinity. Ruth and I sat for hours in a dark cubicle to read entries. Some were in Polish—no problem for me, but most were in Russian. Here I needed help from my Russian friends in Oak Ridge. I remember my excitement when I found the entry of the birth of my paternal grandfather, Efraim Ryczke, signed by my great-grandfather, Benyamin Ryczke. Now I had one piece of information, but not enough. Where was Benyamin born? Who were his parents? My eyes were giving me trouble. I could not sit for hours and read reels. Finally I decided to hire a professional genealogist, Nicki Russler. It took her months. Eventually she did find the common denominator: it turned out that Theo's, David's, Ronnie's, and my ancestors came from a tiny *shtetl* called Golina (about sixteen miles from Konin). Here my great-grandfather Benyamin Ryczke was born. I never heard of Golina and promised myself that on my next trip to Poland I would look up this small town. In May 1999 I drove with my cousin Alina Szmant from Gdańsk to Kalisz and stopped in Golina, a charming small town dating from the fourteenth century. Golina is now a bedroom community for the thriving big city of Konin. There are no Jews left. Most of them moved to Konin, Kolo, Kalisz, or Lodz before World War II. Why the Ryczke family ancestors decided to settle in Golina I will never know.

By the year 2000, I was able to mail the Ryczke family tree to all my cousins—Theo, David, and Ronnie. We now know that Theo, David, Ronnie, and I have a common great-great-grandfather, Mosiek Ryczke, who lived and died in Golina. My father was right; we are all related.

Chapter 21

THE RYCZKE FAMILY REUNION

"Welcome to London"—these words greeted me as I entered the lobby of the Hampton Quality Motel in London in September 2002. I arrived here for the Ryczke family gathering, so capably and efficiently planned by David Richke for the last weekend in September of 2002. David had selected London as the most accessible city for all concerned.

The idea that he and I discussed in Israel in 2001 became reality. He had a list of Ryczke family members scattered all over the globe, and here we were—twenty people from six countries. David did more research and found another Ryczke in Brussels, another first cousin in France, and a Ryczke in Toronto. All local arrangements were made by Theo's son-in-law Neil Vickers, who teaches English literature at one of the universities in London.

The warm greetings in the hotel lobby, the embracing, kissing, and hugging, made it from its inception a family affair. There was David, with his wife, Varda, and their two daughters, Noa and Smadar, from Israel. David's brother, Chanoch Richka, from Florida; Helene Ryczke Vautrin, (David, Theo, and Chanoch's first cousin) and her husband, Jacques, from France; Madeleine Ryczke Najman and her daughter Paulette from Brussels (we were not able to place her relationship to us); Mike (Moshe) Ryczke with his wife, Ariela, and daughter Orit from Toronto; yours truly Mira Ryczke Kimmelman from Oak Ridge, Tennessee; and Theo and Lee Richmond, their sons Jonathan, Simon, and Daniel, with wife, Maya, daughter Sarah and her husband, Neil Vickers, and their sons Noah and Samuel Terence. A total of twenty-two Ryczke family members (including Theo's two grandsons).

The reunion took quite some planning and endless e-mailing and telephoning to the members of the Ryczke clan. Thanks to David and Neil it all came together. Connected by a common surname, very soon we felt a kinship and closeness to each other. Except for Helene and Jacques (who only spoke French), all of us spoke English. Madeleine and Paulette helped to translate English into French and French into English. Madeleine sweetened our get-together with delicious Belgian chocolates—a box for each of us.

For Friday night dinner we walked to an Italian restaurant. The young people occupied a long table and were able to get acquainted, while the mature Ryczke family members engaged in conversation to get to know each other, too. A happy and relaxing evening with delicious food and much wine came to a close too soon. We walked back to our hotel knowing that the highlight of our reunion would follow the next day.

Neil made the arrangements for all of us to meet on Saturday morning at the Swiss Cottage, which we rented for the morning hours. The weather was just delightful—clear and crisp and sunny as we walked (some drove) to the cottage. The entire second floor was occupied by our family. David had prepared huge charts with the Ryczke family tree and handed out smaller copies for each one of us. A few of us contributed to this almost complete family tree, which made it easier for David. We could follow the lines of our relationships quite easily: from great-great-grandfather Mosiek Ryczke all the way to us. Only two families present—Mike Ryczke and Madeleine Ryczke—are still not sure how they fit into the puzzle that is the Ryczke family tree. One thing is sure—we are related.

Ryczke family reunion, London, September 2002. Mira in center rear.

Theo Richmond, author of *Konin,* greeted us as our official London host. He is such a warm and charming person; his words came from the heart. This reunion must have been a wonderful fulfillment. What started for Theo as a quest for family and the *shtetl* of Konin with the writing of his book reached its zenith with this reunion of the Ryczke family. All of us agreed that Theo's book *Konin* was the major factor in the search of family and our gathering here in London.

A few of us spoke about our lives. These were very moving personal stories. Mike Ryczke from Toronto shared his life story with us. He was born in Poland in 1939, a few months before the outbreak of World War II. His father, Aaron Ryczke, was a wealthy lumber merchant in Konin and owner of a sawmill. Both he and Mike's mother, Janka, were quite assimilated. In 1941 Aaron Ryczke was killed by the Nazis. Mike (Mietek as he was called) was placed by a Polish uncle (not Jewish) in a Catholic orphanage near Kraków. Only the priest in the orphanage knew of Mike's Jewish origin, but he never disclosed the secret. Until the war ended Mike did not know that he was Jewish. His mother, Janka, was hiding during the war years with Aryan papers. After the war, she and Mike left for Israel, where one of her sisters lived. In Israel, Mike was put into a Youth Aliyah village. Raised in an orphanage and later with other refugee children, Mike had a difficult childhood. His mother never told him anything about his background, about his father, or about his grandparents. She told him that there were no Ryczke family members alive. Mike told us about his lonely childhood and his yearning for family. With his mother marrying and remarrying several times, he looked for family elsewhere. His wife, Ariela, told us jokingly that Mike married her because she had a large family. I think this is actually true. We could not place Mike's family on our chart; nobody seemed to know anything about his background. A year later, in 2003, Mike sent me his family tree. He and I are direct descendents of Mosiek Ryczke and his second wife, while Theo, David, Chanoch, and Helene are descended from Mosiek Ryczke and his first wife. Only one person did remember Aaron Ryczke, the wealthy sawmill owner. Henry Kaplan told me in 1999 in London that he knew Mike's father, who belonged to "the other Ryczkes." What he meant was that Mike's father was assimilated and wealthy. Divisions among Ryczke family members were by profession. Some were in the dairy and egg business (like Theo's grandfather), the lumber business (Mike's father), grain and seed business (my father and also Ronnie's grandfather). Other divisions were between the religious and the assimilated members of the family. Mike thinks that his family was different because of the material wealth. Today Mike is a successful businessman in Toronto. His wife, Ariela, and daughter, Orit, work in his office. Energetic and ingenious, Mike owns a company that provides nannies, caregivers, and companions for people and institutions. He and Ariela also have a son, Aaron (Ronnie) Ryczke, who is married and has four daughters. He did not come to our reunion.

Next spoke Madeleine Ryczke Najman from Brussels. Madeleine (I call her Malka) and I made contact in July 2001, speaking over the telephone every few weeks. Because my French is almost zero, Malka and I converse in Yiddish. When I called her the first time, her late husband, Felix, answered. Being from Lodz, he spoke with me in Polish. He told me that Malka's father never spoke about the Ryczke family. He died in 1968, and Malka knew very little about her background. In November 2001, Felix Najman passed away and Malka was heartbroken. We spoke often. I urged her to look for old documents. Now she had more time, and while cleaning out drawers she found her parents' marriage certificate and knew now that her father was born in Golina. In the late 1920s he came to Belgium and married her mother. Malka was born in 1930. She had one brother who died a few years ago. Malka and her two daughters live in Brussels. The younger one, Paulette, came to London for the reunion. The older daughter, Jeanine Najman, has two daughters. They could not join us. Madeleine and her family were saved during the war by decent Belgian neighbors who knew about their being Jews but did not betray them to the Nazis.

All of us were very moved by what Helene Ryczke Vautrin told us. Paulette Najman was the translator. "My father was Shimshon Ryczke, the brother of Haskel Ryczke (father of David Richke) and of Simcha Ryczke (father of Theo Richmond). My father left Konin and came to France. On a business trip to Belgium he met my mother, Myriam. They were married and had two children—my brother, Benjamin Ryczke, who died last year at the age of sixty-two, and in 1942 I was born. We lived in France, and when the Germans came, the family went into hiding. In 1943 someone denounced my father to the Nazis. He was picked up and sent to Poland. After the war we found out that in 1945 he was sent to Auschwitz and from there to the concentration camp Mauthausen in Austria. [Ironically, in 1944 my brother, Benno Benjamin Ryczke, was sent from Auschwitz to Mauthausen.] My father was killed in this camp in 1945 at the age of forty-five. [My brother was killed near Mauthausen in April 1945 at the age of seventeen.] In the early 1970s I married my husband, Jacques. We have one son, Gerald, who was born in 1974. Unfortunately, while giving birth to Gerald, the doctors gave me a spinal injection that left me handicapped. I have never been the same since. Gerald is a famous jazz musician. He has many records. I am so sorry that my only brother, Benjamin, did not live to see this reunion."

David and Chanoch told us about their lives. David, the older son of Haskel Ryczke, was born in 1947 in Palestine. Chanoch was born in the new State of Israel in 1949. Both of them are very close. I have never seen such devoted brothers. Their parents left Konin in the 1930s for Palestine. They struggled as pioneers. David lives in Israel and is very successful in his own consulting business. Chanoch left for the United States and settled in Florida, where he is in the air-conditioning business. He also flies his own plane. Both David and Chanoch have two daughters. David's daughters, Noa and Smadar, came to London; Chanoch's daughters, Rachela and Michal, could not be with us. David's wife, Varda, worked hand in hand with David to help with the reunion. She is a wonderful person.

When my turn came, I shared my life in a nutshell with my newly found relatives. I brought to the reunion a folder for each family. It had the family tree that I was able to complete (not 100 percent), many copies of birth, marriage, and death certificates of some of our common ancestors (the first one was the death certificate of Benyamin Haze, who was the father of Mosiek Ryczke and who died in Golina in 1830. It was signed by our common great-great-grandfather, Mosiek Ryczke). Also in the folder were photos I took in Golina in 1999 and a poem I wrote in memory of my brother, Benno Benjamin Ryczke. There was a puzzle as to the surname "Haze," the father of Mosiek Ryczke. What does all this mean? We can only guess. The most probable answer is a political one. Golina, Konin, and surrounding small towns were part of Poland before the partition in 1772. Then this part of Poland was annexed by Prussia. Surnames were given, most of them were German-sounding ones, like "Haze" (probably spelled "Hase"). When Napoleon, on his march east, created the "Duchy of Warsaw" (1807–13), Golina, Konin, and vicinity became part of the independent Polish Duchy of Warsaw. Many Jews with German-sounding names were changing their surnames to Polish-sounding ones. *Ryczke* is an old Polish word for some kind of grain. And so Mosiek, who was born Haze, changed his name to Ryczke. Evidently some of the Ryczkes were in the grain business or had flour mills. My branch of the family—Great-Grandfather Benyamin Ryczke (named after Benyamin Haze); Grandfather Efraim Ryczke; my father, Moritz (Moshe) Ryczke; and Uncle Aron Ryczke (Ronnie's grandfather) all were in the grain business. As far as I am concerned, this can be the only logical explanation for the change in the surname.

It was truly amazing—suddenly there is indeed a Ryczke family. When the war ended, my father thought that he and I were the only remnants of the Ryczke family. Then he found in Israel his cousins Adam and Cesia Ryczke (children of Aron Ryczke of Kolo). Mike Ryczke in Toronto told me that his mother told him after the war that there are no members of the Ryczke family left alive. And he lived in Israel on the same street as the son of Adam Ryczke, Ronnie Ritchke. They never met, and did not even know of each other's existence.

The book written by Theo Richmond (his father's name was Ryczke) triggered the desire of the scattered members of the Ryczke clan to meet each other. I found out that Theo Richmond's first cousin David Richke and Chanoch Richka are part of this family. Helene in France was born Ryczke and so was Madeleine in Brussels. Spread over three continents, the members of the Ryczke/Richke/Richka/Richmond families are now in close contact. I speak to all of them over the telephone, and with Helene I correspond via my French-speaking friends. Yes, there certainly is a Ryczke family. How lucky we are to have found each other.

The hours went fast. Drained and emotionally exhausted, we finally stopped for lunch and to rest in our hotel until dinner at the Richmonds'. The grand finale was truly great. While Friday was a prelude filled with anticipation and the excitement of meeting each other, Saturday morning was the realization of finding the links that bind us as a family. It also was the heartwarming experience of learning about each other. Saturday night was the culmination of it all.

From our schedule we knew that Theo and Lee were opening their hearts and home to host all of us for dinner. They live in a beautiful old remodeled coach house in Richmond-upon-Thames. The house is surrounded by a charming English garden. From the moment we entered their home, the atmosphere was filled with friendship, love, and good cheer. The wonderful food, drinks, many jokes, and endless toasts were exhilarating. Theo and Lee were the "host and hostess with the mostest." Even the not-so-reliable English weather cooperated with us—from start to finish we had sunshine and good, crisp autumn weather. The gods were good to us. We could have eaten and talked way into the night, but some of us had to take the last tube (subway) to London. I had to leave the next morning before 8 a.m., which meant getting up at 6 a.m. We said good-bye to our kind and loving host and hostess and to each other. In our hearts each and every one was thinking, "When will we see each other again? Will we be able to get together for another reunion?" Well, I do not make long-range plans any more. At eighty-one I am grateful for every day. Now that we know each other in person, we shall exchange thoughts, wishes, and ideas by mail or telephone (I am a noncomputer person). We shall recall the highlights of our wonderful reunion and exchange photos. But most of all we shall be forever grateful to our newly found family members for coming to this unique and important reunion. And to David and Neil I can only say—you have done a swell job, thanks a million. A dream came true because of you two.

A Footnote

To get to Richmond, I was lucky to travel by car with Neil Vickers, Sarah's husband (Theo Richmond's son-in-law). The ride took about forty-five minutes and Neil and I talked a lot. Almost every issue under the sun was discussed; Neil knew so much about everything. He mentioned that he came from Ireland. I told him that I have a cousin living in Northern Ireland who went there shortly before World War II. Neil asked, "Where in Northern Ireland does your cousin live?" I said, "In Portadown. His name is Bloch, and his grandmother was a born Ryczke." "I know a Michael Bloch from Portadown," Neil answered. Well, what a small world. Michael Bloch is the son of my distant cousin Richard. Michael came with me to Poland in 1999. "Neil, I just had lunch with Michael. We celebrated his forty-ninth birthday in a Polish restaurant. How do you know Michael?" "He and I belong to the same literary club (Michael is a writer), I have known him for many years." In a city the size of London it is unusual to find people who know each other. Now Neil will know that in Michael Bloch he has another Ryczke connection. What a small world, indeed.

Part 8

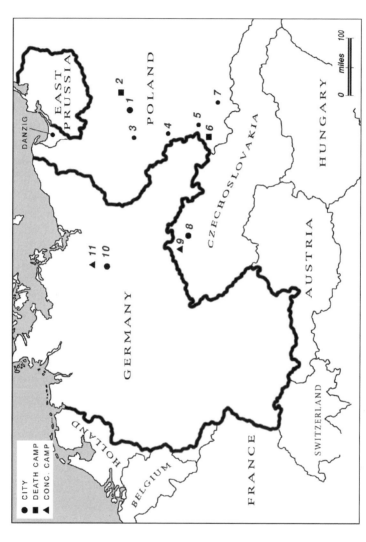

Mira's first return to Eastern Europe: (1) Warsaw; (2) Treblinka; (3) Piotrkow-Trybunalski; (4) Częstochowa; (5) Kraków; (6) Auschwitz (Oswiecim); (7) Krosno; (8) Prague; (9) Terezin (Theresienstadt); (10) Berlin; (11) Sachsenhausen.

Chapter 22

SEARCHING FOR CLOSURE

While Max was alive, we often spoke about the possibility of returning to places in Europe where our families once lived. In June 1973 during our visit to Denmark to see Gene and meet his Danish family, we made a trip to Flensburg, Germany. Once we got there, Max became nervous and visibly agitated. "This one must have been in the SS," he said, pointing to an elderly German. He saw in each one the "enemy" and became actually sick. We had to leave and return to Denmark. I knew that he could not face a return to places of suffering and pain after this brief encounter. Yet I wanted so much to show him the city where I grew up, the places where I had a happy childhood. "I will never go back. After I am gone you can return to Poland and Germany. I am not able to do it," were Max's words. We never spoke about it again. Max was unable to forgive. His pain was too deep.

In 1990, after Max passed away, I was approached by two of the teachers in Oak Ridge who were teaching Holocaust studies, Martha and Jinx. They belonged to the organization Facing History and Ourselves, which was planning a trip to Eastern Europe, and they invited me to join them and other teachers on this historic journey. With Max gone, there was nobody to hold me back. Looking over the itinerary, I realized that this trip would take me back to places where I suffered most, to places where Max's family came from, where his parents and sisters were buried. And I recalled Max's words uttered many years before: "I wish I could visit my mother's grave one more time." These were the decisive factors in my agreeing to make this journey. Was I overestimating my physical and emotional strength? Was I foolish to undertake such a painful journey?

I met the group in Boston and we flew to Warsaw. By making this pilgrimage, I was seeking closure and saying good-bye to my dear departed relatives who perished during the Holocaust. While on the plane, my thoughts went back to the end of May 1941, when my father and I took the bus from Tomaszow-Mazowiecki to Warsaw.[1] This was forty-nine years ago, when we still had hopes of getting out of occupied Poland. How different this trip would be.

On the plane, I heard for the first time announcements in Polish. It sounded so strange, yet it felt so good. Looking out of the window I could see the undulating outlines of the Vistula River. We flew over Sopot (the city of my birth) and Gdańsk—places where I spent the first fifteen years of my life.

When we landed at Warsaw's Okecie Airport, I noticed how shabby and old the terminal looked. Right away one could see how poor the country was. It was five months since Max had passed away, and here I was in Warsaw without him. To me this was almost unreal. The sky was blue, the weather beautiful. Riding through the streets of Warsaw I realized that this was a different city—the Warsaw that I knew from before the war no longer existed. Buildings were dull gray blocks that already showed signs of decay; everything seemed so lifeless. People were rushing back home from work; streetcars and trolleys were filled to capacity. Very few smiling faces; life was hard in Poland.

I wrote a month prior to this trip to Jozio Pruc, the adopted son of Max's sister Hela. He was to come and meet me the first evening of my arrival. We had never met and only knew each other from letters and from photographs.

As we checked into the Forum Hotel, Rachel, my roommate, and I were amazed at the comfort of the room. The hotel, located in the center of the city, was surrounded by many big stores. The exchange rate was mind-boggling—9,600 zlotys for each dollar. The food we were served in the hotel was excellent, the service very good. Knowing that the meat would be mostly pork, I decided to stay away from meat. All I wanted was potatoes with good Polish butter. And potatoes I ate. They tasted as good as I remembered them from my childhood, and I could not get enough of them.

While at dinner, I noticed a man entering our dining room. "This must be Jozio," I thought. And it was. I got up from the table, and we fell into each others arms—both of us crying. I asked Jozio to wait for me in the lobby until I finished my dinner. A few minutes later I went to the lobby, where Jozio waited for me with a bouquet of roses. We went upstairs to my room so that we could talk undisturbed. Jozio told me about the changes in Poland, how very difficult life was, and how the new political system might affect his life. Jozio is a mining engineer. Having worked for years in the Ministry of Mining he had to join the party. Now there was a trend to dismiss all who had been party members. He was scared to lose his job, because this would also affect his wife's job. These were very difficult times in Poland. We spoke of the economic situation, and he told me that the wages of his wife, Krysia, were just enough to pay the utility bill. But because he held a high position for many years, they saved some money and were using some of the reserves now. Their only son, Czarek, and his wife, Monika, went to Sweden for the summer to earn foreign currency picking berries. This is how most of the Poles try to supplement their earnings.

Then Jozio spoke about his stepmother, Hela (Max's sister), about the time when she was hiding in their house during the war years. We spoke about Max's brother Michael (Leon Sroczynski) and his wife, Ewa. Jozio remembered visiting them in Lodz with Hela. And he told me that when Leon, Ewa, and her daughter, Elzunia, received their permit to leave Poland for Israel, they wanted Hela to go with them. She told them that she would never leave Jozio and her husband. This he never forgot. He spoke of Hela with such love and adoration. We sat and chatted for almost two hours. It was an emotional evening, and both of us were drained. When we parted, Jozio

Jozio Pruc and son
Czarek, Warsaw, 1970.

said that he felt like a close relative of mine. After all—I was his adopted aunt and he my adopted nephew.

The first night in Poland we hardly got any sleep. At 1:30 a.m. Rachel and I decided to talk. Both of us had the need to open up. We knew very little about each other and it felt natural to talk about ourselves and our families. I told her about Max, Benno, Joy, Melanie, and Gene. I shared the story about Jozio, how his father, Stefan Pruc, hid Hela during the war (by the way, Hela's Polish name was Hela Rudycka), and about my life in Oak Ridge. Rachel told me about her family. She is an only daughter of survivors, both now deceased. She and her husband have two sons, as I do. Rachel, who lives in Memphis, Tennessee, works in Jewish education, and at that time she was president of her synagogue. We talked until 3 a.m. Rachel went back to sleep, and I decided to write down the impressions of this first day of my return to Poland.

Our first stop in Warsaw was the former small ghetto. At 55 Sienna Street we entered the yard and found the remnant of the ghetto wall. It was on Sienna Street that I stayed with my father in May 1941, at the apartment of my aunt Hela Krzewin, the mother of Gutek. Now I was back after forty-nine years. We walked the streets of the small ghetto, then we took the bus to what once was the large ghetto.

Here, in the large ghetto, I did not recognize a single street. I lived with my parents and brother from October 1939 until January 1940 in the house at 19 Nowolipiki, apartment 21, in the apartment of my mother's sister Gucia Lachman and her husband, David. Their daughter, Marysia, was already married; their son, Mietek (Michael, now in Israel), had left for Bialystok. The streets now were lined with trees, and all houses were "new" buildings. The ghetto was completely burned by the Nazis in May 1943. Not one house was left.[2] Nothing was recognizable.

Our next stop was the *Umschlagplatz*—the place from where my family living in Warsaw was sent to Treblinka. Over 350,000 Jews were shipped to their deaths from here—David and Gucia Lachman, Marysia, and her husband and baby son, Hela Krzewin (my mother's youngest sister), Rozka Hammer and her son Jasio, age eight, and many of our friends, such as the Bieloguski family from Danzig, the Kronman family (Marychna and Hanka) from Zoppot, Marian Lipski and his mother from Gdynia, and many, many others. We said Kaddish at the monument that stood at the once infamous *Umschlagplatz*. The white marble walls bear names in alphabetical order— Jewish as well as Polish first names of the victims.

From there we walked near the railroad tracks that took the victims to Treblinka. We entered Zamenhofa Street and saw many monuments to the fighters of the ghetto uprising. One was in honor of Janusz Korczak,[3] one in honor of Shmuel Zygelboym, who killed himself in London after learning of the fate of the Jews in Poland from Jan Karski. Most impressive was the large monument to honor Mordecai Anielewicz, leader of the Warsaw Ghetto Uprising in 1943. Now we stood in front of this powerful monument by Rappaport to the ghetto uprising. One side depicts the families walking together, guarded by Nazis; the front of the monument depicts the heroes of the uprising.

Next we approached the famous "Mila 18," which once housed the head-quarters of the ghetto uprising; no house is left. Now it is a mound, with a very stark and modest monument to those who took their lives in the bunker rather than fall into the hands of the Nazis. This was the modern Masada.

Memorial marble wall at the *Umschlagplatz* in Warsaw.

Mira lighting a candle at the Warsaw Ghetto Fighters Memorial, August 1990.

Monument at Mila 18, headquarters of the Ghetto Fighters, in Warsaw.

Our group visited the old Jewish cemetery. Here are buried Polish Jews dating back to the beginning of the nineteenth century. Gravestones for Jewish writers like An-ski and Perec, one in memory of Janusz Korczak, the grave of Dr. Emanuel Ringelblum, and many, many others. One could learn the history of Warsaw Jewry by reading the names on the tombstones. At the very end of the lane was a huge field covered with wild flowers. This was the place where in 1941/42 Jews from the ghetto were buried in mass graves. Somewhere here there was a grave where my maternal grandmother Sarah Hammer born Szmant was buried in the winter of 1941, and my maternal grandfather Shlomo Hammer in spring of 1942. In the mass grave my aunt Rosa Przedecka neé Ryczke (my father's only sister) and her two daughters— my cousins Halina and Gina—are buried. Here I was able to pay my respects to those members of our family who met their tragic deaths in Warsaw. (My aunt Rosa took her own life, after learning that both her daughters had been recognized as Jews and were shot.)

I spent the evening with Jozio and Krysia. Krysia is a good-looking and charming woman. I felt right away very much at home in their small apartment. It was so clean and neat—the walls were covered with oil paintings by Krysia. This is her way to relax. I have to mention that both Jozio and Krysia smoke a great deal. I had to beg them to wait until I left, as I am allergic to smoke. Krysia set the table with pastries and homemade cherry preserves; she is an excellent homemaker. We talked for several hours. The flat was dim, because electricity was so expensive. Krysia also worked in a government position. She is a geologist by profession.

While still in Oak Ridge, I made plans to go to Krosno, where Hela, Max's sister, is buried. I mentioned this to a friend of mine, Danusia Jagla, a young Polish doctor in Knoxville. She spoke to her brother Bogus in Kraków about my plans. He was so kind as to offer to drive me to Krosno once we arrived in Kraków. This I mentioned to Jozio. I needed his help, because I did not know where the cemetery is located. Jozio promised to take the train and meet me in Kraków. Together we planned to go with Danka's brother to Krosno. We parted, to meet again in Kraków.

Then came the day I dreaded most, the day we were to go to Treblinka. Since 1942 when my family was taken away from me, I was haunted by the thought of visiting the place of their tragic deaths. Until now I knew this diabolic place only from books and the film *Shoah*. But I had to be there. I had to touch the ground and breathe the air. This horrible place is only seventy miles from Warsaw. We boarded the bus early in the morning for this highly emotional journey. Going west we crossed the Vistula River and drove through Praga, a suburb of Warsaw.

After crossing the Bug River, our eyes met the sight of the railroad tracks leading to Malkinia and Treblinka. These were the tracks on which our dear ones traveled toward their tragic deaths. In my mind I was traveling with them. Did they see the beautiful Polish landscape through the tiny openings in the cattle cars? Did they see the blue sky and the glorious wild flowers? Or were they gasping for air—100–150 in a car, thirsty and hungry, but most of all bewildered and scared? My heart and mind were with those of my family who traveled this last road from the *Umschlagplatz* in Warsaw, but most of all with my dear mother, my paternal grandparents Efraim and Esther Ryczke, my uncle, Markus Przedecki, the whole family Kolski (my friend Eva's parents, two sisters, and two brothers), and many, many more who were "resettled" from the ghetto in Tomaszow-Mazowiecki on October 31 and November 2, 1942. I also thought about Max's first wife, Roma, and their eight-year-old daughter, Maryla (Malka), who were taken from the Piotrkow-Trybunalski ghetto in October 1942 to be killed in Treblinka. My heart was heavy and I knew that the purpose of my trip to Treblinka was to say a final good-bye to all those who died here. I had to do it not only for myself but also for Max and for my father.

We finally arrived in Treblinka and started our walk to the actual site where the camp was. Walking in complete silence through the young pine forest, planted by the Nazis after the camp was leveled to cover up all traces of their atrocities, this tranquil beauty greeted all visitors. One would never know that almost 850,000 Jews marched this road and met their deaths here. I looked at this peaceful panorama in deadly silence with a pounding heart. Could this be the place of such unspeakable crimes? We walked the cobblestones in a funeral-like procession, each one of us immersed in our own thoughts, many of us in our personal grief. Once we made the left turn toward the camp, our eyes saw this tremendous field with thousands of broken stones, large ones and small ones. This Sea of Broken Stones represents the more than 1,300 destroyed Jewish communities in Europe. We had come to this killing field, where the ashes of our dear ones are mixed into the soil, a place that was witness to one of the most hideous crimes committed by human beings.

Treblinka was the place where I wanted to be for so many years—since the fateful day of October 31, 1942, when the ghetto of Tomaszow was liquidated and my dear mother, grandparents, and other relatives were sent here. At that time we were told that the Jews were being relocated east to work for the Nazis. Only later did we learn the terrible truth about Treblinka.

I walked this path, the road of tears and blood, thinking of those thousands of innocent men, women, and children, of the old and sick, of the unborn, all killed by poisonous gas, on whose ashes we were now walking. This was almost an unreal panorama, as if we were on another planet. I could feel the suffering that must have taken place here. How many did survive the terrible train ride? Did my grandfather get here alive? He suffered from asthma; could he breathe in an overcrowded cattle car? How did my dear mother, whose health was not the best, arrive here? I will never know, but the questions keep coming.

Now we began the search for stones with names of communities we wanted to honor and memorialize. The stone in memory of the Piotrkow Jewish victims was very close to the entrance, a few yards to the right. The Birnbaums (he was born in Piotrkow) and I lit the memorial candle, and all of us said Kaddish. There was not a dry eye; tears were flowing like a stream. In silence I stood at this stone and said my prayer for Max in memory of his first wife and daughter. This is their only "grave," and I came here to mourn them.

Before entering Treblinka, I looked on the map for the stone representing the Tomaszow-Mazowiecki community. It was marked No. 107. It was the hardest one to find. Friends helped me locate it, and after twenty minutes of wandering among the stones, we found it in the northwestern part, way in the back. I lit the memorial candle and put pebbles around the stone. As I never said good-bye to my beloved mother, I had to come here to do it. For the past forty-eight years I was thinking of doing it, and did not know how. Now was the chance and I felt that I came here on this pilgrimage of sorrow to attend the funerals that never took place. I came to mourn for my and Max's family. There was no hatred in my heart, only immense pain and endless sorrow, and I could feel Max's presence the whole time. He never wanted to return, but I could do it for him. And so I paid my last respects to our dear ones, and I felt at peace. The circle was slowly closing, yet the pain will remain forever. The sight of Treblinka never leaves me; this is my family's final resting place.

Mira in front of the "broken stone" for Tomaszow-Mazowiecki at the Killing Field of Treblinka.

Treblinka and other places of Nazi atrocities are being cared for by the Polish authorities. We met elderly Polish peasant women who lived near Treblinka during the Nazi era. They were young then but remembered what was going on. They told us that it was dangerous for Poles to even look in the direction of the camp. Once a young Polish woman went to the pasture with her cow and looked toward the camp; she was shot dead on the spot. These women are now cleaning and weeding the place. The pay is meager and we gave them some money. At least someone cares to keep this place neat. But what will be in ten or twenty years? Will all this be forgotten?

Friday night was spent at the only synagogue in Warsaw, the Nozyk Synagogue. During the war it served as a stable for horses. It was sad to see so very few local Jews attend services. If not for us and a few Israelis, there would not have been a *minyan* (quorum). Warsaw has almost two thousand Jews, but the only time one sees them in the synagogue is on Rosh Hashanah and Yom Kippur. Even our Polish taxi driver remarked, "Are Jews ashamed to show their religion? Why are there so few here for services?" This was a valid remark. The truth is that many of the Jews in Poland today are still afraid to openly show their religion.

Our next stop was Piotrkow-Trybunalski, on the way to Kraków and only 82 miles from Warsaw. Here we stopped for a few hours. How many times did I hear Max speak of and describe this city? I remembered the street names, especially the street where his parents lived, 7 Starowarszawska. The only time I saw this medieval city was as a child of almost ten, when the bus that took me to Wlodzimierzow stopped at the market place in Piotrkow. This was in 1933. Now I was walking the streets of the city that Max loved so much. Today, Piotrkow's population is fifty thousand, and only one Jew lives there. Before the war, one-third of its population was Jewish.

We stopped in front of the old synagogue. This once beautiful structure built in the Moorish style is now a library. In front one can still see the two stars of David, which are part of the lamps in front of the building. We entered what once was the sanctuary. Traces of the women's gallery can still be seen. On the eastern wall, behind shelves of books, was the only painting left: the Ark with the Ten Commandments, with lions and crowns painted and now restored. This is the only reminder of the once well-known synagogue. The walls still have holes in them from the time in 1943 when the Nazis and Ukrainians shot through the wall, injuring and killing the Jews who were found in the city after the resettlement and who were locked up in this synagogue by the Nazis.

From the synagogue we walked to the old castle, where King Lokietek hid from the approaching enemies in the fourteenth century. Here the city of Piotrkow has organized an exhibit, where pictures of Nazi crimes are displayed. They are also collecting Jewish artifacts, especially pictures and religious objects from Piotrkow. Candlesticks, silver pointers, and menorahs were found in the wall of the synagogue when it was being remade into a library. These items are now on display. While we were in the castle, Roman (Ruben) Hibszer met us—he is the only remaining Jew in Piotrkow. It is he who takes care of the Jewish cemetery. I wrote to him a few months earlier, asking him to find the graves of Max's parents, who are buried in the Piotrkow cemetery. Two of Max's sisters were also buried there, but Roman told me when we met that he could not find any traces of their graves. Once we visited the cemetery, I understood why.

Roman Hibszer came dressed in a black suit, wearing a large black felt hat. He was so excited. Evidently he was awaiting us for hours. He led the way to the cemetery, and there we were met by a delegation of Poles, former fighters of Nazism, headed by Mr. Koza. They prepared a wreath of white and red carnations to be laid on the grave of the victims of mass murder in the Rakow Forest in 1943. Their bodies were exhumed after the war and buried in the cemetery. We said Kaddish and placed the wreath on the grave. From there we started our walk to the actual old cemetery. Weeds were growing knee high, the tombstones were covered with moss, and the names were almost impossible to read. No wonder that Roman could not find the graves I asked him to look for. Now he led us to a tomb in memory of the members of the *Bund* and prominent members of the Jewish community who were executed by the Gestapo after a runner sent by the *Bund* from Warsaw was caught with false papers. Under torture she gave away their names. Standing at the base of this monument, my eyes caught the name Kimmelman. It said, "Leon Kimmelman and wife." This was Max's older brother, who with his wife, Gucia, was killed in Treblinka in 1942. What a shock it was to see the name, to come to this place and be able to pay tribute to part of Max's family. Not being able to find the graves of his parents, I said my prayers at this memorable place, where the names of Leon Kimmelman and his wife are forever engraved. This episode touched me deeply and was one of the most moving ones for me.

From the cemetery I went to search for the street where Max's family had lived. After asking a few people, I walked through the streets of Piotrkow until I came to Starowarszawska Street. The house number 7 looked well preserved. It was freshly painted, a medium grey color. The balcony was in good shape, and the railings were freshly painted black. I stood in front of this house thinking of Max, his parents, and his siblings. How many times did he walk this way? Through the gate I entered the courtyard. Here I could see how neglected and old the house actually was. Only the front was well kept. While in Piotrkow I knew that in spirit Max walked with me. I could feel his presence.

A very interesting experience was the visit to Czestochowa, which was on the way to Kraków. One of the participants on our trip was Father Bob Bullock, a Catholic priest. He wanted to visit the Jasna Gora Monastery in Czestochowa and see the Black Madonna. Once we arrived here, I was asked to be the translator for the group. It is hard to describe the multitude of people that came on a pilgrimage to the monastery at Jasna Gora. The church was completely filled. The priest who took us around showed us the magnificent interior of the church. The picture of the Black Madonna was covered with gold and precious stones. I have never seen such splendor. Ironically, now I could visit the monastery and see the Black Madonna. While attending the Polish *Gimnazjum* in Danzig, Jewish students were excluded from excursions to Czestochowa!

On everybody's mind now was Auschwitz. Some of us feared this visit, and there was a need to talk about it. Once we were settled in our Kraków hotel, five of us went to the room of one of the organizers, Paul, to talk about Auschwitz. We were trying to sort out our feelings so that we could face the next day's pilgrimage. It was good to be able to let our emotions go, and all of us felt much better.

This day was to be my return to this hell on earth known as Auschwitz. In my mind, it was August 1, 1944, a steamy hot day when our cattle cars were opened at the station in Birkenau/Auschwitz II. My thoughts returned here many times, and I never forgot the moment when I parted here from my father and brother. The three of us were together in the closed cattle car from Blizyn/Majdanek to Auschwitz. I still had many pictures of my family, and my father had some documents from Danzig. All this my father put into my aluminum canteen, the one that was used for food, for me to keep and protect. Through the slots in the cattle car we could see the peasants in the field gathering hay. Everything looked so tranquil. Many of them pointed to the ground when they saw our train. What did they mean? Why were they pointing with their thumbs down? Only later did we understand—they were showing us that we would be dead and buried.[4]

Flashing before my eyes were memories of our three-day journey in unspeakable conditions . . . parting from my father and brother . . . selections telling us to go left or right, which meant who was to live and who was to die . . . the horrible stench of this place . . . the chimneys belching thick, black smoke . . . the bathhouse and the miraculous episode with my canteen . . . my fear of being all alone now . . . my ignorance of the true purpose of this place called Auschwitz. And I tremble now to face this place after so many years.

We entered the city of Oswiecim (Auschwitz) by bus. All the time during our trip through Poland I missed seeing red poppies in the field. All of a sudden I noticed a field filled with beautifully blooming poppies at the entrance to Oswiecim. They looked like drops of blood in the field of wheat.

The familiar gate with the words "Arbeit Macht Frei" (Work Liberates) came into sight. From now on we walked the rest of the day. After entering Auschwitz through this infamous gate, we visited the blocks—these were brick buildings from the time when Auschwitz was a military garrison for the Austrian army before World War I and for the Polish army before World War II. We went into the block where the Catholic priest Maximilian Kolbe had been imprisoned and murdered.[5] In another block was the exhibit of mountains of shoes, shorn human hair, brushes, and household goods. Suitcases bearing the names of their former owners still told the place of their origins—Berlin, France, Holland, Czechoslovakia, Poland, Belgium, Greece, etc.

Now I walked the road that I remembered so well—we entered Birkenau at the site of the ramp where we arrived forty-six years ago. Our group turned left, to see some of the barracks that are still in their original state. Everything was clean, sanitized. We saw the washrooms, where we had only cold water, no soap, and only a few seconds to wash ourselves. And the latrines. These holes were always occupied because most of us suffered from dysentery and spent a lot of time in the "toilets." All this was seen by me now like through a split screen. On one side I saw things as I remembered them, on the other, as they are today. The only difference was that the barracks were clean and the smell was gone; there was no smoke and stench of burning flesh from the chimneys. Now there was grass and wildflowers all over the place. In 1944, we never saw grass, nor flowers, nor trees. Whatever grew here was eaten by the prisoners.

We walked by the remains of the gas chambers and Crematoria II and III. Railroad tracks led here so that people did not have to walk far from this ramp to the gas chambers. A large monument is standing here now.

Turning right we saw the remains of the burned-out Crematorium IV, where inmates plotted to destroy this place with dynamite on October 7, 1944.[6] A little further on was the pond where the ashes of the victims were dumped. We saw the remains of the place called "Kanada," a sorting depot where the belongings of all who arrived here were stored, sorted, and sent to Germany. Working in "Kanada" was like a ticket to life. If someone found some food that the victims brought from their homes, they had something to eat or to barter for bread. It was one of the most privileged places in which to work.

Now we returned to Auschwitz I and toured the first gas chamber, which has been left as it was, also the first crematorium. I was overcome by the ever-present feeling of guilt—the guilt of surviving. How many times did I or my father ask ourselves, why am I alive? Why not Benno, my mother, and other family members? Only a survivor can understand this never-ending feeling of guilt. It overwhelmed me as I walked among the thousands of broken stones in Treblinka. And it was again fortified as I entered the gates of Auschwitz. The feelings of pain and the torture of guilt never left me; they are buried deep inside me and never stop haunting me.

On our way back to Kraków, we stopped at a Youth Center in the city of Oswiecim, where a group of dedicated members of Action Reconciliation— young German men and women—volunteer to work for two years. Here they take care of the only Jewish cemetery in the town of Oswiecim, clean the paths, the tombstones, make sure that the place is in good shape. Others volunteer in Israel and work there in old-age homes or on kibbutzim.

After our return to the hotel, and after a quiet dinner, our group had a long discussion to help us sort out our feelings and thoughts after Auschwitz.

The next morning I had a visit from Bishop Szotmiller, to whom I wrote that I would be in Kraków. He came by car from Czestochowa to see me. The last time I saw him was in February 1982, when he came with his cousin Helen from Peoria to visit Yvonne Foster in Oak Ridge and was a frequent guest in our house. I remember how he and Max were singing Polish songs, how I prepared a Polish meal with Kapusniak and Kielbasa for him, Helen, and Yvonne. After he returned to Poland, he wrote to us, often sending Max postcards from Piotrkow and Polish books for me.

While in Kraków, we toured Kazimierz, the old Jewish quarter. We walked through this very old part of Kraków, where Jews lived since the fourteenth century. We visited the Remo Synagogue and the adjacent oldest Jewish cemetery. Nobody has been buried in the old cemetery for the past 250 years; the newer one is outside of Kraków. A few older Jewish men were sitting around, actually asking for money. There are about two hundred Jews now living in Kraków; in 1939 there were sixty-five thousand Jews. The synagogue has six Torah scrolls, but three of them are *posel,* or unfit.

In the old city we visited St. Mary's Cathedral with the world-famous altar carved by Wit Stworz. We waited for the hour when the bugle player would play out the time, stopping in the middle. This was a tradition from the time when the Tartars invaded the city and shot the bugle player with an arrow while he was in the middle of warning the people about the approaching danger. This happened in the fourteenth century, and the tradition is still carried on. Each step in this beautiful old city of Kraków taught me something new about Polish history.

In the afternoon we walked to the Wawel Castle, and to the famous cathedral, where most of the Polish kings are buried. The castle was closed, but we could still see the moat, the walls, and the fortifications. The cathedral was most impressive, with the sarcophagi of kings, queens, and famous people. In the lower part was the tomb of Marshall Joseph Pilsudski, who died on May 12, 1935. I recall this day quite clearly. On this day—it was a Sunday—I participated in a *Bar Kochba* recital in honor of Lag b'Omer. Pilsudski's body was buried in this place, but his heart was buried in Wilno, next to his mother's grave.

While walking the streets of Kraków, we noticed the first and only graffiti against Jews. It said, "Polska dla Polakow, Zydzi do Israela," which means, "Poland for the Poles, Jews go to Israel." I felt hurt after so many years of "Poland almost without Jews." Why is there still anti-Semitism? This was a painful encounter.

The next day Jozio was to come from Warsaw and we were to drive to Krosno. Jozio met us at the hotel, and a short time later Bogus and his mother, Mrs. Jagla, arrived to take us to Krosno. It was a 137-mile ride, and I knew that we would need the whole day. The weather was fantastic; we had not seen a cloud since we had arrived in Poland.

Mrs. Jagla prepared sandwiches and cake for the trip so that we did not have to stop and lose time. The Polish countryside was enchanting. Haystacks were lined up on every field, and so many wildflowers and poppies were growing all along the road. I asked them to stop at one spot, where there was a field of oats full of poppies. We got out of the car and gathered a large bouquet of poppies, which I wanted to place on Hela's grave.

Thereafter we continued and finally came to Krosno. A few miles before we entered Krosno, Jozio pointed to a large field on our left at a place called Szebnie. Here, he said, the Nazis shot and burned thousands of Jews in 1943. He still remembers the dark smoke from the burning of bodies; he must have been nine years old.

Jozio showed the way to the cemetery. The city of Krosno has grown twice in size since Hela lived here. Now they are drilling for oil all around here; this has become a great industrial city. We entered the Catholic cemetery. Jozio led us to the grave of his parents—both are buried here together. He had a white marble plate put on the grave—no monuments, no holy figures, just a very simple, thin cross at the left side of this plate. The inscription reads,

Helena Pruc—born 18.XI.1905 died 15.V.1965[7]
Stefan Pruc—born 28.XI.1888 died 19.VII.1966

For my dearest parents—son

I laid the poppies on the grave and put a few pebbles next to them. Jozio said his prayer, and I silently said Kaddish. This was Tisha B'Av, the day of mourning for the destruction of the Temple in Jerusalem. Here I was, at Max's sister's grave, saying the prayers for him. How many times did he regret that he did not see his sister after the war? But Max could not bring himself to even think of returning to Poland.

Back in Kraków I said good-bye to Bogus and Mrs. Jagla, whose kindness I shall never forget. It was also time to part from Jozio, who returned home to Warsaw. I found him to be a dear and devoted friend and "relative."

The next seven days took our group to Prague and Terezin (Theresienstadt) and to Berlin and Sachsenhausen.

When I returned to the United States, it felt that I was coming to the nicest place on earth—to another world. It was like coming from darkness into light. Although I was physically and emotionally exhausted, I would have never forgiven myself had I not made this trip. In spite of all the hardship, the many tears, and painful memories, this will be a journey that I shall never forget.

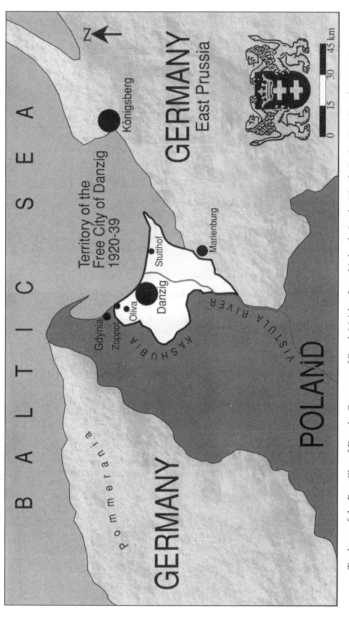

Territory of the Free City of Danzig. Courtesy of Frank Meisler, from his book *On the Vistula Facing East* (London, 1996).

Chapter 28

RECAPTURING MY YOUTH

There was a dream I had for many years, a dream I could not fulfill on my first return to Europe. My children were aware of this dream—a return to my hometown of Danzig (now Gdańsk) and to the city of my birth, Zoppot (now Sopot). In 1991 my dream was made possible first by my son Gene and two years later by my son Benno.

What was it about this city that I could not get out of my mind? I recall the dreams I had during the war years about being back in Danzig. In my fantasies I saw the streets I once walked. I was back in Zoppot, where I was born and lived until I was almost five. I could hear the sound of waves, taste the salty air of the Baltic Sea. These fantasies kept me going, they gave me the strength to endure hardship, to survive. In my imagination I drew the skyline of Danzig with its patrician houses, steeples of churches, majestic city hall, and mysterious Stockturm. These memories were precious. Nobody could touch them, nobody could take them away. Among the photographs and papers my father gave me for safekeeping was a clipping from a German newspaper with a view of Danzig. Like the photographs of my dear ones, I guarded it with my life and looked at it in secrecy. To this day I have this faded but precious picture of Danzig.

Not until the end of the eighteenth century were Jews allowed to reside in the city of Danzig. Five Jewish communities with synagogues and cemeteries existed from the seventeenth to the nineteenth century, all located outside the city walls. Jews were only allowed to enter the city on market days and at the time of the Dominik Fair in August. But they were not allowed to stay overnight. The citizens of Danzig, mostly German and Dutch, were merchants and craftsmen and feared Jewish competition. Although Danzig at that time was part of the Polish Kingdom, it had the status of a free city and Polish kings never could change the Danzig laws pertaining to Jews. In Poland, Jews enjoyed autonomy and freedom, but not so in Danzig. As in many cities in Germany, no synagogue could face the front of a street or be entered directly. Most of them were hidden behind a front building. This was the case with the synagogue my parents belonged to. It was one of the oldest ones in Danzig, one of the five that existed for a long time. The Mattenbuden Synagogue was strictly Orthodox. It had been rebuilt many times, because the old structures were made of wood and burned down quite frequently. A beautiful building had been dedicated in 1838 with dignitaries of the city of Danzig present. But the structure burned down a few years later. The new one was built out of brick and cement. This was the building I remember so vividly. It was the synagogue I attended with my family. Because it was one of the oldest synagogues, we had to enter through a gate, until we reached the synagogue standing in the courtyard. Being an Orthodox house of prayer, men and women were seated separately. Men on the ground floor, women in the balcony. How well I remember the wooden benches with a stand and little cupboard where my father kept his *tallit* (prayer shawl). Men in silk top hats, women dressed in their fineries, and children running around. Next to my mother in the balcony sat Mrs. Przysucher, the cantor's wife. I remember two rabbis—Rabbi Jacob Sagalowitsch and Rabbi Mordechai Golinkin. They sat near the Ark, by the eastern wall. The Torah scrolls were read from a table located on the platform in the center of the synagogue. All prayers were in Hebrew, sermons were in Yiddish interwoven with Hebrew and German. To be truthful, I understood very little of what was going on, but I loved the atmosphere. Especially wonderful were the celebrations at *Simchat Torah,* when all the young ones danced and sang in the courtyard of our synagogue. These were happy times, times that I recalled often during the years of the Holocaust. These happy memories sustained me and helped me to cope with adversity. I could close my eyes and see the old synagogue filled with worshippers, I could see my father wrapped in his huge wool *tallit,* and I could see the children carrying little flags topped with apples, catching candies that were thrown by mothers and sisters from the balcony.

By the middle of the nineteenth century, all five Jewish communities merged, and the Great Synagogue on Reitbahn became the unifying Jewish community center. The Mattenbuden Synagogue, the only Orthodox one in Danzig and vicinity, remained until it was destroyed in November 1938. The synagogue in Langfuhr was heavily damaged but not destroyed. The Reitbahn Synagogue escaped destruction when Jewish war veterans took turns guarding the building from those who wanted to set it on fire. It was later sold to the City of Danzig. Money from the sale of this synagogue and other Jewish properties was to be used to help the Jews of Danzig to emigrate. The building of the Reitbahn Synagogue was dismantled brick by brick in May of 1939. Only the empty lot remains as a reminder of what once was there. This, in a nutshell, is the history of the Jewish community of Danzig.

Years went by. In 1965 I read Günter Grass's *The Tin Drum* and a few years later *From the Diary of a Snail.* While reading these allegorical master-pieces, my desire to see Danzig again was rekindled. I "walked" again the streets of Danzig, and the past became alive. Günter Grass was the first German author who described *Kristallnacht* in Danzig. He wrote about the fate of the Jews of Danzig in *From the Diary of a Snail,* where he mentioned people I knew before the war. These books brought Danzig again to the forefront of my mind. When, in 1980, the exhibit "Danzig, a Destroyed Community" opened in New York and later in Atlanta, I knew that someday I would return to Danzig, my hometown. I wanted to share my memories with Max, but Max could not bear the thought of ever going back. During my first trip back to Europe in August 1990, I did not go back to Danzig. But my dream to revisit the city of my youth never stopped.

In 1945 Danzig had been a heap of ruins and burned-out houses. My father's words—"Do not go back to Danzig—it is a *Trümmerhaufen*, a heap of rubble. You will not recognize the city"—were still ringing in my ears. I heard his description of Danzig after the war. I wondered what I would find. How much would I be able to show my children? Would Danzig still be in ruins?

It was not. The Polish government made the greatest effort to rebuild and restore this historic, beautiful city. Today it is again one of the most beautiful and charming cities in Poland. My father would have been pleasantly surprised had he lived to see Danzig today. I disobeyed my father; I did return to Danzig. I hope that he would have forgiven me. Not once, not twice, but three times in the last decade was I able to revisit Danzig to fulfill my dream. Danzig was in my blood, as my dear friend Brigitte once told me. Each of my three journeys was different. Each one was special. By being able to share my memories, my childhood recollections with my two sons, my daughter-in-law, and Alina Szmant and Michael Bloch, my mission was accomplished; my dreams were fulfilled. I was able to walk with my children down the streets of the city of my childhood and share memories with them. With Gene and Caroline in 1991 and with Benno in 1993, I relived my childhood years in Danzig and Zoppot. Not all memories were happy ones, but to me life in Zoppot and Danzig until 1935 was carefree and good. And I wanted my children to know about this life in Danzig "once upon a time." More than anything I wanted to share with my children the Jewish part of my life in Danzig. Unfortunately, nothing was left of the two synagogues in Danzig and the one in Zoppot. I could only point to the sad, empty lots and tell some of the history of the Jews of Danzig.

My sons knew how much I desired to return to my hometown. Gene and Caroline were to be married in September 1991. But they had something else planned prior to their forthcoming wedding. "How would you like to go with us to Danzig, Zoppot, and on?" They asked me. Both wanted to make this journey back into my past with me. I was deeply touched. The trip was planned for August 1991, and I was excited beyond words. Plans had to be made, an itinerary was left to me.

How do I describe my emotions, my hesitation, and my anticipation while planning this sentimental return to my hometown after fifty-two years? For all these long years the dream of seeing the places of my childhood and youth was in the back of my mind.

The planning started in March 1991—the tickets were ready by May. Now I had the task of preparing myself not only physically but also emotionally. The journey was to take us first to Warsaw. Right away, I wrote to Jozio Pruc letting him know about our planned visit.

In August 1991, Gene, Caroline, and I met at New York's Kennedy airport. Waiting to board the plane for Warsaw we heard more Polish spoken than English. Many Poles were returning home. They had bags and pouches filled to the brim. Everything in Poland was very expensive. They were bringing home as much as they could carry.

After an eight-hour flight, our plane landed at Okecie Airport in Warsaw. Jozio waited for us at the airport; we would stay with him and his wife, Krysia. She was already waiting for us with their son Czarek and daughter-in-law Monika. I had not met the children the previous year and was so glad that this time we all had a chance to get to know each other.

Krysia had prepared a true feast, a most delicious lunch. It was so good to be with them and I felt so much at home. Jozio told us after lunch that their son Czarek would be our driver to Piotrkow and Tomaszow. They had everything planned for us. The distance from Warsaw to Piotrkow was eighty-two miles. Tomaszow would be on our way back—fifteen miles east of Piotrkow. It was around 1 p.m. when we started for Piotrkow. Leaving Warsaw we ran into thousands of people marching to Czestochowa on their annual pilgrimage to see and pray at the shrine of the Black Madonna. It was raining. People on crutches, in wheelchairs—young and old, were singing hymns and marching on. It was quite a sight. Some of the people had to walk a week to reach Czestochowa and the monastery on Jasna Gora. The previous year while in Czestochowa I saw the very crowded monastery but not the march of the pilgrims. The pilgrims slowed us down and we arrived in Piotrkow later than planned.

Jozio parked the car not far from the street where the Kimmelman family lived one hundred years ago. I led them to 7 Starowarszawska, the house where Max's family had their restaurant. I showed them the windows where the business was and upstairs where the family lived. These were the streets where Max walked. I pointed out the old castle and we walked to the once beautiful synagogue. Built in the Spanish style over two hundred years ago, it now houses the public library. When we approached the synagogue, I noticed right away that something was different from the previous year. The side wall that previously still had holes from bullets had been painted over. There were no signs of bullet holes left.

We walked the streets of Okopowa. Remnants of the old city wall are still standing. We saw a statue of Mikolaj Kopernik (Copernicus) in front of the *Gimnazjum* and walked on Rynek Trybunalski. Unfortunately, there was no time to visit the Jewish cemetery where Max's parents and sisters are buried. Our time was too limited.

The streets of Piotrkow were clean but deserted. In each window was a flower box with the most beautiful geraniums, roses, and other bright flowers. The people we saw looked sad and depressed. The poorest people are now living where the ghetto once was. We left Piotrkow—the city so dear to Max—and headed for Tomaszow. It was only a distance of fifteen miles.

Here my family and I had lived from 1940 till May 1943. Tomaszow-Mazowiecki was a fairly new town established in the nineteenth century. It was a textile center with many ethnic Germans employed in factories before the war. I have not been back since we (my father, brother, uncle, and I) were shipped from here to the concentration camp Majdanek/Blizyn in May 1943, over forty-eight years ago.

Entering the city on Pilsudskiego Street, I remembered that the street where we lived in the ghetto was to the right. I found it right away; 37 Zgorzelicka Street was the last house close to the ghetto gate. Coming from Pilsudskiego Street, it was the first house on the left. It had not changed; it looked like the house I lived in forty-eight years ago. I pointed to the second-floor windows on the right side of the building. On the floor above us, the five windows belonged to the apartment where the Kolski family lived. From this building Eva's parents, two sisters, and two brothers were taken to the death camp of Treblinka. She was the sole survivor of her family.[1] I was overwhelmed by feelings of sadness and grief. Here was the house where we lived together as a family for the very last time. Here we experienced some of the most difficult times in our lives. In this building I spent part of my youth, years that normally would be the best and happiest years of growing up. We lived in this house when in January 1941 my brother Benno was observing his becoming a Bar Mitzvah, celebrated with a meager lunch at the apartment of the Kolski family on the third floor. From this house my brother tried to run away in January 1942 with a Polish friend who lived across the street (I showed the children the small house where this boy lived). My brother Benno was a dreamer, an idealist. He wanted to be free. He felt that if he could escape, he had a chance to fight the Nazis. Benno had a premonition of doom. He spoke to me about it while in the camp of Blizyn (Majdanek).

Straight ahead from Zgorzelicka Street we drove toward Wiecznosc Street. This street has been renamed Slowackiego Street. We turned at the corner where there once was a bakery in the ghetto. I wanted to show the children the little white church that stood on this street on the right hand side. In front of it I was separated from my mother on October 31, 1942, when the ghetto was being liquidated. Here I saw my dear mother for the last time. Now shocked I was—the little white church now is a huge modern white church, three times the size of the old one that stood here in 1942. Next I wanted to retrace the road that I traveled with my mother, our last walk together.

We came to the corner of Stolarska Street and turned onto the street in search of the Dietz factory, where our family spent the last night before the liquidation of the ghetto. The factory is gone. A warehouse now stands in its place. In my mind I could still see the factory building. For me it will always remain there. From Stolarska Street we turned onto Poludniowa Street, to No. 5, where my parental grandparents lived. The little house is still there. It has been painted a bright pink and looks beautiful. The small garden to the right of the house where my father, brother, and I grew some vegetables during the years of hunger in the ghetto is still there. How many hours did we spend turning the ground, planting potatoes and carrots, onions and cabbage so that the family would have some additional food? These were years of starvation and fresh produce helped us survive. Here I visited my grandparents every Saturday afternoon. My last visit took place the day before the ghetto was liquidated on October 31, 1942. From here they marched toward the railroad station. They walked the same road my mother and I walked. This, too, was their last walk in the ghetto.

From Poludniowa Street we drove to the other side of the city to 5 Warszawska Street. Czarek parked the car so that we could walk to the house where we lived from May 1940 till November. On the third floor of this house lived the Weiskopf family. The parents Michael and Lisa were dentists. Their children were Zygmunt (a medical student at the university in Montpelier), Salka (my age), and Zosia, the youngest daughter. The Weiskopf family was one of the well-known Jewish families in Tomaszow before the war. Their house was on Plac Kosciuszki and was requisitioned by the Nazis in October 1939. Zygmunt, who came home from France for the summer of 1939, was caught here and never left. Salka and I became close friends.

Salka and I volunteered to work in the kitchen for refugees as waitresses. My aunt Rosa Przedecka (my father's only sister) who was in charge of the kitchen hired us. She gave us the opportunity to help out, and we received soup as our payment. This was so important, as we were constantly hungry. Salka's father Michael Weiskopf was shot in the ghetto during the bloody April pogroms in 1942. Her mother, Lisa, died of typhoid fever a few months later. Salka, Zosia, and Zygmunt became orphans. Zygmunt joined the ghetto police (called *Ordnungsdienst*) so that he could protect his sisters. Salka and Zosia were with me in the camps of Blizyn and Birkenau. We were liberated together in Bergen-Belsen in 1945. After the war, Zygmunt finished his medical studies in Germany, married Lotka, and moved to the United States. Zosia moved to Israel. Salka married Leon Grabowski and moved to Philadelphia, where they lived with their two children, Lisa and Michael. Salka passed away in 1990.

In the next house at 7 Warszawska Street, Dr. Stefan Giebocki and his wife, Maria, lived on the second floor during the war years. They came to Tomaszow as refugees from Bydgoszcz. Both were Polish Catholics and very soon both became our good friends.[2] When we were forced to move into the ghetto, Dr. Giebocki came many times to treat my mother. We learned after the war that he died and were told that he was poisoned.

On the ground floor at 9 Warszawska Street was a hardware store that belonged to the Lipszyc family. Estusia, her husband, and their little son, Pinio,[3] were with us in the ghetto and later in the camp of Blizyn. It was here that seven-year-old Pinio was taken from them and shot in the forest with the rest of the Jewish children. Estusia was the only survivor. She moved to Israel after the war and remarried. We saw each other each time I came to Tel Aviv. Estusia died in 1989. On Warszawska Street lived another good friend, Lolka Rosenbaum. Their family had a haberdashery store on Plac Kosciuszki. When the ghetto was created, they moved to Poludniowa Street. Lolka and I shared the experiences in the Dietz factory on the day when the ghetto was being liquidated.[4] She gave birth to a baby girl in the Bergen-Belsen camp and moved with her daughter to Israel after the war. Lolka died in June 1991. Another good friend from Warszawska Street is gone.

The four of us drove toward the railroad station ready to leave Tomaszow. As I saw the station, my thoughts returned to the bitterly cold day in February 1940 when my parents, my brother, Benno, and I arrived in Tomaszow from Warsaw. The joys and pains of my years in Tomaszow, my secret involvements in the Zionist youth movement *HaShomer Hatzair*, the clandestine schooling—all these memories accompanied me on this pilgrimage to Tomaszow. But most of all I relived the tragic parting from my dearest mother and family members. Now the circle was closing on another chapter of my life.

It seemed almost unreal that on this first day in Poland we saw so much, shared so many memories. It was an unforgettable experience not only for Gene and Caroline but also for Czarek.

Our plan for the following morning was to visit the Jewish cemetery in Warsaw and to see the places I visited a year earlier and to explain them to my children. In the afternoon after visiting the cemetery and after saying good-bye to Krysia, Monika, and Czarek, we left Warsaw for Gdańsk. Jozio was now our driver. We made only one stop near Mlawa. It was here in

September 1939 that the Polish army courageously defended the country against the invasion by the mighty German army. A monument stands by the road in memory of the fallen heroes.

As we were getting closer to Gdańsk my anxiety was building up. I had such mixed feelings. For years I dreamt of returning to the city of my youth. Now after fifty-two years I was to see the city again. The sun was setting. It was bright orange when I saw from afar the skyline once so familiar to me—the steeples of the Marienkirche and the Rathaus (city hall). Driving toward the city we passed the coffee roasting factory just behind the Polish *Gimnazjum*. It was hard for me to see all the familiar places while sitting in the fast-moving car. I knew that we would walk in the city and that I would be able to point out many things. We passed the old Dominikswall, the street where we lived when war broke out. Now it is called Waly Jagiellonskie. This street had been completely destroyed by Russian artillery in March 1945 and is a brand-new street now. I also saw the park across the street where we lived. It was called Irrgarten. The railroad station was now in full view. It had not changed at all. Turning right, we reached our hotel, the Hevelius. I could hardly wait to register and check in so that we could walk the streets of Gdańsk. Since all of us were quite hungry, we had supper in the hotel restaurant. Then we took a short walk. It was dark but the streets were full of people. We made plans to get up early the next morning so that we could see as much as possible.

I suggested that we devote the first full day to driving to Sopot, where I was born almost sixty-eight years earlier and where my parents were married on September 16, 1921—seventy years before. From there we would visit Orlowo and Gdynia.

Passing the Olivaer Tor in Gdańsk, we drove past Halbe Allee, Steffens-park, Langfuhr (now Wrzeszcz), the suburb of Oliva, with its famous cathedral and palace. Here in the seventeenth century the Swedish king Gustav Adolph had his headquarters when the Swedish navy invaded Gdańsk and Poland. Napoleon also stopped here on his way to Russia. In this park my father took a picture of me when I was three years old. The background was a waterfall in the park, and I was holding an apple in my right hand. This picture was enlarged and hung in our living room (*Herrenzimmer*). I was not sure that we would have the time to visit the park. The next stop was Sopot. I asked Jozio to park on Nordstrasse across from the Kasino Hotel (now Grand Hotel). I knew that we were very close to the street where I was born: 14 Promenadenstrasse.

The first street did not look familiar to me and we turned into the next one. I stopped right away in front of house No. 14 and recognized the little garden in front of it. The street is now named ulica Majowieckiego. Although I was only four-and-a-half years old when we moved from this house to Danzig, I have many vivid memories of this place where I was born.

From here we had only a short walk to the beach and sea. The place near the Kasino Hotel, where concerts took place, and where people came to dance, was still there. As we entered the park with the famous pier (over a half mile long), the arcades that once had benches for people to sit on and to listen to concerts were now filled with stalls, peddlers, and merchants. We walked all the way to the end of the pier and saw many swans swimming in the sea. The Baltic Sea has a very low percentage of salt, so swans and ducks thrive here. Seagulls were everywhere waiting for people to feed them. The beaches were deserted. The once beautiful and clear Danzig Bay is so polluted that there are signs everywhere prohibiting swimming. The weather was absolutely beautiful, the sky so clear. From the pier we walked back toward Südstrasse. We passed the house where the Kronman family had lived before the war. Roman and Marychna, originally from Kolo, were close friends of my parents. They had a son, Jurek (George), and a daughter, Hania. Only Jurek survived; he left Zoppot in 1938 for England. I saw him in Belsen, where he found me in 1945 after liberation. Jurek served with the British army. Unfortunately, his parents and only sister met their death in Treblinka.

Then we turned to what once was Eisenhardtstrasse, now ulica Szopena. Here I found the house that my family rented for the summer of 1936. The side street now called ulica Dabrowskiego was once Roonstrasse, where the only synagogue in Sopot stood. It was here that my parents were married. There was no trace of the synagogue. It was set on fire in November 1938 after the Nazis orchestrated *Kristallnacht* in Germany and the free city of Danzig. Now an apartment building stands in its place. There was another task I wanted to accomplish: to find records of my and my brother's birth registry. We were close to city hall; Gene and I went to the proper office. The records of our births were found by the clerk right away. I was only disappointed that she could not find my parents' civil marriage records. Hungry and tired, we walked down the former main street of Sopot—Seestrasse. Today it is a pedestrian mall with many small cafes and restaurants. Jozio, Gene, and Caroline sat down at one of the cafes to eat while I went to look for a bookstore to purchase some Polish books. Then we were ready to continue our trip.

Next on our agenda was the resort town Orlowo near Gdynia. In the early 1920s Orlowo was a small village. By 1932 this small village became a summer resort famous for its white beaches, nice pier, and magnificent woods all around the seashore. When the Nazis came to power in Danzig, many of the Jewish families living there spent the summer months in Orlowo instead of Zoppot, as did my family. I remembered it full of life, filled with vacationers. Now it looked like a ghost town. This once thriving resort was completely deserted. We could actually count the people there. First we walked to the places I wanted to find—the two summer homes where my family spent three months in the summers of 1933, 1934, and 1935. I found the first house right away on the main street leading to the sea. It did not change much and looked newly painted. The next goal was to find the house where we spent the summers of 1934 and 1935. I remembered the paths and led the children and Jozio to the place.

We took the steep walk downhill. I very vividly remember when my father was driving his car down the steep road. On the left stood the house where the owners by the name Czoske once lived. Some people were in the yard. I asked them if they knew anything about the Czoske family. "They are all gone," was their reply. "Only one daughter who married a Pole came back a few years ago to see the house." I wondered if the daughter was my friend Ursula Czoske. The Czoskes were a large family with eight children. I hoped to find at least one member of the Czoske family here, but they, too, were gone.

Now we walked toward the little house that we called "Villa Czoske." Actually, it was a small cottage. How many fond memories I have of the two happy summers spent here with my family and friends. In 1934 my parents invited my cousin Mietek Lachman to spend the summer as a high school graduation gift. In 1935 my cousin Halina Przedecka from Lodz was invited to spend the summer with us. The house looks old and neglected now. I can still see it as it looked almost fifty-eight years ago.

We walked back to the sea and sat on the pier looking at the shoreline, enjoying the beauty and tranquility of this place. My thoughts went back to the years when my parents, my brother, Benno, and I came here and walked on the pier, enjoying the carefree summer months before the storm.

Next on our agenda was Gdynia, the third of the tri-cities. We lived in Gdynia in 1938, when my father opened his office here. Gdynia was a fishing village until 1924. By 1929 it became a new and modern Polish city and port. We entered Gdynia on Swietojanska Street, the street where we once lived. I found the corner house, No. 68, where the department store Bon Marché stood before the war. Now it is a bookstore. Next to it, in No. 66, we lived on the third floor. I recognized the five large windows facing the street. They were from our dining room, living room, and my parents' bedroom. When we resided here fifty-three years ago it was a brand-new building with an elevator and carpeted marble staircase. Now it looked drab and neglected. Next to it, No. 64, was the house where the Ebin family lived. They left Gdynia on August 25 on the last ship (*Batory*) and came to New York when the war was already in progress. The younger daughter Gala Ebin was my very close friend. She died in September 1976. There was one more stop I had to make in Gdynia. I wanted to see the house at 12 Skwer Kosciuszki, where my father's office was in 1938. We found the house without difficulties.

In one day I found so many places—the house where my brother and I were born, the houses where we spent our summers in 1933, 1934, 1935, and 1936, the house in Gdynia where we lived in 1938, and my father's office. Unfortunately, only memories and places are left, the people and family so dear to me are gone. The next search would be in Gdańsk.

Upon our return to Gdańsk, we rested and then went to the old city for dinner. We were told that Pod Wierza (Under the Tower) was a good restaurant. It was located on Jopengasse (now Piwna) very close to the church of St. Mary's. The food proved to be very good. The restaurant was in a four-hundred-year-old restored building. Now we were very close to the street where my family lived after we left Zoppot in March 1928. The street then was Brotbänkengasse (now ulica Chlebnicka). All old patrician houses have been restored to their old glory. I found the house without difficulty. The facade and the building have been beautifully restored. Here we lived from 1928 until early summer of 1933. I started school in April 1930 while we lived in this house. So many childhood memories suddenly came back.

Only a few yards from the house was Brotbänkentor—Brama Chlebnicka. It led us to the Mottlau (Motlawa) River. Across from this gate were the famous Danzig granaries, where grain and seeds were stored. Here once stood the granary "Deo Gloria," which burned down before the war. In one of these granaries my father was storing seeds and grain for export. All is now gone. There are only a few restored granaries on the other side of the bridge (Grüne Brücke). We walked through the famous Grünes Tor (upstairs were quarters where kings visiting Gdańsk resided) and we entered the heart of the old city—Langer Markt (Dlugi Rynek).

The children and Jozio were breathless. One house was more beautiful than the next. The sight of these artistically restored buildings was indescribable. Gene and Caroline were completely enchanted by the charm of the old city. I showed them Artushof, where the daily commodity market met and the Börse (stock exchange), attended daily by my father. I recall the many times he took me with him. In front of it stands the famous Neptunbrunnen (Fontanna Neptuna). Then came city hall—one of the landmarks of Gdańsk. On top of the Rathaus (city hall) is the reconstructed statue of the Polish king Zygmunt II. It was getting late and we could not visit the inside of the building. The city hall has ceilings painted with the old view of the city, scenes from the Old Testament, and on one of the pictures the artist painted with Hebrew letters the Tetragrammaton. At the corner of Postgasse and Hundegasse I found the house where my father's brother Heinrich Ryczke lived. Today this building looks old, dark, and very depressing. As another landmark was rediscovered, more bittersweet memories came back to me. Tired after a long day, and a lot of walking, we returned to our hotel.

The next day at breakfast, Gene told me about a very early telephone call. He was awakened at 5 a.m. by someone who spoke only Polish. He could understand but was not able to converse. He understood that some friends of mine will visit us in the hotel between 8 and 9 a.m. It dawned on me that I had written to the Rode family in Tuchola about my coming to Gdańsk. They are relatives of Yvonne Foster of Oak Ridge. For the past ten years I have been translating Yvonne's letters to them and theirs to her. They live on a farm near Tuchola about ninety-five miles from Gdańsk. The farm belonged to their family for almost seven hundred years. Finally I would be able to meet them.

They arrived after 9 a.m.—Maria Rode, the mother, her son Janek, daughter Wanda, and granddaughter Beatka. I knew so much about the family, they were no strangers to me. First I invited them for coffee, then we went to my room to talk. Maria Rode came with a basket filled with fried chicken and a cooked carp from their pond. There was no need to order lunch. They came fully equipped. We spent the morning talking. As a gift they left two porcelain vases, one for Yvonne and one for me. They were beautiful, but what a burden to carry. Gene urged me many times during our trip to "just drop them"—but I could not do it. Maria gave them to me with such love, and I wanted to take them back to Oak Ridge.

After the Rode family left, we decided to use the afternoon driving to the former concentration camp in Stutthof, only twenty miles from Gdańsk. I felt that being so close to it, Gene and Caroline should have the opportunity to see at least one former camp. This was one of the hardest things we did. I had a special reason for going there. While living in Gdynia in 1938, I met my first boyfriend. He had already graduated from the *Gimnazjum* and worked in Gdynia for a firm my father knew from Danzig. He and I belonged to the same Zionist organization. His name was Bruno (Bronek) Chaim. The family originally came from Rzeszow and settled in Gdynia in 1930. When the Germans entered Gdynia on September 1, 1939, Bruno was taken prisoner. By September 10 he was sent to Stutthof. I corresponded with his sister Linka and his mother, who left Gdynia for Rzeszow when war was imminent. For months they tried to find out what happened to their only son. In July 1940 I received a letter from Linka. The family had been notified that Bruno had died of "heart failure" in the camp of Stutthof. He was twenty years old. This was the first time I had heard of Stutthof.

Before we left for Stutthof, I wanted to show Gene and Caroline some more places. Not far from the hotel was the former Pfefferstadt (now Korzenna). Here stood the old city hall completely undamaged. A few yards from this old city hall is the stream Radaune (Radunia). It looked dirty and terribly polluted. The waters from this stream were used by the Grosse Mühle (Duzy Mlyn), a huge old mill. On the other side of the Radunia was the house where the Zionist organization *Habonim* had held meetings. The street was called Am Sande (Na Piaskach). I belonged to *Habonim* from 1934 till 1938 and attended many meetings in the building. The house now looks better, having been painted and redone. So here I found another place to remind me of my youth.

The ride to Stutthof was an hour long. It was not easy to find the camp, as it was located in a well-secluded area. This part of the free city was called Danziger Niederung (low country), where brown coal was claimed from the clay in the marshes and swamps. The climate was unhealthy. It was humid and known for the many mosquitoes that bred near the swamps. Here the Nazis opened the Stutthof camp on September 2, 1939. At first it was a detention camp for Jews, Poles, and anti-Nazis. Soon it became a slave labor camp and later a concentration camp. The site of Stutthof was selected in 1939 by Albert Forster, who was the Gauleiter of the Free City of Danzig. He had his people compile names of Poles that he wanted interned, and as soon as the Nazis officially occupied the once Free City of Danzig, the arrest of Poles and Jews began. At first all arrested Poles and Jews were brought to the former Victoria Schule, which I attended until 1935. After a few days they were sent to Stutthof. Leon Lendzion and his father (who was later shot in Stutthof) as well as his brother were arrested and brought to this place. Now a street in Wrzeszcz is named in honor of Mr. Lendzion, Leon's father. Barracks had to be built by prisoners, as it was completely empty here in September of 1939. On September 2, 1939, of the 1,500 Poles arrested in Gdańsk, 150 were brought to Stutthof. This was the beginning of the tragic story of this camp. Stutthof at first served mainly to eliminate the most patriotic Poles, from the educated circles of Gdańsk and the Pomorze region. At the beginning plans were to imprison about 3,500 prisoners. As more Poles and later prisoners from twenty-three European countries were sent here, by 1944 the camp had 57,000 inmates. The main camp was here in Stutthof, but it had thirty-nine subcamps (*Aussenkommandos*) where prisoners were forced to work. By the time the Soviets were approaching East Prussia, before the camp was slowly evacuated, it had 110,000 men, women, and children. During the years 1939–45, 65,000 persons died as a result of shootings, hangings, gassing (Zyklon B), beatings, and phenol injections (to stop the heart). Jewish women, who were brought here from Baltic countries, from Hungary and Lodz, were taken to the gas chamber and killed. In some instances, when they hesitated to walk toward their deaths, railroad cars were brought. The women were told that they would be taken by train to a place where they would have better working conditions. They were tricked. As soon as they entered the cattle cars, doors were hermetically closed and poison gas was thrown into the crowded cars. All of them perished. There were three evacuations from Stutthof—in January 1945, in March 1945, and the last one in early April 1945. Most of the evacuated prisoners died. The few that survived and are still alive today are being interviewed so that the history of this camp can be accurately compiled. We toured the museum and the many barracks and saw names of prisoners and death notices. Then we walked into the camp where the gas chamber and crematorium were located. Everything is well preserved. Adults and school children were visiting this place of horror. Around the large monument in memory of the victims were pieces of human bones taken from the crematorium and enclosed in glass. The layout of the camp showed us that the Jewish barracks were completely separate. Even in camps Jews were isolated. It was interesting to read that quite a large contingent of Danes were in this camp. As we later learned in Denmark, the Danish police stood up to the Nazis. These men were sent to Stutthof. We left the camp in a subdued mood. For Gene, Caroline, and Jozio, this was a moving experience, as it was the first and only concentration camp they had seen. Our hearts were filled with sadness—it was a painful afternoon for all of us.

Stutthof concentration camp crematorium.

Stutthof concentration camp gas chamber. Railroad tracks where prisoners were unloaded for gassing are directly outside the gas chamber.

On the way back to Gdańsk we saw many nests with storks. We even saw three of them standing in one nest. It was harvest time in Poland, and hundreds of storks and other birds were in the fields, looking for leftover wheat and barley kernels.

Back in Gdańsk, Caroline, Gene, and I wanted to find the grade school that Benno and I attended. I knew it was not very far from our hotel. The street was called Wallgasse, in Polish ulica Walowa. Walking past two churches dating from the fourteenth century, St. Brigit and St. Bartholomew, I noticed the sign ulica Walowa. I told the children where to look for my old grade school. We found it—there was the dark red brick building on the left side of the street. It was already quite dark but we could read the plaque. I told Gene the school was Szkola Maciezy Polskiej w Gdańsku, and this is exactly what was written on the plaque. Another landmark was discovered. Not far from the school lived our Hebrew teacher, Mr. Glückmann. Twice a week Benno and I walked to his house to take Hebrew lessons and religious instruction. The house looked exactly the way I remembered it. This part of the city was untouched by the war.

We walked some more toward the Markthalle (market hall), St. Catherine's church, toward Breitgasse (Szeroka). Here was the famous Unter dem Lachs house, where the well-known Danzig liqueur Goldwasser was produced. Gene knew all about this drink, as my father brought a bottle of this delicious liqueur from Europe many years ago. Today Pod Lososiem is one of the best-known restaurants in Gdańsk. The place was jammed. We stepped inside so that the children could see the luxurious interior and decided to make our reservations for the following evening, our last evening in Gdańsk. It was already close to 10 p.m., yet the streets were still full of people. We walked back to the hotel to retire after a day filled with many emotions.

The following day Jozio had to return to Warsaw. With tears in his eyes Jozio said goodbye to us. Now we were on our own.

We planned to walk first to the railroad station, then toward the street where my family lived until war broke out. It was drizzling but very warm. This kind of weather is typical for Gdańsk, but I knew that soon the sun would come out. We passed St. Elizabeth church. Not far from it was the street where we once lived. Then it was called Dominikswall; now it is known as Waly Jagiellonskie. Our side of the street has been rebuilt. I showed the children exactly where the house we lived in was once located. All of the houses on the opposite side of the street were destroyed. Here the Bloch family once resided. Kazik Bloch was my father's second cousin. His mother, Zosia Bloch, and my grandfather Ryczke were first cousins. The Bloch family lived in Zoppot, Danzig, and finally in Gdynia. From there they left for England in 1939. I am in touch with the older son, Richard.

Next I wanted to retrace with my children the road to the Polish *Gimnazjum*. We walked by what once was the Polizeipräsidium, the police headquarters. From Karenwall the Great Synagogue on Reitbahn could once be seen. The street and synagogue are gone now. New streets and highways have been built. As we passed St. Trinity Church, I knew that we were getting close to my old *Gimnazjum*. I told the children that near the school was a white tower on a street called Am Weissen Turm. Lo and behold, here was the white tower in front of us, and on the other side of the street the large brick building that once housed the Polish *Gimnazjum*. A plaque is attached to the front of the building stating that in 1922 this building was erected as the only Polish *Gimnazjum*. The street has been named after the last school principal, Jan Augustynski. How well I remember him. He was killed during the war. Now we saw everything we had planned to see.

It was still early, and we wanted to do some shopping. The month of August was always the time for St. Dominik's Fair. The city was full of stalls with all kinds of wares displayed on tables and in the streets. We saw so many books for sale, all printed in German. I bought two small books about Gdańsk and then we went to the stall with sweaters. Gene bought one for me for my birthday and I got one for Caroline's birthday. We walked toward the Kohlenmarkt (Rynek Weglowy) where once the Gdańsk theater was located. Under the Stockturm (Katownia)—the "tower of torture"—we found a stand with carved wooden articles. I wanted to get some gifts that would not break. And here the nightmare began.

As I was paying for my purchases, I noticed that my passport was missing. It had been in a special leather wallet and someone took it out of my bag. The rest is hard to describe. We had to go to the police station and report the theft. Gene and Caroline returned to the place of the crime to look in garbage cans for my passport while I stayed at the police station. We rushed back to our hotel once the theft was reported. I placed a telephone call to the American Embassy in Warsaw telling them about my predicament. The following day we were supposed to leave by ferry for Sweden, and I would not be able to travel without a passport. The woman at the embassy told me that they were open only until noon on Friday (this was Thursday) and that it takes three working days to issue a passport. Finally I asked to speak with the American consul, who was a woman. Using psychology, I asked my son, "the lawyer," to speak to her. At first she gave him the same story about three working days needed for issuing a passport. After much deliberation, Gene asked her if he could swear to the fact that I was a U.S. citizen. She agreed, but we would have to report to her office in the morning with three photographs, which I quickly managed to obtain. We hurried to the hotel to pack, checked out, and took a taxi to the train station. There was one express train leaving at 3 p.m. We got on it and within four hours arrived in Warsaw.

On the train we studied a map of Warsaw. We had to find a hotel close to Aleje Ujazdowskie, where the embassy was located. Luckily we found one hotel and checked in. It was close to 8 p.m. We had not eaten a decent meal all day and were starved. But it was important for us to find the exact location of the embassy. We walked from the hotel on Marszalkowska Street to the embassy. We timed it—it was a good twenty-minute walk. On the way back we stopped at a small sidewalk café and had something to eat and drink. Our hotel was located on a very noisy street with buses and trams running all night long. I could not sleep. Not only was I upset because my passport was gone, but also I had spoiled the children's vacation. All I wanted now was for them to be able to return to Gdańsk and catch the ferry for Sweden. It would be hard for me to remain in Warsaw alone, but at least I could speak the language. I never prayed as hard as that night hoping that things would turn out all right.

The next morning, we took off for the embassy. Arriving much too early, we waited for the gate to open. We were the first ones to enter, and after filling out many forms and Gene swearing that I was a citizen, within one hour I was the happiest person—I had a brand-new U.S. passport. There was not much time to lose. The only train to take us to Gdańsk in time to catch the ferry was leaving Warsaw at 12:20 p.m. Rushing to our hotel to pick up our belongings and catching a taxi to the station, we had just enough time to purchase the tickets and to get something to eat.

The train to Gdańsk was a local, filled to capacity. We stood in the corridor for four of the five hours and finally arrived in Gdańsk. Happy to be back, we took a taxi to the port, arriving just in time to board the ferry to Sweden. Someone "Upstairs" was watching over us. Soon I would part company with Gene and Caroline and travel to Malmö to visit my distant cousin Halinka Gelles.

In Malmö, I was met by my cousin Halinka. We walked to the car where her husband, Werner, was waiting for us. Despite being partially paralyzed on his left side from a stroke, he continued to drive a car. From now on our conversation would be in German, so that Halinka's husband would be able to participate.

Their house was in a quiet neighborhood outside the city. Outside the house was a charming garden with the most beautiful flowers. These are nursed by Halinka, who does all the yard work. Besides flowers they have raspberry and gooseberry bushes, dill, onions, other spices and a huge plum tree. Taking care of the house and garden keeps Halinka busy, but most of her time has to be devoted to taking care of her semi-invalid husband.

The next two days were spent reminiscing about our families and about Halinka's life in Sweden. I shared with her details about my life in America. We spoke at great length about our children and husbands. Halinka had the need to talk. So every evening, after she put Werner to bed, we sat in Halinka's room and she opened her heart. She told me about her present life with Werner. Werner is seventy-six years old and can barely walk. Her whole life revolves around Werner, having to do almost everything for him. Halinka's health is not the best. She developed a hernia and will not undergo surgery. Her only worry is, "What will happen to Werner if I get sick?" She told me over and over, "I only hope that I will survive him. Who will take care of Werner if I am gone?" Her thoughts were very gloomy. Most of the time she recalled the great love she felt toward her two brothers, Pawel and Rafal.

We saw each other three times after the war—in 1945 in Belsen, in 1971 in Israel, and now in 1991. I will never forget this visit and will have very fond memories of our reunion. How good that we had at least two days together.

After leaving Halinka and Werner in 1991, I visited my good friend from Danzig, Janka Krakowska Waril, in Stockholm for a few days. Then I left for New York, happy to see my children. After spending a few days with Benno, Joy, Melanie, and Michael, I returned to Oak Ridge.

Now I had to sort out my feelings and impressions from and reflect on this memorable journey into my past. I arrived back home on September 1, 1991. Exactly fifty-two years ago World War II began. I was not quite sixteen years old, but the life I knew was shattered. The next five-and-a-half years were one nightmare after another. Fifty-two years earlier I had a family. When the war was finally over, only two of our eighteen family members survived: my father and I. We had to rebuild our lives. The memories of my happy childhood in Danzig sustained me during the war years. These were the memories I tried so desperately to recapture during this trip back to Gdańsk/Danzig. The absence of any signs of Jewish life in Gdańsk, Sopot, Gdynia was most painful. I tried to remember not only my dear family but also friends who lived here. And I was glad to be able to share my memories and feelings with Gene and Caroline.

While in New York, I told Benno some of the experiences we had in Poland. By now Benno and Joy were parents of two children, and Benno, too, wanted to visit my hometown. I wished he could have gone with Gene and Caroline, but Benno could not leave Joy alone with two small children. So the two of us decided to plan a trip "just like Gene's" for 1993. Benno in the meantime wanted to brush up on his Polish (he understands and speaks a little), but he wanted to be more fluent in the language.

I had ample time to plan my return to Poland with Benno. I notified Jozio about our intentions, and he promised to "do for Benno what he had done for Gene and Caroline." There was nothing to worry about—Jozio would be in charge. It was May 1993 when Benno and I met at Kennedy Airport. We had tickets on the Polish airline LOT. The waiting room was very crowded; almost all passengers were Poles returning from a visit to the States, or Americans of Polish origin flying to visit Poland. The service on this flight was one of the best I ever experienced. With just a few minutes' delay, we landed at the newly built airport at Okecie in Warsaw.

Leaving the baggage claim, I heard someone shout: Mira. It was Jozio waiting for us. How good it was to see him again. From now on I knew that we would be in good hands and could depend on him. As soon as we were together, Jozio told me some bad news. Krysia had just returned from the hospital. She suffered from high blood pressure and circulatory problems and had to be hospitalized for one week. The second shock was the news that Monika left Czarek (Jozio's son) two weeks earlier, after almost four years of marriage. This probably contributed to Krysia's sudden illness. I was very upset. We arrived here at a time when Jozio and Krysia had many problems. Jozio assured me that everything was under control; he did not want us to worry.

The weather was perfect. Jozio drove us home, not through the city, but the back way, which was much shorter. Krysia and Czarek greeted us at the door. I was shocked to see Krysia's white face. She looked so pale and frail, and her hands were cold as ice. She definitely was not well, and I felt bad to have come to their home at this time.

An elaborate brunch awaited us. It was good to see that Benno enjoyed the Polish food. I did worry that he might not like the kind of food that was served here. I could hardly wait for the good Polish bread and butter. This alone would have been enough for me. Jozio arranged for Czarek to take us to Piotrkow and Tomaszow while he stayed with Krysia. I was able to show Benno what Gene and Caroline saw two years before in Piotrkow and Tomaszow. But there were some places that only Benno would have a chance to visit.

This time, while in Piotrkow, I wanted to see Leonarda Street. This street has been renamed, but we had no trouble finding it. Here Max and his family lived with Hela, when the ghetto was established in Piotrkow in 1939. From here Hela left the ghetto in 1942, traveling on false Polish papers to Krosno. In one of her letters to Max after the war she reminded him of the time when they said good-bye on Leonarda Street. I also wanted to show Benno Bugaj, where Max worked before the war. It was only a few miles from here, a huge complex of red brick buildings. This was once the most important textile mill in the city. The Nazis took it over and converted it into a plant that produced tents for the army as well as prefabricated houses. Here Max worked after the liquidation of the ghetto in 1942, until he together with the remaining Jews was shipped to Buchenwald in November 1944. We saw almost everything we wanted to see, except for the Jewish cemetery. There was no time left, because we wanted to stop in Tomaszow Mazowiecki on our way back to Warsaw.

In Tomaszow, Benno retraced the same places with me that were filled with memories I shared with Gene and Caroline in 1991. On the way to Warsaw we stopped to get fresh cherries and to relax at a nice inn. Czarek took us for a short walk to Puszcza Kepinowska, not very far from their home. It was getting late, and we knew that Krysia and Jozio would be worried if we did not return on time. Indeed they worried, and when we came into their home we were greeted with joy. A feast of chicken soup, turkey, marinated mushrooms, and more was waiting for us. I felt terrible that Krysia worked so hard to prepare such an elaborate meal, but Jozio told me that he had helped, and that most of the cooking was done before. Although we were dead tired, we felt the need to talk. We sat for a few hours in the living room and talked about so many things—politics, the economy, Czarek's future, and about our lives in the United States.

Benno and I decided to write down all details of this journey. At 4 a.m. I began to write and woke up Benno after 6 a.m., so that he, too, could write down his impressions. Our plans for the first day were slightly changed. Instead of touring Warsaw, Jozio wanted to leave for Gdańsk after breakfast and leave the touring of Warsaw for the end of our stay. Lech Walesa, Poland's president, dissolved the *Sejm* (parliament), and there was talk of strikes. A strike could mean road blocks. The sooner we could get to Gdańsk, the more we would be able to see. Jozio and I also decided that it would be better for us to stay at the hotel in Gdańsk instead of Sopot, where we originally planned to stay. We took off for Gdańsk, while Czarek was left in charge of taking care of Krysia, who had this whole week to recuperate. It would be very peaceful at home with the three of us gone. Krysia really needed peace and a lot of rest. Jozio followed the same route to Gdańsk that took us there two years earlier.

While driving, we looked at the map, and I mentioned to Jozio that the old fortified city of Malbork (former Marienburg) was only about fifteen miles from Gdańsk, and that it would be nice for Benno to see it. Gene and Caroline saw the fortifications only from the train when we traveled to Warsaw two years earlier. Jozio said that this would be a special gift from him. We arrived after 1 p.m. in Malbork. This part of Poland is called Zulawy, and it is situated below sea level. Malbork castle traces its beginnings from the end of the thirteenth century, when the Teutonic Order—of Crusader fame—after crushing the second uprising of the Prussian population, erected this stronghold originally named Marienburg. First they built the High Castle, the headquarters of the Grand Commander and his convent. The first half of the fourteenth century marked an expansion of the castle connected with the transfer of the order's seat from Venice to Malbork in 1309. It became the strongest fortified castle in medieval Europe. As a result of the Treaty of Torun in 1466, finishing the thirteen-year war between the Teutonic Order and Poland, Malbork was incorporated into the Kingdom of Poland. For over three centuries the castle had served as the residence of Polish kings while visiting Pomerania and as the biggest arsenal in Poland. After the first partition of Poland in 1772, Malbork came under Prussian rule. Before World War I, restoration of this former Teutonic castle was carried out with very good results by German experts. In 1945 the castle was substantially destroyed by Soviet artillery. This time Polish experts restored the splendor of this old castle. Today Malbork is one of the greatest tourist attractions in Poland. Since 1961 it houses the Castle Museum, which shows research done in the fields of Eastern Pomeranian history and culture and houses collections of old and contemporary works of art. Malbork is famous for its unique collection and display of artistic objects made of amber. Most of the older tourists we saw in Malbork were Germans, some of whom may have once resided here. Buses with children from different schools were arriving, and we toured this remarkable place listening to the tour guides. As a schoolgirl I came here many years ago, but I saw so much more this time.

We had to leave if we wanted to get to Gdańsk by 4 p.m. These were the last fifteen miles. Soon the skyline of my Gdańsk was before us. Benno recognized it from pictures and was anxious to see the city. It was an easy drive to the hotel Novotel; we spotted the sign as soon as we entered Gdańsk. This hotel is situated on ulica Chmielna, former Hopfengasse, between the old and the new Mottlau (Motlawa) River. Once it was called Speicherinsel—the isle of granaries. The rooms were ready for us, all on the same floor. My window faced the old city, and I could not have dreamed of a better view. Benno and Jozio's windows faced what once was Mattenbuden, where the synagogue my family attended once stood (destroyed in 1938). They also could see the Milchkannenturm. Without wasting any time we began touring the city on foot. Everything that Gene and Caroline had seen, Benno saw too. There were just a few extras.

As we walked down Jopengasse (ulica Piwna) toward Frauengasse (Mariacka ulica), I found the house where my father had his office from 1923 to 1928 (while we lived in Sopot, he commuted to this place). It was getting close to dinnertime, and I suggested that we try to eat at Pod Lososiem, the famous restaurant on Breitgasse (ulica Szeroka), where once the Goldwasser liqueur was produced. It was Danzig's trademark. Today this liqueur is produced in Germany and sold in the best liquor stores throughout the world. Two years earlier we could not get a table here, the restaurant was so crowded. This time the place was empty, as it was still early in the season. Elegant, and very attractive, the food was served without much enthusiasm by a young waiter. Most of the guests were Germans, who constitute 95 percent of all tourists in this city. With Gene and Caroline we missed the opportunity to dine here because of my stolen passport.

It was 7 p.m. when we left Pod Lososiem. The day was still young, and we wanted to see more of Gdańsk. We stopped at the Marienkirche and entered to see the splendor of this famous church. Built in the early fourteenth century as a Catholic church, it later became a Protestant church and is now again a Catholic church. Most of the interior was destroyed during the last days of March 1945. The organ and the altars have all been reconstructed. The size of this church is enormous, its beauty is hard to describe. Walking toward the Markthalle (Hale Targowe) I pointed to the older tower called Kuck in die Kück, which means in Low German, "Look into the Kitchen." Now it was pitch dark, time to return to our hotel.

Gdańsk Waterfront at Motlawa River (crane in background dates from sixteenth century), 1993.

The following morning I woke up early to another beautiful day. The view of the old city from my hotel window was breathtaking. Clearly outlined were the steeples of the Marienkirche, the Royal Chapel, and the city hall. What a view. I tried to take a picture of it, but I was not sure that it would come out. So I sketched the panorama of old Gdańsk on a piece of paper— not really a piece of art, but something to remember. For two hours I wrote down impressions of my return to Gdańsk and at 6 a.m. made a wake-up call to Benno. He was already up. His room faced east, and the sun woke him up very early. He, too, was busy writing about this trip. Benno and I began touring the city at 6:30. He took endless pictures of the beautifully restored patrician houses, their splendor shining in the morning sun. One cannot really describe what these buildings look like, the sight was one of absolute beauty. Each one was adorned with sculptures, figures, and pictures. By now the streets were filling with people walking to work. It was 7:30 a.m. and time to return to the hotel where Jozio was waiting for us. Most of the guests in the hotel were Germans, and German was the language we heard spoken in Gdańsk. Bringing currency to Poland, the Germans are one of the best sources of income. (Especially in Gdańsk, where tourism is the most important industry). All stores, all public places advertise in German for the benefit of these tourists.

Next we took off for Sopot, Orlowo, and Gdynia, just like two years before. This time, when we approached the house where I was born, I dared to go upstairs and knock on the door to the apartment that was once ours. Two years earlier I was too excited to even think of entering this house. Now I walked into the entrance hall and up the three flights of steps that have not changed since we lived here from 1923 to 1928. While walking up the steps, I stopped for a few seconds on the second floor. Here the Bloch family once lived. I had to think of the many times when I visited them with their sons, Richard and George. Knocking on the door, an elderly man opened it. I explained who I was and why I had come here and asked if it would be all right to see the apartment for just a few minutes. His wife joined him, and they looked at each other and agreed that I could enter their apartment. They were originally from Torun and Poznan and had lived in this house since 1948. I recognized right away the room to the right, which once was my room. Even the view from the window of this room was so familiar. The larger room across from the entrance was our living room. The windows have been changed and the furniture was quite modern. The owners of this apartment were retired professional people and seemed very pleasant. Both spoke of their suffering during the war years after they learned that I was in Auschwitz. At one point they asked me what I was (how well I understood what they meant), and I answered straightforward—I am Jewish. I do not think that they asked me the question in malice, and I had no reason to think so. They continued to be very pleasant, asking me if I wanted to see the rest of their apartment, but I did not want to intrude on their privacy. It is hard to describe my feelings while standing in the place where I was born, where the very first memories of my early childhood are still vivid in my mind and heart. There was so much here that reminded me of the years I lived here—the time when my aunt Rosa Przedecka and cousins Halina and Gina came here to visit us, the day when my brother, Benno, was born in this apartment on January 24, 1928. All these moments flashed through my mind—it was like a dream of long, long ago. I thanked the couple for their kindness and walked down the familiar stairs to join Benno and Jozio. I was glad that Benno, too, had the opportunity to see the house in which his mother was born.

It was time to show Benno the famous Sopot pier. We walked down the old Seestrasse (now Bohaterow Monte Casino) toward the sea. The weather was a little breezy but warm. The streets and pier were crowded with children—this day being the "Day of the Child." The sea seemed dirtier than two years earlier, and there were fewer swans. The beaches were empty, and it was absolutely forbidden to enter the water because of heavy pollution. Then we drove to Orlowo and Gdynia, just like two years before.

When we arrived in Gdańsk, I called Leon Lendzion. He invited us to his home in Oliwa, and I promised to visit him on our way back from Gdynia to Gdańsk. It was only a twenty-minute drive from Gdynia. We found the street and house without any difficulties. Leon Lendzion came out to greet us. Oliwa is a quiet suburb, and the house they live in is a nicely remodeled two-story house. Leon's wife, Hela, went to school with me until 1937, then she transferred to the Wyzsza Szkola Handlowa (higher trade school) in Gdańsk. They invited us into their living room, and Leon right away gave me some books as gifts, including a book to take back for Harry Szmant. Leon and Harry went to school together for many years, and in 1936 they graduated together from the Polish *Gimnazjum*. I brought some gifts for Hela and Leon, which were greatly appreciated. They tried to contact some of the former students of the *Gimnazjum* that were in my class, but they could only get hold of Stefa Bierska. Stefa came, and to my surprise brought a picture taken in school in 1938. On it was Gala Ebin, Tula Dlugolecka, and me. It was even signed by me. I really could not recall when this picture was taken, but what a surprise this was. Stefa also brought a bouquet of lilies of the valley—my favorite flowers. Leon Lendzion produced a book from before the war, where streets were listed, and a directory with names of people living in them. He opened it to Dominikswall, and surely under No. 10 was listed Moritz Ryczke, my father. This book was printed in 1939. Hela asked me if I still remembered our telephone number in Gdańsk, and without thinking

I said (in German) 27537 and 27538. Hela checked the book: I was right. Somehow after so many years these numbers were embedded in my memory. It is strange, but I do not recall any other telephone numbers, only those from my childhood in Gdańsk. The table was set in the dining room, Hela prepared delicious cakes and we continued talking while enjoying the dessert. Leon and Hela insisted that we stay for supper. While in Oliwa, I wanted to visit the Oliwa Schlosspark, with the famous cathedral and castle. Leon told us that he would be glad to be our guide and show us around. We wanted to do it before it got dark and we left. Hela remained at home to prepare the meal.

At the home of the Lendzion family, Oliva, May 1999. *Left to right:* Jacek Lendzion, Hela Lendzion, Alina Szmant, and Leon Lendzion.

With Gene and Caroline we talked about going to Oliwa, but we did not have the time. On this trip we would visit this famous park. First we went to the cathedral built as a church in the twelfth century by a Cistercian order. This impressive building became the cathedral of the diocese of Danzig in 1926. Its beautiful organ and altar are truly to be admired. We left the cathedral once mass started and walked toward the park. We passed the castle, which has been restored to its former glory. Here the "Peace of Oliwa" was signed between Poland and Sweden, after the Swedes invaded Poland in the seventeenth century. I remembered a waterfall in the park, where my father took a picture of me in 1927. We found the small waterfall; somehow it was much smaller than I remembered. Then I recalled the whispering grotto. It was dirty, but I wanted to try it out on Benno. For some reason it did not work: he could not hear what I said in a whisper, although he was supposed to hear it clearly on the opposite side. The park is well kept and is almost like a botanical garden. It was a special treat to be able to visit this place I had not seen since 1938.

It was getting dark and time to return to the Lendzions' for supper. Hela prepared two kinds of delicious fish. She knew that I would not eat meat, and she had a variety of salads and the good Polish bread. Hela and Leon received us with so much warmth and genuine Polish hospitality, we shall never forget this day. We talked for many hours and told them about our plans for the following day. We wanted to visit the concentration camp of Stutthof again. Here Leon was a prisoner for a few months in 1939. Benno also wanted to see the Polish *Gimnazjum*. Leon asked us if he could go with us. We were thrilled, because in him we had a perfect guide. We agreed that Leon would meet us at our hotel in two days. I said good-bye to Hela and promised to write and send some of the pictures I had taken. It was a perfect day, filled with so many emotions and memories. How glad I was that I was in touch with Leon Lendzion and had the opportunity to see old friends and share memories with them.

While discussing the fate of the Polish post office in September 1939 at the Lendzions', we were told about the very meaningful monument that stood in front of this building to memorialize the fallen Polish post office workers. The following day Benno and I found it—a most impressive sculpture. It shows a fallen Polish mailman, his pouch with letters on the ground and pieces of letters scattered around and above him. These pieces of paper looked like doves. Another postman was defending his fallen friend with a rifle. I remembered so vividly the old Polish post office. Many times I had to walk here in the evening with letters my father wanted mailed. Danzig had two post offices: this Polish one and the one of the Free City on Langgasse (ulica Dluga). All mail that went to Poland, if mailed from the Polish post office, left the city before 10 p.m., to arrive in Poland the next day. It was important for my father to have these letters mailed before collection time, and he gave them to me to take to this post office. In winter, when it was getting dark by 4 p.m., I made this walk very reluctantly. To tell the truth, I was scared. Then I asked my brother, Benno, to accompany me on these walks. The Polish post office was the scene of a fierce battle on September 1, 1939, when the Nazis officially annexed Danzig. Most of the defending Polish postal workers were killed or wounded.

From here we walked back toward the center of the old city, through Mariacka Gate. We turned to Chlebnicka Street to look again at the site where the house we lived in stood. I told Benno that from the window of the children's room (I shared a large room with my brother while living here) I recalled the glass roof of a factory. This was a low building, and as children we looked through our window and could see through the glass roof people working below. To find this building we had to enter through the side street Kürschnergasse (ulica Kusniarska). As soon as we reached the gate to the backyard, I saw the glass-covered structure; the roof was the glass roof that I remembered. Another proof that my childhood memories had not misled us.

Our hotel was close to the former Milchkannengasse (now ulica Stagiewna). The houses on the left side of this street were all replaced by ugly warehouses. Here was once the jewelry store of Mr. Passierschein, where my father purchased my first watch for my thirteenth birthday. It was a chrome-plated Optima. A few houses farther lived the Krakowski family, the Szmants, the Feuersteins, and my first music teacher, Lucie Jung. On the opposite side of the street (the right side coming from the Green Bridge) in number 1A was my father's office. While we resided on Dominikswall, my father had his office there. By 1935 my father needed more space and moved his office to

1A Milchkannengasse. All houses on this street were destroyed. We heard that the city wanted to restore this street as soon as funds would be available. They did indeed. When I was in Gdańsk in 1999, the houses were beautifully restored in their original style. We turned toward the former Mattenbuden, now Szopy. I showed Benno the spot where once the synagogue stood to which we belonged. The Mattenbuden Synagogue was an old Orthodox house of prayer, built at the end of the eighteenth century. At that time Jews were not allowed to reside in the city proper, only in the outskirts like Mattenbuden, or in Langfuhr. We were told by the Lendzions that in Langfuhr there still is a synagogue, but we had no time to see it. According to the Lendzions, there are no Jews in Gdańsk per se. Maybe there are some hidden Jews, who bear Polish names and are afraid to admit their Jewish roots. While visiting here in 1999, I heard that Gdańsk and vicinity had three hundred Jews.

Benno also had the opportunity to see the Polish *Gimnazjum*. The day we came here students had their final exams. It felt so strange to enter this building after almost fifty-four years. Because of Leon Lendzion we were allowed to see the exhibit of pictures of the school before the war, photos of professors that I remembered, and a plaque on the wall with the names of teachers and students of this school who were killed or who died during World War II. From the exhibit we walked upstairs. I walked the same steps so many times as a young student. Now I wanted to see the room in which I attended classes in 1939; it was situated on the far end of the second floor. Unfortunately, the door was locked. The hall looked old, neglected, and dingy. There are no funds to keep old buildings in good shape, as the economy of the city is geared mainly to restore historical sites and to keep streets and roads in good shape.

The Stutthof concentration camp was next on our agenda. On the way to Stutthof, now Sztutowo, Leon Lendzion pointed out to us unusually styled houses built in the seventeenth century by Mennonites who came here from Holland. In Danzig they were persecuted and settled here in the Werder (Zulawy). They later became Germans but kept their religion. Strangely enough, these formerly Dutch people were among the first to embrace Nazism. Their old houses are now historical relics and under the protection of the state. Their columns are characteristic. Their number tells the amount of land they have. It was interesting to learn about these people. Leon is quite a historian. We arrived at the former concentration camp in Stutthof. Two years earlier we visited this place with Jozio, Caroline, and Gene, and became very depressed. For Benno this would be his first camp to see. Again we were fortunate. Leon knew Mrs. Grabowska, the director of this camp turned museum. She invited us into her office and gave us a detailed history of this gruesome place. I told the director the story of Bruno Chaim and asked her if there are lists of people who perished in this camp. Indeed they had such lists, but these were from the years after 1941. Especially missing were the lists of Jews who were killed at the very beginning. She wrote down all the details, and these will be entered into the history of Stutthof. At least Bruno Chaim's name will be mentioned in the books on Stutthof.

Through the Death Gate (which lead to a gas chamber), we walked to the barracks that serve now as a museum. Here Benno could read the details of this horrible camp. Then we proceeded toward the gas chamber. Two years earlier there was only a large cross. Now there was also a large blue Star of David to memorialize the Jewish victims who met their death here. Next to the gas chamber is the crematorium. We entered and read all the details of Nazi brutality. Next to the crematorium stands the gallows. This one was used for the public hanging of prisoners.

Shocked by what we saw, we walked toward the Stutthof monument. Unveiled in 1968, it consists of two huge blocks: the horizontal one is a wall 157 feet long and 11 feet high. Its artistic form expresses the martyrdom of the camp prisoners. Encased in the back of it is a reliquary of not completely burned human bones taken from a stake, where in 1944–45 the Nazis burned the bodies of their victims. It is a gruesome sight; one cannot erase it from memory. The vertical block is thirty-six feet high, depicting faces of victims. It symbolizes their fight and final victory over evil. The space in front of this impressive monument has become a Forum of Nations, a site where memorial events take place. The first Sunday in September has been designated for this observance. A huge map at the side of the road shows where prisoners lived and the plan of the camp. Jewish prisoners were right away separated from other nationalities. They had to perform the hardest work and received the worst treatment. They were the first to be gassed. It was heartwarming to see groups of schoolchildren as well as adults coming to this place to learn about horror, injustice, and inhumanity. As long as people are willing to come and see places like Stutthof, Auschwitz, Buchenwald, and Dachau, we may be able to prevent future holocausts.

Although I had been to Stutthof before, I was deeply moved by what we saw. My thoughts were with the thousands upon thousands of innocent people whose lives were taken so brutally by the Nazis. I had to think of all those whose bodies had been turned to ashes in this crematorium, who perished because they were Jews or Gypsies (Sinti and Roma), too old or too young, too weak or too sick. I think that Benno, too, was overwhelmed with feelings of sadness and injustice. We hardly spoke on the way back to Gdańsk; each of us was affected and touched by what we saw and heard. Benno was especially touched by the history of the camp told to us by its director, Mrs. Grabowska.

Back in Gdańsk, Benno and I had the opportunity to visit city hall. Construction of this landmark started in the fourteenth century. Gdańsk was then under the rule of the Polish kings after the Teutonic Knights were defeated. Artists, artisans, and painters were brought to Gdańsk from Holland, Flanders, and Italy, and sculptors came from Augsburg, Dresden, Antwerp, and other places. An era of making this Hanseatic city the "pearl of the Baltic" began. The city hall was only one example of how much work went into making Gdańsk famous for its architecture and beauty. As we entered the hall, we saw the famous winding staircase leading to upper floors. One is not allowed to walk on it, but its sight is very impressive. We entered the famous Red Room, depicting the history of Gdańsk on its fabulously painted ceiling. I was able to show Benno the word *Adonai* in Hebrew towering over the painted city of Gdańsk. As we walked from room to room, we saw where the city council gathered in the winter months (more windows in the room to let in the sun), and where they met in the summer. Beautifully carved tables, chairs, and cabinets made by famous Danzig craftsmen reminded me of the cabinets I saw in the Piotrkow castle, which I visited in 1990. Drawings and sketches by Günter Grass were on exhibit.

These were well done but depressing. The tour of the city hall was worthwhile. I am only sorry that Gene and Caroline did not have the chance to see all this splendor. They missed it because of the episode with my stolen passport. Mea culpa.

Now we had some time left to do our shopping—this was the only time we had to purchase gifts. Benno wanted to get something for Melanie, toys for Michael, and something very special for Joy. When our shopping was done, I wondered how on earth we would pack it all. Somehow we would have to squeeze everything into our bags. It was close to 6 p.m. and time for dinner. We found an Italian restaurant next to the Marienkirche on ulica Piwna (Jopengasse) and had quite a tasty meal. Looking out of the window of this restaurant, I recognized where we were—across from us was the police station, where two years ago I had to report my stolen passport. This time I asked Benno to carry it, so that there would be no accidents.

The next day we would have a long day driving all the way to Kalisz and Lodz. Benno and I walked to see some more of Gdańsk, and I took him to places we had not seen before. Walking down Langgasse through the Golden Gate, we turned left to the former Reitbahn. The Great Synagogue, built in the second part of the nineteenth century, once stood here. In 1939, after the Nazis tried to burn the building down (they did not succeed), Jewish war veterans guarded the building all night. The Jewish community of Gdańsk then decided to sell this and other Jewish properties in the city. Now there is an empty space; no sign informs the passersby that here once stood such an impressive Jewish house of prayer.

A substantial collection of Judaica objects as well as precious religious items were crated and sent to New York for safekeeping. The stipulation was this: Should there be no active Jewish community in Gdańsk in fifteen years (this meant by 1954), those objects were to remain in the Jewish Theological Seminary in New York City. In January 1939 those crates with precious objects belonging to the Jewish community in Gdańsk arrived in New York and were stored in the basement of the seminary. For many years nobody knew about them. They remained forgotten until 1966, when a fire broke out in the basement. Some of the crates were heavily damaged, and many Torah scrolls were destroyed by fire. When the salvaged crates were opened, someone remembered the shipment from Gdańsk. Items were repaired, restored, and cleaned. In 1980 the Jewish Museum in New York opened the "Danzig Exhibit"—the Judaica collection from the destroyed Jewish community of Danzig. For the first time people in the United States heard about Danzig and the Jewish community that had once existed there.

Next Benno saw the Polizeipräsidium, the main police station, which I passed on my way to school. We turned toward the former Dominikswall and passed the Hohes Tor (High Gate), where before the war Lloyds of London had its office. Before World War I German sentries guarded the city here. We walked by what once was 10 Dominikswall, and I had to think of the many times when my family and I walked this street. From here we turned to Holzmarkt (Rynek Drzewny) where the Szmants lived from 1934 to 1938. It had changed; new houses were everywhere. Most of the original buildings were destroyed by the Soviet artillery. We turned into the former Töpfergasse. Here once was the famous ice cream parlor Toscani; on the opposite side was the kosher butcher Drucker and next to it a store with pastry. A little farther on was a stationery store and a bookstore. I showed Benno the house on Töpfergasse (Garncarska), where the family Samet lived; they were friends of my parents. Their son Rudolph was my age, their daughter Halina a few years younger, and their youngest daughter was Benno's age. Not a trace is left of this family.

Walking down the street toward the railroad station, I told Benno of the two large movie houses that once stood here: on the left the UFA Palast, to the right UT Lichtspiele. Nothing is left of these buildings. New modern office buildings occupy these spaces. Benno looked again at the Gdańsk railroad station, then we turned back. Passing the St. Elizabeth church, Dominikswall (Waly Jagiellonskie), we stopped at the Stockturm (Tower of Torture), walked past the Kohlenmarkt with the theater through the Golden Gate to Langgasse. Here we found a place that sold ice cream with real whipping cream and sat down to relax. This would be our last evening in Gdańsk. It was getting dark. The post office was still open (they close at 9 p.m.), and we got some stamps and postcards and mailed them from here. By now it was night and time to return to our hotel. We still had to do our packing. Tomorrow would be a day of traveling. This last day in Gdańsk was filled with so many impressions, so many emotions, and so many memories.

Up at the usual 4 a.m., I described in my diary the happenings and impressions of the previous day. In a few hours we would be leaving the city of my youth. Benno and I wanted to utilize every minute here. I made the usual 6 a.m. wake-up call to Benno, and by 6:20 a.m. we were walking the streets of Gdańsk. We walked the streets of the old city for the last time. By now Benno was very familiar with every street, every building. Both of us admired the charm and beauty of this city, wondering if and when we would be back here. Maybe Benno would be able to visit here with his wife and children. Would he remember the stories and history he had heard from me? We returned to the hotel, paid the bill, and met Jozio for breakfast. All our bags were packed, and we were ready to leave. Our destination was Kalisz, a drive of more than 250 miles from here. We had the last view of the Gdańsk panorama and headed south.

It was a very warm day. We passed the cities of Grudziadz, Torun (where Copernicus was born), Inowroclaw, and Konin. The last time I was in Konin was in July 1933 with my paternal grandmother. This was the summer when we moved from Brotbänkengasse to Dominikswall, and my grandparents invited me to spend a month with them. My grandmother took me to the town where my father was born, Slupca. Here I met some of the members of my father's family, all very old people. Then we went to Konin, where my grandmother's cousin (Ciocia Andzia) lived. That was sixty years ago.

We stopped on the way in a forest to rest and to have some of the sandwiches we took along with us. I gathered pine cones and leaves from different trees. The leaves will be dried and will go into the album. When we continued our drive toward Kalisz, we came upon some of the most glorious wheat fields filled with ruby-red poppies. The field looked like a red carpet. The view was breathtaking, and we had to stop and take pictures. The drive lasted over five hours. Finally we arrived in Kalisz. One of Poland's oldest cities, it also has the oldest Jewish cemetery. Here in Kalisz lived my paternal and maternal grandparents before the war. In this city my dear mother was born. When we entered Kalisz and parked the car, I wanted to locate the house at 9 ulica Targowa, where my maternal grandparents lived. From the time I was six years old, we came here each spring for the Passover holidays. The first Seder was always spent with my grandparents Ryczke, the second one with grandparents Hammer. My last visit to this city was fifty-five years earlier, in 1938. We came with my mother a few days before the holidays because my uncle Heniek Hammer's son, who was born prematurely, was to have his circumcision before the holidays. His name was Teos (Theodore). Heniek had lived in Kalisz with his family in the same house as my maternal grandparents Shlomo and Sarah Hammer. As I walked the crowded streets of this city with Benno at my side, I told him some of the details about family members who lived here. Jozio stayed with the car. He was told that there are so many car thefts that he had better watch his car. The air was heavy with humidity and heat, and the streets were crowded with people. Names of streets have been changed, and I had to ask people who looked older if they knew the names of streets I was looking for. The car was parked on Plac Kilinskiego, and we walked down Zamkowa Street toward Targowa Street. Everything looked very familiar. Turning right, we found Targowa Street. Unfortunately, the house No. 9 was gone. It had been destroyed during the war. We walked back to Zamkowa Street, passing the side street where my uncle Zygmunt Krzewin had his printing shop. Zygmunt was the husband of my mother's youngest sister, Hela. They had one son, Gutek. Only Gutek survived the war (on Polish papers), he died in London in 1986.[5] Hela and Zygmunt were killed during the Holocaust.

Turning onto Zamkowa Street, we crossed the bridge over the Prosna River, and now the street changed to Staromiejska Street. I remembered that there was a second bridge, which we had to cross before coming to the street where once my paternal grandparents lived. Sure enough, we found the second bridge. The River Prosna was so dirty we could smell the polluted water. Now we were very close to Wiejska Street, where I wanted to see the house my grandparents Ryczke once lived in. I stopped a man and asked him if he lived in Kalisz before the war. He was insulted, asking me, "Do I look that old?" But he did know the name Wiejska Street. It is now ulica Pulackiego. Turning left on the former Wiejska Street, we found the house No. 5. My grandparents lived here on the second floor from 1920 until 1934. We walked into the yard, I showed Benno the balcony on the second floor. This was where the kitchen once was, and on this balcony my grandfather had built his sukkah, when the holidays of Sukkoth were celebrated. As a young child I sat on the balcony, and once I saw a rat in the yard running into a hole. This had been the first time I saw a rat, and later I told my friends in Danzig about "the rat in Kalisz." This old house brought back memories of my early childhood. In 1934 grandparents Ryczke moved into a modern apartment on ulica 6-go Sierpnia. I could not recall the house number, but I did remember what the house looked like. We walked back from Pulackiego (Wiejska) Street and came to the former ulica 6-go Sierpnia, now Zamkowa Street. I did recognize the house. Benno wanted to get some pastry or rolls, but it was noon and everything was already sold out. We returned to Plac Kilinskiego, where Jozio was guarding his car. It was so hot that we gave up the idea of walking to the park for which Kalisz was famous. Ever since my early childhood, the Passover holidays meant a visit to Kalisz. Even today, whenever I prepare for this festive holiday, I have to think of the many years that I spent with my grandparents Ryczke and Hammer in Kalisz. And so this sentimental return to another place where I spent part of my childhood stirred many emotions. It is true, Kalisz today is different than the one I used to know—the names of the streets have been changed and many houses have disappeared. But to me it still is a familiar place filled with happy child-hood memories. Exhausted from the heat, we left Kalisz.

Our next destination was the city of Lodz. It was only a sixty-mile drive from Kalisz to Lodz. Here we would spend the night, after finding the places I wanted to see. I told Benno that Lodz was Poland's second largest city, but it was not very attractive. The center of Poland's textile industry before the war, it was smelly from all the chemicals used in the manufacturing of tex-tiles. It had a large Jewish population, almost 30 percent of the residents were Jews. A great number of ethnic Germans lived here. They were the tex-tile experts in factories and also the best mechanics to repair the many machines. As we had no hotel reservations, Jozio stopped to find out about accommodations. He was directed to the Hotel Swiatowit on the corner of Kosciuszki Street and Zamenhofa Street. Driving through the main street, ulica Piotrkowska, we turned toward the hotel and checked in. After deposit-ing our bags in our rooms, we went out to see Lodz. The hotel registration had a map of the city, but I could not find the name of Zawadzka Street, where my paternal grandparents once lived. We were told that this street is now called ulica Prochnika. I knew where to find it, and we walked down

Piotrkowska Street until we reached Prochnika Street. Turning left, we crossed Gdańska and Zeromskiego Streets. It was very obvious that this had become a very bad neighborhood. The faces of people, the behavior of the youth, and the state of the street and houses was appalling. Jozio said that he would never venture here in the dark. It was still daytime, and we found the house at 49 Zawadzka Street. My grandparents Ryczke moved into this house from Kalisz in 1938 to be close to their only daughter, Rosa Przedecka, who lived just around the corner with her husband and two daughters. Here in this house I spent a few months in the summer of 1939, before returning to Gdańsk. The house had not changed. I remembered the two windows in the front on the ground floor, where my grandparents' bedroom was. The entrance to this apartment faced the backyard. As we took pictures, a man came toward us. He said that he was the administrator and wanted to know what we were looking for. Not a pleasant fellow, he told us that some time ago the daughter of the former owner came by. I assured him that we did not come here to claim the house, explaining that my grandparents rented their apartment here from 1938 till 1940, and that I was writing about that period. I assured him that we were not here to take anything away from him. What a character. I think that Jozio was ready for a fight with him.

Now we went on toward Aleja 1-go Maja Street, just around the corner where my aunt, uncle, and cousins Halina and Gina Przedecka resided. The house is still there, but it has aged. In 1938 it was almost a new house, one of the first high-rises. We found houses and streets, only the Jews were gone. As we walked on toward Zeromskiego Street, Jozio remembered that in 1950 he visited here with Hela, Max's sister. Michael (Leon Sroczynski), Max's brother, and Ewa with Elzunia lived here before emigrating to Israel. Hela brought Jozio here to say farewell to her brother.

Walking back toward ulica Piotrkowska we saw some very nicely renovated buildings, but all of the nice ones were government houses. The rest looked ugly, neglected, and dirty. The city has no funds to do anything about these buildings, and some streets resemble slums. I could see that Benno was very uneasy about walking here, and we decided to leave the side streets. As it was getting dark, and we had not eaten for a long time, we asked for a good restaurant. The information we got was not very promising, but we knew that the Grand Hotel was on Piotrkowska Street and that we could probably eat dinner there. On the corner of Traugutta Street and Piotrkowska Street was the hotel. We had no trouble getting a table there—the dining room was empty. This was once the most elegant hotel, and it still is very impressive. The food and service were very good. After walking the streets of this city we were glad to be in such luxurious surroundings. When we left the Grand Hotel it was close to 9 p.m. and pitch dark. This part of Piotrkowska Street is now a walking mall, so there was no traffic. Street names have been changed, and many streets are named after Polish Jews—Artur Rubenstein (pianist), Julian Tuwim (poet), Ludwig L. (Lazar) Zamenhof (inventor of Esperanto), etc. The Jews of Lodz are gone, but now some of the streets are named after them. We returned to the hotel, eager to leave this city early in the morning. Benno suggested that if we left early enough, we could stop in Piotrkow on the way to Warsaw. He wanted to see the inside of the old synagogue and also visit the Jewish cemetery. Jozio promised to study the map and see to it that we would stop in Piotrkow. What would we have done without Jozio and his car? All these visits to places like Gdańsk, Sopot, Kalisz, Lodz, Piotrkow, and Tomaszow would have been impossible to accomplish without the help of Jozio. I shall be grateful to him forever for all the assistance he gave us. Because of Jozio's help, Benno, Gene, and Caroline were able to see so much of our family's past.

In Piotrkow Jozio stopped in front of the old castle, the same spot where Czarek parked the previous Sunday (was it only last Sunday that we were here?) It seemed so long ago, we had been to so many places and seen so much. We walked toward the synagogue (now a library). The sign said that the library opened at 10 a.m., but we saw a lady entering the building. Jozio followed her and told her the purpose of our visit. She was very kind and invited us inside. In the entrance hall we saw the large plaque that the former Piotrkow Jews brought here in April, when the group came to Poland to commemorate fifty years of the Warsaw Ghetto Uprising. Ben Giladi, who organized the tour, was instrumental in having this plaque made. Sure enough, his name was on it. While we were here, Benno was able to see the inside of the synagogue and the paintings on the doors to the Ark.

I mentioned to the lady that in 1990 I met the editor of the local paper, Mr. Kobalczyk, who wrote some books about Piotrkow. I wondered if I could obtain the books. The director of the museum, which is located in the old castle, happened to be in his office. He told us that they had some books in the museum and he would ask someone to bring them here. Then he asked us if we would like to see the new exhibit: "500 Years of the Polish *Sejm.*" This was a very special treat, and we walked back with him. First we purchased a few books, then we entered the castle. I had been inside before, had seen some of the exhibits, but what we were shown now was of immense interest. The director was the most knowledgeable historian, and every piece of the exhibit was explained to us in detail. Then we walked into the rooms once occupied by kings, and here we saw the magnificent handcrafted oak furniture made in Gdańsk. Some were of the same style Benno and I saw in the Gdańsk city hall. We were also shown the exhibit I saw in 1990 about the history of Piotrkow during the Nazi occupation. Jozio spotted one Nazi announcement prohibiting Poles from helping and hiding Jews under the penalty of death. This was the first time Jozio saw the original announcement. This being the "Week of the Child," the museum had an exhibit of paintings, sculptures, and art all made by children ages eight to fourteen. Poland is very supportive of its children and promotes their developing talents. We thanked the director. It was time for us to leave.

I felt that Jozio, who had never been to this city, should walk with us to Starowarszawska Street. We wanted him to see house No. 7, where Hela, his adopted mother, was born. Today the streets of the former ghetto were crowded with people, and the stores, too, were very busy. Benno wanted me to find some fresh pastry, and we even went to the bakery, but by this time everything was sold out. In one of the stores on Jerozolimska Street we found a few hard rolls and bars of Wedel chocolate. The last stop we wanted to make was at the Jewish cemetery. I wanted Benno to see the grave with the names of Leon Kimmelman (after whom he was named) and his wife, Gucia.

Directions to the cemetery were given to us at the library, but somehow we got lost and had to ask again. We stopped near the gate and saw the small house where the caretaker lives. She told us to come in and opened the side door for us. Here in this old cemetery are buried Max's parents, Yitzhak and Malka Kimmelman, and Max's sisters Regina and Eva (Abramek's mother). When I was here in 1990, I looked in vain for the graves. Everything was overgrown with moss and weeds, and the grass was so high that I could hardly walk to the back of this two-hundred-year old cemetery. Jozio stayed behind with the caretaker, while Benno and I went to see the grave I told him about. We had no difficulties finding it, and I was amazed how some of the paths had been cleared of the overgrowth. It was so peaceful here. We wandered from one row of graves to another, looking for the names we wanted to see. Not finding them, we returned to see the caretaker. She mentioned to us that the name Kimmelman was familiar, and she brought out a small notebook. Here she had listed names of people and rows where they were buried. From her mother, who worked for Jewish families before the war, she learned to read the Hebrew alphabet and was able to read the names on the old tombstones. Suddenly she pointed in her notebook to the name Malka Kimmelman. This was Max's mother. The caretaker took us to the grave. I cannot describe my feelings: here we stood at the grave of Max's mother, Benno's grandmother, after whom his daughter Melanie is named. Providence must have brought us back today, so that Benno and I could be at this grave. Max said many times that he only regretted that he could not be at his mother's grave after the war. So here we were fulfilling his wish. The headstone was very tilted and will probably fall over in the near future. The caretaker told us that her son is restoring old stones and would gladly restore this tombstone. The price would be $250. She wanted the money in advance, but I had only traveler's checks. Benno wanted to think it over; somehow he did not trust the lady. I knew that this is what Max would want me to do, and I told her that I would send her the money soon. She promised to mail me a photo of the restored tombstone. Before leaving the cemetery I gathered some earth to place on Max's grave at home. It was very hard to get over the excitement and deep feelings of this encounter. I never thought that we would discover the grave of Malka Kimmelman. We left this place overcome with emotions. Back in Warsaw we shared our experiences with Krysia. I think that finding the grave in Piotrkow will remain one of the high points of this journey.

It was Friday night, and I asked Krysia if I could light candles in honor of Shabbat. She set the table with a sparkling white tablecloth, and two candles adorned the table as we sat down to supper. I had such a warm feeling toward Jozio, Krysia, and Czarek as we sat at the table talking about the events of the day. After the meal we listened to the tape of a concert given by Pavarotti and Domingo and turned in to sleep. The next day would be our last full day in Poland. It would also be one of the most difficult days of our trip—the day when we would make the pilgrimage to Treblinka.

We left early in the morning. On the way we saw fields that looked so peaceful, with haystacks and flowers everywhere. From the car we could see the railroad tracks, the very same tracks that took the cattle cars with innocent Jewish men, women, and children to their deaths in Treblinka. From Tomaszow the trip to Treblinka lasted much longer than from Warsaw. Many times I wished to know what my family members had felt during this last journey. Every time I think about their last journey, in my mind I am with them in the cattle cars and I suffer terrible mental anguish and physical pain. As we were approaching Treblinka, we passed the railroad station, came to Poniatowo, and turned toward the camp.

An eerie feeling overcame us. Among the young pine trees I could see in my mind columns of Jews being chased from the train, walking the same road we were walking now. We stopped at the kiosk that had the map of the memorial and of Treblinka. We needed to know the location of the stones for the victims from Piotrkow and Tomaszow. Last time the Piotrkow stone was close to the entrance; this time we could not locate it on the map. But we did find the location of the Tomaszow stone. As we entered the camp, the sight of the large monument surrounded by 1,300 broken stones was overwhelming. Benno, Jozio, and I walked among this sea of broken stones in complete silence. There was a deadly quiet over Treblinka. We were surrounded by the memories of the more than eight hundred thousand Jewish victims of Nazi brutality. This silence was screaming to us: DO NOT FORGET WHAT HAPPENED HERE. I stood at the stone for the Warsaw victims, and at the Tomaszow stone, praying silently for my dear ones. Treblinka is our family's resting place, ashes of my dear ones were scattered and mixed in the ground we were walking on. On August 2, 1943, a revolt broke out in this death camp.[6] Only about one hundred Jews escaped; the rest were killed, and the camp was destroyed. I pointed out to Benno the pit with simulated black coal. Here the bodies were stacked between rods and burned when the crematoria could not burn the victims fast enough. After the revolt, the Nazis erased all traces of their crimes, and all the ashes of the victims were plowed under. Most of the Jews who were killed here were from Warsaw and other Polish towns. But Jews from Austria, Belgium, Czechoslovakia, France, Greece, Germany, the Soviet Union, and Yugoslavia also met their deaths here. May the memories of these victims be forever recalled, and may their souls be blessed. We left this place of sorrow with heavy hearts and drove home. Very little was said on the way home, each of us had to deal with Treblinka and what it represents for our family.

When we were planning this trip, I asked Jozio in my letter if it would be possible to see a performance at the Yiddish Theater. Krysia was able to obtain tickets for all four of us. The play was a reading of poems written by Julian Tuwim and Yitzchak Kacenelson. Tuwim was an assimilated Jew— never very interested in the fate of Polish Jewry. He left before the war, went to Brazil, and returned to Lodz in 1946. The Holocaust changed Tuwim. He started to write about Jews and became active in Jewish literary circles. One of his most famous documents about Polish Jews was called *My Zydzi Polscy* (We, the Polish Jews). It was written in Polish in 1944 and was translated into Hebrew the same year. Tuwim died in Poland in 1953.

Now in the theater these poems were recited in Polish, the writing by Kacenelson in Yiddish. Yitzchak Kacenelson was born in what now is Lithuania, near Nowogrodek. He came from a very religious and observant Jewish family, his father, too, was a writer of Hebrew and Yiddish books. Kacenelson moved with his family to Lodz, where his father opened a Hebrew high school and Yitzchak became a teacher. He not only wrote poetry but also plays and songs and translated them into Yiddish. When the German army entered Lodz, Yitzchak left first for Kraków, then for Warsaw. Here he lived with his wife and three sons. In the ghetto Kacenelson risked his life by teaching in secret "schools," giving readings of his poetry, and writing for secret newsletters. When the ghetto was liquidated in July 1942, Yitzchak buried most of his writings at 34 ulica Dzielna (where they were found after the war). In August 1942 his wife and two younger sons (eleven-year-old Josele and fourteen-year-old Ben-Tzion) were taken to Treblinka. Yitzchak became active in the planning of the uprising of the ghetto but left with his oldest son, Tzvi, for the "Aryan side," helped by the Jewish Underground. The Nazis devised tricks to get to Jews who were hiding on the Polish side and announced that there would be an exchange between Jews and German prisoners of war. Jews believed it, and Yitzchak and his son Tzvi were among those who reported for this exchange. They were sent to Vittel, a concentration camp in France. Here they spent ten months, and Yitzchak wrote more poetry. Desperate and aware of what was awaiting him, he buried some of his writing in three bottles under the stump of a pine tree. These poems were found after the war. On April 17, 1944, the Gestapo surrounded the camp and deported 173 prisoners; among them were Yitzchak and Tzvi Kacenelson. They were shipped first to the camp of Drancy, then to Auschwitz on April 27. The transport arrived there on May 1, 1944, and on the same day all of the people in this transport perished in the gas chambers.

How can I describe the performance in the Yiddish Theater? Most of the actors were Poles who had to learn Yiddish in order to perform here. Very few of the attending people were Jewish, as the public was mostly Polish. What irony: there are barely any Jews left in Poland, yet the state supports this theater. The opening started with the Polish reading by Tuwim. The scene was a cemetery, dark and awesome. Tuwim's poem deals with the fate of the Polish Jews and was very well done. The next scene, too, represented the cemetery, with actors reciting very moving poems about the Jews who perished; the actors represented their ghosts. The words were so touching, so tragic—tears were running down my cheeks. The tragedy of the Jewish people was portrayed here—from deepest agony and despair to new hope when the Jews took up arms against the Nazis. The singing of the partisan songs brought back so many memories. We sang these songs in secrecy in the camps. This evening at the Yiddish theater followed our day in Treblinka and was the emotional culmination of this memorable day. My heart was breaking, but I would have never missed this experience. It will stay with me forever.

Krysia was not feeling well. I suspect that this was too much of an emotional evening for her. We drove home in a hurry, so that she could take her medicine. Krysia fell asleep right away, while Jozio, Benno, and I sat in the living room and talked. This was our last evening here. The next day, early in the morning, we would pack our belongings and leave. I could not fall asleep, and I started to write down the happenings of the day. Benno too was writing a diary, so that at some later time we would be able to compare our notes, our observations, and our feelings.

Early the next morning I started to pack my bags. In my foresight I had taken an extra bag with me from home. This came in handy, because all the glass we had purchased as gifts had to be carried as hand luggage. Everything fit perfectly. Benno, too, had room for all the gifts he was taking home. Jozio placed the dried leaves and flowers that I gathered between some plastic sheets so that they would not be damaged. Our plane was leaving at 12:40 p.m. There was plenty of time, so we did not have to rush. Krysia came with us to the airport, and we spent the last few minutes with Jozio and Krysia. No words can express our gratitude. They have opened their home and hearts to us. Their warm hospitality and generosity cannot be described. I hope that they feel our friendship, admiration, and gratitude toward them and know how much they mean to us. Jozio learned about Hela's past by traveling with us to Piotrkow. He understands now so much better the history and tragedy of the Jewish people by having been to Stutthof and Treblinka. It was not easy for him, but as he said—he will take Krysia and Czarek to some of those places and explain things to them.

In three years I was with Jozio and Krysia three times, and they became very dear to me. I know that Gene and Benno will stay in touch with them and will see the Pruc family again. Jozio promised to go to Piotrkow and see if the tomb of Malka Kimmelman has been refinished and repaired. I left the money for this job with him. Knowing Jozio, he will not pay a penny until the job is done well. I trust Jozio completely. We shall continue to write to each other. We parted at the gate of the airport and checked our bags. In an hour we would board the LOT plane and begin our journey back.

Benno and I talked most of the time. We talked more on the flight home than during the seven days we spent together. What Benno saw, what he learned, what he heard during these seven days will stay with him for the rest of his life. In time he will share all of it with Joy and his children. And who knows, someday he may want to return with his family and travel to some of the places we saw. From generation to generation (*le dor va dor*), as it is written in the Torah—it is our obligation to transmit to the next generation our knowledge, our experiences, our feelings, our tradition. Thank you, Benno and Gene, from the bottom of my heart for enabling me to make these journeys with you. I know that Max's spirit was with us all through these odysseys.

In May 1999 I traveled for the fourth time to Poland. Why another trip in 1999? This time I had two very different reasons. While visiting Sopot and Gdańsk with my children, I found no evidence of Jewish life, no sign that Jewish houses of prayer ever existed. We visited the place where once the synagogue in Sopot stood, now replaced by an apartment building. Again, in Gdańsk, where one of the oldest synagogues in the city once flourished, a row of apartment buildings stood. No sign or plaque indicated that a synagogue or Jewish life existed and thrived in these cities in pre–World War I and World War II Danzig and vicinity. This fact was to haunt me. I kept wondering what and how something could be done to memorialize the Jewish houses of prayer in Gdańsk and Sopot.

In October 1995 I visited my second cousin Harry Szmant in Miami. His daughter, Alina, was interested in the family history. In 1997 Alina, at the time professor of marine biology at the University of Miami (presently she has the same position at the University of North Carolina in Wilmington), contacted me to ask whether I would be willing to travel to Gdańsk with her. My cousin Harry Szmant told her very little about his past, and now he was ill and unable to travel. The family had moved to Gdańsk when Harry was only three years old. He and his sister, Celina, were born in Kalisz, as was my mother. A traditional Jewish family, his parents attended the Mattenbuden Orthodox Synagogue in Gdańsk, and the children graduated from the Polish *Gimnazjum.*

During World War II, Celina and her parents lived in the Lodz ghetto while her husband, as a Polish soldier, fought the Germans. Having survived the fighting, he went to the Soviet Union to escape Nazi persecution as a Jew.

But Harry's parents and sister succumbed to the Nazis. His pain was great. He became an atheist, refusing to believe in a God "who could allow my family to perish." This was undoubtedly the reason he never talked to his children about his past nor visited Gdańsk. But Alina wanted so much to see the places where her father and aunt and grandparents had lived. With no hesitation, I promised to go with her. We agreed to plan for 1999.

Meanwhile, my thoughts about doing something to memorialize the destroyed Gdańsk synagogues plagued me. I began writing to the municipalities in Gdańsk and Sopot, asking for permission to have plaques attached to the houses that now occupy the places where the synagogues once stood. First and foremost, I hoped to memorialize the Roonstrasse Synagogue in Sopot, founded in 1914 and destroyed by the Nazis in November 1938. Secondly, I wanted to memorialize the old Mattenbuden Synagogue in Gdańsk, where my family and I worshiped from 1930 to 1938. Not an impressive building but one of the oldest synagogues in Gdańsk, it was completed in 1834 and also destroyed by the Nazis in 1938. I can still visualize my father praying there and recall my mother praying in the gallery, the two separated in worship by gender in the Orthodox tradition.

After ten months of writing and making endless telephone calls, only the Sopot municipality, with the help of my Polish writer friend, Hanna Domanska, agreed to have a tablet with a proper inscription attached to the house where once the Roonstrasse Synagogue stood. I would pay an artist to design and construct the plaque.

Because Alina could only leave for Poland in late spring, we planned the trip for the end of May 1999. In the meantime, I heard that Pope Paul II was to visit Poland, with Gdańsk his first stop. Knowing how hectic it would be during the Pope's visit, we changed our travel plans to May 21–29. I notified the authorities in Sopot about the date of my arrival to be sure that the plaque would be ready in time. Reassured, Alina and I finalized our plans, making sure that all the places she wanted to see were on our agenda. Then a third person asked to join us.

Michael Bloch, who lives in London, is the son of my third cousin Richard. Richard and I were born in the same house in Sopot. We attended the same *Gimnazjum* and belonged to the same Zionist Youth Movement,

Habonim. Richard's family left Gdynia for England in 1939, then moved to Northern Ireland to open an embroidery factory; although we were only distant relatives, we were friends and kept in touch after the war. Suddenly, I had a letter from Richard's son, Michael, whom I had never met. He now realized that he had a relative in Tennessee. His father had never mentioned me. As Michael put it, "I was stone-walled. My questions were never answered." Like Alina, he wanted to learn more about his father's younger years and to see the places where he had grown up. Michael, who is a writer, had sent me some of his books, all biographies. I promised to stop in London to meet him on my next trip to Israel, which I had done. While in London I told Michael about my plans to visit Gdańsk with Alina the following spring. He asked if he could join us. Knowing how eager he was to see the places where his father grew up, I welcomed him to come with us. Alina would travel from Miami via Brussels where I would meet her to travel on to Warsaw, and from there we would take the train to Gdańsk. Michael would meet us two days later at our hotel in Gdańsk.

I would revisit the city of my youth with two of my cousins, two people who are not related to each other. Alina is my third cousin on my mother's side: her grandmother was the sister of my grandfather, and her grandfather was the brother of my grandmother. And Michael is related to me on my father's side: his great-grandmother and my grandfather were first cousins. One of the reasons for this journey was to help them reconstruct the early years of their fathers' lives in Gdańsk. And the second reason—to memorialize the Sopot Synagogue. With this twofold purpose in mind, I was eager to embark on this important pilgrimage.

Alina Szmant and I met for the first time in Miami in October 1995 when I visited Harry. I stayed in her house and met her husband and their daughter. Although Alina and I spoke frequently by telephone, we really did not know one another well. Now we would travel and be together for eight days and nights.

I had to fly to Boston to catch the Sabena flight to Brussels. Alina and I met in the terminal. Her plane from Atlanta was on time, and now we were together. I told her about the plans for Sunday and for Monday. She did not know about the dedication of the memorial plaque. I had never mentioned it because until the last moment I was not sure that it would be ready by the time we planned to be in Sopot. I assured Alina that we would have ample time for the people and things she wanted to visit and see.

At the Warsaw Airport we were once again met by my adopted nephew, Jozio Pruc, who had been my host and guide during the 1991 and 1993 trips. Jozio would drive us from the airport to the railroad station.

We exchanged dollars for Polish zloty and enjoyed a beautiful sunny afternoon drive with Jozio through the streets of Warsaw. I had to translate every word for Alina as Jozio pointed out famous landmarks. After a snack at the railroad station, we boarded the train that would take us to Gdańsk. Alina had purchased reserved first-class seats via the Internet. Since the train was completely full, without those seats in the first-class compartment we would not have been able to board the train.

Looking through the train window, we saw fields filled with golden flowers. Alina wanted to know what those flowers were. They were rape (*Raps*), whose seeds produce oil. The Polish scenery was breathtaking. Endless fields covered with golden rape. It made me recall my father's seed business before the war, where I became familiar with the rape seeds. Soon we saw the castle and fortification of the Teutonic stronghold, Malbork (Marienburg). Getting close to Tczew, there was the Vistula River, and soon the rooftops and church gables of Gdańsk were in full view.

When the train stopped in Gdańsk, I caught sight of my old friend, Leon Lendzion, the husband of my school friend, Hela, and a classmate of Alina's father. She had heard so much about him from her father and was excited to finally meet him. Leon greeted each of us with a rose and accompanied us to a taxi that drove us to the Hevelius Hotel, a stone's throw from the station. Our room was on the thirteenth floor, and from our window we had a most glorious view of the city of Gdańsk.

No sooner had we returned to our room after a fine dinner in the hotel dining room than Hanna Domanska telephoned. She wanted me to know that the unveiling of the synagogue memorial plaque would take place on Monday morning, May 24, and that we should be ready by 10 a.m. The Sopot municipality would send a minibus to take us to Sopot city hall, where there would be a small reception and interviews with the press and

Gdańsk (Danzig), May 1999.

local television. It sounded all so formal. I never expected anything like this. But I now knew that my dream would come true. The plaque would be placed where the synagogue once stood to demonstrate that a Jewish community once existed and flourished there.

Refreshed after a night's sleep, we looked out of the window: the sun was shining, and the rooftops were glistening in the sunshine. What a spectacular view! We went downstairs for a huge breakfast consisting of different cheeses, eggs, herring, vegetables, dry and fresh fruits, and all kinds of delicious Polish breads and pastry. Everything tasted too good, and we ate too much. At 10 a.m. I called Dr. Apoloniusz Goebel in Orlowo. His daughter, Marta Pietrasz, and her husband, Lech, reside in Oak Ridge and we have become good friends. When Dr. Goebel and his wife, Basia, visited their children in Oak Ridge, I invited them to lunch in my home. Knowing of my plans to visit Gdańsk, the Goebels wanted me to reserve one day to spend with them. Sunday, May 23, was the day we would spend with the Goebels. Dr. Goebel was waiting for us in the hotel lobby at 11 a.m. His plan was to drive us to Gdynia and then to Orlowo, to their home for lunch. On the way,

Dr. Goebel picked up his ninety-year-old mother-in-law, who rode with us. While we were riding with Dr. Goebel, I pointed out to Alina places that her father knew so well while living in Gdańsk: the suburbs of Wrzeszcz, Oliwa, and the city of Sopot. The weather was perfect and the majestic chestnut trees were in full bloom. The chestnut blossoms varied in color: white, pink, and red. The road from Gdańsk to Oliwa was lined with these tall impressive trees all in bloom.

We arrived at the Polish port in Gdynia. Once a fishing village, today it is a major industrial city, the largest of the Tri-Cities: Gdańsk, Sopot, Gdynia. Then we continued on to Orlowo. Orlowo has become a bedroom community of Gdynia, with impressive villas and apartment buildings. Dr. Goebel told us that apartments here are now as expensive as in New York. Orlowo became a community for wealthy people. The pier at the seashore has been rebuilt (in 1991 and 1993 we saw how it had deteriorated). Now everything looked very neat. We arrived at the Goebel's home. As soon as we entered, Basia Goebel greeted me with tears in her eyes; she had fallen in the bathroom. (Basia had hip and leg surgery and walks with crutches.) Her right arm was in a sling; she broke it in the fall. Her elderly mother prepared lunch for us; Basia was in great pain and barely touched the food. She had to go to the hospital in Gdańsk, and on the way Dr. Goebel dropped Alina and me off at the Lendzions' in Oliwa.

Hela and Leon Lendzion greeted us with great warmth. Another old school friend of mine was waiting to see me. Stefa Bojarska, Hela Lendzion, and I were in the same class in the Polish *Gimnazjum* before the war. Stefa is a retired lawyer, and like me she is a widow. We correspond and keep in touch with each other. After Stefa left, Alina had a chance to get to know the Lendzions. Hela liked Alina right away. Alina was overwhelmed by the hospitality, which in Poland was the normal hospitality among friends.

Leon had some old school pictures of Harry as a young boy, which he handed to Alina. They were a real treasure because she had no picture of her father when he was young. The only photos were the few that Harry brought with him from Gdańsk when he came to this country.

Alina knew that Harry came from Danzig but was born in Poland, and, therefore, to her he was Polish. "Until I was eighteen I did not know my father was Jewish," she said. "Apparently he wanted to be considered Polish." Leon and I tried to explain that even if some Jews thought of themselves as Poles, they were almost always considered Jews. In Poland before World War II, Jews were about 10 percent of the population; they were an ethnic minority and always called Jews.

The conversation turned to Leon's and Harry's school years. While we sat and talked, Alina heard from Leon for the first time how much anti-Semitism we experienced in the Polish *Gimnazjum* and how her father had been subjected to it in class. I do not think that Alina realized how hard it was to be Jewish even in a Polish school. There Harry Szmant was a Polish Jew, but a Jew nonetheless.

Leon and Hela's son came over for supper, and we had a true Polish meal. Hela's delicious pastry and tea followed, and we toasted our getting together with champagne. It was late, time for us to return to Gdańsk. The next day we would meet the Lendzions in Sopot at the unveiling of the tablet. Leon accompanied us by train all the way to Gdańsk and made sure that we were safe in our hotel. Then he returned home.

The long-anticipated day finally arrived. I woke up early, knowing that Michael Bloch would call our room as soon as he got to the hotel. Sure enough, at 8 a.m. sharp he rang our room. I told Michael to wait in the lobby and I would join him shortly. We had only met once, in London, the previous November. But I had a feeling of closeness, not only because we were related but because we had become friends. Michael looked well. He was dismayed that the room I reserved for him was not ready. The hotel was filled with German tourists. Each morning buses from Germany brought people to Gdańsk; each morning buses left with their guests. Michael would have to wait until a room had been cleaned and made ready for him. In the meantime, Alina came downstairs to join us and to meet Michael. I hoped that my two unrelated cousins would like each other. Luckily they did.

Michael was told about the plans for the day. He had no idea that there would be a dedication of a plaque in Sopot. I was not sure of the exact plans that had been made by the Sopot municipality. All I knew was that the three of us would be picked up at 10 a.m., driven to Sopot, and that there would be some interviews. We needed some free time in Sopot so that I could show Michael the house where his father and uncle were born. I also wanted to show Alina the beautiful resort of Sopot at the Baltic Sea.

The driver from the Sopot municipality showed up at the appointed time. Not very friendly, he probably wondered why he had to pick up "those foreigners" and deliver them to city hall in Sopot. During the twenty-five-minute ride I pointed out to Michael some of the most memorable places Michael's father knew so well. When we arrived at city hall, an elderly lady approached me and asked if I was Mira Kimmelman. It was Hanna Domanska. How did I get to know her? Upon my return from the Passover holidays with my children in New York (April 1998), I found a letter from the United States Holocaust Museum in Washington, D.C. They informed me that someone was looking for former Jewish residents of Gdańsk. The museum is not permitted to give out addresses, so they sent the letter of inquiry to me. The letter was from Hanna Domanska in Sopot, the author of a few books about the Jews in Gdańsk. She asked to be contacted by those who grew up in prewar Gdańsk. She included her address and telephone number in her letter. Without even thinking twice, I dialed her number. Hanna Domanska told me that she had written more than fifty letters to former Jews from Gdańsk—to Israel, England, and the U.S.A. Only I responded. And so we have been in close contact for over one year. It was Hanna Domanska who helped me get in touch with the Sopot municipality. The vice president of the city was her personal friend, and I petitioned him to have a plaque made. Hanna and I spoke often by telephone. She needed information about Jews who resided in Gdańsk and vicinity. She asked me if I knew other former Danzigers who could answer some of her questions. Obviously, she needed help since she did not know prewar Gdańsk or Jews who lived there. Hanna is not Jewish and was born in Poznan. Without the permission of some of my Gdańsk friends I was not free to give her names or addresses. I had a friend in New York who was the daughter of Paul Anker, a business friend of my father. Both were in the seed business. Brigitte Anker Kaufmann and I found each other when she attended a book fair in Beverly Hills and found my book. This was how the two of us became reacquainted, how we became close friends. I called Brigitte and told her about Hanna Domanska. Could I give her name and address to Hanna? She agreed right away. There was one problem, however: Hanna speaks and understands only Polish. I had to translate all the letters from Brigitte Anker Kaufmann into Polish and Hanna's letter to Brigitte into English. I was glad that now

Hanna had another source of information. Some of my friends did not wish to correspond with Hanna. I mailed a copy of my book to Sopot so that Hanna could ask someone to translate the chapter about Gdańsk into Polish. She in turn sent me two of her books. In one of the books I found the picture of the Roonstrasse Synagogue. This was a treasure—I had seen this house of prayer for the last time in July 1938. It was destroyed by fire in November 1938. Now Hanna and I met in person for the first time. She introduced me to an elderly man, her husband, Leon Lifsches. He was much older than Hanna and very kind to her. Hanna had knee trouble and walking was difficult. She used a cane and walked slowly. I introduced Alina and Michael to Hanna, who knew from my letters that my two cousins with ties to Gdańsk would accompany me. She already had the background on the Szmant and Bloch families; I had supplied her with all details.

At the city hall, we were ushered first to the office of the vice president of the city council and from there to a meeting hall. Tables were set up in a square, where members of the press and radio as well as some important citizens of the city of Sopot were seated. My friend Leon Lendzion sat between Alina and Michael so that he could serve as their interpreter/translator from Polish to English. Then the president and vice president entered—both very polite gentlemen.

After a short while the president excused himself; he had to attend another meeting. Wojciech Fulek, the vice president, presided over the ceremony. He was a most pleasant cultured young man who had helped me greatly to realize my dream. I was so pleased to meet him and expressed my thanks for all the help he had extended to me. There were many speeches, each one ending with a presentation of a bouquet of flowers to me. There were bouquets of roses, orchids, and more roses. Then one man stood up and introduced himself as Bruno Wandtke, an architect. I noticed him because of his deformed nose. Mr. Wandtke asked for permission to read a letter he had written to me.

The letter was very moving. Bruno Wandtke wrote about his parents, who had resided at Roonstrasse next to the synagogue since 1920. His father worked for the Polish railroad; his mother cleaned and took care of the synagogue. In 1938 when the synagogue was set on fire for the first time, his father noticed the flames and called the fire department. The fire was extinguished. When the Nazis set fire to the synagogue for the second time, Mr. Wandtke's father tried in vain to call the fire department. This time he was severely beaten for interfering with the anti-Semitic policy of the Nazis. As a gift, Bruno Wandtke handed me a framed picture of the now nonexistent Roonstrasse Synagogue. What a precious gift. I had tears in my eyes and thanked him for his thoughtfulness.

Then some members of the press asked questions. Finally I was asked to say a few words. In Polish, a language I do not use often, I expressed my deep gratitude and appreciation to the City of Sopot, especially to Mr. Fulek, for enabling me to place a tablet on the building where the Sopot synagogue once stood. Then I explained why it was necessary to remember that there once was a Jewish religious, cultural, and economical life in prewar Gdańsk and prewar Sopot. More than four thousand Jews had resided in Sopot. Today there is no Jewish community there. I told them of my visits to Gdańsk and Sopot in 1991 and 1993 with my sons and how I had looked in vain for a trace of Jewish life. That is when the idea of donating a plaque occurred to me. I told them how much I wanted to see a tablet on the place of the destroyed Sopot synagogue as well as the Mattenbuden Synagogue in Gdańsk. Only the first materialized, thanks to the friendly administration of the Sopot municipality, especially the support of Mr. Fulek.

We left city hall and proceeded to the house on ulica Dabrowskiego, the former Roonstrasse where the unveiling of the attached plaque would take place. We were driven with Mr. Fulek in the van. Some of the members of the press had their cars, others walked. The street is only a ten-minute walk from city hall (Gene, Caroline, and I walked here in 1991). When we arrived, there were more than twenty people assembled around the building.

The flag of Sopot (blue and yellow with a seagull) covered the tablet. My heart was beating fast: what would the plaque look like? The moment of unveiling came; I was asked to pull the string holding the flag. Nothing happened. The string was caught at the edge of the tablet. Someone had to climb up to remove the flag.

No words can express my emotions—to finally see this beautifully executed tablet, much larger than I originally thought. It had the image of the

Roonstrasse Synagogue at the top, a Polish inscription, and then an English one: "Here stood the Jewish House of Prayer, the Roonstrasse Synagogue, dedicated in 1914, destroyed by fire by the Nazis in November 1938." Without my prior knowledge, they had put my name at the bottom: "Donated by Mira Ryczke Kimmelman." I never wanted my name on it, but they explained that this was the proper way to acknowledge the donor. For a few minutes I stood speechless. I was thinking of my family, of my dear parents, of my brother.

Dedication of plaque in Sopot, May 1999. *Left to right:* Leon Lifsches, Barbara Rybczynska, Mira, and Hanna Domanska.

Tears welled up in my eyes, but I did not want to cry. This was a somber yet happy moment. Polish television was there to ask questions, and friends came with flowers. I finally met the artist: Barbara Rybczynska, a young and pretty woman and already quite an established artist. Now I had to pay her for the beautifully executed tablet. We stepped aside so that I could pull out the cash I had been carrying on me since I left home. Truly I was so grateful to this young lady for the excellent job she had done. I never imagined such an impressive plaque.

Mr. Fulek wanted to show us around Sopot. Again we boarded the van and drove first to the race track. I remembered it well. My mother used to attend horse races in Sopot quite often. Now this place was being prepared for the pope's imminent visit. The city of Sopot was getting ready for over six hundred thousand people who would come to attend High Mass conducted by the pope. An altar had been erected with many crosses and statues of saints. Barbara Rybczynska told me that her husband is also an artist, that all the statues were made by him. How interesting: the wife made a tablet for the memorialization of the Jewish house of prayer while her husband made statues of Catholic saints. How very ecumenical.

Next we drove to the seashore of Jelitkowo—formerly Glettkau. This was once a famous fisherman's village; the old original houses dating back to 1870 are still in use and in good shape. In the book *The Tin Drum*, Günter Grass (from Gdańsk) mentioned Glettkau when he described the episode with the eels. The sea was as blue as the sky and the sand very clean and white. Jelitkowo is now a fashionable sea resort near Sopot.

We returned to Sopot where Hanna Domanska wanted us to see the only remaining Jewish cemetery. Indeed it was clean and neat. I had never been here as a child because then Jewish children were not supposed to enter a cemetery if their parents were still alive. This was a tradition, maybe even some superstition. Some old tomb stones still have the inscription in Hebrew, German, and some in Polish. They are old and almost illegible. A quiet and tranquil place, I was amazed that the Nazis had not destroyed it. Thanks to volunteers like Hanna and Leon, the cemetery represents the only place to remind people that Jews once lived and died here. Hanna and Leon met here while cleaning the cemetery. After Leon's wife passed away, they married.

On the way from the cemetery we stopped at the street where I was born. Formerly 14 Promenadenstrasse (now ulica Majkowskiego), here not only I and my brother, Benno, but also Richard, Michael's father, and George Bloch, Michael's uncle, were born. Michael saw for the first time the house where his grandparents resided and where his father and uncle were born.

Mira and Michael Bloch in Glettkau at the Baltic Sea in May 1999.

Hanna was getting tired. She and her husband returned by van to city hall, and at 2 p.m. we were to join them at a restaurant. With Mr. Fulek leading, Alina, Michael, and I took a walking tour of Sopot. I was very thankful that he gave us so much of his time. Afterward, we met Hanna and Leon at city hall and had a nice meal with them. We then walked to their home and spent the afternoon talking. I felt guilty: poor Alina and Michael sat there while I tried to translate most of our conversation. By 5 p.m. we were ready to return to Gdańsk and parted from Hanna and Leon.

Our plans for the next few days were not certain, but one thing was sure: we would not have enough time to return to Sopot. Hanna and I would not have a chance to see each other again. We would continue to write to each other. I hope that her new book will meet with success. Books on Jewish life are subsidized by the Ministry of Culture, and Hanna Domanska is well known for her work. I wish her good health so that she can continue her writing.

After we arrived at the hotel, all three of us decided to rest for a few hours and meet again in the lobby to have a light supper. Then I would take them on a short tour of Gdańsk. Since it did not get dark until after 9 p.m., we had time to see some of the important Gdańsk landmarks. The true exploration of Gdańsk would begin the following day.

The next day had been designated to show my two cousins places or buildings where their families once lived. I also wanted them to see the city of Gdańsk in its glory. The weather was perfect, good for a lot of walking. From the hotel we walked toward the train station and then to the old city. The first building we passed was the house where Alina's aunt, Celina Szmant, once worked. This building is located next to St. Elizabeth Church, which is in fairly good condition. We did see a few traces of damage caused by Soviet artillery in March 1945. Because of her knowledge of languages, Celina Szmant worked at a responsible job with the Spanish consulate in Gdańsk. The building I showed Alina was where the consulate was once located. Celina and my mother were very close. They were first cousins, genetically almost siblings. They met quite often in coffee houses or visited each other's homes.

Our next stop was at Waly Jagiellonskie, formerly Dominikswall. This street had been completely demolished by Soviet artillery in March 1945.

Only the left side of the street (coming from the station) has been rebuilt. A row of many look-alike apartment houses now occupy this side of the street. How different they are from the impressive patrician houses that stood there before the war. There in house No. 10 my family lived until war broke out.

Across the street, houses have not been rebuilt. Only trees line that side of the street. At number 4 the Bloch family lived until 1938. There was no house to show, no building for Michael to see—only an empty space. At least he had an idea where his father lived and grew up. Many times Richard (Michael's father) and I had walked to the Polish *Gimnazjum* together—all he had to do was cross the street. Once upon a time Dominikswall was an attractive tree-lined street. But that was in the past.

We proceeded to walk toward the former Reitbahn, where once the Great Synagogue stood. Built in 1868, it became the largest liberal synagogue in Gdańsk and vicinity. It was not as reformed as temples in the United States but much more progressive than Orthodox synagogues. Many concerts, lectures, and other cultural events took place in the Reitbahn Synagogue. In May 1939, exactly sixty years earlier, the Great Synagogue was dismantled; it was torn down brick by brick. Now only an empty lot remains. Michael's family lived two houses from the Reitbahn Synagogue. They moved here from Sopot in 1929 and resided here till 1933. Again, only an empty space remains where the house once stood. Now Michael had seen two places in Gdańsk where the Blochs once lived.

It was Alina's turn now. The Szmant family lived from 1934 until 1938 at 27/28 Holzmarkt (now Rynek Drzewny). It was a corner house. Holzmarkt was built in a semicircle and was a very beautiful street. It was heavily damaged in the last weeks of March 1945. Some of the old buildings have been restored. But the house where Alina's grandparents and father lived is no more. There is only a patch of grass with some flowers at the corner where the house once stood. It was the corner of Holzmarkt and Altstädtscher Graben. Again, Alina had only an inkling, an idea of the house. I did have a clipping from an old book of Gdańsk with a picture of the house, which I gave Alina. The Szmant family moved to this house from Milchkannengasse (now ulica Stagiewna). To get there, we walked through many streets of the old city and crossed the Green Bridge over the river Motlawa. We entered the former Milchkannengasse. Most of the houses on this street were destroyed by the Soviets. The Szmants lived on the left side of the once busy street at No. 26. I had other friends who once lived on this street. My father had his office on the opposite side in the corner house of No. 1A. When the Szmant family came to Danzig from Kalisz, Celina was eleven and Harry was three years old. In the same building where the Szmants resided, my first piano teacher, Lucie Jung, also lived. She was Celina's best friend.

Again, Alina saw only the place but no house. Warehouses occupy this side of the street; the city is planning to build a tourist center there. On the opposite side are now beautifully built houses, all in the old style. Six years ago this side of the street was empty—only stones and sand. It was a nice surprise to see that the city is trying to rebuild streets that have been demolished. And it is being done in the prewar style.

A block away from the former Milchkannengasse we walked over a short bridge, passing the medieval Milchkannenturm (tower) and came to Mattenbuden. On this street there once had stood one of the oldest synagogues. This was the synagogue my parents and I attended. The families Szmant, Feuerstein, and Lipinski also worshiped there. A row of large apartment buildings occupies the place where the synagogue once stood. I hoped so very much to be able to have a tablet or stone attached to one of these buildings, just like I did in Sopot. With obstacles and bureaucracy in the Gdańsk municipality this project has to wait. I would love to see any sign here that would tell about this old house of prayer, one of the first synagogues in Gdańsk.

By now Alina and Michael had seen all I could show them that would link them to their families' past. The three of us decided to meet for supper in the hotel dining room. We would remain in the hotel because I had some important information I wanted to share with Alina and Michael after supper. We went to our room and I gave each of them charts with their family trees, letters, and clippings I had collected for many years. These would be helpful to Alina and Michael in sorting out their family past. I had made all these copies in Oak Ridge so that I could explain family links to my two cousins. We spent the evening studying these papers. I hoped that Alina and

Michael would find them interesting as well as valuable. The next day would be our last day in Gdańsk. Michael wanted to visit the monument near the former Polish Post Office honoring the Polish heroes who fought the Nazis in September 1939. I promised to take Alina and Michael there first thing in the morning. The next day Leon Lendzion had arranged for us to meet with the director of the school that occupies the former Polish *Gimnazjum*. He and Hela would meet us in the hotel at 10 a.m. Michael was planning to leave by train at 10 p.m.; Alina and I would leave by rental car Thursday morning.

After breakfast the three of us went to see the monument honoring Polish heroes who fought and died in September 1939. Wherever we went, whatever we saw, we captured with our three cameras. We returned to the hotel to wait for the Lendzions. As planned, Leon, Hela, and another school friend of mine arrived at the hotel. They came with flowers and gifts for all of us. Leon had arranged for us to tour the former Polish *Gimnazjum*. He wanted Alina to see the Memorial Room that has a tablet with the names of teachers and students who were killed during the war or died after the war. Leon and I visited this place six years ago and I mentioned to him that Celina Szmant, who graduated from this school, perished during the war. Leon promised to add Celina's name to the tablet. Now he wanted Alina to see it.

Leon suggested that we place the flowers under the memorial tablet in memory of my cousin and Alina's aunt, Celina. Carrying the flowers, we took taxis to my former *Gimnazjum*. The director met us in a small and unattractive meeting room. He offered us tea or coffee, but we declined. The building smelled stale and looked neglected and run down. We walked to the Memorial Room, where Leon pointed out to Alina the tablet with Celina Szmant's name. With tears in her eyes she placed her flowers beneath the tablet, so did I. Here for the first time Alina came in contact with Celina's name. In memory of her father's sister, she had named the daughter from her first marriage Celina.

We left the Memorial Room and the director took us to the once beautiful *Aula* (auditorium). The school is in the process of restoring this room. Once it was covered with very nice paintings on the ceiling and on all its walls. Former students will be contacted to contribute to this project.

The day of our leaving Gdańsk arrived. Alina insisted that we stop in Kalisz, where her father was born. We packed the rest of our belongings, had breakfast, and walked to the Hertz car rental office. All kinds of stories were told to discourage us from driving to Kalisz and Warsaw. In an early morning telephone call, Dr. Goebel warned us that the farmers of Poland had declared a strike and would be blocking major roads. I felt a little uneasy and asked Alina whether she would be upset if we took the train directly to Warsaw instead of driving through Kalisz to Warsaw. She suggested that we ask the people at Hertz about the danger or risks we were taking. Should they discourage us, we would take the train. The people at the Hertz office laughed at us. The roads were safe they said. We decided to take a chance and Alina would drive the rented car. As we were leaving Gdańsk, deep in my heart I had a feeling that for me this was my last visit to "my Danzig."

On the way to Kalisz we made one stop—in Golina—located twenty-five kilometers from Konin. When a genealogist researched the Ryczke family tree, she discovered that my great-great-grandfather had lived in Golina. This was the first time that I had heard about my ancestors coming from this small town. I knew that some came from Konin and some from Kolo and Slupca. Golina was an unknown place to me. When Alina suggested that we drive to Kalisz, I knew that we would have to pass Konin. Now I had the opportunity to see Golina. It is a fairly small town. There are only a few streets and a market square. Some of the houses are very old, many in need of repair. But there are streets with new houses, some quite pretty. The marketplace is called Plac Kazimierza Wielkiego, named after the Polish king who ruled in the fourteenth century. It was he who issued the order to invite the Jews into Poland. A statue of this king adorns the market place.

I took a few pictures of Golina and we left in the direction of Kalisz, an hour's drive from Konin. The houses in Kalisz looked clean and the streets were without litter. There were flowerpots on most of the balconies. Looking for postcards, we were told they could be obtained in a small store next to the post office on ulica Zamkowa. It so happened that this store was in the same building where my grandparents Ryczke resided from 1934 to 1938. At that time the name of this street was ulica 6-go Sierpnia. How strange:

Alina wanted postcards of Kalisz, and coincidentally I saw again the familiar house where I spent many happy holidays.

We wanted to reach Warsaw before dark and took the secondary highway toward Warsaw to avoid the strikers. By now we had already traveled eight hours. With heavy traffic we did not know how long it would take us to reach Warsaw. Trucks were everywhere. Alina skillfully tried to overtake them, but an accident on the road cautioned us to slow down. Finally we saw the outskirts of Warsaw.

We checked into our hotel, the Forum. Our room was on the nineteenth floor. After settling in we went downstairs to dine. Alina was exhausted and hungry. She deserved a good meal and a good drink after so many hours behind the wheel. After we returned to our room, we discussed plans for the next day. That would be our only full day in Warsaw. The hotel was crowded with tourists, the dining room uncomfortable, and the food just fair. I stayed in this hotel in 1990 when I traveled with the teachers from "Facing History." It was just as crowded then as now, only the tourists were from different countries. Then we heard a lot of Italian spoken, now it was German. Alina and I signed up for a tour of Warsaw. In three hours we would see some of the most important landmarks.

Although both of us were invited for supper to Jozio's on our last evening in Warsaw, I accepted the invitation, while Alina decided to spend the evening with a girl from Indiana whom we had met. I think she really wanted me to have some private time with Jozio and Krysia.

When I went to the lobby to get some flowers for Krysia I found Jozio already waiting. He had come early and had a surprise for me. His son, Czarek, would meet us, too. Czarek is now married to a physician and they have a little son. I was anxious to see Krysia. This was her first day at home after two weeks in the hospital. She greeted me warmly yet looked tired and drawn. The table was beautifully set. Czarek could not stay long. He had to return to work, and we said good-bye. The three of us sat around the dining room table and I recalled 1991 and 1993 when I was here with my sons and Caroline, when Krysia and Jozio were such good hosts. It was again Friday night, as during my visit here in 1993, and I asked Jozio if I could light candles. Right away he produced candlesticks and even a bottle of wine.

Afterward we talked about the past. Jozio loved Hela, his adopted mother and Max's sister dearly and shared his memories with me.

We also talked about politics and the present situation in Poland. I told them how different I found the Poland of today from the Poland I visited in 1990, 1991, and 1993. Today the country is prosperous. People work hard and have the money to buy cars and homes. Construction is booming in Poland, the stores are filled with good merchandise, and groceries carry food from around the world. The Poles enjoy freedom, and one can see that democracy works. The influence of the Western world is visible everywhere. German, Swedish, and American companies are heavily investing in Poland's economy. What a difference from the Poland I saw years ago. Jozio did not agree with me; he claimed that under the "old" (Communist) system things were better.

By 9 p.m. I was ready to return to my hotel and Jozio drove me back. He promised to pick up Alina and me the next morning and drive us to the airport. I thanked him for everything. He was always most helpful.

On our last morning in Warsaw, Alina and I went outside to explore Warsaw. We had a few hours left and wanted to see the Palace of Culture. A short walk from our hotel, this huge complex is despised by the Poles mostly because it was presented to them by the Soviets. Many buildings are joined to comprise the Palace of Culture. There are theaters, concert halls, auditoriums, and a large reception hall. Polish architecture is graceful, but this place was built in the heavy style used by the Soviets. Statues of Marx and Lenin as well as of Polish writers and poets surround the Palace of Culture. Since this was Saturday, thousands of schoolchildren with their teachers were visiting this place. Alina and I decided to take the elevator to the top floor. From the top we could see Warsaw's panorama. We saw the Vistula River with many bridges, the railroad station, and the suburb Praga, even though the weather was hazy. Back at the hotel we gathered our bags and suitcases when Jozio called our room. He and Krysia were downstairs waiting to take us to the airport. Our baggage was placed in Jozio's car and off we drove to the airport, again through heavy traffic. The weather was very warm and humid and Krysia felt uncomfortable. The normal twenty-minute ride took almost one hour, but we still had some time to check in.

I advised Jozio to take Krysia home. She could barely breathe in the heavy humid air. We said our farewells and thanked them for all their help. Who knows if we shall see each other again?

Alina and I had spent eight days together. We shared a hotel room, and we ate all our meals together. The experiences, our emotions, and feelings will remain with us forever. Although a generation apart, we understood and respected each other. Alina is a strong and determined and very independent woman. She reminded me of her aunt Celina Szmant. It was Alina who was determined to go to Gdańsk and Kalisz to search for her roots. If only her father had taken her back to Poland years ago, it would have been more meaningful to Alina. I tried my best to do what Harry Szmant would have done. This journey was filled with moments of high emotion—we laughed and we cried together. The memories will stay with us forever.

Epilogue

Dear Reader,

I have taken you from liberation to a life of freedom. I shared with you first my life alone, my reunion with my father, and my meeting of the man I loved and married. You traveled with me from devastated Europe to the New World. I told you about the lives of relatives and their survival. And you journeyed with me back to Europe, where I sought to find closure and mourn my losses. You were with me as I returned to my hometown Gdańsk/Danzig to recapture my childhood and youth. Almost every person I wrote about had been given the gift of life by a friend or stranger, by a compassionate person. Some were Germans, some Poles. Others were comrades in camps, friends. They all came from different backgrounds and were of different nationalities and religions. One thing they had in common: they dared to help, they had empathy.

My religion teaches that deeds are more important than words. Good intentions without action are meaningless. We have to be sensitive to people's suffering, act justly, and treat all people with dignity. Our legacy is to repair the world, in Hebrew *Tikkun Olam*. There is goodness in every person; all we have to do is seek it out. Let us listen to our hearts, fight injustice and discrimination, and remember that hatred is a disease that destroys people. These values we have to live by and teach to the next generation. The world is beautiful; there is much goodness. We have to learn from the past, but we also have to strive for a better future. And we must never, ever lose hope!

Editor's Introduction

1. Menachem Z. Rosensaft, ed., *Life Reborn: Jewish Displaced Persons, 1945–1951,* Conference Proceedings, Jan. 14–17, 2000 (Washington, DC: USHMM/AJJDC, 2001), 5.
2. See this volume, chap. 6.
3. See also U.S. Holocaust Memorial Commission (USHMC), *1945: The Year of Liberation* (Washington, DC: U.S. Holocaust Memorial Museum, 1995), 23.
4. See Angelika Königseder and Juliane Wetzel, *Waiting for Hope: Jewish Displaced Persons in Post–World War II Germany* (Evanston, IL: Northwestern Univ. Press, 2001), 33.
5. Ibid., 3.
6. USHMC, *1945,* 23.
7. Rosensaft, *Life Reborn,* 91.
8. USHMC, *1945,* 25.
9. Königseder and Wetzel, *Waiting for Hope,* 15.
10. Ibid., 28, 29.
11. Leonard Dinnerstein, *America and the Survivors of the Holocaust* (New York: Columbia Univ. Press, 1982), 198.
12. See USHMC, *1945,* 26, and Dinnerstein, *America and the Survivors,* 10.
13. Königseder and Wetzel, *Waiting for Hope,* 21–22.
14. USHMC, 1945, 26; also Dinnerstein, *America and the Survivors,* 11.
15. See Königseder and Wetzel, *Waiting for Hope,* 57.
16. USHMC, *1945,* 27.
17. Ibid.
18. Ibid., 302; see also Königseder and Wetzel, *Waiting for Hope,* 55.
19. USHMC, *1945,* 27.
20. See also Königseder and Wetzel, *Waiting for Hope,* 18.
21. USHMC, *1945,* 26.
22. Ibid.
23. See Rosensaft, *Life Reborn,* 54, and Königseder and Wetzel, *Waiting for Hope,* 3.

24. Bartley C. Crum, *Behind the Silken Curtain* (Jerusalem: Milah Press, 1996), 13.
25. USHMC, *1945*, 26.
26. See also Dinnerstein, *America and the Survivors*, 33.
27. Ibid., 33.
28. Königseder and Wetzel, *Waiting for Hope*, 172.
29. Dinnerstein, *America and the Survivors*, 14, 15.
30. USHMC, *1945*, 26.
31. Dinnerstein, *America and the Survivors*, 11.
32. Königseder and Wetzel, *Waiting for Hope*, 7.
33. See also USHMC, *1945*, 28.
34. Königseder and Wetzel, *Waiting for Hope*, 6.
35. Ibid., 79.
36. Rosensaft, *Life Reborn*, 6; see also Königseder and Wetzel, *Waiting for Hope*, 169.
37. Königseder and Wetzel, *Waiting for Hope*, 178.
38. USHMC, *1945*, 27.
39. Ibid., 23.
40. See also Königseder and Wetzel, *Waiting for Hope*, 171.
41. Ibid., 193.
42. See Königseder and Wetzel, *Waiting for Hope*, 6, 27, and USHMC, *1945*, 26.
43. Königseder and Wetzel, *Waiting for Hope*, 27.
44. Ibid., 6.
45. USHMC, *1945*, 26.
46. Königseder and Wetzel, *Waiting for Hope*, 22.
47. Ibid., 18; Dinnerstein, *America and the Survivors*, 201.
48. USHMC, *1945*, 27.
49. Dinnerstein, *America and the Survivors*, 16.
50. USHMC, *1945*, 27.
51. Dinnerstein, *America and the Survivors*, 16.
52. Königseder and Wetzel, *Waiting for Hope*, 27.
53. Ibid., 81.
54. See Königseder and Wetzel, *Waiting for Hope*, 19, 80.
55. Ibid., 19.
56. USHMC, *1945*, 289.
57. Königseder and Wetzel, *Waiting for Hope*, 19–20.
58. Ibid., 81.
59. USHMC, *1945*, 28.
60. Dinnerstein, *America and the Survivors*, 15; Königseder and Wetzel, *Waiting for Hope*, 31.
61. USHMC, *1945*, 28.
62. Dinnerstein, *America and the Survivors*, 120.
63. USHMC, *1945*, 30.

64. Dinnerstein, *America and the Survivors,* 113.
65. USHMC, *1945,* 30.
66. Dinnerstein, *America and the Survivors,* 163.
67. Königseder and Wetzel, *Waiting for Hope,* 37, 38.
68. See also USHMC, *1945,* 224–25.
69. Howard M. Sachar, *A History of Israel from the Rise of Zionism to Our Time,* 2nd ed., rev. and updated (New York: Alfred A. Knopf, 2002), 258–64.
70. See Königseder and Wetzel, *Waiting for Hope,* 50, 201–4.
71. USHMC, *1945,* 28.
72. See this volume, chap. 15.
73. USHMC, *1945,* 30.
74. Yaffa Eliach, *There Once Was a World: A 900-Year Chronicle of the Shtetl of Eishyshok* (New York: Little, Brown & Co., 1998), 663–69.
75. See also Dinnerstein, *America and the Survivors,* 110; Königseder and Wetzel, *Waiting for Hope,* 47.
76. Michael Berenbaum, *The World Must Know: The History of the Holocaust as Told in the United States Holocaust Memorial Museum* (New York: Little, Brown & Co., 1993), 207.
77. Dinnerstein, *America and the Survivors,* 109.
78. Königseder and Wetzel, *Waiting for Hope,* 45.
79. Ibid., 46.
80. See also Königseder and Wetzel, *Waiting for Hope,* 5, 44, 46.
81. Dinnerstein, *America and the Survivors,* 117.
82. Ibid., 46.
83. USHMC, *1945,* 30.
84. Dinnerstein, *America and the Survivors,* 181.
85. Ibid.
86. Ibid., 255.
87. Victor E. Frankl, *Man's Search for Meaning,* rev. and updated (New York: Washington Square Press, 1984), 105.
88. Ibid., 111.
89. Ibid., 109–10.
90. Rosensaft, *Life Reborn,* 91.
91. Frankl, *Man's Search for Meaning,* 110.
92. Rosensaft, *Life Reborn,* 92.
93. Frankl, *Man's Search for Meaning,* 113–14.
94. Ibid., 96–97.
95. Ibid., 97.
96. Rosensaft, *Life Reborn,* 93.
97. See this volume, chap. 6.
98. Rosensaft, *Life Reborn,* 92.

99. Frankl, *Man's Search for Meaning*, 133.
100. Königseder and Wetzel, *Waiting for Hope*, 100.
101. Rosensaft, *Life Reborn*, 5.
102. Ibid., 62.
103. Königseder and Wetzel, *Waiting for Hope*, 181.
104. Ibid., 183; see also Rosensaft, *Life Reborn*, 7.
105. Frankl, *Man's Search for Meaning*, 135.
106. Ibid.
107. Ibid., 104.
108. Rosensaft, *Life Reborn*, 65–66, my emphasis.
109. Ibid., 93.
110. Jacob Rader Marcus, *This I Believe: Documents of American Jewish Life* (Northvale, NJ: Jason Aronson, 1990), 255–57.
111. Jacob Rader Marcus, *The Jew in the Medieval World: A Source Book, 315–1791* (Cincinnati: Union of American Hebrew Congregations, 1990), 311–16.
112. R. Nathan of Nemirov, *Rabbi Nachman's Wisdom: Shevachay HaRan and Sichos HaRan*, trans. Aryeh Kaplan, ed. Zvi Aryeh Rosenfeld (New York: Sepher Hermon Press, 1973), 149.
113. Ibid., 150. My deep gratitude to my colleague David Patterson for his sensitive reading of this manuscript and his insightful and helpful comments on the importance of names in Judaism.
114. See this volume, chap. 7.
115. Wendy Lowe Besmann, *A Separate Circle: Jewish Life in Knoxville, Tennessee* (Knoxville: Univ. of Tennessee Press, 2001), 146–47.

CHAPTER 3

1. Typhoid fever is caused by polluted water and food. "DBMD — Typhoid Fever— General Information," Center for Disease Control, http://www.cdc.gov/ncidod/ dbmd/diseaseinfo/typhoidfever_g/htm (accessed Dec. 1, 2003). Typhus in connection with the Holocaust was caused by the bite of lice in unsanitary living conditions in the concentration camps. "Typhus," *Yahoo! Health Encyclopedia*, http://health.yahoo.com/health/encyclopedia/001363/0.html (accessed Dec. 1, 2003).

CHAPTER 4

1. For a detailed account of Mira's Holocaust experience, see *Echoes from the Holocaust: A Memoir* (Knoxville: Univ. of Tennessee Press, 1997).
2. In 1998, I visited the Bergen-Belsen memorial site and asked for Mira's name. It was not on their list. I asked that it be added and brought back forms for Mira to fill out and send in, along with a copy of her book.
3. See Kimmelman, *Echoes from the Holocaust*, chap. 7.

Chapter 5

1. There are many different types of Zionists. Pre-1948, a Zionist was an individual who adhered to the philosophy of a Jewish homeland in Palestine and often participated in its realization. Today a Zionist is a person who supports the State of Israel ideologically and materially. See Raphael Patai, ed., *Encyclopedia of Zionism and Israel*, 2 vols. (New York: Herzl Press, 1971).

Chapter 6

1. The *Bund* was a Jewish socialist labor organization founded in Vilna in 1897. It was not Zionist-oriented. See USHMC, *1945*, 303.
2. *Kapo* is a generic term for a concentration camp inmate functionary, such as prisoner camp police. See USHMC, *1945*, 308.
3. Lag b'Omer is on the eighteenth of Iyar. It is a joyous day in the forty-nine-day period of semi-mourning between Passover and Shavuat.

Chapter 7

1. In his memoir, *Displaced Persons,* Joseph Berger writes, "The Marseilles, on 103rd Street, had been bought up by HIAS and filled with survivors. Its lobby could seem like Rick's café in *Casablanca,* with refugees scouting for jobs or apartments or trying to make a little money by selling a watch or camera they had picked up cheaply in the black market of the DP camps. Everyone hunted for any information, any lead that could help locate a missing brother or sister or parent or even a hometown friend." Joseph Berger, *Displaced Persons* (New York: Washington Square Press, 2001), 28–29. In *America and the Survivors,* Dinnerstein writes, "Like the JDC and HIAS, USNA [United Service for New Americans] spared no expense, and at one point purchased the Hotel Marseilles on New York City's upper west side to house temporarily the new comers awaiting trains or buses to the hinterlands" (203).
2. See chap. 6 about Max Kimmelman's experiences.
3. On April 12, 1951, the Knesset (Israeli Congress) declared the twenty-seventh of the Jewish month of Nissan as *Yom HaShoah U'Mered HaGetaot* (Holocaust and Ghetto Revolt Remembrance Day), later shortened to Yom HaShoah. See Irving Greenberg, *The Jewish Way: Living the Holidays* (New York: Simon & Schuster, 1988), 333.

Chapter 9

1. From the German *Muselmänner, muselman* is a Holocaust-era term that refers to a person who has become a walking skeleton due to starvation and psychic exhaustion.

2. Lowell E. Perrine, "Morris Ryczke Is a 'Big Egg' Man," *New Jersey Farm and Garden*, March 1954, 54–55.

CHAPTER 15

1. The Warsaw Uprising is not to be confused with the Warsaw Ghetto Uprising. The latter was a resistance effort by the Jews living in the Warsaw ghetto from the second day of Passover, April 19, 1943 to May 16, 1943. The Warsaw Uprising occurred on August 1, 1944, in Polish Warsaw, with assistance from surviving Jews. This uprising was crushed in early October 1944. Martin Gilbert, *The Holocaust: A History of the Jews of Europe during the Second World War* (New York: Holt, Rinehart, and Winston, 1985), 557–67, 714–18.

CHAPTER 16

1. Wladyslaw Anders (1892–1970) was born near Warsaw and served in the Tsar's army during World War I. Subsequently, he joined the newly formed Polish army. By the mid-1930s, Anders was promoted to general. His cavalry brigade fought the Nazis in 1939 when they invaded Poland. He was captured and imprisoned by the Soviets. When the Nazis invaded Russia, Anders was freed to command an army of Poles freed from Siberia on Russian soil. As the Second Polish Corps, Anders and his army were sent to Iran by the British and later to Italy. After World War II, Anders lived in England until his death. "The Path of Anders," *Anders' Army: The Eagles in Exile*, http://andersarmy.com/anders-bio.htm (accessed Dec. 1, 2003).

CHAPTER 22

1. See Kimmelman, *Echoes from the Holocaust,* chap. 4.
2. See *The Pianist* (2002), directed by Roman Polanski and written by Ronald Harwood.
3. Janusz Korczak (Henry Goldschmidt) was a Jewish educator who ran an orphanage in Warsaw. On August 6, 1942, he and nearly two hundred children, as well as his staff, were deported to Treblinka, where they were all murdered by gas. Michael Berenbaum, *The World Must Know* (Boston: Little, Brown & Co., 1993), 77–80.
4. For Mira's Holocaust journey to Auschwitz, see Kimmelman, *Echoes from the Holocaust,* 55–58.
5. Maximilian Kolbe (1894–1941) was a Catholic monk in Poland of the Conventual Franciscan Order. Cofounder of the "Immaculata" movement in 1917, he was ordained in Rome in 1918. He returned to Poland to teach history in the Kraków seminary in 1919 and received his doctorate in theology in

1922. Traveling to Japan and India in the early 1930s, he returned to Poland in 1936. The Nazis imprisoned him in 1941 and sent him to Auschwitz the same year. After an escape attempt by prisoners, Kolbe took the place of a young father who was to be shot in retribution. He died on August 14 by lethal injection. Kolbe was beatified in 1971 and canonized by Pope John Paul II in 1982. "Saint Maximilian Kolbe," *Catholic Community Forum,* http://www.catholicforum.com/ saints/saintm01.htm (accessed Dec. 1, 2003).

6. The revolt did not succeed in the way planned. The Sonderkommando was able to set the building of Crematorium IV on fire, but not to use the explosives they had been collecting for this purpose. They did damage Crematorium III and blow up Crematorium II. See Rittner and Roth, *Different Voices,* 138–42; also Gilbert, *The Holocaust,* 743–50.

7. Helena (Hela) was actually born in 1900, but the Polish papers she survived on gave the year of birth as 1905.

CHAPTER 23

1. Eva Kolska Horwitz died in 1993.
2. See Kimmelman, *Echoes from the Holocaust,* chap. 3.
3. Ibid., chap. 9.
4. Ibid., chap 6.
5. See this volume, chap. 17.
6. For details see Gilbert, 597.

Glossary

Aliyah Bet
Illegal immigration into Palestine

Akiba
Zionist youth group

Anschluss
Annexation of Austria by Nazi
Germany

Bar/Bat Mitzvah
Son/daughter of the Commandments,
Jewish coming-of-age ceremony

Betar
Zionist youth group

Blau-Weiss
Zionist youth group Blue-White

Blockälteste
Barracks supervisor

Brichah
Escape, flight; Jewish group facilitating
escape from eastern Europe

Brit Milah
Circumcision

Bund
Socialist labor organization

Cheder
Jewish elementary school

Chevrah Kadisha
Burial Society

DAW *Deutsche Ausrüstungswerke*
Supplier of clothing for military

DPC
Displaced Persons Commission

Einsatzgruppen
Mobile killing squads

Eretz Israel
Land of Israel

Final Solution
State-sponsored plan for the murder
of European Jewry

Führer
Title Adolf Hitler bestowed upon
himself

Gestapo/Geheime Staatspolizei
Secret police

Get
Jewish religious divorce

Gimnazjum
Polish high school

Habonim
Zionist youth group The Builders

Hadassah
Hebrew name for Esther; Zionist
women's organization

HIAS
Hebrew Immigrant Aid Society

IRO
International Refugee Organization

Jewish Brigade
Jewish soldiers from Palestine serving
with British forces during World War II

JJB *Jung-Jüdischer Bund*
Zionist youth group

"Joint"
American Jewish Joint Distribution Committee (AJJDC)

Kaddish
Jewish prayer for the dead

"Kanada"
Warehouses with deportee belongings in Auschwitz

Kapo
Inmate camp police

Ketubah
Jewish marriage contract

Kibbutz
Communal settlement in Israel

Kindertransport
Transport of Jewish children from the continent to England

Kristallnacht
Organized attacks by German mobs on Jewish communities throughout Germany on November 9–10, 1938

Lag b'Omer
18th of Iyar in Jewish calendar

Lagerschutz
Inmate camp police

Mikvah
Jewish ritual bath

Minyan
Quorum for worship service

Mohel
Jewish ritual circumciser

Muselman
A skeleton-like human being

Operation Reinhard
Deportation of Jews to death camps

OT *Organisation Todt*
Military supply company

Reichstag
German parliament and building in which parliament meets

Rosh Hashanah
Jewish New Year

Sherit HaPLetah
Saved Remnant (survivors)

Simchat Torah
Jewish holiday of rejoicing in the law

Tallit
Prayer shawl

Tikkum olam
Hebrew expression for the Jewish way to repair or complete the world

Tisha B'Av
Commemoration of the destruction of the Jewish Temples

Turnverein Bar Kochba
Bar Kochba Gymnastics Society

Tzedakah
righteous giving and living

UAHC
Union of American Hebrew Congregations

Ulpan
Intensive Hebrew language program

Umschlagplatz
Collection point for deportees in a town

UNRRA
United Nations Relief and Rehabilitation Agency

WIZO
Women's International Zionist Organization

Yeshivah
Jewish religious high school

Yom Hashoah
Holocaust Remembrance Day

Yom Kippur
Day of Atonement

Zionist
Individual who helped build and/or supports the modern state of Israel

Bibliography

Berenbaum, Michael. *The World Must Know: The History of the Holocaust as Told in the United States Holocaust Memorial Museum.* New York: Little, Brown & Co., Boston, 1993.

Berger, Joseph. *Displaced Persons: Growing Up American After the Holocaust.* New York: Washington Square Press, 2001.

Besmann, Wendy Lowe. *A Separate Circle: Jewish Life in Knoxville, Tennessee.* Knoxville: Univ. of Tennessee Press, 2001.

Crum, Bartley C. *Behind the Silken Curtain.* Jerusalem: Milah Press, 1996.

Dinnerstein, Leonard. *America and the Survivors of the Holocaust.* New York: Columbia Univ. Press, 1982.

Eliach, Yaffa. *There Once Was a World: A 900-Year Chronicle of the Shtetl of Eishyshok.* New York: Little, Brown & Co., 1998.

Facing History and Ourselves National Foundation. *The Jews of Poland.* Brookline, MA: Facing History and Ourselves National Foundation, 1998.

Frankl, Victor E. *Man's Search for Meaning.* Rev. and updated. New York: Washington Square Press, 1984.

Gilbert, Martin. *The Holocaust: A History of the Jews of Europe during the Second World War.* New York: Holt, Rinehart & Winston, 1985.

Greenberg, Irving. *The Jewish Way: Living the Holidays.* New York: Simon & Schuster, 1988.

Kimmelman, Mira Ryczke. *Echoes from the Holocaust: A Memoir.* Knoxville: Univ. of Tennessee Press, 1997.

Königseder, Angelika, and Juliane Wetzel. *Waiting for Hope: Jewish Displaced Persons in Post–World War II Germany.* Evanston, IL: Northwestern Univ. Press, 2001.

Marcus, Jacob Rader. *The Jew in the Medieval World: A Source Book, 315–1791.* Cincinnati: Union of American Hebrew Congregations, 1990.

——. *This I Believe: Documents of American Jewish Life.* Northvale, NJ: Jason Aronson, 1990.

Meisler, Frank. *On the Vistula Facing East.* London: Andre Deutsch, 1996.

Nemirov, R. Nathan of. *Rabbi Nachman's Wisdom: Shevachay HaRan and Sichos HaRan.* Trans. Aryeh Kaplan. Ed. Zvi Aryeh Rosenfeld. New York: Sepher Hermon Press, 1973.

Patai, Raphael, ed. *Encyclopedia of Zionism and Israel.* 2 vols. New York: Herzl Press, 1971.

Perrine, Lowell E. "Morris Ryczke Is a 'Big Egg' Man," *New Jersey Farm and Garden,* March 1959.

Rittner, Carol, and John K. Roth, eds. *Different Voices: Women and the Holocaust.* St. Paul, MN: Paragon House, 1993.

Rosensaft, Menachem Z., ed. *Life Reborn: Jewish Displaced Persons, 1945–1951.* Conference Proceedings Jan. 14–17, 2000. Washington, DC: USHMM/AJJDC, 2001.

Sachar, Howard M. *A History of Israel from the Rise of Zionism to Our Time.* 2nd ed., rev. and updated. New York: Alfred A. Knopf, 2002.

Smith, Helmut Walser, ed. *The Holocaust and Other Genocides: History, Representation, Ethics.* Nashville: Vanderbilt Univ. Press, 2002.

U.S. Holocaust Memorial Commission. *1945: The Year of Liberation.* Washington, DC: U.S. Holocaust Memorial Museum, 1995.

Index

LOT Polish Airline, 277, 303
Louisville, Ky., 64, 95, 151
Lüneburg 12

Macy's, 81
magazines, xxii
Majdanek, xv, xxxvi–xxxvii
Malbork (Marienburg) Castle, 280, 307
Malmö, 211, 213, 276
malnutrition, 11
Mandate in Palestine, xx
Marcus, Rabbi Robert, 98, 154
Mariacka Gate, 287
Marienkirche, 264, 281–82, 291
Markthalle (Hale Targowe) 273, 281
Marseilles, Hotel, 66, 70–71, 331n1
Marszalkowska Street, 275
martial law, xxxiii
Mauthausen, 18, 28, 30, 32–33, 227
Medical Corps, 10, 12
Menuhin, Yehudi, 15
Messer, Uri, 187
Messerschmitt factories, 28, 30
mikvaot (ritual baths), xxii, 336
Mila 18: headquarters of ghetto fighters, 237, 240
Milchkannengasse (ulica Stagiewna), 201–2, 287–88, 318–19
Milchkannenturm, 281, 319
military chaplains, Jewish, xxi, 328n47
military, xviii, xxii, 328n60; government, 12, 38
minyan (quorum), 245, 336
Mlawa, 263
mobile killing squads, xxxvi
Morek, Jan, 174,183, 192–93
Mormon Church, 220–21
Mottlau (Motlawa) River, 268, 281–82, 319

Munich, 46, 59, 61, 151
muselman, 331n1, 336
My Zydzi Polscy (We, the Polish Jews), 301

Nachman of Bratzlav, Rabbi, xxix
Nagasaki, xxxix
Najman, Felix, 226–27
Najman, Jeanine, 227
Najman, Madeleine (Malka) Ryczke, 224, 226–27, 229
Najman, Paulette, 224, 227
Nazi(s), xv, xvii, xxii–xxiv, xxix, xxxiii, xxxv–xxxix, 5, 12, 28, 30, 36, 39, 51, 53, 68, 74, 86, 133–35, 139, 146–47, 149, 174–75, 179, 186, 202, 225, 227, 237, 242–46, 251, 261–62, 265, 270, 279, 287, 289–91, 301–2, 305, 312, 314–15, 320, 333n5; quarters, xviii; victims of, xv, xviii
Neptunbrunnen (Fontanna Neptuna), 268
New York City, 9, 45, 48–49, 65–68, 70–71, 80–81, 83–84, 114–16, 160, 163, 181, 210, 213, 215–16, 218, 257, 259, 267, 277, 291–92, 311
Niewiarowski, Bolek, 175–76
Night of Broken Glass, xxxii. See also Kristallnacht
Nixdorf, 46, 58–59, 70, 147–48, 157
nonaggression treaty, xxxvi
Nordstrasse, 265
Normandy, xxxvii; invasion of, xv
Northern Ireland, 306
Novotel Hotel, 281
Nowolipki Street, 173, 185, 237
Nuremberg Laws, xxxiii

Postgasse, 268
Potsdam Agreement, xix, xxxviii, xxxviii
Poznan (Posen), 128, 133, 283, 311
Praga, 176, 242, 323
Prague, 46, 59, 62, 148, 232, 252
prisoners: psychology, xxvi; revolt,
    xxxviii; Soviet, xxxvi; of war, xvi
Prochnika, ulica, 295–96
Promenadenstrasse (ulica
    Majowieckiego), 265, 316
Prosna River, 137, 294
Pruc, Czarek, 235–36, 259, 262, 263,
    278–79, 297, 300, 322
Pruc, Helena (Hela Kimmelman), 251,
    296, 298, 303, 323, 333n7. *See also*
    Kimmelman, Hela (Rydecka)
Pruc, Jozio, 61, 234–36, 241, 251–52, 259,
    263, 265–66, 271, 273, 277–82, 284,
    289, 293–98, 300, 303, 307, 322–24
Pruc, Krysia, 235, 241, 259, 263, 278–79,
    299–303, 322–24
Pruc, Monika, 235, 259, 263, 278
Pruc, Stefan, 61, 111, 236, 251
Prussia, 228; East, 271
Przedecka, Gina, 130, 168, 241, 283, 296
Przedecka, Halina, 130, 168, 241, 267,
    283, 296
Przedecka, Rosa Ryczke, 130–31, 168,
    241, 262, 283, 296
Przedecki, Markus, 133, 242
Puerto Rico, 206
Purim, 120, 127, 129

Radaune (Radunia), 270
Rakow Forest, 208–9, 246
Rashkovsky, Rabbi Victor, 107, 161, 163
Rathaus (city hall), 264, 268; ceiling
    painting with Tetragrammaton, 268

Ravensbrück, 209
Red Cross, British, 12–13, 16
refugees, xvii, xxv, 80; Jewish, xxiii, xxxiv;
    questions about, xxii
Regensburg, 60, 179–80
Reich Citizenship Law, xxxiii
Reichstag, xxxiii, 336
Reitbahn, 291, 318
reparations, xvii, 86
repatriated, xviii
restitution, 86, 118, 155–56
revolt, Auschwitz, xxxviii
Richka, Chanoch, 224, 226–29
Richka, Michal, 228
Richka, Rachela, 228
Richke, David, 216–17, 219–21, 223–24,
    226, 230
Richke, Noa, 223, 228
Richke, Smadar, 223, 228
Richke, Varda, 223, 228
Richmond, Daniel, 224
Richmond, Jonathan, 224
Richmond, Lee, 216, 224, 229
Richmond, Maya, 224
Richmond, Sarah (Sarah Richmond
    Vickers) 224, 230
Richmond, Simon, 224
Richmond, Theo, 215–17, 220–21,
    223–27, 229–30
Righteous Gentiles, 5
Ringelblum, Emanuel, 241
Risley, New Jersey, 115
Ritchke, Orly (Gutfreund), 218–20
Ritchke, Ronnie, 169, 217–21, 228–29
Robertsville Junior High School, 94
Rockdale Avenue, 76, 83
Rockwood, 90, 92–93, 96
Roonstrasse (Dabrowskiego Street), 265

Life beyond the Holocaust was designed and typeset on a Macintosh computer system using QuarkXPress software. The body text is set in 10.5/13 Minion and display type is set in Carpenter. This book was designed and typeset by Kelly Gray and manufactured by Thomson-Shore, Inc.